by John McPhee

Irons in the Fire
The Ransom of Russian Art
Assembling California
Looking for a Ship
The Control of Nature
Rising from the Plains
Table of Contents
La Place de la Concorde Suisse
In Suspect Terrain
Basin and Range
Giving Good Weight
Coming into the Country
The Survival of the Bark Canoe
Pieces of the Frame
The Curve of Binding Energy
The Deltoid Pumpkin Seed
Encounters with the Archdruid
The Crofter and the Laird
Levels of the Game
A Roomful of Hovings
The Pine Barrens
Oranges
The Headmaster
A Sense of Where You Are

The John McPhee Reader
The Second John McPhee Reader

THE SECOND
JOHN McPHEE
READER

Selected by

David Remnick and Patricia Strachan

Edited by Patricia Strachan

With an introduction by David Remnick

Farrar, Straus and Giroux

New York

THE SECOND JOHN McPHEE READER

Library of Congress Cataloging-in-Publication Data
McPhee, John A.
The second John McPhee reader / selected by David Remnick and
Patricia Strachan ; edited by Patricia Strachan ; with an
introduction by David Remnick.—1st ed.
p.   cm.
I. Strachan, Patricia.   II. Remnick, David.   III. Title.
AC8.M267   1996   081—dc20   95–33519   CIP

In memory of Anne Sullivan

The big year for the New Journalism was 1965. A *Journal of the Plague Year, Homage to Catalonia,* and even Joseph Mitchell's foretaste of the post-modern, "Joe Gould's Secret," had been published before this momentous date, but that wasn't the point. "New" was the point. In the spring, Tom Wolfe hurled a two-part pie in the face of *The New Yorker* with his send-up, "Tiny Mummies! The True Story of the Ruler of 43rd Street's Land of the Walking Dead!" It was Wolfe's thesis that the magazine had devolved into a humorless, genteel museum piece of middlebrow culture living off the literary capital accumulated in the days of Harold Ross. Years later, Wolfe would claim that his mockery of the magazine and the eccentricities of its famously shy editor, William Shawn, was no more wicked or out-of-bounds than Wolcott Gibbs' 1936 parody of Henry Luce and the syntax of *Time* ("Backward ran sentences until reeled the mind"). After having taken his whacks in other pieces at slumming debs, Murray the K, Junior Johnson, and other totems of the Zeitgeist, Wolfe figured that *The New Yorker* would be just one more overripe target. And why the hell not? Who would take offense if Wolfe administered Eustace Tilley a good zetz? Hadn't Lillian Ross, in her *New Yorker* profile of Ernest Hemingway, made Papa out to look like an infantile ass? Fun's fun, no?

Apparently not. The uproar after Wolfe's piece appeared in *The Herald Tribune* was astonishing and across-the-board, coming, as it did, from everyone from J. D. Salinger to Walter Lippmann. In the windiest of the attacks, Dwight Macdonald, a regular contributor to *The New Yorker*, ventilated in *The New York Review of Books* against Wolfe and what he called "parajournalism." "It is a bastard form, having it both ways," Macdonald declared, "exploiting the factual authority of journalism and the atmospheric license of fiction."

A few months later, Shawn made mush of Wolfe and Macdonald both, publishing every word of what remains a classic of non-fiction writing, Truman Capote's *In Cold Blood*. Capote's work was built on the sheer exertion of painstaking reporting; at the same time, it possessed all the texture and narrative energy of the best novels. No ladies' magazine stuff here, Mr. Wolfe. Nothing "para" or quasi or faux about it, Mr. Macdonald. Both sides of the argument, Wolfe and Macdonald, eventually betrayed some regret at their initial salvos. Wolfe never put "Tiny Mummies!" in his collections. Macdonald, who had been touching in his defense of Shawn but hopelessly muddled in his arguments, seemed to recognize his own errors as he added a series of footnotes to the original essay, admitting that, yes, "parajournalism" was, in fact, "a legitimate art form": witness, he said, Norman Mailer's *Armies of the Night*, James Agee's *Let Us Now Praise Famous Men*, and, yes, Tom Wolfe's *Radical Chic*.

In that same noisy year, 1965, *The New Yorker* published "A Sense of Where You Are," a seventeen-thousand-word-long profile of the Princeton University basketball star Bill Bradley. It was, in many ways, a traditional piece for *The New Yorker*: understated, measured, a sustained work of admiration centered on a Caucasian paragon of Ivy League polish and Calvinist habit. And yet the author, John McPhee, then in his early thirties and a "back-of-the-book" writer at *Time*, had, in his quiet way, accomplished something of distinction.

To begin with, he had found a perfect subject, one who could articulate his distinctive character, verbally and physically. Bradley would later go on to win two National Basketball Association championships with the New York Knickerbockers and then a seat in the U.S. Senate, and yet his accomplishments were never so pure as they were when he was an undergraduate. McPhee, with Bradley's help, wrote with insight and precision about the mechanics of basketball, an immensely complicated game that, unlike baseball or boxing, had yet to attract its bard; even the great Red Smith had dismissed basketball as the "up and down" sport.

In Bradley, McPhee discovered a banker's son from Missouri who was able to overcome the liabilities of winters in Palm Beach and "the white man's curse" (a limited vertical jump), to become one of the most technically accomplished players in the history of the college game. What was more, Bradley, even as a collegian, was unusually self-conscious, able to move well beyond the standard cliché of the contemporary athlete ("Well, Bud, God just blessed me with these talents") and explain his craft, the economy of his moves, the thinking behind his work habits. In Bradley, McPhee found an artist in absolute touch with his materials (his teammates, the court, his own body) and willing to describe them.

McPhee did not let Bradley merely talk about his sense of the game; he let him show it. By staying close to Bradley, day after day, McPhee accumulated the details necessary to describe Bradley's quest for perfection. With McPhee's gift for the telling anecdote, Bradley's game and his acute awareness of its angles came alive even to a reader who would never think, otherwise, to care:

Last summer, the floor of the Princeton gym was being resurfaced, so Bradley had to put in several practice sessions at the Lawrenceville School. His first afternoon at Lawrenceville, he began by shooting fourteen-foot jump shots from the right side. He got off to a bad start, and he kept missing them. Six in a row hit the back rim of the basket and bounced out. He stopped, looking discomfited, and seemed to be making an adjustment in his mind. Then he went up for another jump shot from the same spot and hit it cleanly. Four more shots went in without a miss, and then he paused and said, "You want to know something? That basket is about an inch and a half low." Some weeks later, I went back to Lawrenceville with a steel tape, borrowed a step-ladder, and measured the height of the basket. It was nine feet ten and seven-eighths inches above the floor, or one and one-eighth inches too low.

Convinced that Bradley's greatest natural gift was his vision, his ability to take in the entire flow of action without betraying his next move, McPhee brought him to an ophthalmologist in Princeton for testing. This is not something that reporters are ordinarily willing to do (nor is it something that hassled and spoiled athletes usually permit), but the results were astonishing:

With both eyes open and looking straight ahead, Bradley sees a hundred and ninety-five degrees on the horizontal and about seventy degrees straight down, or about fifteen and five degrees more, respec-tively, than what is officially considered perfection. Focused horizon-tally, the typical perfect eye, according to the chart, can see about forty-seven degrees upward. Bradley can see seventy degrees upward. This no doubt explains why he can stare at the floor while he is waiting for lobbed passes to arrive from above. Dr. Abrams said that he doubted whether a person who tried to expand his peripheral vision through exercises could succeed, but he was fascinated to learn that when Bradley was a young boy he tried to do just that. As he walked down the main street of Crystal City, for example, he would keep his eyes focused straight ahead and try to identify objects in the windows of the stores he was passing. For all this, however, Bradley cannot see behind himself. Much of the court and, thus, a good deal of the action are often invisible to a basketball player, so he needs more than good eyesight. He needs to know how to function in the manner of a blind man as well. When, say, four players are massed in the middle of things behind Bradley, and it is inconvenient for him to look around, his hands reach back and his fingers move rapidly from shirt to shirt or hip to hip. He can read the defense as if he were reading Braille.

In *A Sense of Where You Are*, McPhee was writing a kind of sports hagiography, but he was not exaggerating. He was not

(Red Smith again) "godding up" the athlete. Instead, he was faithfully describing a particular set of physical gifts and an artistic discipline. Bradley's warm-up sessions, as McPhee portrayed them, were more interesting to watch than most players' games. With an audience or without one, Bradley worked, over and over again, on the footwork for simple, but essential, moves: the pivot, the crossover. He was almost suicidally unselfish. Here was an All-American in the athletically deprived Ivy League, and yet he instinctively gave up the ball to teammates even though their shots ten feet away from the basket were probably less accurate than his from twice the distance. McPhee's profile was filled with such precise physical detail and description of his subject's work habits that they added up, in the end, to a picture of Bradley's game and, more so, his character.

Read nearly thirty years and twenty-three books later, *A Sense of Where You Are* also appears to have an autobiographical dimension, a McPhee manifesto on how to approach the difficulty of any art, non-fiction writing very much included. McPhee's virtues as a reporter and writer are much like Bradley's as a basketball player: thorough preparation in the reading and reporting, an uncanny sense of structure and form, an elegant and useful economy.

McPhee's reputation is substantial, far from a secret. He is a favorite of other writers, the sort of figure who is so good that he is beyond envying, and in recent years he has sold enough books to compel his publisher to reissue all his books in a handsome paperback series. His classic account of life in Alaska, *Coming into the Country*, and his four books on geology are among his bestsellers. All the same, McPhee's reputation should be greater still. While much of the New Journalism of the sixties and seventies has long felt mannered or hysterical in the rereading, McPhee's work has the quality of permanence. Like Edmund Wilson's *Apologies to the Iroquois*, John Hersey's *Hiroshima*, Mitchell's *McSorley's Wonderful Saloon*, Janet Malcolm's *Psychoanalysis*, Mark Singer's *Mr. Personality*, or Ian Frazier's *Great Plains*, McPhee's books represent the innovations in non-fiction writing and the best of what has been in *The New Yorker*.

I should come clean. This is not, if there is such an animal, an entirely objective introduction. Fifteen years ago, in college, I took a twelve-week writing course with McPhee at Princeton. I received a "P"—for "Pass." This was a mercy. McPhee has been teaching the course, so far as I know, since the Silurian Period. More than half of his former students have gone on to work at various magazines and newspapers, to write books. Actually, only a small percentage of McPhee's students studied with him at Princeton; he has been for dozens and dozens of non-fiction writers what Robert Lowell used to be for poets and poet wannabes of a certain age: the model.

To the degree that he revealed himself in the classroom, McPhee showed himself to be not unlike his first subject, Bill Bradley—conservative about, and immersed in, the fundamentals of his craft. That is, he is conservative, blessedly conservative, where it comes to fact. His principle is that non-fiction can, and should, borrow the varied structures of fiction, but not its license. A reader has a right to know if a book presenting itself as non-fiction is permitting itself the liberties of fiction. Books labeled "non-fiction novel" or somesuch at least admit to the fudge factor. It was not always thus. By way of commenting on a change in journalistic mores and not to tar any reputations, it's probably fair to say that the standards of mainstream, non-tabloid American journalism have grown stricter. No editor at *The New Yorker*, or at any other decent magazine I can think of, would knowingly tolerate some of the abuses and seeming abuses of the past. Piped quotes, invented scenes, conflated characters were once a matter of regular use and not, as they are now, a subject of scandal.

McPhee could not be more different from such contemporaries in New Journalism as Wolfe or Joan Didion or Michael Herr. He is not a writer of the Zeitgeist. His tone, which is at once rather formal and still all his own, has always been something apart from the current moment. It does not absorb the hysteria or static of the prevailing breeze. Over the years, McPhee's less insightful reviewers, even by way of admiration, have said he is too distant from politics, preferring to make something of very little. In the midst of Vietnam or Watergate, it may have seemed that McPhee's subjects were insubstantial: a profile of a kindly prep-school autocrat (*The Headmaster*), a journey in the forests of New Jersey (*The Pine Barrens*), a narrative about a bizarre aeronautical experiment (*The Deltoid Pumpkin Seed*), and, most famously, a book about a fruit (*Oranges*).

If the same critics believe that McPhee is somehow aloof from the perils of the real world, that he is some sort of platonic version of a *Yankee* magazine staff writer, sweet and oblivious, they have him wrong. McPhee is drawn to craftsmen, it is true, experts who open up a world for him and his readers, but these voices invariably point their way toward questions large and, not infrequently, political. It soon became clear (or should have) that amid all of McPhee's pursuit of personal pleasures in his choice of subjects (canoes, the wilderness, food, sport) he was steadily developing a remarkable political literature. Over time he has become the most effective literary advocate for environmentalism. The subject has, for some reason, spawned one unbearably sanctimonious and sensationalist book after another. McPhee, however, does not preach, nor does he shout doomsday in a crowded room. He tells stories—stories that, in the margins, fairly bark the most important ecological questions. In *The Curve of Binding Energy*, his subject, the physicist Ted Taylor, presciently raised the specter of nuclear-weapons proliferation. In *Encounters with the Archdruid*, McPhee and the environmental activist David Brower went on three journeys with three different men of industry to provoke debates on issues of preservation versus economic growth.

Over the years, McPhee's writing, on all subjects, has evolved. His characters and narrative structures are more complicated and surprising. He is looser, funnier, and, at the same time, his engagement with the physical world and moral problems consistently deepens. The first John McPhee Reader mined its gold in the books leading up to, but not including, his commercial breakthrough and literary masterpiece, *Coming into the Country*, which was published in 1977. A book like this Reader should act as a kind of tasting menu (sample, by the way, the tasty profile "Brigade de Cuisine"), and the sections published here from *Coming into the Country* should, at the very least, provide the flavor of this more ambitious phase of McPhee's career, its radiant maturity.

The Second John McPhee Reader is not without its uncomplicated pleasures; for example, "Heirs of General Practice," a piece about doctors in Maine, is almost a throwback to work like *The Pine Barrens* and *The Crofter and the Laird*. But, more often, the pieces and excerpts gathered here show off a writer who not only is in absolute command of his craft—his sentences, his structures, his sense of humor—but also revels in the pleasures of a fragile world and makes sure we take note. Vanity, thy name is Man, his books tell us. McPhee makes his case not at the lectern but rather, the way the engaged novelist does, through the wielding of his art. Read his set piece on the bear in *Coming into the Country* and your sense of man's place in the wild is forever changed; read about the rock avalanche in "Los Angeles Against the Mountains" and no sense of security in the face of nature's strength is ever possible again: "Boulders bigger than cars ride long distances in debris flows. Boulders grouped like fish eggs pour downhill in debris flows. The dark material coming toward the Genofiles was not only full of boulders; it was so full of automobiles it was like bread dough mixed with raisins."

This Reader includes, as it well should, a dose of McPhee's geology books, known collectively as *Annals of the Former World*. It is not a secret to McPhee that even some of his most loyal fans have hoped he would finally get off his "rocks" books; these books are not always easy, filled as they are with great Whitmanic catalogues of minerals and pyrotechnic attempts to explain nothing less than the textures and the movements of the earth. What is too often forgotten is that the "rocks" books are, in many ways, McPhee's most interesting in a *literary* sense. Watch the way he weaves biography, diary, and science in *Rising from the Plains*. Not long ago, a friend of mine and fellow McPhee fan suggested that his career has been Joycean and that the geology books are his *Finnegans Wake*. When I heard this I blanched; when McPhee hears it, he will turn the color of claret. But there is sense in it: the books of *Annals of the Former World* attempt to explain all that we stand on, coast to coast and beyond; and, as literary experiments, filled with the beautiful but foreign language of geology, they sometimes risk losing the reader. The samples here will, I am willing to bet, send many to the four complete volumes.

McPhee's sense of literary fun is everywhere. He likes to play the simpleminded reporter sometimes, and yet he has included here a piece of writing that is nothing less than a post-modern romp, a story with more traps than a Chinese box. Watch what he is up to in "North of the C.P. Line." Here he is, in a piece utterly factual, writing about a bush pilot and game warden who wrote him letters at *The New Yorker* complaining that he was "using" his name. His name is John McPhee, John's real-life double, his doppelgänger. Shades of *The Double*, shades of *The Secret Sharer*. McPhee visits his namesake and the result is delight.

The Second John McPhee Reader closes with healthy chunks of McPhee's latest long piece, *The Ransom of Russian Art*, a thirty-thousand-word profile of an eccentric art collector. It is a piece that has all the qualities of precision and praise that *A Sense of Where You Are* has. Every sentence seems to deliver another pleasure, in detail or language. In a way, *Ransom* is for McPhee what Graham Greene used to call "an entertainment," a temporary turn from the more obviously ambitious, darker stories.

Norton Townshend Dodge is an American original, an eccentric loaded with advanced degrees in Russian studies and a gilded stock portfolio. Between 1956 and the rise of glasnost under Mikhail Gorbachev, Dodge spirited out of the Soviet Union hundreds of underground artworks. His collection, the largest of its kind by far, is a phantasmagoric jumble of greatness and garbage, art and protest. In its political moment, the artwork Dodge made available to the outside world represented a form of contrary spirit that was enormous in scope; nearly all of the art is now in the art museum at Rutgers University; the rest is still housed on his 960-acre farm in southern Maryland.

McPhee has once more found an ideal subject. Sometimes it seems that he does not have to invent his Falstaffs and Pips: with the other John McPhee, he had only to open his mail; other times, as with Norton Dodge, McPhee is bound to meet his characters on public transport.

"I met him on an Amtrak train in Union Station, Washington, in January, 1993. Casual as that," he writes of his first meeting with Dodge. "He came into an empty car and sat down beside me, explaining that the car would before long fill up. It did. He didn't know me from Chichikov, nor I him. His button-down buttons weren't buttoned. He wore khaki trousers, a green tie, a salmon shirt, a tweed jacket with leather elbows, and a rubber band as a bracelet. An ample fringe of hair all but covered his collar. His words filtered softly through the Guinness Book mustache. It was really a sight to see, like a barrel on his lip. Two hundred miles of track lie between Union Station and Trenton, where I got off, and over that distance he uttered about forty thousand words."

His interest whetted, McPhee sets off to visit Dodge on the farm in Maryland and, through Dodge and meetings with artists and hangers-on, he illuminates part of an era that now seems so long ago, the underground art scene in the old Soviet Union. There is no evidence in *The Ransom of Russian Art* that McPhee visited the former Soviet Union as part of his research, and so it is a testament to his skill as a reporter—to his ability to listen to informants—that he has managed to deliver such a vivid picture of a distant and particular world. Relying on Dodge and other interview subjects for information and a sense of place and character, McPhee brings us into rickety artists' lofts in Moscow, and I swear you can smell the turpentine and the bad cigarettes and the garbage down the hall.

As McPhee paints him, Dodge cuts a rather strange figure. He has the bad habit of trying to write or read while driving his car down the thruway. He has the housekeeping habits of the Collier brothers. He resembles a friendly walrus—"with his grand odobene mustache, he had everything but the tusks"—and "is absent-minded to a level that no competing professor may yet have reached. He has called a locksmith to come and get him out of a situation that could have been alleviated by a key he found later in his pocket." Mainly, Dodge is a hoot, a comic presence with serious intentions and amazing successes. He enters the great gallery of McPhee's characters—not the last, of course, but rather a marker before the writing that will go into another book worth waiting for: The Third John McPhee Reader.

Fini 4/19/01 while Dave & Lisa took a golf class.

CONTENTS

With the exception of "Under the Snow,"
which is here in its entirety,
all titles are represented by excerpts.

FROM

COMING INTO

THE COUNTRY

(1 9 7 7)

[This is John McPhee's longest book, his most popular to date. It is about
Alaska—Arctic Alaska, urban Alaska, bush Alaska, its inventive people, its
incomparable places. What follows here is a montage of the people and the
places, in segments of varying length. The montage begins with a sketch of
Anchorage, where Alaska forms its first impression on visitors. "Just getting
up there is a long do," McPhee has remarked elsewhere. "If you happen to
leave Seattle at, say, nine o'clock some summer night, you fly out in darkness
over the Olympic Peninsula. In an hour or so, you look down through total
blackness at scattered points of light on the Queen Charlotte Islands. Another
hour goes by. Now—if you are on the right-hand side of the plane—you look
ahead and see what appears to be a small semicircle of intense blue light,
like the end of a tunnel, hundreds of miles away. As you keep on going, that
small concentration of light spreads laterally and becomes a thin blue band.
More distance, and a pink band develops above the blue one. The farther
you go, the more the bands of blue and pink expand upward into the black.
Between midnight and 1 a.m., you land in Anchorage in daylight."]

4/19/01

Begum

4/19/01

If Boston was once the most provincial place in America, Alaska, in this respect, may have replaced Boston. In Alaska, the conversation is Alaska. Alaskans, by and large, seem to know little and to say less about what is going on outside. They talk about their land, their bears, their fish, their rivers. They talk about subsistence hunting, forbidden hunting, and living in trespass. They have their own lexicon. A senior citizen is a pioneer, snow is termination dust, and the N.B.A. is the National Bank of Alaska. The names of Alaska are so beautiful they run like fountains all day in the mind. Mulchatna. Chilikadrotna. Unalaska. Unalakleet. Kivalina. Kiska. Kodiak. Allakaket. The Aniakchak Caldera. Nondalton. Anaktuvuk. Anchorage. Alaska is a foreign country significantly populated with Americans. Its languages extend to English. Its nature is its own. Nothing seems so unexpected as the boxes marked "U.S. Mail."

[*Juneau, in the Alexander Archipelago, is the capital of Alaska. In an on-again off-again manner, Alaskans for decades have addressed themselves to building an entirely new capital city in wild terrain in a more central part of the state.*]

There are those who would say that tens of thousands of barrels of oil erupting from a break in the Trans-Alaska Pipeline would be the lesser accident if, at more or less the same time, a fresh Anchorage were to spill into the bush. While the dream of the capital city plays on in the mind, Anchorage stands real. It is the central hive of human Alaska, and in manner and structure it represents, for all to see, the Alaskan dynamic and the Alaskan aesthetic. It is a tangible expression of certain Alaskans' regard for Alaska—their one true city, the exemplar of the predilections of the people in creating improvements over the land.

As may befit a region where both short and long travel is generally by air, nearly every street in Anchorage seems to be the road to the airport. Dense groves of plastic stand on either side —flashing, whirling, flaky. HOOSIER BUDDY'S MOBILE HOMES. WINNEBAGO SALES & SERVICE. DISCOUNT LIQUORS OPEN SUNDAY. GOLD RUSH AUTO SALES. PROMPT ACTION LOCKSMITHS. ALASKA REFRIGERATION & AIR CONDITION. DENALI FUEL . . .

"Are the liquor stores really open Sundays?"

"Everything in Anchorage is open that pays."

Almost all Americans would recognize Anchorage, because Anchorage is that part of any city where the city has burst its seams and extruded Colonel Sanders.

"You can taste the greed in the air."

BELUGA ASPHALT.

Anchorage is sometimes excused in the name of pioneering. Build now, civilize later. But Anchorage is not a frontier town. It is virtually unrelated to its environment. It has come in on the wind, an American spore. A large cookie cutter brought down on El Paso could lift something like Anchorage into the air. Anchorage is the northern rim of Trenton, the center of Oxnard, the ocean-blind precincts of Daytona Beach. It is condensed, instant Albuquerque.

PANCHO'S VILLA, MEXICAN FOOD. BULL SHED, STEAK HOUSE AND SONIC LOUNGE. SHAKEY'S DRIVE-IN PIZZA. EAT ME SUBMARINES.

Anchorage has developed a high-rise city core, with glass-box offices for the oil companies, and tall Miamian hotels. Zonelessly lurching outward, it has made of its suburbs a carnival of cinder block, all with a speculative mania so rife that sellers of small homesites—of modest lots scarcely large enough for houses—retain subsurface rights. In vacant lots, queen-post trusses lie waiting for new buildings to jump up beneath them. Roads are rubbled, ponded with chuckholes. Big trucks, graders, loaders, make the prevailing noise, the dancing fumes, the frenetic beat of the town. Huge rubber tires are strewn about like quoits, ever ready for the big machines that move hills of earth and gravel into inconvenient lakes, which become new ground.

FOR LEASE. WILL BUILD TO SUIT.

Anchorage coins millionaires in speculative real estate. Some are young. The median age in Anchorage is under twenty-four. Every three or four years, something like half the population turns over. And with thirty days of residence, you can vote as an Alaskan.

POLAR REALTY. IDLE WHEELS TRAILER PARK. MOTEL MUSH INN.

Anchorage has a thin history. Something of a precursor of the modern pipeline camps, it began in 1914 as a collection of tents pitched to shelter workers building the Alaska Railroad. For decades, it was a wooden-sidewalked, gravel-streeted town. Then, remarkably early, as cities go, it developed an urban slum, and both homes and commerce began to abandon its core. The exodus was so rapid that the central business district never wholly consolidated, and downtown Anchorage is even more miscellaneous than outlying parts of the city. There is, for example, a huge J. C. Penney department store filling several blocks in the heart of town, with an interior mall of boutiques and restaurants and a certain degree of chic. A couple of weedy vacant lots separate this complex from five log cabins. Downtown Anchorage from a distance displays an upreaching skyline that implies great pressure for land. Down below, among the high buildings, are houses, huts, vegetable gardens, and bungalows with tidy front lawns.

Anchorage burst out of itself and left these incongruities in the center, and for me they are the most appealing sights in Anchorage. Up against a downtown office building I have seen cordwood stacked for winter.

BIG RED'S FLYING SERVICE. BELUGA STEAM & ELECTRIC THAWING. DON'T GO TO JAIL LET FRED GO YOUR BAIL.

There is a street in Anchorage—a green-lights, red-lights, busy street—that is used by automobiles and airplanes. I remember an airplane in someone's driveway—next door to the house where I was staying. The neighbor started up its engine one night toward eleven o'clock, and for twenty minutes he ran it flat out while his two sons, leaning hard into the stabilizers, strained to hold back the plane. In Alaska, you do what you feel like doing, or so goes an Alaskan creed.

There is, in Anchorage, a somewhat Sutton Place. It is an enclave, actually, with several roads, off the western end of Northern Lights Boulevard, which is a principal Anchorage thoroughfare, a neon borealis. Walter Hickel lives in the enclave, on Loussac Drive, which winds between curbs and lawns, neatly trimmed, laid out, and landscaped, under white birches and balsam poplars. Hickel's is a heavy, substantial home, its style American Dentist. The neighbors' houses are equally expensive and much the same. The whole neighborhood seems to be struggling to remember Scarsdale. But not to find Alaska.

Books were selling in Anchorage, once when I was there, for forty-seven cents a pound.

There are those who would say that the only proper place for a new capital of Alaska—if there ever has to be one—is Anchorage, because anyone who has built a city like Anchorage should not be permitted to build one anywhere else.

At Anchorage International Airport, there is a large aerial photograph of Anchorage formed by pasting together a set of pictures that were made without what cartographers call ground control. This great aerial map is one of the first things to confront visitors from everywhere in the world, and in bold letters it is titled "ANCHORAGE, ALASKA. UNCONTROLLED MOSAIC."

The first few days I spent in Alaska were spent in Anchorage,

[6]

and I remember the increasing sense of entrapment we felt (my wife was with me), knowing that nothing less than a sixth of the entire United States, and almost all of it wilderness, was out there beyond seeing, while immediate needs and chores to do were keeping us penned in this portable Passaic. Finally, we couldn't take it any longer, and we cancelled appointments and rented a car and revved it up for an attempted breakout from town. A float plane—at a hundred and ten dollars an hour— would have been the best means, but, like most of the inmates of Anchorage, we could not afford it. For a great many residents, Anchorage is about all they ever see of Alaska, day after day after year. There are only two escape routes—a road north, a road south—and these are encumbered with traffic and, for some miles anyway, lined with detritus from Anchorage. We went south, that first time, and eventually east, along a fjord that would improve Norway. Then the road turned south again, into the mountains of Kenai—great tundra balds that reminded me of Scotland and my wife of parts of Switzerland, where she had lived. She added that she thought these mountains looked better than the ones in Europe. Sockeyes, as red as cardinals, were spawning in clear, shallow streams, and we ate our cheese and chocolate in a high meadow over a torrential river of green and white water. We looked up to the ridges for Dall sheep, and felt, for the moment, about as free. Anchorage shrank into perspective. It might be a sorry town, but it has the greatest out-of-town any town has ever had.

[*This next scene is about eight hundred miles out of Anchorage, with not much between but black spruce and mountains and rivers and streams. With five other people, the author is near the headwaters of a Brooks Range river on a canoe-and-kayak reconnaissance trip. Three of them take off from the river one afternoon to make a long walk and have a look around. They are perhaps six or seven miles into that walk.*]

We passed first through stands of fireweed, and then over ground that was wine-red with the leaves of bearberries. There were curlewberries, too, which put a deep-purple stain on the

[7]

hand. We kicked at some wolf scat, old as winter. It was woolly
and white and filled with the hair of a snowshoe hare. Nearby
was a rich inventory of caribou pellets and, in increasing quantity
as we moved downhill, blueberries—an outspreading acreage of
blueberries. Bob Fedeler stopped walking. He touched my arm.
He had in an instant become even more alert than he usually
was, and obviously apprehensive. His gaze followed straight on
down our intended course. What he saw there I saw now. It
appeared to me to be a hill of fur. "Big boar grizzly," Fedeler
said in a near-whisper. The bear was about a hundred steps away,
in the blueberries, grazing. The head was down, the hump high.
The immensity of muscle seemed to vibrate slowly—to expand
and contract, with the grazing. Not berries alone but whole bushes
were going into the bear. He was big for a barren-ground grizzly.
The brown bears of Arctic Alaska (or grizzlies; they are no longer
thought to be different) do not grow to the size they will reach
on more ample diets elsewhere. The barren-ground grizzly will
rarely grow larger than six hundred pounds.

"What if he got too close?" I said.

Fedeler said, "We'd be in real trouble."

"You can't outrun them," Hession said.

A grizzly, no slower than a racing horse, is about half again
as fast as the fastest human being. Watching the great mound of
weight in the blueberries, with a fifty-five-inch waist and a neck
more than thirty inches around, I had difficulty imagining that
he could move with such speed, but I believed it, and was without
impulse to test the proposition. Fortunately, a light southerly wind
was coming up the Salmon valley. On its way to us, it passed
the bear. The wind was relieving, coming into our faces, for had
it been moving the other way the bear would not have been
placidly grazing. There is an old adage that when a pine needle
drops in the forest the eagle will see it fall; the deer will hear it
when it hits the ground; the bear will smell it. If the boar grizzly
were to catch our scent, he might stand on his hind legs, the
better to try to see. Although he could hear well and had an
extraordinary sense of smell, his eyesight was not much better

[8]

than what was required to see a blueberry inches away. For this reason, a grizzly stands and squints, attempting to bring the middle distance into focus, and the gesture is often misunderstood as a sign of anger and forthcoming attack. If the bear were getting ready to attack, he would be on four feet, head low, ears cocked, the hair above his hump muscle standing on end. As if that message were not clear enough, he would also chop his jaws. His teeth would make a sound that would carry like the ringing of an axe.

. . .

Like pictures from pages riffled with a thumb, these things went through my mind there on the mountainside above the grazing bear. I will confess that in one instant I asked myself, "What the hell am I doing *here?*" There was nothing more to the question, though, than a hint of panic. I knew why I had come, and therefore what I was doing there. That I was frightened was incidental. I just hoped the fright would not rise beyond a relatively decorous level. I sensed that Fedeler and Hession were somewhat frightened, too. I would have been troubled if they had not been. Meanwhile, the sight of the bear stirred me like nothing else the country could contain. What mattered was not so much the bear himself as what the bear implied. He was the predominant thing in that country, and for him to be in it at all meant that there had to be more country like it in every direction and more of the same kind of country all around that. He implied a world. He was an affirmation to the rest of the earth that his kind of place was extant. There had been a time when his race was everywhere in North America, but it had been hunted down and pushed away in favor of something else. For example, the grizzly bear is the state animal of California, whose country was once his kind of place; and in California now the grizzly is extinct.

If a wolf kills a caribou, and a grizzly comes along while the wolf is feeding on the kill, the wolf puts its tail between its legs and hurries away. A black bear will run from a grizzly, too. Grizzlies sometimes kill and eat black bears. The grizzly takes what he happens upon. He is an opportunistic eater. The predominance of the grizzly in his terrain is challenged by nothing but men and ravens. To frustrate ravens from stealing his food, he will lie down and sleep on top of a carcass, occasionally swatting the birds as if they were big black flies. He prefers a vegetable diet. He can pulp a moosehead with a single blow, but he is not lusting always to kill, and when he moves through his country he can be something munificent, going into copses of willow among unfleeing moose and their calves, touching nothing, letting it all breathe as before. He may, though, get the head of a cow moose between his legs and rake her flanks with the five-inch knives that protrude from the ends of his paws. Opportunistic. He removes and eats her entrails. He likes porcupines, too, and when one turns and presents to him a pygal bouquet of quills, he will leap into the air, land on the other side, chuck the fretful porpentine beneath the chin, flip it over, and, with a swift ventral incision, neatly remove its body from its skin, leaving something like a sea urchin behind him on the ground. He is nothing if not athletic. Before he dens, or just after he emerges, if his mountains are covered with snow he will climb to the brink of some impossible schuss, sit down on his butt, and shove off. Thirty-two, sixty-four, ninety-six feet per second, he plummets down the mountainside, spray snow flying to either side, as he approaches collision with boulders and trees. Just short of catastrophe, still going at bonecrushing speed, he flips to his feet and walks sedately onward as if his ride had not occurred.

His population density is thin on the Arctic barren ground. He needs for his forage at least fifty and perhaps a hundred square miles that are all his own—sixty-four thousand acres, his home range. Within it, he will move, typically, eight miles a summer day, doing his travelling through the twilight hours of the dead of night. To scratch his belly he walks over a tree—where forest exists. The tree bends beneath him as he passes. He forages in the morning, generally; and he rests a great deal, particularly after he eats. He rests fourteen hours a day. If he becomes hot in the sun, he lies down in a pool in the river. He sleeps on the tundra—restlessly tossing and turning, forever changing position. What he could be worrying about I cannot imagine.

His fur blends so well into the tundra colors that sometimes it is hard to see him. Fortunately, we could see well enough the one in front of us, or we would have walked right to him. He caused a considerable revision of our travel plans. I asked Fedeler what one should do if a bear were to charge. He said, "Take off your pack and throw it into the bear's path, then crawl away, and hope the pack will distract the bear. But there is no good thing to do, really. It's just not a situation to be in."

We made a hundred-and-forty-degree turn from the course we had been following and went up the shoulder of the hill through ever-thickening brush, putting distance behind us in good position with the wind.

. . .

"It's amazing to me," Fedeler said. "So large an animal, living up here in this country. It's amazing what keeps that big body alive." The barren-ground bear digs a lot of roots, he said—the roots of milk vetch, for example, and Eskimo potatoes. The bear, coming out of his den into the snows of May, goes down into the river bottoms, where over-wintered berries are first revealed. Wolf kills are down there, too. By the middle of June, his diet is almost wholly vegetable. He eats willow buds, sedges, cotton-grass tussocks. In the cycle of his year, roots and plants are eighty per cent of what he eats, and even when the salmon are running he does not sate himself on them alone but forages much of the time for berries. In the fall, he unearths not only roots but ground squirrels and lemmings. It is indeed remarkable how large he grows on the provender of his yearly cycle, for on this Arctic barren ground he has to work much harder than the brown bears of southern Alaska, which line up along foaming rivers—hip to hip, like fishermen in New Jersey—taking forty-pound king salmon in their jaws as if they were nibbling feed from a barnyard trough. When the caribou are in fall migration, moving down the Salmon valley toward the Kobuk, the bear finishes up his year with one of them. Then, around the first of November, he may find a cave or, more likely, digs out a cavern in a mountainside. If he finds a natural cave, it may be full of porcupines. He kicks them out, and—extending his curious relationship with this animal—will cushion his winter bed with many thousands of their turds. If, on the other hand, he digs his den, he sends earth flying out behind him and makes a shaft that goes upward into the side of the mountain. At the top of the shaft, he excavates a shelf-like cavern. When the outside entrance is plugged with debris, the shaft becomes a column of still air, insulating the upper chamber, trapping the bear's body heat. On a bed of dry vegetation, he lays himself out like a dead pharaoh in a pyramid. But he does not truly hibernate. He just lies there. His mate of the summer, in her den somewhere, will give birth during winter to a cub or two—virtually hairless, blind, weighing about a pound. But the male has nothing to do. His heart rate goes down as low as eight beats a minute. He sleeps and wakes, and sleeps again. He may decide to get up and go out. But that is rare. He may even stay out, which is rarer—to give up denning for that winter and roam his frozen range.

      .   .   .

Another two miles, descending, and we were barefoot in the river, with pink hot feet turning anesthetically cold. We crossed slowly. The three others were by the campfire. On the grill were grayling and a filleted Arctic char. The air was cool now, nearing fifty, and we ate the fish, and beef stew, and strawberries, and drank hot chocolate. After a time, Hession said, "That was a good walk. That was some of the easiest hiking you will ever find in Alaska."

We drew our route on the map and figured the distance at fourteen miles. John Kauffmann, tapping his pipe on a stone, said, "That's a lot for Alaska."

We sat around the campfire for at least another hour. We talked of rain and kestrels, oil and antlers, the height and the headwaters of the river. Neither Hession nor Fedeler once mentioned the bear.

When I got into my sleeping bag, though, and closed my eyes, there he was, in color, on the side of the hill. The vision was indelible, but fear was not what put it there. More, it was a sense of sheer luck at having chosen in the first place to follow Fedeler and Hession up the river and into the hills—a memento not so much of one moment as of the entire circuit of the long afternoon. It was a vision of a whole land, with an animal in it. This was his country, clearly enough. To be there was to be incorporated, in however small a measure, into its substance—his country, and if you wanted to visit it you had better knock.

[Coming into the Country *consists of three separately structured compositions. The first describes a journey in Arctic Alaska, the second has to do with the search for a new capital, and the third describes the people and terrain of the eastern interior. In Alaska, the term "interior" refers to the country that lies between the Brooks Range and the Alaska Range, the highest mountain range in North America. The interior—divided and drained by the Yukon River—is the warmest and the coldest part of Alaska. In the eastern interior, a great deal of gold mining has occurred—on Mammoth Creek, on Mastodon Creek, on the Fortymile River. Next door is the Canadian Yukon (Bonanza Creek, the Klondike). The great gold rushes occurred in the eighteen-nineties, of course, and soon after the turn of the century the numbers of people fell away. Remarkably, though, miners have been in that Alaskan country working the creeks in every year of every decade since 1893. In Alaska, there are ten or twelve small communities along the Yukon in something above a thousand river miles. The first two—Eagle and Circle—are a hundred and sixty miles apart. Their combined population is under three hundred. A very small number of people, spread out, live in the country between.*]

With a clannish sense of place characteristic of the bush, people in the region of the upper Yukon refer to their part of Alaska as "the country." A stranger appearing among them is said to have "come into the country."

.   .   .

New miners come into the country every year—from Nevada, Montana, Oregon, wherever. They look around, and hear stories. They hear how Singin' Sam, on Harrison Creek, "hit an enrichment and took out nuggets you wouldn't believe." They hear about "wedge-shaped three-quarter-inch nuggets just lying there where water drips on bedrock." They hear about a miner in the Birch Creek district pulling nuggets from the side of a hill.

"I have always been mining, always preparing ground. I'm not telling you how much money I've got ready to dig up. She's in the bank. Trouble is, there's too much gravel with it."

In tailing piles left behind by dredges, people hunt for nuggets that were *too big* to get stopped in the sluice boxes and went on through the dredge with the boulders. People reach into their shirt pockets and show you phials that are full of material resembling ground chicken feed and are heavier than paperweights. Man says he saw a nugget big as a cruller tumbling end over end in the blast from a giant hose. It sank from view. He's been looking for it since. Man on Sourdough Creek, working for someone else, confessed he had seen a nugget, and reached to pick it up, and found it was connected by a strand of wire gold to something much larger and deeper. He broke off the nugget and reported nothing. He could hardly mark the spot. Later, he went back to try to find what was there—he knew not where.

To stories of such nature Stanley and Ed Gelvin have not always been immune. Son and father, deep-rooted in the country (the one by birth, the other since long before statehood), they live in Central, a community with a Zip Code and a population of sixteen, so named because it was the point on the Birch Creek supply trail from which the miners fanned out to the gulches. Some went surprisingly far. Both Stanley and Ed Gelvin are, among other things, pilots, familiar with the country from the air; and some years ago they became more than a little interested in certain conjunctive stream courses in high remote terrain, where they saw aging evidence of the presence of miners. The site is—they request that I not be too specific—somewhere in the hundred-plus miles of mountain country that lies between Eagle and Central. Along a piece of valley floor more than three thousand feet high they noticed, among other things, a wooden sluice box weathered silver-gray, a roofless cabin, a long-since toppled cache. The old-timers did not build cabins, caches, and sluice boxes just in hopes of finding worthwhile concentrations of gold. Having found it, however, they lacked the means to remove anything like the whole of what was evidently there, even when they dug down in winter into places where flooding would stop them in warmer weather—thawing frozen deep gravels with fires and hoisting it up in buckets for sluicing in the spring. Under the stream beds were soaked unfrozen depths known as live ground, where the old-timers could not have worked at all. While some Alaskan streams freeze solid, most continue to run all winter under phenomenally increasing layers of ice and snow. The phenomenon is overflow, which has so often been lethal to people travelling streams on foot—soaking themselves, freezing to death. Water builds up pressure below the ice until it breaks through a crack and spreads out above. When the pressure is relieved, the flow stops and the water becomes a layer of ice. Before long, snow falls, and compacts. More pressure builds, and water again flows out on top. Through a winter, these alternating layers of snow and ice, white and blue, can build up to great confectionery thicknesses—but the stream below remains liquid to bedrock. With appropriate earthmoving equipment, Stanley pointed out, a guy could go into that live ground and scrape up what lay on the rock. No such machine had ever reached these alpine streams, as a glance at their unaltered state confirmed. They were much too far from the mining road and the dredged and bulldozed creeks of the district. It was almost too bizarre to imagine—a bulldozer in the roadless, trail-less wilderness of those mountains. The price of gold, on the other hand, had lately quintupled. Maybe going in there was worth a try. Over the Gelvins' kitchen table, father and son kept talking, and a program gradually evolved. Attention became focussed on the family backhoe. The first necessity would be to sample the deep gravels and see what was there. That long steel arm and big steel bucket could reach many feet into the bottom of a stream. If a guy wanted to have a look at what was lying on the bedrock, that backhoe would be the thing. Maybe a guy could fly it up there. The backhoe was a modified tractor that had once belonged to the United States Air Force and had hauled bombers around in Fairbanks. It weighed five thousand seven hundred pounds. A guy could take it apart. Reduce it to many pieces. Fly it, in the family airplanes, like birds carrying straws, nut by bolt in fragments into the hills.

When I first met the Gelvins, in the early fall of 1975, pieces of backhoe were strewn all over the ground beside the airstrip behind their cabin. The machine itself was still recognizable but was fast melting away under the influence of the wrench. The airstrip looked like a dirt driveway scarcely ten feet wide, with weeds upgrown on either side almost to the level of a Cessna's wings. The runway had a dogleg. Every so often, Stanley or Ed would stuff some parts into an airplane, roll off in a plume of dust, disappear around the bend, and reappear eventually, rising, to clear a backdrop wall of spruce. Stanley—tall, lanky, still in his middle twenties—being of the country, was a gold miner almost by nature. His father, Ed Gelvin, was more diversified. Over the years, he had become, it seems safe to say, as much as anyone in Alaska an example of what Steve Ulvi has in mind when he speaks so admiringly of "the man of maximum practical application." Mining, as it happened, was what first drew Ed and his wife, Ginny, into the country. In the early nineteen-fifties, he worked some claims on Squaw Creek, near Central. He moved a lot of gravel but not a lot of gold. They liked the country, turned to other things, and stayed. Trapper, sawyer, pilot, plumber, licensed big-game guide, welder, ironworker, mechanic, carpenter, builder of boats and sleds, he suffered no lack of occupation. I once asked him if there was anything that could go wrong around his place that would cause him to seek help from elsewhere. He looked off into the distance and carefully thought over the question—this compact and gracefully built man of fifty or so with thick quizzical bifocals, a shy smile, a quiet voice. Finally, he said no, he guessed there wasn't. Ginny hunted with him, and ran the traplines as well. They raised a son and three daughters, who were so fond of moose and caribou they never much cared for beef. Over all the years, meanwhile, and despite the multifarious activities which followed that first attempt at mining, Ed had more trouble getting gold out of his mind than he had had getting it out of Squaw Creek. He had contracted gold fever, the local malaria; and he passed it on to Stanley.

If they were teased by the sight of the old relics they saw in that high nameless valley, there were stories around that were stimulating, too. Old miners in the district said they had always heard it was shallow ground up there, with good colors near the surface—and not much developed by the real old-timers. It had been the valley of, among others, Pete the Pig. That would be his cache lying on its side. Pete the Pig Frisk was a savvy prospector, an efficient miner, not one to waste his time where there was no pay. He found a good pay streak there, and not a few bears. He was a clean, attractive man, Pete the Pig—but he grunted while he worked, while he rooted for gold. When he opened his mouth to speak, he grunted first. When he got old, he went to the Sitka Pioneers' Home. From time to time, the miners out in the country saw a published list of who was there. One year, Pete Frisk's name was gone from the list. In 1962, a man named Brown—from Oregon or "somewhere down near there"—had had himself flown to Pete Frisk's valley in a helicopter. He had a partner with him, two pet Airedales, and a set of miniature sluice boxes that were innovative and effective as tools for prospecting. He also had a .357 Magnum for grizzlies, of which he killed three. When the partners left, they attempted to walk out, by crossing mountains to the Yukon. Because the creeks and streams of Alaska have a geminate quality that can fool even people who know them well, the two men thought they were on Coal Creek headed for the big river when in fact they were on Hanna Creek headed somewhere else. Brown's partner came out weeks later, with an injured leg, floating on a raft he had made on the Charley River. Brown, for his part, "stayed" in the high country; that is, he apparently died there. He was never heard from again. His partner said they had separated after the injury, as Brown went on for help. All that was ever found was the carcass of an Airedale, butchered out as for the table, but uneaten. Possibly, a bear ate Brown. His widow suspected something worse. She thought there had been more than just colors found up there in Pete Frisk's valley.

A dozen years later, Stanley Gelvin, in his Aeronca Champ with its dunebuggy tundra tires, flew so low he skimmed the dwarf willows, hunting the valley for a place to land. Thirteen treeless

summits, each about the height of the high Adirondacks, surrounded the three confluent streams there, and down from this
nippled coronet ran sweeping tundra fells deceptive to view. They
appeared to be as smooth as fairways, but with their sedge tussocks
and fissured soils they were in fact as rough as boulderfields.
Flying near stallout speed, Stanley followed one creek and another, studying the ground. Finally, he saw a place he thought
he could get out of if he were to set the plane down. The walk
would be long if he couldn't—not to mention what to do about
the plane. Rising, circling, returning, he gingerly put his wheels
on the ground and jumped back at once into the air. Felt pretty
good. He circled again. He rolled his wheels on the tundra twice
more. It was thumping rough, but it seemed negotiable. He set
the Aeronca down.

Taking off successfully, he went home and told his father, and
they began to advance their plans. First, they should improve the
landing place. They had a little Ranger—a diminutive tractor,
like a Cub Cadet—which they had used to like purpose when
they built a cabin on the Charley River years before. Ed cut the
Ranger in half. They flew it to the mountains, and he welded it
back together. The backhoe before long followed, and when it
was at last reassembled they scooped into the center of a stream.
Bedrock was eight feet down. Even at six, they panned the colors
they had hoped to see.

They had intended to spend the whole of the following season
ranging with the backhoe around the claims they had made, trying
out pieces of seven miles of streams, but early results were so
encouraging that they sharply foreshortened the tests. To put it
conservatively, a pay streak appeared to be there, and what was
needed now—since the backhoe was just a fifty-seven-hundred-
pound shovel—was a means of moving gravel in a major way.
The Caterpillar Tractor Company produces the eponymous Cat
in seven sizes—styled D3, D4, and so on to D9. Most gold miners
use something less than the largest, but the Gelvins—forming a
partnership with two friends in Fairbanks—decided to go all the
way. The supreme Cat, twenty-seven feet long, eleven feet high,

with a blade of fourteen feet, could sweep forty yards of gravel before it—possibly a hundred dollars a shove. Ed Gelvin went to Los Angeles to shop for a used D9.

With his partners in Fairbanks putting up the money in return for a half interest in the claims, he paid forty-seven thousand five hundred dollars for a ten-year-old machine—D9, Series G. In the fleets of general contractors, it had spent its lifetime ripping raw California land, making freeways, and preparing building sites on beaches and deserts. Who, watching it there—clanking, dozing, wheezing, roaring, grunting like Pete the Pig—could ever in farthest-fetched imaginings have guessed where it would go? It went to Seattle by train, and by barge to Whittier, in Prince William Sound. There the Alaska Railroad picked it up and took it to Fairbanks, where, in early April, a lowboy hauled it up the dirt road north. Forty miles from Central, the haul stopped—blocked by the still unbroken winter snows. The road had been smothered since October. Ed Gelvin, who was observing from the air, landed on the road and with Stanley put the blade on the Cat. The weather in a general way was warming. Snow was melting. Ice was beginning to rot. If the D9 was going to move up frozen stream beds and climb into the mountains, it had to keep going now. If the road was closed, the Cat would open it.

When Stanley Gelvin was a small boy and did his elementary-school work by correspondence from the kitchen table in Central, he was from time to time required to draw a picture. When the choice of subject was his to make, he always drew a Cat. He operated one before he drove anything else. Now, with a Cat all around him, he knew where things were. He sensed like an athlete the rhythm of the parts—the tilt cylinders, the blade-lift arms. A good Cat skinner is a Cat mechanic, and, from the torque converter to the sun-and-planet gears, he knew what was making the moves. "I know what's inside the thing—everything—and what makes it work. My father knows how the stuff goes together, too. If the thing needs work, we do it."

The snow-obscured road leading on toward Central was—even at its best, in summer—a tortuous trail. In several high places, it traversed the flanks of mountains as a fifteen-foot shelf with no rail of any kind and a precipitous plunge on the outboard side. On the last of these mountain passes, twenty miles from home, Stanley encountered drifts that were thirty feet deep. To keep going, he had to bite into the snow, doze some to the brink, send it avalanching down, then turn and bite some more—all the while feeling for the road, feeling with his corner bits (the low tips of the blade) for the buried edge where the road stopped and the plunge began. A D9 is in some ways the most difficult Cat to operate. "You've got so much iron in front of you you can't see what you're doing." It is also his favorite size, because it is so big it does not bounce around. This one weighed a hundred and ten thousand pounds. Its balance point was ten feet back of the blade. Repeatedly, Stanley moved the blade eight feet over the edge. He knew where it was. If he had gone off the mountain, he would have raised one fantastic cloud of snow. Instead, he trimly dismantled the prodigious drifts and dozed on down to Central.

To the pads of the track Ed Gelvin welded ice grousers. They would keep the Cat from sliding. They were small pieces of steel, protruding like hyphens from the tracks. Ed and Stanley had built a steel slick plate and a steel sluice box, and Ed had rearranged them as a huge loaded sled—eight feet wide and twenty-four feet long: I-beams, H-beams, three-sixteenths-inch plate. He had made a thousand-gallon fuel tank. It was full and on the sled. Here and there, he slipped in snowshoes, gold pans, a two-hundred-amp generator, a welding tank and torch. Finally, he secured to the top of the load a plywood wanigan—that is, a small hut, with three bunks, propane, and a cupboard full of food. The rig, composed, weighed about twelve tons. When it was hooked to the D9, Stanley left for the mountains.

He crossed low terrain at first. His mother rode with him. His father hovered in the air. Then he changed passengers, taking on a friend named Gary Powers, and they began to move up Woodchopper Creek. His altitude at the start was nine hundred feet. The highest point on the trip was well above four thousand. They travelled five days, fourteen hours a day. There was plenty of wind. The highest temperature they experienced was zero. They stopped to cut their way through trees with a chain saw (fearing to doze them because the wanigan might be crushed). The Cat fell twice through rotting ice. With no difficulty, it climbed out of the water. There was some luck in the conditions, but not much. With less ice in Woodchopper Canyon, Stanley might have been stopped. But successive overflows on the creek had built the ice thickness in places to thirty feet. Nearing the head of Woodchopper, he moved the Cat slowly up a steep slope of ice, slid back, crept again, slid back, and thought for a while he wouldn't make it. Without the grousers, the big rig would have been stopped, but they held just enough, and gradually he crawled out of the head of the creek—only to move into snow so deep the D9's steel tracks spun out. Stanley thought it wise to stop for the night. For one thing, all this was happening in a blizzard. Next day, the sky was clear, the air colder, and Stanley moved on a contour through the deep snow until he found an uphill route. Steadily, he climbed ridges, sometimes in little snow, sometimes in seven-foot drifts. At one point, the going was so steep that he disengaged the sled and tried first to clear a trail. "I knew that ridge was too steep to go over, because it was almost vertical. So I went around to the right. Without them ice grousers, the machine would have slid sideways and straight to the bottom as if it was on skates. Gary was scared to death. I went real slow now, and slipped some, and then went down to a dead crawl. I had it idled as low as it would go. I went on a half a mile or so. When I saw it was possible, I went back for the sled."

Landing on skis, his father would fly him out, and the D9 would sit idle in the mountains until summer. Meanwhile, there was one last ridge to cross. "One side was sheer, and the other had deep snow and was very steep. It must have been forty-five degrees. A guy could have maybe gone around one side—if you'd left the wanigan, dug the snow, and plowed a road. But I didn't want to make a horrible-looking mess. I moved slowly up. The track did spin a bit. I couldn't go straight up. It was too steep. I

couldn't go sideways too well. I couldn't go back, because I had
the sled. I'd have been afraid to back down. You can cut a road
into the side of a mountain if you want to with a Cat like that,
but I just inched up the thing, and over. I didn't want to dig up
the country."

[*What follow are three fragments of the winter and the summer.*]

When I have stayed with the Gelvins, I have for the most part
occupied a cabin toward the far end of the airstrip—a place they
acquired not long ago from an old-timer named Curly Allain,
who was in his seventies and went south. He had no intention
of returning, but he left his cabin well stocked with utensils, food,
and linen—a tin of coffee close to the pot, fifty pounds of flour,
five pounds of Danish bacon, firewood in three sizes stacked
beside the door. Outside, some paces away, I have stood at a
form of parade rest and in the broad light of a June midnight
been penetrated in the most inconvenient place by a swarm of
indecent mosquitoes, and on the same spot in winter, in a similar
posture at the same hour, have stared up in darkness from squeaky
snow at a green arch of the aurora, green streamers streaming
from it all across the sky. At home, when I look up at the North
Star I lift my eyes but don't really have to move my head. Here,
I crane back, lift my chin almost as far as it will go, and look up
at the polestar flirting with the zenith. The cabin is long and low,
and its roof is loaded white—mantled eighteen inches deep. Its
windows are brown-gold from the light of burning lamps. The
air is so still I can hear the rising smoke. Twenty-two degrees
below zero. Balls of ice are forming in the beard. I go back inside
and comb it off, and jump into a bag of down.

[*22*]

The spruce in their millions are thick with snow, but not heavy snow—a light dry loaf on every bough, with frost as well, in chain crystals. Just touch one of these trees and all of its burden falls, makes craters in the snow of the ground. The load is so delicately poised a breath can break it, a mild breeze denude the forest. Day after day, the great northern stillness will preserve this Damoclean scene, while the first appearance of each February dawn shoots pink light into the trees, and colors all the blanketed roofs, the mushroom caps on barrels and posts. Overhead, sometimes, a few hundred feet above the ground stillness, the wind is audibly blowing.

Brad Snow said that if the canoe were to tip over, it would have to be abandoned, because the river, even now, in June, was too cold to allow the usual procedure of staying with the boat and kicking it to shore. "Keep your clothes on in the river. They provide some insulation, and you will need them later on. It's a good idea to have some matches tucked away in a dry container. We would need a drying fire." With luck, and fair probability, the canoe would go into an eddy, he said, and might be recovered there.

Nothing much was going to turn us over, though. Only at one or two points in a hundred and sixty miles did we see anything that remotely suggested rapids, and these were mere drapefolds of white in the otherwise broad, flat river. Sleepers were in the water—big logs flushing down out of Canada and floating beneath the surface—but they were going in our direction and were much less dangerous than they would have been had we been heading upstream. The great power of the Yukon—six and more fathoms of water, sometimes half a mile wide, moving at seven knots—was unostentatiously displayed. The surface was deceptively calm—it was only when you looked to the side that you saw how fast you were flying.

From the hull, meanwhile, came the steady sound of sandpaper, of sliding stones, of rain on a metal roof—the sound of the rock in the river, put there by alpine glaciers. Dip a cupful of water and the powdered rock settled quickly to the bottom. At the height of the melting season, something near two hundred tons of solid material will flow past a given point on the riverbank in one minute. Bubbling boils, like the tops of high fountains, bloomed everywhere on the surface but did not rough it up enough to make any sort of threat to the canoe. They stemmed from the crash of fast water on boulders and ledges far below. Bend to bend, the river presented itself in large segments—two, three, six miles at a stretch, now smooth, now capped white under the nervously changeable sky. We picked our way through flights of wooded islands. We shivered in the deep shadows of bluffs a thousand feet high—Calico Bluff, Montauk Bluff, Biederman Bluff, Takoma Bluff—which day after day intermittently walled the river. Between them—in downpourings of sunshine, as often as not—long vistas reached back across spruce-forested hills to the rough gray faces and freshly whitened summits of mountains. Some of the walls of the bluffs were of dark igneous rock that had cracked into bricks and appeared to have been set there by masons. Calico Bluff—a sedimentary fudge, folded, convoluted in whorls and ampersands—was black and white and yellow-tan. Up close it smelled of oil. It was sombre as we passed it, standing in its own shadow. Peregrine falcons nest there, and—fantastic fliers—will come over the Yukon at ballistic speeds, clench their talons, tuck them in, and strike a flying duck hard enough (in the neck) to kill it in midair. End over end the duck falls, and the falcon catches it before it hits the river. As we passed the mouth of the Tatonduk, fifteen ducks flew directly over us. Brad Snow reached for his shotgun, and quickly fired twice. Fifteen ducks went up the Tatonduk. Above the Nation, steep burgundy mountainsides reached up from the bright-green edges of the river, then fell away before tiers of higher mountains, dark with spruce and pale with aspen, quilted with sunlight and shadow. Ahead, long points of land and descending ridgelines reached toward one another into the immensity of the river, roughed now under a stiff wind. Filmy downspouts dropped from the clouds. Behind the next bend, five miles away, a mountain was partly covered with sliding mist. The scene resembled Lake Maggiore and might have been the Hardanger Fjord, but it was just a fragment of this river, an emphatic implication of all the two thousand miles, and of the dozens of tributaries that in themselves were major rivers—proof and reminder that with its rampart bluffs and circumvallate mountains it was not only a great river of the far northwestern continent but a river of preëminence among the rivers of the world. The ring of its name gave nothing away to the name of any river. Sunlight was bright on the mountains to both sides, and a driving summer rain came up the middle. The wind tore up the waves and flung pieces of them through the air. It was not the wind, though, but the river itself that took the breath away.

Dick Cook has sometimes handed the sled over to me for two and three miles at a time, he and Donna walking far behind. On forest trails, with the ground uneven, the complexity of the guess-work is more than I'd have dreamed. We come to, say, a slight uphill grade. I have been riding, standing on the back of the sled. The dogs, working harder, begin throwing glances back at me. I jump off and run, giving them a hundred-and-fifty-pound bonus. The sled picks up speed in reply. Sooner or later, they stop—spontaneously quit—and rest. Let them rest too long and they'll dig holes in the snow and lie down. I have learned to wait about forty-five seconds, then rattle the sled, and off they go. I don't dare speak to them, because my voice is not Cook's. If I speak, they won't move at all. There are three main choices—to ride, to run behind, or to keep a foot on the sled and push with the other, like a kid propelling a scooter. The incline has to be taken into account, the weight of the sled, the firmness of the trail, the apparent energy of the dogs, the time since they last rested, one's own degree of fatigue. Up and down hill, over frozen lakes— now ride, now half ride, run. Ten below zero seems to be the fulcrum temperature at which the air is just right to keep exertion cool. You're tired. Ride. Outguess the dogs. Help with one foot. When they're just about to quit, step off and run. When things look promising, get on again, rest, look around at the big white country; its laden spruce on forest trails; its boulevard, the silent Yukon. On a cold, clear aurorean night with the moon and Sirius flooding the ground, the sound of the sled on the dry snow is like the rumbling cars of a long freight, well after the engine has passed. According to Harry David, dogs run faster in moonlight, because they are trying to get away from their shadows.

[*This is about Harry David and his sons Michael and Minicup.*]

By a campfire near the boundary—the north-south Canadian boundary—Michael John David reads aloud to me and to his brother from "Lame Deer Seeker of Visions." It is one of several books he carries in his pack. Around us are tall spruce that Michael means to cut and float six or eight miles down the Yukon to become the walls of his new cabin. He is the chief of Eagle Indian Village. " 'I think white people are so afraid of the world they created that they don't want to see, feel, smell, or hear it,' " he reads. He has turned with no searching to what is obviously a favorite passage. " 'The feeling of rain and snow on your face, being numbed by an icy wind and thawing out before a smoking fire, coming out of a hot sweat bath and plunging into a cold stream, these things make you feel alive, but you don't want them anymore.' " He pauses to chuckle, to flash a grin. "Do you like this?"

I tell him he hasn't read enough of it to me. The book was written by John Fire/Lame Deer and Richard Erdoes, and is dedicated to Frank Fools Crow, Pete Catches, George Eagle Elk, Bill Schweigman, Leonard Crow Dog, Wallace Black Elk, John Strike, Raymond Hunts Horse, Charles Kills Enemy, and Godfrey Chips. Such names are as unfamiliar to Michael as they are to me, for they belong to the Minneconjou Sioux, in the Lower Forty-eight, and he is of the Hungwitchin of the Athapaskans. His family came into the country in immemorial time. Long before their settlement became known as Eagle Indian Village, it was known as David Camp. David, Juneby, Malcolm, and Paul are the four major families of the Village now. Michael throws a stick onto the fire and continues: " 'Living in boxes which shut out the heat of the summer and the chill of winter, living inside a body that no longer has a scent, hearing the noise from the hi-fi instead of listening to the sounds of nature, watching some actor on TV having a make-believe experience when you no longer experience anything for yourself, eating food without taste—that's your way. It's no good.' " He laughs aloud—a long, soft laugh. His voice is soft, too—fluid and melodic, like nearly all the voices in the Village. The contrast with my own is embarrassing. No matter how I try to modulate it, to experiment with his example, my voice in dialogue with Michael's sounds to me strident, edgy, and harsh. He is twenty-five years old. His body is light, his face narrow, his nose aquiline. His hair, black and shining, passes through a ring behind his head and plumes between his shoulder blades. He wears a khaki jacket, patched pink denim trousers, leather boots, a belt-sheathed jackknife. He may be an Indian, but he looks like a Turk. On his head is a fur hat that has the shape of an inverted flowerpot—a long-haired fez. His thin, Byzantine mustache droops at the wing tips. He has a miniature beard, scarcely a quarter inch long, tufting from the point of his chin. His brother, Minicup, teen-age, wears bluejeans, a red headband. Minicup is taciturn but obviously interested and even inquisitive, his eyes moving back and forth between Michael and me. He was baptized Edward David. Minicup is a name he gave to himself years ago.

We are finishing dinner, a common enterprise. It began, after
making camp, with a mutual presentation of what each of us had
to offer. Michael and Minicup set out Spam, Crisco, Sanka,
fresh carrots, onions, and potatoes. I set out tins of beef stew,
and corn, tea, sugar, raisins, nuts, chocolate, and cheese. Michael, opening the Spam, said, "I remember when it cost a
dollar." Between us there has been a certain feeling out of ways
and means. It is my wish to follow Michael's lead, to see how
he will go about things in the woods. To some extent, he seems
to want to do the same with me. It was he who chose this campsite—a couple of hundred yards into the forest and away from
the Yukon's right bank, on flat ground covered with deep sphag-
num, close to the edge of a small, clear stream. Wicked thorns
grow out of the moss on long roselike stems. We hacked at them
with our knives until we had cleared an area big enough for my
small nylon A-frame and the brothers' wall tent—an orange Canadian affair that Michael, for privacy, often stays in at the Village. Before building the fire, he turfed out the moss, cutting
eight inches down and removing a five-foot square. Even so, he
did not get to the bottom of the moss. I then, automatically,
without pausing to think, went off to the river for rocks. I brought
back two or three in my arms, like loaves of bread, and dropped
them on the moss. I returned to the river. The brothers followed.
We all collected rocks and carried them back into the woods—
gathering, in several trips, more than enough for a fireplace. I
was about to begin building one but checked myself and relin-
quished the initiative. Why should I build the sort of three-walled
fireplace I would make in Maine? I wanted to see what they would
do. I fiddled with my pack and left the rocks alone. Michael and
Minicup laid them out singly—one after another, scarcely
touching—in the closest thing possible to a perfect circle. I could
not see what the purpose of such a circle might be. It could not
shield the fire from wind, nor could it support the utensils of
cooking. Possibly it was to retain the spread of smolderings
through the moss, but it seemed awfully large for that. Why had
they made it, unless purely as an atavistic symbol, emplaced by
what had by now become instinct?

Now Michael, finishing his dinner, has a question for me. He says, "Why did you go get the rocks?"

A few days ago, when I heard that Michael was going up the Yukon for cabin logs, I went to ask if I could join him. In a canoe, I approached the Indian Village, which sits on the left bank—twenty, thirty feet above the river. It is a linear community: cabins spaced along the river a third of a mile, facing, across the water, a six-hundred-foot bluff. In front of each cabin, the steep slope of the riverbank glitters with broken glass—micaceous flakes, the Indian midden. I kept the canoe close under the bank, sliding below the Village. When the youth above are drinking, they like to shoot over the river at the bluff—a .30-calibre declaration of joy. That is what they were doing at the time, so it was prudent to be under the bullets. Harm, of course, was not intended. In 1898, one Angus, who lived up there, organized what he hoped would be a massacre of the whites of Eagle, but, like many projects that have got started in the Village, it was not carried out, it was merely conceived. The Hungwitchin appear to be characteristically passive. When and if they do go on what Michael likes to call "the warpath," their preferred weapons are legal briefs and lobbies—supplied by the native regional corporation that stands behind them. I went up the bank and found Michael alone in a cabin, sober and disconsolate, sitting in a chair, looking straight ahead. His face seemed less alive than cast. The cabin was spotless and almost empty, with psychedelic posters on the walls. It is shared by Village bachelors, of whom he is one. He was anxious to go upriver and to get back well in advance of the next session of the Village Council, he said. It would be of great importance to him, because it would have to do with control of alcohol. When I left him there, he was still staring straight ahead, listening to the reports of the rifles.

A door or two away was the cabin in which Michael grew up. Like most cabins in the Village, it is essentially one room, twenty by twenty feet, with a storm vestibule full of dog harnesses, guns, mukluks, parkas. In the main room, all furniture is against the walls, which are insulated with carton cardboard ("Burger King

Frozen Shoestring Potatoes"). There are three beds, a bench and a table, a tall oval heat stove, a propane oven and range. Cordwood, stacked waist-high, is inside the cabin as well. Yet the first two impressions the cabin gives are a sense of neatness and a sense of space. Michael, three brothers, and two sisters are grown and away now, if not altogether gone. So his parents, Bessie and Harry David, have only four children at home with them still. The beds touch like dominoes. The three youngest sleep in one, parents in another, Minicup in the third. Clothes are in boxes under the beds. A broom hangs by the door. Coming inside in winter, you sweep your legs free of snow before it melts.

No one seems to knock. People just come in and sit down and don't say much until something occurs to be said. Harry, on the bench by the table, may be slowly sharpening a saw, Bessie pouring cups of tea. A radio plays rock. Charlie Juneby, big as a bear, comes in with a frozen mop, and without explanation sits and drinks tea. He is joined later on by his brother Isaac. Stay in one place long enough and almost the whole Village appears and visits and goes. If consumed time is the criterion, visiting is what the Hungwitchin mainly do. They tell about hunting. Jacob Malcolm impressively describes himself stalking moose on snowshoes—successfully running them down. In the phenomenal stillness of the winter air, he lights a match to see how the flame may bend, then he chooses his direction of approach. Jimmy David comes in, and drops a pair of bloody white ptarmigan on the floor, presenting them to his mother. A fresh snowshoe hare already hangs from a wire on the wall. Bessie wears slacks, has a ready grin. Her hair is tied behind her head. Her oldest child is in his thirties, her youngest is eleven. She is some years younger than Harry. Harry is as trim as a coin. He is short and grayhaired, wears glasses. He is intense, and is known for working hard. "I work hard, come in, take a god-damned good shot before I eat. I like coffee, too, soon as I get up." Harry is the kind of man who shakes Tabasco on his beans. "At home, I'm kind of hazy like, don't feel very good, no satisfaction with anything. I enjoy myself outside, across the Yukon River, feel fine, feel full of hell and vinegar, full of life, energy—lots of energy." So saying, one February day he went out of the cabin and walked seven miles in the snow. I went behind him, in his tracks. We are the same size; he has a rolling gait, a shorter stride than mine, but he made the going easier for me. He wore rubber boots, rubber trousers, a blue down jacket, a dark-brown leather hat. In his cheek he had a dip of Copenhagen snuff. When he stood still, to talk, he leaned forward. We walked some distance on the Yukon River, which, under the snow, was now smooth and now mountainously jagged where the ice floes at freeze-up had jammed. Gradually, we crossed over, and then went up a crease in the bluff—Harry without the slightest pause, as if he were ascending stairs, when in fact the snow on that precipitous ground was underlaid with ice, and a slip could mean a long fall down. He carried a stick. "This is a good place to go up from the Yukon River," he said, reaching back for me with the stick. Beyond the top, he had cut a maze of trails, miles through a forest burn. He works six and seven days a week cutting cordwood for sale. He does not use a power saw. "John Borg lost his way one time, coming to get some wood, and he said, 'God damn it, Harry, you got too many trails up here'—but he got a good trail to here, don't kick about that." We passed a large pile of whole spruce trunks—up to thirty feet long, their bark blackened—that Michael had cut and had stacked by himself. "He's a young boy. By God, he handle it," Harry said. "He's a well-liked boy. The girls are crazy for him. He is the chief. He has done his country good. By talking, you know—making everything go nice. I think he's got a little college in him. He studies the right way for his people. He like to see people get along together, make no enemy with nobody."

Fifteen years ago, Harry was the chief. "Anyone interfere with our country, we got a right to pitch in and kick like hell about it. You white people butt in, take our traplines, our fishing. That's what we try to stop."

"How do you feel about independence for Alaska, Harry?"

"That's the best way to look at it."

Making a long loop through the burn, we came out eventually
at the highest part of the bluff, directly opposite the Village: a
panoptic aerial view, of such height and distance, taking in so
much river and mountain land, that it emphasized the isolation
and the elongate symmetry of the Village by the river and—what
is not apparent up close—its beauty. For Harry, this was obviously
the supreme moment in the country—the sight of his village from
the air. He was born, he said, far down the Yukon River, at the
mouth of the Kandik, in 1913. "They kept on moving in those
days. They don't stay one place. They lived off the country. They
lived in tents, ten by twelve, the biggest they ever had. They just
keep on moving. They don't stay in town all the time, like we
do." Harry's father, Old David, died when Harry was six, and he
was raised for a time by Chief Alec, at Fortymile, but when "the
flu came up the river" Chief Alec died, and so did his wife, Mary
Alec. Harry was returned to his mother, at Eagle, and lived with
her until she died. In the same year, his stepfather drowned.
Harry was by now a young man. He hauled wood for the river-
boats, and he worked aboard them, too, until they stopped running, "when the Jap tried to take Alaska." At Moosehide one
time, near Dawson, he met Bessie. "She is what they call a Crow,
I think. One day, I bought two bottles of Hudson Bay rum—a
hundred and fifty proof—and a keg of beer, and I married her."
Looking across at their cabin, in miniature, in the third of a mile
of cabins all touched with smoke, he said he had cut its logs by
Eagle Creek and floated them down the Yukon River. For a time,
he made his living as a trapper and in summer fished, with a
wheel, on Goose Island. He pointed. "That is Goose Island, in
the Yukon River—there." He soon went to work, seasonally, for
the gold-mining operations at Woodchopper, Coal Creek, and
Chicken. "For many years, my work and unemployment just
connected." His and Bessie's children were born in the cabin—
Michael in 1951, "clever, too, just like Howard, quick." Harry
pointed toward the school, at the upstream end of the Village,
and said Bessie taught Han there. Han is the language of the
Hungwitchin. There are about thirty people in the world who

speak it. A few are upriver, in the area of Dawson, but virtually all of them are in Eagle Indian Village. Han is one of the smallest subdivisions of the great Athapaskan language family, which reaches contiguously from Nulato and Koyukuk, in western Alaska, to southern Alberta and east to Hudson Bay—and makes a surprising jump, as well, across twelve hundred miles to the isolated Southwestern enclave of the Apache and the Navajo, which, among Athapaskans, are by far the most numerous. High on a pole outside the school we could see a small, dark movement—the flag of Alaska flying. The flag, as it happens, was designed by a native. It is lyrically simple, the most beautiful of all American flags. On its dark-blue field, gold stars form the constellation of the Great Bear. Above that is the North Star. Nothing else, as the designer explained, is needed to represent Alaska. It was the flag of the Territory for more than thirty years. Alaskans requested that it become the flag of the new state. The designer was a thirteen-year-old Aleut boy.

Michael went to high school in Tok, and he was "clever for anything," his father said. "With no trouble, he got into the Army. One day, he said, 'Dad, I'm going far to Anchorage with my friend.' He went far to Anchorage with his friend, and he got through the examination clean as a dollar. He went to California." Michael spent almost all of his two service years at the Presidio of San Francisco, where it never snowed, and he missed the winter. He also missed Sophie Biederman. She was a tall, slim, beautiful girl in brightly beaded moccasins. She had an outreaching smile, black hair, a complexion light and clear, notwithstanding that she went around with a can of soda pop almost constantly in her hand, and—eating virtually never—seemed to live on Coca-Cola alone. Harry told her she smoked too much marijuana. (Harry, for his part, does not even smoke tobacco.) Sophie's childhood had been roiled in her parents' troubles with alcohol. Nonetheless, she emerged with a joy in living, a fondness for excitement, a love of games. Her life and Michael's seemed to be spiralling upward through the summer of his return. Spilling Coke, she would dash into his arms. They planned a wedding, and he went to the North Slope to collect money to begin their married life. While he was there, she died of a gunshot wound, an apparent suicide. "Michael got broke down over her."

[*Even before the large expansion of national parkland in Alaska in 1980, the federal government tried hard to discourage new people, most of whom were in their twenties, from building or occupying cabins on Alaskan federal land. As a result, the following story came to be held in special regard by young people in the upper Yukon.*]

The country is full of stories of unusual deaths—old Nimrod Robertson lying down on a creek in overflow and letting it build around him a sarcophagus of ice; the trapper on the Kandik who apparently knocked himself out when he tripped and fell on his own firewood and froze to death before he came to—and of stories also of deaths postponed. There are fewer of the second. I would like to add one back—an account that in essence remains in the country but in detail has largely disappeared.

On a high promontory in the montane ruggedness around the upper Charley River lies the wreckage of an aircraft that is readily identifiable as a B-24. This was the so-called Liberator, a medium-range bomber built for the Second World War. The wreckage is in the dead center of the country, and I happened over it in a Cessna early in the fall of 1975, during a long and extremely digressive flight that began in Eagle and ended many hours later in Circle. The pilot of the Cessna said he understood that the crew of the Liberator had bailed out, in winter, and that only one man had survived. I asked around to learn who might know more than that—querying, among others, the Air Force in Fairbanks, the Gelvins, various old-timers in Circle and Central, some of the river people, and Margaret Nelson, in Eagle, who had packed parachutes at Ladd Field, in Fairbanks, during the war. There had been one survivor—everyone agreed. No one knew his name. He had become a symbol in the country, though, and was not about to be forgotten. It was said that he alone had come out—long after all had been assumed dead—because he alone, of the widely scattered crew, was experienced in wilderness, knew how to live off the land, and was prepared to deal with the hostile cold. Above all, he had found a cabin, during his exodus, without which he would have died for sure.

"And the government bastards try to stop us from building them now."

"Guy jumped out of an airplane, and he would have died but he found a cabin."

If the survivor had gone on surviving for what was now approaching thirty-five years, he would in all likelihood be somewhere in the Lower Forty-eight. When I was home, I made a try to find him. Phone calls ricocheted around Washington for some days, yielding only additional phone numbers. The story was just too sketchy. Did I know how many bombers had been lost in that war? At length, I was given the name of Gerard Hasselwander, a historian at the Albert F. Simpson Historical Research Center, Maxwell Air Force Base, Alabama. I called him, and he said that if I did not even know the year of the crash he doubted he could help me. Scarcely two hours later, though, he called back to say that he had had a free moment or two at the end of his lunch hour and had browsed through some microfilm. To his own considerable surprise, he had found the survivor's name, which was Leon Crane. Crane's home when he entered the Army Air Forces had been in Philadelphia, but Hasselwander had looked in a Philadelphia directory and there was no Leon Crane in it now. However, he said, Leon Crane had had two brothers who were also in service—in the Army Medical Corps—during the Second World War. One of them was named Morris. In the Philadelphia directory, there was a Dr. Morris Crane.

When I called the number, someone answered and said Dr. Crane was not there.

I asked when he would return.

"I don't know" was the reply. "He went to Leon's."

The Liberator, making cold-weather propeller tests above twenty thousand feet, went into a spin, dived toward the earth, and, pulling out, snapped its elevator controls. It then went into another spin, and the pilot gave the order to abandon ship. There were five aboard. Leon Crane was the co-pilot. He was twenty-four and he had been in Alaska less than two months. Since the plane was falling like a swirling leaf, he had to drag himself against heavy centrifugal force toward the open bomb bay. He had never used a parachute. The outside air temperature was at least thirty degrees below zero. When he jumped, he forgot his mittens. The day was December 21st.

The plane fiercely burned, not far away from where he landed, and he stood watching it, up to his thighs in snow. He was wearing a hooded down jacket, a sweater, winter underwear, two pairs of trousers, two pairs of socks, and felt-lined military mukluks. He scanned the mountainsides but could see nothing of the others. He thought he had been the second one to go out of the plane, and as he fell he thought he saw a parachute open in the air above him. He shouted into the winter silence. Silence answered. Months later, he would learn that there had been two corpses in the aircraft. Of the two other fliers no track or trace was ever found. "Sergeant Pompeo, the crew chief, had a hell of a thick set of glasses. He must have lost them as soon as he hit the airstream. Without them, he really couldn't see. What was he going to do when he got down there?"

For that matter, what was Crane going to do? He had no food, no gun, no sleeping bag, no mittens. The plane had been meandering in search of suitable skies for the tests. Within two or three hundred miles, he had no idea where he was.

Two thousand feet below him, and a couple of miles east, was a river. He made his way down to it. Waiting for rescue, he stayed beside it. He had two books of matches, a Boy Scout knife. He started a fire with a letter from his father, and for the first eight days he did not sleep more than two hours at a time in his vigilance to keep the fire burning. The cold awakened him anyway. Water fountained from a gap in the river ice, and that is what he lived on. His hands, which he to some extent protected with parachute cloth or in the pockets of his jacket, became cut and abraded from tearing at spruce boughs. When he spread his fingers, the skin between them would split. Temperatures were probably ranging between a high of thirty below zero and a low around fifty. The parachute, as much as anything, kept him alive. It was twenty-eight feet in diameter, and he wound it around him so that he was at the center of a great cocoon. Still, he said, his back would grow cold while his face roasted, and sparks kept igniting the chute.

He was telling me some of this on a sidewalk in Philadelphia when I asked him how he had dealt with fear.

He stopped in surprise, and looked contemplatively up the street toward Independence Hall, his graying hair wisping out to the sides. He wore a business suit and a topcoat, and he had bright, penetrating eyes. He leaned forward when he walked. "Fear," he repeated. "I wouldn't have used that word. Think about it: there was not a hell of a lot I could do if I were to panic. Besides, I was sure that someone was going to come and get me."

All that the search-and-rescue missions had to go on was that the Liberator had last been heard from above Big Delta, so the search area could not be reduced much below forty thousand square miles. Needless to say, they would not come near finding him. He thought once that he heard the sound of an airplane, but eventually he realized that it was a chorus of wolves. In his hunger, he tried to kill squirrels. He made a spear, and threw it awkwardly as they jumped and chattered in the spruce boughs. He made a bow and arrow, using a shroud line from his parachute, but when he released the arrow it shot off at angles ridiculously oblique to the screeching, maddening squirrels. There was some rubber involved in the parachute assembly, and he used that to make a slingshot, which was worse than the bow and arrow. When he fell asleep by the fire, he dreamed of milkshakes, dripping beefsteaks, mashed potatoes, and lamb chops, with lamb fat running down his hands. Awake, he kicked aside the snow and found green moss. He put it in his mouth and chewed, and chewed some more, but scarcely swallowed any. Incidentally, he was camped almost exactly where, some twenty-five years later, Ed and Virginia Gelvin would build a cabin from which to trap and hunt.

Crane is a thoroughly urban man. He grew up in the neighborhood of Independence Hall, where he lives now, with an unlisted number. That part of the city has undergone extensive refurbishment in recent years, and Crane's sons, who are residential builders and construction engineers, have had a part in the process. Crane, more or less retired, works for them, and when I visited him I followed him from building to building as he checked on the needs and efforts of carpenters, bricklayers, plumbers. He professed to have no appetite for wild country, least of all for the expanses of the north. As a boy, he had joined a city Scout troop, and had become a First Class Scout, but that was not to suggest a particular knowledge of wilderness. When he flew out of Fairbanks that morning in 1943, his lifetime camping experience consisted of one night on the ground—with his troop, in Valley Forge.

He decided on the ninth day that no help was coming. Gathering up his parachute, he began to slog his way downriver, in snow sometimes up to his waist. It crossed his mind that the situation might be hopeless, but he put down the thought as he moved from bend to bend by telling himself to keep going because "right around that curve is what you're looking for." In fact, he was about sixty miles from the nearest human being, almost a hundred from the nearest group of buildings large enough to be called a settlement. Around the next bend, he saw more mountains, more bare jagged rock, more snow-covered sweeps of alpine tundra, contoured toward another river bend. "Right around that curve is what you're looking for," he told himself again. Suddenly, something was there. First, he saw a cache, high on legs in the air, and then a small cabin, with a door only three feet high. It was like the lamb chops, with the grease on his fingers, but when he pushed at the door it was wood and real. The room inside was nine by ten: earth floor, low ceiling, a bunk made of spruce. It was Alaskan custom always to leave a cabin open and stocked for anyone in need. Split firewood was there, and matches, and a pile of prepared shavings. On a table were sacks of dried raisins, sugar, cocoa, and powdered milk. There was a barrel stove, frying pans on the wall. He made some cocoa, and, after so long a time without food, seemed full after a couple of sips. Then he climbed a ladder and looked in the cache, lifting a tarp to discover hammers, saws, picks, drills, coiled rope, and two tents. No one, he reasoned, would leave such equipment far off in the wilderness. "I figured civilization was right around the corner. I was home free."

So he stayed just a night and went on down the river, anxious to get back to Ladd Field. The moon came up after the brief light of day, and he kept going. He grew weak in the deep cold of the night, and when the moon went below the mountains he began to wander off the stream course, hitting boulders. He had been around many corners, but no civilization was there. Now he was sinking into a dream-hazy sleepwalking numbed-out oblivion; but fear, fortunately, struck through and turned him, upriver. He had not retraced his way very far when he stopped and tried to build a fire. He scraped together some twigs, but his cut and bare hands were shaking so—at roughly fifty below zero—that he failed repeatedly to ignite a match. He abandoned the effort, and moved on through the snow. He kept hitting boulders. He had difficulty following his own tracks. He knew now that he would die if he did not get back to the cabin, and the detached observer within him decided he was finished. Left foot, right foot—there was no point in quitting, even so. About noon, he reached the cabin. With his entire body shaking, he worked at a fire until he had one going. Then he rolled up in his parachute and slept almost continuously for three full days.

In his excitement at being "right around the corner from civilization," he had scarcely looked in the cache, and now he found rice, flour, beans, powdered eggs, dried vegetables, and beef—enough for many weeks, possibly months. He found mittens. He found snowshoes. He found long johns, socks, mukluks. He found candles, tea, tobacco, and a corncob pipe. He found ammunition, a .22. In the cabin, he mixed flour, peas, beans, sugar, and snow, and set it on the stove. That would be his basic gruel—and he became enduringly fond of it. Sometimes he threw in eggs and vegetables. He covered his hands with melted candle wax, and the bandage was amazingly effective. He developed a routine, with meals twice a day, a time for hunting, a fresh well chopped daily through the four-foot river ice. He slept eighteen hours a day, like a wintering bear—not truly hibernating, just lying there in his den. He felt a need to hear a voice, so he talked to himself. The day's high moment was a pipeful of tobacco puffed while he looked through ten-year-old copies of *The Saturday Evening Post*. He ransacked the magazines for insights into the woods lore he did not know. He learned a thing or two. In a wind, it said somewhere in the *Post*, build your fire in a hole. He shot and ate a ptarmigan, and had the presence of mind to look in its stomach. He found some overwintering berries there, went to the sort of bushes they had come from, and shot more ptarmigan. Cardboard boxes, the magazines, and other items in the cabin were addressed to "Phil Berail, Woodchopper, Alaska." Contemplating these labels, Crane decided that Alaska was a fantastic place—where someone's name and occupation were a sufficient address. One day, an old calendar fell off the wall and flipped over on its way to the floor. On the back was a map of Alaska. He stared at it all day. He found Woodchopper, on the Yukon, and smiled at his foolishness. From the terrain around him, the northward flow of the stream, the relative positions of Fairbanks and Big Delta, he decided—just right—that he was far up the Charley River. The smile went back where it came from.

He decided to wait for breakup, build a raft, and in late May float on down to the Yukon. After five or six weeks, though, he realized that his food was going to give out in March. There was

little ammunition with which to get meat, and he had no confidence anyway in his chances with the rifle. If he stayed, he
would starve. He felt panic now, but not enough to spill the care
with which he was making his plans. He had set off willy-nilly
once before and did not want to repeat the mistake. He patched
his clothes with parachute cloth, sewing them with shroud lines.
He made a sled from some boards and a galvanized tub. He
figured closely what the maximum might be that he could drag
and carry. On February 12th, he left. The sled would scarcely
budge at first, and snow bunched up before it. Wearing a harness
he had made, he dragged the sled slowly downriver. Berail's
snowshoes had Indian ties. Try as he would, he could not understand how to secure them to his feet. The snowshoes were
useless. Up to his knees, and sometimes to his hips, he walked
from dawn until an hour before dark each day. He slept beside
bonfires that burned all night. Blizzards came up the river some
days, and driving williwaws—winds of a force that could literally
stop him in his tracks. He leaned against the wind. When he
could, he stepped forward. Once, at the end of a day's hard
walking, he looked behind him—on the twisting mountain
river—and saw where he had started at dawn. The Charley in
summer—clear-flowing within its canyon walls, with grizzlies
fishing its riffles, Dall sheep on the bluffs, and peregrines above
it in the air—is an extremely beautiful Alaskan river (it has been
called the loveliest of all), but for Leon Crane it was little more
than brutal. He came to a lead one day, a patch of open water,
and, trying to use some boulders as stepping stones, he fell in up
to his armpits. Coming out, barging through snowdrifts, he was
the center of a fast-forming block of ice. His matches were dry.
Shaking as before, he managed this time to build a fire. All day,
he sat steaming beside it, removing this or that item of clothing,
drying it a piece at a time.

After a couple of weeks on the river, he found another cabin,
with a modest but welcome food cache—cornmeal, canned vegetables, Vienna sausage. He sewed himself a backpack and abandoned his cumbersome sled. Some seven or eight days on down

[*41*]

the river, he came around a bend at dusk and found cut spruce tops in parallel rows stuck in the river snow. His aloneness, he sensed, was all but over. It was the second week of March, and he was eighty days out of the sky. The arrangement of treetops, obviously, marked a place where a plane on skis might land supplies. He looked around in near darkness and found a toboggan trail. He camped, and next day followed the trail to a cabin— under smoke. He shouted toward it. Al Ames, a trapper, and his wife, Neena, and their children appeared in the doorway. "I am Lieutenant Leon Crane, of the United States Army Air Forces," he called out. "I've been in a little trouble." Ames took a picture, which hangs on a wall in Philadelphia.

Crane remembers thinking, Somebody must be saving me for something, but I don't know what it is. His six children, who owe themselves to that trip and to Phil Berail's fully stocked Charley River cabin, are—in addition to his three sons in the construction business—Mimi, who is studying engineering at Barnard; Rebecca, who is in the master's program in architecture at Columbia; and Ruth, a recent graduate of the Harvard Medical School. Crane himself went on to earn an advanced degree in aeronautical engineering at the Massachusetts Institute of Technology, and spent his career developing helicopters for Boeing Vertol.

"It's a little surprising to me that people exist who are interested in living on that ground up there," he told me. "Why would anyone want to take someone who wanted to *be* there and throw them out? Who the hell could *care?*"

Al Ames, who had built his cabin only two years before, harnessed his dogs and mushed Crane down the Yukon to Woodchopper, where a plane soon came along and flew him out.

Crane met Phil Berail at Woodchopper, and struggled shyly to express to him his inexpressible gratitude. Berail, sixty-five, was a temporary postmaster and worked for the gold miners there. He had trapped from his Charley River cabin. He was pleased that it had been useful, he said. For his part, he had no intention of ever going there again. He had abandoned the cabin four years before.

Earl Stout, a former miner, is too old to be concerned with all the new government regulations, with settling ponds or enforcement orders or turbidity units in any form. He worked Sly Creek, Fourth of July Creek—and in 1959 he retired to his cabin on Crooked Creek, in Central. He eats potatoes. They are the fundaments of his breakfasts, his lunches, and his dinners. "I ain't too heavy on the meat situation. I never was. I get my outfit in the fall of the year. Potatoes." He is in ruddy health, white-haired, of medium height, a little stooped—eighty-five years old. He smokes a pipe. In his cabin are three calendars and three clocks. He gets up at exactly five-thirty every morning. Evenings, just before he goes to bed at nine, he goes to the calendars and crosses off the day.

This is a Friday in winter, as it happens. Sometime this morning, he filled his gas lantern. That is about all he has accomplished today. "In fact, I ain't done a whole lot since I retired in '59," he says, and in the silence that follows the ticking of his clocks sounds like the puffing of locomotives. There is an iron bed, a couple of chairs, and a big galvanized tub full of melted stream ice. When he needs more, he will cut it out of Crooked Creek and haul it on a go-devil behind his old Oliver Cat. In his Bean's boots, open wool shirt, and gray trousers, he sits and sleeps and reads—*Newsweek, Popular Science, National Geographic, Prevention.* On a shelf beside him is a book called "Upper Tittabawassa Boom Towns," in a couple of which (Hope and Sanford, Michigan) he grew up. He came to the upper Yukon fifty years ago.

On Fridays now, at precisely four o'clock, he goes down the

road to collect his mail. He could run this errand at almost any time and on almost any day. In good weather, the mail plane arrives three times a week. But Earl Stout likes to gather mail in weekly units. "What's the use of getting it," he explains, "before it's all in?" Saturday nights, he used to play pool at the Central store—stick in hand, cigar in mouth, brandy on the cushion. "That was until the old Chevy went out. Now I stay home. All the years I was on the Yukon, there was no place to go. The nearest person was five miles away. You got to get used to staying home." He sorely misses Bob. A black, short-haired mongrel, Bob was for many years Earl's only companion. Five wolves running on the creek overtook Bob not long ago. They left his collar and a small piece of his tail. After finding the blood and the fragments, Earl drank a bottle of rum. It is 3:45 P.M. He gets up and pulls denim overalls over his trousers. He ties strings around the ankles. He puts on mittens and a wool cap, and he says, "I can't take the cold the way I used to." The air outside is ten below zero. I make a move to leave. "You don't have to go," he says. "It isn't time yet. There's still ten minutes." He waits until the clocks say four. "Now," he says, "it's time to go."

GIVING GOOD

WEIGHT

(1 9 7 9)

[Giving Good Weight *is a five-part collection with highly varied themes. In the title piece, McPhee is working for a farmer in the Greenmarkets of Harlem, Brooklyn, the Upper East Side. "While I was writing* Coming into the Country," *he recalls, "the long strain of the effort was so great that I kept promising myself that if I ever finished it I'd never write another line. That was a way of getting through. A couple of weeks after I completed the manuscript, in midsummer, I went to New York to do a Talk of the Town piece about the Greenmarket, a city program in which farmers were—as they still are—permitted to sell their produce from their trucks in designated lots and blocks, on a different site each day of the week. I intended a one-day reportorial visit, no more. But selling beans beats writing, hands down (or so it seemed to me at the time), and on the third day—after I'd gotten to know some of the people—I put on an apron and started to weigh produce and make change. I began commuting from my home in New Jersey to the BAM parking lot at Flatbush and Atlantic, to 102nd and Amsterdam, to 137th Street and Adam Clayton Powell; and I was still there when snow was falling on the pumpkins."*]

Giving Good Weight

You people come into the market—the Greenmarket, in the open air under the downpouring sun—and you slit the tomatoes with your fingernails. With your thumbs, you excavate the cheese. You choose your stringbeans one at a time. You pulp the nectarines and rape the sweet corn. You are something wonderful, you are—people of the city—and we, who are almost without exception strangers here, are as absorbed with you as you seem to be with the numbers on our hanging scales.

"Does every sink grow on your farm?"

"Yes, ma'am."

"It's marvellous. Absolutely every sink?"

"Some things we get from neighbors up the road."

"You don't have no avocados, do you?"

"Avocados don't grow in New York State."

"Butter beans?"

"They're a Southern crop."

"Who baked this bread?"

"My mother. A dollar twenty-five for the cinnamon. Ninety-five cents for the rye."

"I can't eat rye bread anymore. I like it very much, but it gives me a headache."

Short, born abroad, and with dark hair and quick eyes, the woman who likes rye bread comes regularly to the Brooklyn Greenmarket, at Flatbush and Atlantic. I have seen her as well at the Fifty-ninth Street Greenmarket, in Manhattan. There is abundant evidence that she likes to eat. She must have endured some spectacular hangovers from all that rye.

Farm goods are sold off trucks, vans, and pickups that come into town in the dark of the morning. The site shifts with the day of the week: Tuesdays, black Harlem; Wednesdays, Brooklyn; Fridays, Amsterdam at 102nd. There are two on Saturdays—the one at Fifty-ninth Street and Second Avenue, the other in Union Square. Certain farms are represented everywhere, others at just one or two of the markets, which have been primed by foundation funds and developed under the eye of the city. If they are something good for the urban milieu—tumbling horns of fresh plenty at the people's feet—they are an even better deal for the farmers, whose disappearance from the metropolitan borders may be slowed a bit by the many thousands of city people who flow through streets and vacant lots and crowd up six deep at the trucks to admire the peppers, fight over the corn, and gratefully fill our money aprons with fresh green city lettuce.

"How much are the tomatoes?"

"Three pounds for a dollar."

"Peaches?"

"Three pounds for a dollar twenty-five."

"Are they freestones?"

"No charge for the pits."

"How much are the tomatoes?"

"Three pounds for a dollar. It says so there on the sign."

"Venver the eggs laid?"

"Yesterday."

"Kon you eat dum raw?"

We look up from the cartons, the cashbox, the scales, to see who will eat the eggs raw. She is a good-looking big-framed young blonde.

"You bet. You can eat them raw."

"How much are the apples?"

"Three pounds for a dollar."

Three pounds, as we weigh them out, are anywhere from forty-eight to fifty-two ounces. Rich Hodgson says not to charge for an extra quarter pound. He is from Hodgson Farms, of Newburgh, New York, and I (who come from western New Jersey) have been working for him off and on for three months, summer and fall. I thought at first that I would last only a week, but there is a mesmerism in the selling, in the coins and the bills, the all-day touching of hands. I am often in charge of the peppers, and, like everyone else behind the tables by our truck, I can look at a plastic sack of them now and tell its weight.

"How much these weigh? Have I got three pounds?"

"That's maybe two and a quarter pounds you've got there."

"Weigh them, please."

"There it is. Two and a quarter pounds."

"*Very* good."

"Fantastic! Fantastic! You see that? You see that? He knew exactly how much it weighed."

I scuff a boot, take a break for a shiver in the bones. There are unsuspected heights in this game, moments that go right off the scale.

This is the Brooklyn market, in appearance the most cornucopian of all. The trucks are drawn up in a close but ample square and spill into its center the colors of the country. Greengage plums. Ruby Red onions. Yellow crookneck squash. Sweet white Spanish onions. Starking Delicious plums.

Fall pippins ("Green as grass and curl your teeth"). McIntoshes, Cortlands, Paulareds. ("Paulareds are new and are lovely apples. I'll bet they'll be in the stores in the next few years.")

Pinkish-yellow Gravensteins. Gold Star cantaloupes. Patty Pan squash.

Burpless cucumbers.

Cranberry beans.

Silver Queen corn. Sweet Sue bicolor corn, with its concise tight kernels, its well-filled tips and butts. Boston salad lettuce.

Parris Island romaine lettuce. Ithaca iceberg crunchy pale lettuce. Orange tomatoes.

Cherry Bell tomatoes.

Moreton Hybrid, Jet Star, Setmore, Supersonic, Roma, Saladette tomatoes.

Campbell 38s.

Campbell 1327s.

Big Boy, Big Girl, Redpak, Ramapo, Rutgers London-broil thick-slice tomatoes.

Clean-shouldered, supple-globed Fantastic tomatoes. Celery (Imperial 44).

Hot Portugal peppers. Four-lobed Lady Bell glossy green peppers. Aconcagua frying peppers.

Parsley, carrots, collard greens.

Stuttgarter onions, mustard greens.

Dandelions.

The people, in their throngs, are the most varied we see—or that anyone is likely to see in one place west of Suez. This intersection is the hub if not the heart of Brooklyn, where numerous streets converge, and where Fourth Avenue comes plowing into the Flatbush-Atlantic plane. It is also a nexus of the race. "Weigh these, please." "Will you please weigh these?" Greeks. Italians. Russians. Finns. Haitians. Puerto Ricans. Nubians. Muslim women in veils of shocking pink. Sunnis in total black. Women in hiking shorts, with babies in their backpacks. Young Connecticut-looking pants-suit women. Their hair hangs long and as soft as cornsilk. There are country Jamaicans, in loose dresses, bandannas tight around their heads. "Fifty cents? Yes, dahling. Come on a sweetheart, mon." There are Jews by the minyan, Jews of all persuasions—white-bearded, black-bearded, split-bearded Jews. Down off Park Slope and Cobble Hill come the neo-bohemians, out of the money and into the arts. "Will you weigh this tomato, please?" And meantime let us discuss theatre, books, environmental impacts. Maybe half the crowd are men—men in cool Haspel cords and regimental ties, men in lipstick, men with blue eyelids. Corporate-echelon pinstripe men.

Their silvered hair is perfect in coif; it appears to have been audited. Easygoing old neighborhood men with their shirts hanging open in the summer heat are walking galleries of abdominal and thoracic scars—Brooklyn Jewish Hospital's bastings and tackings. (They do good work there.) A huge clock is on a tower high above us, and as dusk comes down in the autumn months the hands glow Chinese red. The stations of the hours light up like stars. The clock is on the Williamsburgh Savings Bank building, a skyscraper full of dentists. They go down at five into the Long Island Rail Road, under us. Below us, too, are all the subways of the city, in ganglion assembled.

"How much are the cabbages?"

"Forty cents a head."

"O.K. Weigh one, please."

We look around at empty storefronts, at J. Rabinowitz & Sons' SECURITY FIREPROOF STORAGE, at three gold balls (Gem Jewelers Sales), at Martin Orlofsky's Midtown Florist Nursery. Orlofsky has successfully objected to our presence as competitors here, and we can sell neither plants nor flowers. "HAVE YOU HAD ANY LATELY? CLAMS, STEAMERS." Across Fourth Avenue from the Greenmarket is the Episcopal Church of the Redeemer, a century and a quarter old, with what seem to be, even in the brightest morning light, black saints in its stained-glass windows. Far down Fourth, as if at rest on the paved horizon, stands a tower of the Verrazano-Narrows Bridge. To the northwest rises the Empire State. Not long after dawn, as trucks arrive and farmers begin to open boxes and set up wooden tables, a miscellany of whores is calling it a day—a gradual dispersal, quitting time. Their corner is Pacific and Fourth. Now and again, a big red Cadillac pauses at the curb beside them. The car's rear window is shaped like a heart. With some frequency, a squad car will slide up to the same curb—a week-in, week-out, endless duet with the Cadillac. The women hurry away. "Here come the law." The Greenmarket space, which lies between Atlantic and Pacific, was once occupied by condemned buildings—spent bars and liquor stores. The block is fenced and gravelled now, and is leased by the Brooklyn Academy of Music, which charges the Green-market seventy-five dollars a Wednesday. The market does not fill the lot—the rest is concession parking. Here in the din of the city, in the rivers of moving metal, some customers drive to the Greenmarket as if it were a roadside stand in Rockland County, a mall in Valley Stream.

On a sidewalk around the corner, people with a Coleman stove under a fifty-five-gallon drum are making sauce with our toma-toes. Tall black man in a business suit now picks up a slim hot pepper. Apparently he thinks it sweet, because he takes most of it with a single bite and chews it with anticipant relish. Three . . . two . . . one. The small red grenade explodes on his tongue. His eyeballs seem to smoke. By the fistful, he grabs cool string-beans and stuffs them into his mouth.

I forget to give change to a middle-aged woman with bitter eyes. I charged her forty-five cents for a pound and a third of apples and she gave me half a dollar. Now she is demanding her nickel, and her eyes are narrower than the sides of dimes. She is a round-shouldered person, beaky and short—shortchanged. In her stare at me, there is an entire judiciary system—accusation, trial, and conviction. "You give me my nickel, mister."

"I'm sorry. I forgot. Here is your nickel."

She does not believe my mistake a mistake. She walks away in a white huff. Now she stops, turns, glowers. She moves on. Twice more, as she departs from the market, she stops, turns, and stares angrily back. I watch her all the way to the curb. She waves at the traffic and gets into a cab.

A coin will sink faster through bell peppers than it will through water. When people lose their money they go after it like splashing bears. Peppers everywhere. Peppers two deep over the apples, three deep over the plums. Peppers all over the ground. Sooner or later, the people who finger the eggs will spill and break the eggs, and the surface they walk on becomes a gray-and-yellow slurry of parking-lot gravel and egg—a Brooklyn omelette. Woman spills a dozen now. Her purse is hanging open and a falling egg plops in. Eleven smash on the ground. She makes no offer to pay. Hodgson, who is young and whimsical, grins and shrugs. He is not upset. He is authentically amused. Always, without a sign of stress, he accepts such losses. The customer fingers another dozen eggs, and asks if we are sure they are good.

I err again, making change—count out four ones, and then a five, "and ten makes twenty."

The customer says, "I gave you a ten-dollar bill, not a twenty."

I look at her softly, and say to her, "Thanks very much. You're very nice."

"What do you mean I'm very nice? I gave you a ten-dollar bill. Why does that make me very nice?"

"I meant to say I'm glad you noticed. I'm really glad you noticed."

"How much are the tomatoes?"

"Weigh these, please."

"Three pounds for a dollar."

"How much the corn?"

"Ten cents an ear. Twelve for a dollar."

"Everything is so superior. I'd forgotten what tomatoes taste like."

"Will you weigh these, please?"

"The prices are so ridiculously cheap."

"How can you charge so little?"

"In nine years in the city, I've never seen food like this."

"How much are these?"

"Fifty-five cents."

"Wow! What a rip-off!"

"Three pounds for a dollar is too much for tomatoes. You know that, don't you? I don't care how good they are."

"How much are these?"

"A dollar-ten."

"A dollar-*ten*?"

"Three eggplants. Three and a half pounds. Three pounds for a dollar. You can have them for a dollar-ten."

"Keep them."

"In the supermarket, the vegetables are unspeakable."

[*53*]

"They are brought in from California."

"You can't see what you are getting."

"When the frost has come and you are gone, what will we do without you?"

Around the market square, some of the trucks have stickers on them: "NO FARMERS, NO FOOD." Alvina Frey is here, and Ronald Binaghi, from farms in Bergen County, New Jersey. John Labanowski and his uncle Andy Labanowski are from the black-dirt country, the mucklands, of Orange County, New York. Bob Engle and Jim Kent tend orchards in the Hudson Valley. Bill Merriman, the honey man, is from Canaan, Connecticut; Joan Benack and Ursula Plock, the bakers, from Milan, New York. Ed and Judy Dart grow "organic" on Long Island, Richard Finch in Frenchtown, New Jersey. John Henry. Vincent Neglia. Ilija Sekulovski. Don Keller. Cleather Slade completes the ring. Slade is young, tall, paunchy, silent, and black. His wife, Dorothy, sells with him. She has a nicely lighted smile that suggests repose. Their family farmland is in Red Springs, North Carolina, but the Slades are mainly from Brooklyn. They make occasional trips South for field peas, collards, okra, yams, and for the reddest watermelons north of Chichicastenango.

Jeffrey Mack works for Hodgson part time. He has never seen a farm. He says he has never been out of the city. He lives five blocks away. He is eight years old, black. He has a taut, hard body, and glittering eyes, a round face. He piles up empty cartons for us and sometimes weighs tomatoes. On his better days he is some help.

"Jeffrey, that's enough raisin bread."

"Jeffrey, how many times do I have to tell you: get yourself out of the way."

"What are you doing here, Jeffrey? You ought to be in school."

He is not often pensive, but he is pensive for a moment now. "If you had a kid would you put him up for adoption?" he asks.

"What is that supposed to mean, Jeffrey? Why are you asking me that?"

"My mother says she's going to put me up for adoption."

With two, three, and four people working every truck, the farmers can occasionally take breaks, walk around—eat each other's apples, nectarines, and pears. Toward the end of the day, when their displays have been bought low and the crowd is becoming thin, they move around even more, and talk in small groups.

"What always surprises me is how many people are really nice here in the city."

"I was born in New York. My roots are here, you know. I'd throw away a bad cantaloupe, anything, so the people would come back."

"We have to leave them touch tomatoes, but when they do my guts go up and down. They paw them until if you stuck a pin in them they'd explode."

"They handle the fruit as if they were getting out all their aggressions. They press on the melons until their thumbs push through. I don't know why they have to handle the fruit like that. They're brutal on the fruit."

"They inspect each egg, wiggle it, make sure it's not stuck in the carton. You'd think they were buying diamonds."

"They're bag crazy. They need a bag for everything, sometimes two."

"They're nervous. So nervous."

"Today I had my third request from someone who wanted to come stay on the farm, who was looking for peace and quiet for a couple of days. He said he had found Jesus. It was unreal."

"I had two Jews in yarmulkes fighting over a head of lettuce. One called the other a kike."

"I've had people buy peppers from me and take them to another truck to check on the weight."

"Yeah, and meanwhile they put thirteen ears of corn in a bag, hand it to you, and say it's a dozen. I let them go. I only get after them when they have sixteen."

"They think we're hicks. 'Yeah,' I say. 'We're hicks and you're hookers. You're muggers and you breathe dirty air.' "

"I hardly smoke in the city. Down home I can smoke a whole

pack of cigarettes and still have energy all night. You couldn't pay me to live here. I can't breathe."

If the farmers have a lot to say about their clients, they have even more to say about each other. Friendly from the skin out, they are deep competitors, and one thing that they are (in a sense) competing for is their right to be a part of the market. A high percentage of them seems to feel that a high percentage of the others should be shut down and sent away.

The Greenmarket was started in 1976. Farmers were recruited. Word got around. A wash of applicants developed. There was no practical or absolute way to check out certain facts about them —nor is there yet. For example, if some of the goods on a truck were not grown by the farmer selling them, who did grow them, and when, and where? The Greenmarket quickly showed itself to be a prime outlet for the retailing of farm produce. On a good day, one truck with an eighteen-foot box could gross several thousand dollars. So every imaginable kind of seller became attracted. The ever-present problem was that anyone in jeans with a rustic address painted on his truck could load up at Hunts Point, the city's wholesale fruit-and-vegetable center, and head out at 5 A.M. for the Greenmarket—a charter purpose of which was to help the regional farmer, not the fast-moving speculator, survive. Authentic farmers, moreover, could bring a little from home and a lot from Hunts Point. Wholesale goods, having been grown on big mass-production acreages (and often shipped in underripe from distant states), could be bought at Hunts Point and retailed—in some instances—at lower prices than the custom-grown produce of a small Eastern farm. Prices, however, were an incidental issue. The customers, the people of the city, believed—and were encouraged to believe—that when they walked into a Greenmarket they were surrounded by true farmers who had grown the produce they displayed and were offering it fresh from the farm. That was the purpose and promise of the Greenmarket—if not the whole idea, an unarguably large part of it—and in the instances where wholesale, long-distance, gassed-out goods were being presented (as some inevitably were) the principle was being subverted. In fact, the term Greenmarket had been coined—and registered in Albany—to set apart these markets in the public mind from certain "farmers' markets" around the city that are annually operated by Hunts Point hicks.

"Are you a farmer, or are you buying from an auction?" was a challenge the farmers began to fling around. Few were neighbors at home—in positions to know about each other. They lived fifty, a hundred, a hundred and fifty miles apart, and came to the city to compete as strangers. They competed in sales, and they competed in slander. They still do. To a remarkable—and generally inaccurate—extent, they regard one another as phonies.

"He doesn't even know what shoe-peg corn is."

"Never trust a farmer who doesn't know shoe-peg corn."

"What exactly is shoe-peg corn?"

"Look at *him*. He has clean fingernails."

"I happen to know he has them manicured."

"I bust my hump seven days a week all summer long and I don't like to see people bring to market things they don't grow."

"Only farmers who are not farmers can ruin this market."

"These hustlers are going to work us off the block."

"There's farmers selling stuff they don't know what it is."

"What exactly is shoe-peg corn?"

"I like coming here. It gets me out of Vineland. Of course, you pick your ass off the night before."

"Look at Don Keller's hands. You can see the farm dirt in them."

"His nails. They'll never be clean."

"Rich Hodgson. See him over there? He has the cleanest fingernails in New York State."

"That Hodgson, he's nice enough, but he doesn't know what a weed looks like. I'll tell you this: he's never even *seen* a weed."

Around the buildings of Hodgson Farms are some of the tallest volunteers in New York, topheavy plants that sway overhead—the Eastern rampant weed. With everybody working ninety hours a week, there is not much time for cosmetics. For the most part, the buildings are chicken houses. Rich's father, Dick Hodgson, went into the egg business in 1946 and now has forty thousand hens. When someone in the city cooks a Hodgson egg, it has quite recently emerged from a chicken in a tilted cage, rolled onto a conveyor, and gone out past a candler and through a grader and into a waiting truck. A possible way to taste a fresher egg would be to boil the chicken with the egg still in it.

Dick Hodgson—prematurely white-haired, drivingly busy—is an agrarian paterfamilias whose eighty-two-year-old mother-in-law grades tomatoes for him. His wife, Frances, is his secretary and bookkeeper. He branched into truck farming some years ago specifically to keep his daughter, Judy, close to home. Judy runs the Hodgsons' roadside stand, in Plattekill, and her husband, Jan Krol, is the family's vegetable grower, the field boss—more than a hundred acres now under cultivation. Rich, meanwhile, went off to college and studied horticulture, with special emphasis on the fate of tropical houseplants. To attract him home, his father constructed a greenhouse, where Rich now grows wandering Jews, spider plants, impatiens, coleus, asparagus ferns—and he takes them with him to Harlem and wherever else he is allowed to sell them. Rich, who likes the crowds and the stir of the city, is the farm's marketer.

The Greenmarket, even more than the arriving Hodgson generation, has expanded Hodgson Farms. Before 1976, the family had scarcely twenty acres under cultivation and, even so, had difficulty finding adequate outlets for the vegetables Jan grew. The roadside stand moved only a minor volume. Much of the rest was sold in New Jersey, at the Paterson Market, with discouraging results. "Paterson is semi-wholesale," Rich says. "You have to sell in units of a peck or more. You're lucky if you get three dollars for a half bushel of tomatoes. You ask for more and all you hear all day is 'That's a too much a money. That's a too much a money.' " (A half bushel of tomatoes weighs twenty-six pounds, and brings at least eight dollars at the Greenmarket, giving good weight.) The Hodgsons tried the fruit-and-vegetable auction in Milton, New York, but the auctioneer's cut was thirteen per cent and the farmers were working for him. They also tried a farmers' market in Albany, but sold three bushels of peppers and a couple of bags of corn in one depressing day. They were more or less failing as small-scale truck farmers. Dick Hodgson's theory of family cohesion through agricultural diversification was in need of an unknown spray. NBC News presented a short item one evening covering the début of the Greenmarket. The Hodgsons happened to be watching.

"The first place we went to was Fifty-ninth Street, and the people were fifteen deep waiting to get to the eggs. I couldn't believe it. There were just masses of faces. I looked at them and felt panic and broke into a cold sweat. They went after the corn so fast I just dumped it on the ground. The people fell on it, stripped it, threw the husks around. They were fighting, grabbing, snatching at anything they could get their hands on. I had never seen people that way, never seen anything like it. We sold a full truck in five hours. It was as if there was a famine going on. The people are quieter now."

Quietly, in a single day in the Greenmarket, Rich has sold as many as fifteen hundred dozen eggs. In one day, nearly five thousand ears of corn. In one day, three-quarters of a ton of tomatoes.

"How much are the tomatoes?"

"Fifteen hundred pounds for five hundred dollars."

Rich is in his mid-twenties, has a tumbling shag of bright-red hair, a beard that comes and goes. When it is gone, as now, in the high season of 1977, he retains not only a mustache but also a pair of frontburns: a couple of pelts that descend from either end of the mustache and pass quite close to his mouth on their way to his chin. He is about six feet tall and wears glasses. Their frames are pale blue. His energy is of the steady kind, and he works hard all day with an easygoing imperturbability—always bemused; always a controlled, sly smile. Rarely, he looks tired. On market days, he gets up at four, is on the Thruway by five, is setting up tables and opening cartons at seven, has a working breakfast around nine (Egg McMuffin), and, with only a short break, sells on his feet until six or seven, when he packs up to drive home, take a shower, drop into bed, and rise again at four. His companion, Melissa Mousseau, shares his schedule and sells beside him. There is no market on Mondays, so Rich works a fourteen-hour day at home. He packs cartons at the farm—cartons of cauliflowers, cartons of tomatoes—and meanders around the county collecting a load for Harlem. The truck is, say, the six-ton International with the Fruehauf fourteen-foot box—"HODGSON FARMS, NEWBURGH, N.Y., SINCE 1946." Corn goes in the nose—corn in dilapidating lath-and-wire crates that are strewn beside the fields where Jan has been bossing the pickers. The pickers are Newburgh high-school students. The fields, for the most part, are rented from the State of New York. A few years ago, the state bought Stewart Air Force Base, outside Newburgh, with intent to lengthen the main runway and create an immense international freightport, an all-cargo jetport. The state also bought extensive farms lying off the west end of the base. Scarcely were the farmers packed up and on the road to Tampa Bay when bulldozers flattened their ancestral homes and dump trucks took off with the debris. The big freightport is still in the future, and meanwhile the milieu of the vanished farms is ghostly with up-growing fields and clusters of shade trees around patches of smoothed ground where families centered their lives. The Hodgsons came upon this scene as farmers moving in an unusual direction. With the number of farms and farmers in steady decline in most places on the urban fringe, the Hodgsons were looking for land on which to expand. For the time being, rented land will do, but they hope that profits will be sufficient to enable them before long to buy a farm or two—to acquire land that would otherwise, in all likelihood, be industrially or residentially developed. The Greenmarket is the outlet—the sole outlet—that has encouraged their ambition. In the penumbral world of the airport land, there are occasional breaks in the sumac where long clean lines of Hodgson peppers reach to distant hedgerows, Hodgson cantaloupes, Hodgson cucumbers, Hodgson broccoli, collards, eggplants, Hodgson tomatoes, cabbages, corn—part vegetable patch, part disenfranchised farm, with a tractor, a sprayer, and a spreader housed not in sheds and barns but under big dusty maples. The family business is integrated by the spreader, which fertilizes the Greenmarket vegetables with the manure of the forty thousand chickens.

Corn in the nose, Rich drives to the icehouse, where he operates a machine that grinds up a three-hundred-pound block and sprays granulated snow all over the corn. Corn snow. He stops, too, at local orchards for apples, Seckel pears, nectarines, peaches, and plums. The Greenmarket allows farmers to amplify their offerings by bringing the produce of neighbors. A neighbor is not a wholesale market but another farmer, whose farm is reasonably near—a rule easier made than enforced. The Hodgsons pick things up—bread included—from several other farms in the county, but two-thirds to three-quarters of any day's load for the city consists of goods they grow themselves.

In the cooler of E. Borchert & Sons, the opiate aroma of peaches is overwhelming, unquenched by the refrigerant air. When the door opens, it frames, in summer heat, hazy orchards on ground that falls away to rise again in far perspective, orchards everywhere we can see. While loading half-bushel boxes onto the truck, we stop to eat a couple of peaches and half a dozen blue free plums. Not the least of the pleasures of working with Hodgson is the bounty of provender at hand, enough to have made the most sybaritic Roman prop himself up on one elbow. I eat, most days, something like a dozen plums, four apples, seven pears, six peaches, ten nectarines, six tomatoes, and a green pepper.

Eating his peach, Rich says, "The people down there in the city can't imagine this. They don't believe that peaches come from Newburgh, New York. They say that peaches come only from Georgia. People in the city have no concept of what our farming is like. They have no idea what a tomato plant looks like, or how a tomato is picked. They can't envision a place with forty thousand chickens. They have no concept how sweet corn grows. And the people around here have a false concept of the city. Before we went down there the first time, people up here said, 'You're out of your mind. You're going to get robbed. You're going to get stabbed.' But I just don't have any fears there. People in black Harlem are just as nice as people anywhere. City people generally are a lot calmer than I expected. I thought they would be loud, pushy, aggressive, and mean. But eighty per cent of them are nice and calm. Blacks and whites get along much better there than they do in Newburgh. Newburgh Free Academy, where I went to high school, was twenty-five per cent black. We had riots every year and lots of tension. Cars were set on fire. Actually, I prefer Harlem to most of the other markets. Harlem people are not so fussy. They don't manhandle the fruit. And they buy in quantity. They'll buy two dozen ears of corn, six pounds of tomatoes, and three dozen eggs. At Fifty-ninth Street, someone will buy one ear of corn for ten cents and want it in a bag. The reason we're down there is the money, of course. But the one-to-one contact with the people is really good—especially when they come back the next week and say, 'Those peaches were really delicious.' "

In the moonless night, with the air too heavy for much sleep anyway, we are up and on the road, four abreast: Anders Thueson, Rich Hodgson, David Hemingway . . . A door handle is cracking my fifth right rib. Melissa Mousseau is not with us today, and for Hemingway it is the first time selling. He is a Newburgh teen-ager in sneakers and a red football shirt lettered "OKLAHOMA." Hemingway is marking time. He has mentioned January half a dozen ways since we started out, in a tone that reveres the word—January, an arriving milestone in his life, with a college out there waiting for him, and, by implication, the approach of stardom. Hemingway can high-jump seven feet. He remarks that the Greenmarket will require endurance and will therefore help build his stamina for January. He is black, and says he is eager to see Harlem, to be "constantly working with different people —that's a trip in the head by itself."

When the truck lurches onto the Thruway and begins the long rollout to the city, Hodgson falls asleep. Anders Thueson is driving. He is an athlete, too, with the sort of legs that make football coaches whistle softly. Thueson has small, fine features, light-blue eyes, and short-cropped hair, Scandinavian yellow. He is our corn specialist, by predilection—would apparently prefer to count ears than to compute prices from weights. When he arrives in Harlem he will touch his toes and do deep knee bends to warm himself up for the corn.

Dawn is ruddy over Tappan Zee, the far end of the great bridge indistinct in mist. Don Keller, coming from Middletown, broke down on the bridge not long ago, rebuilt his starter at the toll-booth apron, and rolled into market at noon. Days later, Jim Kent's truck was totalled on the way to Greenmarket—Hudson Valley grapes, apples, peaches, and corn all over the road. Gradually now, Irvington and Dobbs Ferry come into view across the water—big square houses of the riverbank, molars, packed in cloud. In towns like that, where somnolence is the main resource, this is the summit of the business day. Hodgson wakes up for the toll. For five minutes he talks sports and vegetable prices, and again he dozes away. On his lap is a carton of double-yolk eggs. His hands protect them. The fingernails are clean. Hodgson obviously sees no need to dress like Piers Plowman. He wears a yellow chemise Lacoste. The eggs are for Derryck Brooks-Smith, a Brooklyn schoolteacher, who is a regular Hodgson city employee. Brooks-Smith is by appearances our best athlete. He runs long distances and lifts significant weights. He and Thueson have repeatedly tried to see who can be the first to throw an egg over an eight-story building on Amsterdam Avenue. To date their record of failure is one hundred per cent—although each has succeeded with a peach.

We arrive at six-fifteen, to find Van Houten, Slade, and Keller already setting up—in fact, already selling. People are awake, and much around, and Dorothy Slade is weighing yams, three pounds for a dollar. Meanwhile, it is extremely difficult to erect display tables, open boxes, and pile up peppers and tomatoes when the crowd helps take off the lids. They grab the contents.

"Weigh these, please."

"May I have a plastic bag?"

"Wait—while I get the scales off the truck." The sun has yet to show above the brownstones.

This is the corner of 137th Street and Adam Clayton Powell Jr. Boulevard, known elsewhere in the city as Seventh Avenue. The entire name—Adam Clayton Powell Jr. Boulevard—is spelled out on the street sign, which, as a result, has a tip-to-tip span so wide it seems prepared to fly. The big thoroughfare itself is of extraordinary width, and islanded, like parts of Broadway and Park Avenue. A few steps north of us are the Harlem Performance Center and the Egbe Omo Nago African Music Center, and just east along 137th Street from our trucks is the Mother A.M.E. Zion Church. For the Tuesday Greenmarket, the street has been barricaded and cars sent out, an exception being an old Plymouth without tires that rests on flaking steel. On the front wall of the church is a decorous advertisement: "Marion A. Daniels & Sons, Funeral Directors." The block has four young sycamores, and contiguous buildings in every sort of shape from the neat and trim to broken-windowed houses with basements that are open like caves. On 137th Street beyond Adam Clayton Powell are two particularly handsome facing rows of brownstones, their cornices convex and dentilled, their entrances engrandeured with high, ceremonious flights of stairs. Beyond them, our view west is abruptly shut off by the City College cliffs in St. Nicholas Park—the natural wall of Harlem.

The farm trucks are parked on the sidewalks. Displays are in the street. Broad-canopied green, orange, purple, and red umbrellas shield produce from the sun. We have an awning, bolted to the truck. Anders Thueson, with a Magic Marker, is writing our prices on brown paper bags, taping them up as signs. "Is plums spelled with a 'b'?" he asks.

Hemingway tells him no.

A tall, slim woman in a straw hat says to me, "I come down here get broke every Tuesday. Weigh these eggplants, please."

"There you are. Do you want those in a bag?"

"You gave me good weight. You don't have to give me bags."

Minerva Coleman walks by, complaining. She is short and acidulous, with graying hair and quick, sardonic eyes. She wears bluejeans and a white short-sleeved sweatshirt. She has lived in this block twenty-three years. "You farmers come in too early," she says. "Why do you have to come in so early? I have to get up at four o'clock every Tuesday, and that don't make sense. I don't get paid."

Not by the Greenmarket, at any rate. Minerva works for Harlem Teams for Self-Help, an organization that is something like a Y.M.-Y.W.C.A. It is housed, in fact, in a former Y, the entrance to which is behind our truck. Minerva is Director of Economic Development. As such, she brought the Greenmarket to 137th Street—petitioned the city for it, arranged with the precinct to close off the street. While her assistants sell Harlem Teams for Self-Help shopping bags (fifteen cents), Minerva talks tomatoes with the farmers, and monitors the passing crowd. As the neighborhood kleptos come around the corner, she is quick to point them out. When a middle-aged man in a business suit appears on the scene wearing a sandwich board, she reads the message —"HARLEM TEAM FOR DESTROYING BLACK BUSINESS"—and at once goes out of her tree. "What do you mean, 'destroying black business'? Who is destroying black business? *What* is destroying black business? Get your ass off this block. Can't you see this market is good for everybody? The quality and the price against the quality and the price at the supermarket—there's no comparison."

Exit sandwich board.

"How much are the apples?"

"Three pounds for a dollar, madam."

"Are they sweet?"

"You can eat them straight or bake them in a pie."

"Give me six pounds of apples, six pounds of tomatoes, and three dozen extra-large eggs. Here the boxes from the eggs I bought last week."

Mary Hill, Lenox Avenue. Florrie Thomas, Grand Concourse. Leroy Price, Bradhurst Avenue. Les Boyd, the Polo Grounds.

Ylonia Phillips, 159th Street. Selma Williamson, 141st Street. Hattie Mack, Lenox Avenue. Ten in the morning and the crowd is thick. The sun is high and hot. People are drinking from fireplugs. A white cop goes by, the radio on his buttock small and volcanic, erupting: ". . . beating her for two hours." In the upstairs windows of the houses across the street, women sit quietly smoking.

"Are these peppers hot?"

"Those little ones? Yeah. They're hot as hell."

"How do you know how hot hell is? How do you know?"

The speaker is male and middle-aged, wears a jacket and tie, and is small, compact, peppery. He continues, "How do you know how hot hell is? You been over there? I don't think you know how hot hell is."

"Fifty cents, please."

The hundreds of people add up into thousands, and more are turning the corner—every face among them black. Rarely, a white one will come along, an oddity, a floating moon. Just as a bearded person becomes unaware of his beard and feels that he looks like everyone else, you can forget for a time that your own face is white. There are no reminders from the crowd.

Middle-aged man with a woman in blue. She reaches for the roll of thin plastic bags, tugs one off, and tries to open it. The sides are stuck together and resist coming apart. She looks up helplessly, looks at me. Like everyone else on this side of the tables, I am an expert at opening plastic bags.

"These bags are terrible," I tell her, rubbing one between my thumb and fingers. When it comes open, I hand it to her.

"Why, thank you," she says. "You're nice to do that for me. I guess that is the privilege of a lady."

Her husband looks me over, and explains to her, "He's from the old school." There is a pause, some handling of fruit. Then he adds, "But the old schools are closing these days."

"They're demolished," she says. "The building's gone."

They fill their sack with peppers (Lady Bell).

The older the men are here, the more likely it is that they are wearing suits and ties. Gray fedoras. Long cigars. The younger they are, the more likely it is that they are carrying shoulder-strapped Panasonics, turned on, turned up—blaring. Fortunately, the market seems to attract a high proportion of venerable people, dressed as if for church, exchanging news and some opinion.

Among our customers are young women in laboratory smocks with small gold rings in the sides of their noses—swinging from a pierced nostril. They work in Harlem Hospital, at the end of the block, on Lenox Avenue.

Fat man stops to assess the peppers. His T-shirt says, "I SUR-VIVED THE BERMUDA TRIANGLE." Little boy about a foot high. His T-shirt says, "MAN'S BEST FRIEND."

Our cabbages are in full original leaf, untrimmed, each one so broad and beautiful it appears to be a carnation from the lapel of the Jolly Green Giant. They do not fit well in collapsible shopping carts, so people often ask me to strip away the wrapper leaves. I do so, and sell the cabbage, and go back to weighing peppers, making change, more peppers, more change. Now comes a twenty-dollar bill. When I go into my money apron for some ones, a five, a ten, all I come up with is cabbage.

I prefer selling peppers. When you stay in one position long enough, a proprietary sense develops—as with Thueson and the corn. Hodgson, the true proprietor, seems to enjoy selling anything—houseplants and stringbeans, squash and pears. Derryck Brooks-Smith likes eggs and tomatoes. Hemingway is an apple man. Or seems to be. It is early to tell. He is five hours into his first day, and I ask how he is getting along. Hemingway says, "These women in Harlem are driving me nuts, but the Jews in Brooklyn will be worse." Across his dark face flies a quick, sarcastic smile. "How *you* doing?" he asks me.

"Fine. I am a pepper seller who long ago missed his calling."

"You like peppers?"

"I have come to crave them. When I go home, I take a sackful with me, and slice them, and fill a big iron skillet to the gunwales—and when they're done I eat them all myself."

[67]

"Cool."

"These tomatoes come from a remote corner of Afghanistan," Derryck Brooks-Smith is saying to some hapless client. "They will send you into ecstasy." She is young and appears to believe him, but she may be in ecstasy already. Brooks-Smith is a physical masterpiece. He wears running shorts. Under a blue T-shirt, his breasts bulge. His calves and thighs are ribbed with muscle. His biceps are smooth brown loaves. His hair is short and for the most part black, here and there brindled with gray. His face is fine-featured, smile disarming. He continues about the tomatoes: "The smaller ones are from Hunza, a little country in the Himalayas. The people of Hunza attribute their longevity to these tomatoes. Yes, three pounds for a dollar. They also attribute their longevity to yogurt and a friendly family. I like your dress. It fits you well."

Brooks-Smith teaches at John Marshall Intermediate School, in Brooklyn. "A nice white name in a black neighborhood," he once remarked. He was referring to the name of the school, but he could as well have meant his own. He was born in the British West Indies. His family moved to New York in 1950, when he was ten. He has a master's degree from City University. "It is exciting for me to be up here in Harlem, among my own people," he has told me over the scale. "Many of them are from the South. They talk about Georgia, about South Carolina. They have a feeling for the farm a lot of people in the city don't have." He quotes Rimbaud to his customers. He fills up the sky for them with the "permanganate sunsets" of Henry Miller. He instructs them in nutrition. He lectures on architecture in a manner that makes them conclude correctly that he is talking about them. They bring him things. Books, mainly. Cards of salutation and farewell, anticipating his return to the school. "Peace, brother, may you always get back the true kindness you give." The message is handwritten. The card and its envelope are four feet wide. A woman in her eighties who is a Jehovah's Witness hands him a book, her purpose to immortalize his soul. She will miss him. He has always given her a little more than good weight. "I love old people," he says when she departs. "We have a lot to learn from them."

"This is where it is, man. This is where it is!" says a basketball player, shouldering through the crowd toward the eggplants and tomatoes, onions and pears. He is well on his way to three metres in height, and his friend is taller still. They wear red shorts with blue stripes and black-and-white Adidas shoes. The one who knows where it is picks up seven or eight onions, each the size of a baseball, and holds them all in one hand. He palms an eggplant and it disappears. "Man," he goes on, "since these farmers came here I don't hardly eat meat no more."

Now comes a uniformed racing cyclist—All-Sports Day at the Greenmarket. He is slender, trained, more or less thirty, and he seems to be on furlough from the Tour de France. He looks expensive in his yellow racing gloves, his green racing shoes. Partly walking, partly gliding, he straddles his machine. He leans over and carefully chooses peppers, apparently preferring the fire-engine-red ones. Brooks-Smith whispers to me, "That bicycle frame is a Carlton, made in England. It's worth at least five hundred dollars. They're rare. They're not made much anymore."

"That will be one dollar, please," I say to the cyclist, and he pays me with a food stamp.

Woman says, "What is this stuff on these peaches?"

"It's called fuzz."

"It was on your peaches last week, too."

"We don't take it off. When you buy peaches in the store, the fuzz has been rubbed off."

"Well, I never."

"You never saw peach fuzz before? You're kidding."

"I don't like that fuzz. It makes me itchy. How much are the tomatoes?"

"Three pounds for a dollar."

"Give me three pounds. Tomatoes don't have fuzz."

"I'm a bachelor. Give me a pound of plums." The man is tall, is wearing a brown suit, and appears to be nearing seventy.

"They're only for me, I don't need more," he explains. "I'm a bachelor. I don't like the word 'bachelor.' I'm really a widower. A bachelor sounds like a playboy."

"Thirty-five cents, please. Who's next?"

"Will somebody lend me a dollar so I can get some brandy and act like a civilized human for a change?" We see very few drunks. This one wears plaid trousers, a green blazer, an open-collared print shirt. He has not so much as feigned interest in the peppers but is asking directly for money. "This is my birthday," he continues. "Happy birthday, Gus. My mother and father are dead. If they were alive, I'd kick the hell out of them. They got me into this bag. For twenty years, I shined shoes outside the Empire State Building. And now I'm here, a bum. I need to borrow a dollar. Happy birthday, Gus."

Slade, opposite, is taking a break. He sits on an upturned tall narrow basket, with his head curled into his shoulder. Like a sleeping bird, he has drifted away. I need a break, too—some relief from the computations, the chaotic pulsations of the needle on the scale.

"Two and a quarter pounds at three pounds for a dollar comes to, let's see, seventy-five cents. Five and a half pounds at three for a dollar twenty-five, call it two and a quarter. That's three dollars."

"Even?"

"Even."

"Y'all going up every week. Y'all going to be richer than hell."

"How much are the nectarines?"

"Weigh these, please."

Turn. Put the fruit in the pan. Calculate. Turn again. Spin the plastic bag. Knot the top. Hand it over. Change a bill.

"You take food stamps?"

"Yes, but I can't give you change."

"How much are the green beans pounds for a dollar and with you in a minute next one—please."

I take off my money apron, give it to Rich, and drift around the market. I compare prices with the Van Houtens. I talk cows with Joe Hlatky. We are from the same part of New Jersey, and he once worked for the Walker-Gordon dairy, in Plainsboro, with its Rotolactor merry-go-round milking platform. Hlatky is a big, stolid man with a shock of blond hair not as neatly prepared as his wife's, which has been professionally reorganized as a gold hive. They work together, selling their sweet white corn and crimson tomatoes—not for nothing is it called the Garden State. Hlatky's twenty-one-year-old daughter, Juanita, often sells with him, too. She is a large-boned, strongly built, large-busted blonde like her mother. Hlatky says that he and his family are comfortable here in Harlem, feeling always, among other things, the appreciative good will of the people. I remember Minerva Coleman telling me that when the farmers came into Harlem the first Tuesday they were "a little nervous—but after that they were O.K." She went on to say, "You can tell when people don't feel quite secure. But now they come in here and go about their business and they don't pay nobody no mind. They like the people here better than anywhere else. I don't know why. I would assume they'd get ripped off a little bit—but not too much." And now Hlatky, standing on 137th Street weighing tomatoes, says again how much he likes this market, and adds that he feels safer here than he does in other parts of the city. He says, "I'll tell you the most dangerous place we sell at. The roughest part of the city we go to is Union Square." So rough, he confides, that when he goes there, on Saturdays, he takes along an iron pipe.

Hlatky today has supplemented his homegrown New Jersey vegetables with peaches from a neighbor in California. They are wrapped in individual tissues. They are packed and presented in a fine wooden box. He bought them at a wholesale market. Robert Lewis, assistant director of the Greenmarket, happens along and sees the peaches. Lewis is a regional planner about to receive an advanced degree from the University of Pennsylvania, a gentle person, slight of build, a little round of shoulder, with a bandanna around his throat, a daypack on his back, steel-rimmed spectacles—all of which contribute to an impression of amiable, academic frailty. He says to big Joe Hlatky, "Get those peaches out of sight!"

With an iron pipe, a single tap on the forehead could send Lewis to heaven twice. Hlatky respects him, though, and is grateful to him, too, for the existence of the market. Hlatky says he will sell off these peaches, with a promise not to bring more— never again to bring to a Greenmarket so much as a single box of wholesale fruit.

"The peaches are from California," says Lewis. "They must go back on the truck."

Hlatky casts aspersions up one side of 137th Street and down the other. Has Lewis noticed Slade's beans, Hodgson's onions, Van Houten's lettuce, Sekulovski's entire load? He says he feels unfairly singled out. He knows, though, that without Lewis and Barry Benepe, who created and developed the Greenmarket, the Hlatky farm in New Jersey would be even more marginal than it is now. ("Here you can make double what you make wholesale. If I sold my stuff in a wholesale market, I couldn't begin to exist.") And while Lewis and Benepe might lack a certain shrewdness with regard to the origin of beans, they contribute an essential that no farmer could provide: a sophisticated knowledge of the city.

One does not just drive across a bridge with a load of summer squash, look around for a vacant lot, and create a farmers' market in New York. Tape of every color is in the way: community boards, zoning committees, local merchants, City Hall. In order to set up even one open-air market—not to mention five or six —it was necessary to persuade, and in many cases to struggle against, nine city agencies, which Benepe describes in aggregate as "an octopus without a head; pull off one tentacle and another has a grip." Benepe is an architect who has worked as a planner not only for the city government but also in Orange County, watching the orchards disappear. When he conceived of the Greenmarket, in 1974, it seemed "a natural answer to a twofold problem": loss of farmland in the metropolitan area and a lack of "fresh, decent food" in the city. Moreover, farmers selling produce from their trucks would start conversations, help resuscitate neighborhoods, brighten the aesthetic of the troubled town. "It seemed too obvious to ignore," Benepe says. "But most obvious things do get ignored." Benepe, like Lewis, is a native of the city. Son of an importer of linen, he studied art history at Williams College (1950) and went on to M.I.T. His dress and appearance remain youthful. To the Greenmarket office, on Fortieth Street, he wears brown denim highwaters, polo shirts, and suède Wallabees. He has long sandy graying hair, a lithe frame, a flat stomach. He rides a bicycle around town. He has a steady gaze, pale-blue eyes. He knows where City Hall is. He once worked for the Housing and Redevelopment Board. To start the Greenmarket, he knew which doors to knock on, and why they would not open. He approached the Real Estate Department. "They seemed to think I wanted to rip them off." He affiliated the project with the Council on the Environment of New York City in order to be eligible to receive foundation funds. He tried the Vinmont Foundation, the Richmond Foundation, the Fund for the City of New York, the America the Beautiful Fund. Finally, the J. M. Kaplan Fund said it would match anything he raised elsewhere. He went back to the others, and enough came through. Of the Greenmarket's overall cost—forty-two thousand dollars in 1977—the farmers, renting space, pay a third.

Lewis, twenty years younger, was a colleague of Benepe in Benepe's urban-planning firm, and helped him start the market. They searched for sites where farmers would be welcome, where neighborhoods would be particularly benefitted, where local fruit-and-vegetable stores were unlikely to open fire. Lewis to a large extent recruited the farmers. He sought advice from Cornell and Rutgers, and wrote to county agents, and interviewed people whose names the agents supplied. He went to roadside-marketing conferences, to farmers' associations, to wholesale outlets. Under his generally disarranged locks, his undefeated shrug, Lewis has a deep and patient intelligence that tends to linger over any matter or problem that comes within its scrutiny. If he is ready to rebuke the farmers (for selling West Coast peaches), he is also ready to listen, without limit, to their numerous problems and even more numerous complaints. Day by day, market to market, he is a most evident link between the farmers and the city. He binds them to it, interprets it for them. Son of a New York University professor, he has no idea what shoe-peg corn is, but he was born in Brooklyn Jewish Hospital, grew up in Crown Heights, and has a sense of neighborhoods, of urban ways, that reaches from Flatbush to the hem of Yonkers. He is not much frightened by Harlem or intimidated by Fifty-ninth Street. He is a city man, and, more important, he is an emeritus city kid.

After staring up the street for a while, Hlatky puts the peaches back on the truck.

"Cigarette lighters! Cigarette lighters!"

The Zippo man did not grow his produce down home. "Cigarette lighters!" Never mind where they're from. They're fifty per cent off and selling fast. While Lewis goes after the Zippo man —effecting an at best temporary expulsion—I return to my peppers.

"Give me two, please. Just two. I ain't got nobody with me. I live by myself. I throw food in the pot. I stick a fork in it. When it gets soft, I eat it."

"Lysol! Lysol!"

A man has come along selling Lysol. He offers cans to Rich Hodgson and, at the same time, to a woman to whom Rich is selling apples. One result of the Greenmarket's considerable success is the attraction it presents to street hucksters, not the Sabrett's-hot-dog sort of street venders, who are licensed by the city, but itinerant merchants of the most mercurial kind. Some conceal things under their jackets. They are readily identifiable because their arms hang straight, as whose would not with five pounds of watches on either wrist? They sell anything—ski hats, tooled-leather belts, turquoise rings, inflatable airplanes. They spread blankets on the sidewalk and sprinkle them with jewelry. Man comes by now selling his dog. They always try to sell to the farmers, who are possibly better customers than the customers. A guy came up to me once in Brooklyn and offered me a case of hot mangoes. I assume they were hot. What other temperature could they be when the case-lot price was two dollars? Another day in Brooklyn, a man pulled up to the curb in an old Chevrolet sedan, opened the trunk, and began selling Finnish porgies. Cleaning them, he spilled their innards into a bucket and their scales fell like snow on the street.

As to nowhere else, though, such people are attracted to 137th Street. All day they come by, selling coconuts, guavas, and terminal-market cucumbers out of carts from the A. & P. "Crabs! Crabs!" The crab man has bright-red boiled blue crabs. Three for a dollar, they dangle from strings. Now a man arrives with a rolling clothes rack crammed with sweaters and pants. He wants eighteen dollars for a two-piece ensemble. "No, thanks," a woman tells him. "I don't want to go to jail." She turns to the peppers and glances up at me, saying, "If a cop came around the corner they'd drop that stuff and run." Now a young man and woman in turtlenecks and Earth shoes wheel up a grocery cart full of comic books, cotton hats, incense, and tube socks. He has a premature paunch. Her eyes are dreamy and the lids are slow. She leans on him in a noodly manner. She looks half asleep, while he looks half awake, as if they were passing each other in the middle of a long journey. "Tube socks! Incense! Tube socks!" The man fixes his attention on Rich. "It's going to get—I'm telling you—*cold* on that farm, man." The socks are still in the manufacturer's package, marked a dollar ninety-five a pair. "Cold, man, I'm telling you. Here's six pairs for five dollars." Sold.

Minerva Coleman, who has been watching, stares after the couple as they go. "That must have been a Long Island girl," she says. "A Harlem girl would know I'd break her ass."

There was a firehouse across the street once. It was razed, and a vest-pocket park is there now, smoothly paved, with a chain-link fence, three strands of barbed wire, and a fan-shaped basketball backboard that (most weeks) has a net. When I am not turned toward the scale, and while I wait for customers to fill their plastic bags, I often watch the games across the street. Some of the boys who play there move like light, their gestures rehearsed, adroit. They go both ways, hit well from the outside. The game they play, almost to the exclusion of any other game, begins from the outside.

Say five, in all, are playing. One starts things off with a set from outside.

"How much are the peppers?"

"Three pounds for a dollar."

"Pick me out three pounds. I'll be back after I get some corn."

"Where are your beans? What happened to your beans today?"

The shooter hits five straight from twenty feet. He is a pure shooter. Now he misses. He and the four others go for the rebound. The one who gets the ball is now on his own to try to score, while everyone else tries to stop him. He dribbles right, into the one-on-four. He stops. Jumps. Shoots. Misses.

"Weigh these, please."

"Weigh mine, please."

Another player grabs the ball. Now *he* makes his moves, trying to score against the four others. The ball pulsates in his hands. His legs are flexed. His feet do not stir. He picks his moment, leaps, arches his back (ball behind his head), scores. The ball is handed to him. He goes outside and shoots an unguarded set. He hits. He shoots another. He misses. Someone else gets the rebound. Now it is four against *that* player as he tries to drive and score. He misses. The player who gets the rebound now faces the four others. . . .

"Mister, will you weigh these peppers? Do you want to sell them to me or not?"

"Sorry. Three and a half pounds. Take them for a dollar." Who wants to make change?

After a reverse pivot that is fluid beyond his years, the kid with the ball scores. He walks to the outside. He takes a free set. Swish. He hits again.

"Weigh these, please."

The shooter misses. The rebound goes high. All five are after it. The boy who grabs it turns and faces the mob.

We see the same game all over the city. Always, the player

with the ball is alone, the isolated shooter, the incubating star—versus everyone else on the court. There is never a pass, a screen, a pick, a roll, a two-on-two, a two-on-three, a three-on-two, a teammate. I turn with some peppers and rattle the scale.

Bartley Bryt comes by and says a cop caught a thief who was ripping off Sekulovski. Bryt is young and white, in bluejeans, Pumas, and a rugger shirt. He is doing a summer job, helping administer the market. He is slim, good-looking, with a shock of light-brown hair—Dalton School, 1977.

I ask him how old the thief was.

"About forty-five," says Bryt. "The only elderly person I've ever seen stealing here. When there's trouble here, it's usually from kids, but there's not much trouble, because the community feeling is so great here. People are so nice to you. Where I live, people go in and turn on their air-conditioners and that's it."

"Where do you live?"

"Seventy-fifth Street between Park and Lexington."

Brigade de Cuisine

*["Brigade de Cuisine" is about a chef who grew up in Spain, was trained at
the Euler in Basel and the Ritz in Paris, and not long ago returned to Europe
after years cooking in rural Pennsylvania. He asked John McPhee to give him
a pseudonym, but as things developed he chose his own.]*

Sometimes, at the height of an evening there are two customers
in his dining room. His capacity is fifty-five, and he draws that
number from time to time, but more often he will cook for less
than forty. His work is never static. Shopping locally to see what
is available today, reading, testing, adding to or subtracting from
a basic repertory of roughly six hundred appetizers and entrées,
he waits until three in the afternoon to write out what he will
offer at night—three because he needs a little time to run to the
store for whatever he may have forgotten. He has never stuffed
a mushroom the same way twice. Like a pot-au-feu, his salad
dressing alters slightly from day to day. There is a couple who
have routinely come to his dining room twice a week for many
years—they have spent more than fifteen thousand dollars
there—and in all that time he has never failed to have on his
menu at least one dish they have not been offered before. "I don't
know if they're aware of this," he has told me. "We owe it to

them, because of the frequency of their visits. They keep us on our toes."

In the evening, when his dining room is filling and he is busy in the rhythm of his work, he will (apparently unconsciously) say aloud over the food, and repeat, the names of the people for whom he is cooking. A bridge-toll collector. A plumber. A city schoolteacher. A state senator—who comes from another state. With light-edged contempt, he refers to his neighborhood as *Daily News* country. There are two or three mobsters among his clientele. They are fat, he reports, and they order their vegetables "family style." There is a couple who regularly drive a hundred and twenty miles for dinner and drive home again the same night. There is a nurse from Bellevue who goes berserk in the presence of Anne's meringue tortes and ultra-chocolate steamed mousse cakes, orders every dessert available, and has to be carted back to Bellevue. There is an international tennis star who parks his car so close against the front door that everyone else has to sidle around it. Inside, only the proprietors seem to know who the tennis star is. The center of attention, and the subject of a good deal of table talk, is the unseen man in the kitchen.

.   .   .

In part, the philosophy of this kitchen rests on deep resources of eggs, cream, and butter, shinbone marrow, boiled pig skins, and polysaturated pâtés of rich country meat. "Deny yourself nothing!" is the motto of one of the regulars of the dining room, who is trim and fit and—although he is executive vice-president in charge of public information at one of the modern giants of the so-called media—regards his relationship with the chef as a deep and sacred secret.

.   .   .

The chef is an athletically proportioned man of middle height—a swimmer, a spear fisherman. One day when he was thirteen he was picking apples in a tree between North Oxford and St. Giles and he fell out of the tree onto a bamboo garden stake. It impaled his cheek at the left corner of his mouth. His good looks are enhanced, if anything, by the scar that remains from this accident. He has dark hair, quick brown eyes, and a swiftly rising laugh. Anne is tall, finely featured, attractive, and blond. Each has eaten a little too well, but neither is falling-down fat. They work too hard. She works in a long ponytail, a cotton plaid shirt, unfaded dungarees, he in old shirts with the sleeves rolled up, rips and holes across the chest. His trousers are generally worn through at the knees. There are patches, sutures of heavy thread. His Herman boots are old and furred and breaking down. He pulls out a handkerchief and it is full of holes. "I don't mind spending money on something that is going to be eventually refundable," he explains. "A house, for example. But not a handkerchief." Most of the time, he cooks under a blue terry-cloth sailor hat, the brim of which is drawn down, like his hair, over his ears.

He was working with a Fulton Market octopus one morning, removing its beak, when he happened to remark on his affection for the name Otto.

"I like Otto," he said. "I think Otto is a sensational name. It's a name you would have to live up to, a challenging name. It suggests aloneness. It suggests bullheaded, Prussian, inflexible pomposity. Someone called Otto would be at least slightly pompous. Intolerant. Impatient. Otto."

Anne said, "He has written his autobiography in that name."

"I like Otto," he said again. "Why don't you call me Otto?"

I said, "Fine, Otto. I'll call you Otto."

Otto stepped outdoors, where he set the unbeaked octopus on a wide wooden plank. "Otto," he repeated, with savor. And he picked up an apple bough, a heavy stick about as long as his arm, and began to club the flesh of the octopus. "Otto," he said again, moving from one tentacle to the next. "I like that very much." Smash. "You do this to break down the fibres." Steadily, he pounded on. In time, he said, "Max is a good name, too—a sort of no-nonsense, straightforward name. Otto sounds humorless, and I don't think I'm humorless."

"Fine, Max. I'll call you Max."

"I like the way Max looks," he said. "It looks wonderful written on paper. You have the imagery of 'maximum,' too. And all the

Maximilians." He struck the octopus another blow with the apple bough. "However," he went on, "I prefer Otto. Otto is autocratic. One word leads to another."

He carried the octopus inside. He said he has a cousin in the Florida Keys who puts octopuses in his driveway and then drives over them. "It's just to break down the fibres. I don't know what happens. I just know that it works." He went into the restaurant bar and took down from a wall an August Sander photograph of an anonymous German chef, a heavy man in a white coat of laboratory length over pin-striped trousers and highly polished shoes. The subject's ears were small, the head a large and almost perfect sphere. On the upper lip, an aggressive mustache was concentrated like a grenade. The man was almost browless, his neck was too thick to permit a double chin, and his tiny black eyes—perhaps by the impertinence of the photographer—were opened wide. In his hammy hands were a bowl and a wooden-handled whip. "This pig-faced guy is a real Otto," said the chef. "When our customers ask who that is in the picture we say he is our founder."

As we returned to the kitchen, I thought about the chef's actual name, which, like the man's demeanor, like the man himself in nearly all his moods, is gentle and unaggressive—an all but dulcet name, ameliorative and smooth, a name like Randal or Malcolm or Neal or Duncan or Hugh or Alan or John. For all that, if he wished to call himself Otto, Otto he would be.

Anne said, "He is less pompous than when I met him."

"Never let it boil," said Otto, lowering the octopus into a pot. "It mustn't boil. It should just simmer."

Nine o'clock in a spring morning and with a big square-headed mallet he is pounding a loin of pork. He has been up for three hours and has made school lunches for the two of his children who are still at home, boned some chicken, peeled potatoes, peeled onions, chopped shallots, shucked mussels, made coffee, swept the kitchen, made stock with the head of a twenty-pound grouper, and emptied outside a pail of scraps for the geese. His way of making coffee is to line a colander with a linen napkin and drip the coffee through the napkin. He ate a breakfast of leftovers—gâteau Saint-Honoré, Nesselrode cream-rum-chestnut mousse. He said, "I always eat dessert for breakfast. That's the only time I like it. For the rest of the day, if I'm working, I don't eat. It's wonderful not to eat if you're in a hurry. It speeds you up."

Anne works late and sleeps late. Otto goes to bed when his cooking is done and is up, much of the year, before dawn. Even at 6 A.M., he is so pressed with things to do that he often feels there is no time to shave. Into the school lunches today went small pork cutlets. He said, "I really don't believe in letting children eat the food served at school. Hot dogs. Baloney. Filth like that." His children carry roast chicken, veal, various forms of fish instead. At home, at the inn, they cook their own meals and eat more or less at random. The family business being what it is, the family almost never sits down at a table together. Sometimes the children, with friends, have dinner in the restaurant. Otto says, "They dress as if they're going to a disco, contemptibly wearing their collars outside their jackets, which is worse than wearing a blazer patch." He charges them half price.

The pork loin flattens, becomes like a crêpe. He dips the mallet in water. "All the cookbooks tell you to pound meat between pieces of waxed paper," he remarks. "And that is sheer nonsense." He is preparing a dish he recently invented, involving a mutation of a favored marinade. Long ago he learned to soak boned chicken breasts in yogurt and lemon juice with green peppercorns, salt, garlic, and the seeds and leaves of coriander, all of which led to a flavor so appealing to him that what he calls chicken coriander settled deep into his repertory. In a general way, he has what he describes as "a predilection for stuffing, for things with surprises inside," and so, eventually, he found himself wondering, "Maybe you could translate a marinade into a stuffing. You could pound a pork loin thin and fold it like an envelope over a mixture of cream cheese, fresh coriander leaves, lemon juice, and green peppercorns. Then you'd chill it, and set it, and later bread it. Sauté it a bit, then bake it. It should have a beguiling taste."

Anne is Latvian and was six when she left the country. Her American-accented English contains no trace of those six years (that I, at any rate, can discern). Her predominant memories of Riga are of food—wide bowls full of caviar, mountained platters of crayfish, smoked lampreys served under crystal chandeliers at banquets in her home. In an album is a photograph of Anne's mother all in white satin among sprays of lilies and roses bending attentively toward a bunting-covered drape-folded canopied bassinet—the day of the christening of Anna Rozmarja. Anna Rozmarja Grauds.

Otto sums it up. "They were rich," he says. "I mean, they were rich rich."

"When I was a little girl, I was swathed in ermine and mink. I don't have a need for it now. It's been done."

"Her family had flocks of money, many ships. It was one of the First Families of Latvia, which is like being one of the First Families of Scranton."

"When the Germans took over the house, they allowed us to live on the top floor."

Words rise quickly in Anne's mind, but in speaking them she often hesitates and stumbles, and most of what she says comes slowly. "When the Russians were after us, we had to hide in the country. I remember the cows and the river and the food. Latvia is rich in milk and cheese and eggs. Even in the war no one was hungry. When we were escaping, we stayed at a farm where there were hams and wheels of cheese and things."

"Was that far from Riga?"

"In LLLatvia, nnnnnnothing is far from Riga."

Tilsit was not far from Riga, and Tilsit was not even in Latvia. Otto's grandfather was an architect in Tilsit. One day, the architect saw an advertisement in a newspaper in which sums of money were mentioned in connection with the connubial availability of a young woman in Salzburg. "Her brother placed the ad, and this chap came down from Tilsit and married her," Otto recounts. "It was the only way she could attract a man. She was quite plain."

"She was a handsome woman," Anne informs him.

Otto says, "She was about as handsome as Eleanor Roosevelt. She was a violent Nazi, that grandmother."

Her husband, at any rate, was excoriated by his family for "promiscuous marrying into the proletariat." Her son, Otto's father, went to *Gymnasium* in Salzburg and was later trained in hotels in Berlin and Munich. By 1936, when he was asked to be manager of the Reina Cristina, in Algeciras, he had been married, in England. The Mediterranean and Iberian Hotels Company, Ltd., an English concern, wanted someone they could trust who could also get on with the Germans. Otto's father carried a German passport during the Second World War.

Otto was born in Buckinghamshire, in July, 1938, and was taken home on a Japanese ship. Food was scarce in Spain for many years thereafter—to the ends of, and beyond, two wars. Gypsies, near starving, came to the hotel, asked for food, performed circus stunts as a way of paying, and then ate less than they were given. Asked why they would ignore food set before them, they said that if they ate a great deal they would soon be hungrier than they would be if they ate little. When Otto was nine, he discovered a boy in a persimmon tree on the hotel grounds stealing fruit. Otto happened to be carrying an air rifle. Pointing it, he ordered the boy to descend. On the ground, the boy "broke for it," and began to climb a garden wall. Otto threw a brick and knocked him down. Proudly, he reported the achievement to his parents. His father cracked him over the head. Otto saw the boy as a thief; his father saw the boy as someone so hungry that he had to steal—and therefore it was proper to let him steal.

"You must remember," Anne will say of her husband, "that he learned early what food really is. He knows what it is to be without it. He has a grasp of the sanctity of food. That is his base. He finds delight just in seeing his ingredients. He goes on to luxury after that. Remember, too, that he ate awful meals endlessly—for years. He was in school in England after the war."

Tutored from the age of three, Otto was sent to Britain a year after the German surrender—to Tre-Arddur House School, on Tre-Arddur Bay, in North Wales, a place that, according to him, "specialized in ridding industrialists' sons of their accents, boys from Yorkshire and Lancashire." Otto spoke Spanish, French, and German, and virtually no English, so he had several accents that were targeted for destruction, too. He was called Dago or Greaser, because he came from "Franco Spain." When he was caught in this or that misdemeanor, the headmaster, gnashing craggily, told him not to "use your Spanish tricks" at Tre-Arddur. "My character was deformed there." Otto's tone is more factual than bitter. "I was a happy kid before then, and I became a morose loner. Eventually, when I was invited to join things, I realized I no longer needed to join." The headmaster whipped the boy for his miserable handwriting. On the rugger field, the headmaster caned anyone who funked a tackle. "We won a lot of rugger matches. I was a hooker—in, you know, the center of the scrum." The Tre-Arddur year had its fine moments. The assistant headmaster fished in Scotland and brought back enough salmon to feed everyone in school.

Otto lived for the long vacs in Spain, for the big sardines on sticks over beach fires, the limpets, the wild asparagus, the fishing, and the catch of red mullet baked on fig leaves and tile. The Reina Cristina was lush beyond thought with its fountains and pools under bougainvillea, its date palms and tangerines, its Islamic arcades and English gardens. "You would have to be a Saudi sheikh to live that life again." English colonials, Andalusians, Murcians, titled and rich, "the whole of the south of Spain knew each other very well, they were very cliquey, and when they came to Gibraltar to clothe their women in English finery they stayed at the Reina Cristina." Above them all stood

Otto's father, six feet five inches, thin and regal, actually a dominant figure among the sherry people and the rest of his distinguished guests. Guy Williams (Williams & Humbert), the Gonzalezes, the Palominos, the Osbornes, the Domecqs. "My father was, you know, *amigo íntimo* with all of them." Having four hundred employees, he was as well a figure of first importance in back-street Algeciras. He and a cork company were the principal employers in the town. He had his standards. He never hired a former altar boy. He felt that altar boys were contaminated by priests. He was scrupulously sensitive to the needs and natures of his staff. When Otto called the chef's son a *mariquita azúcar*, his father made him write a calligraphically perfect note of apology. On a tour of countries to the north, the family went out of its way to stop in Lourdes, because the Reina Cristina's housekeeper had mentioned that she would like some holy water with which to cure her black dog, which had come down with terminal mange. Approaching home through dry hundred-degree heat on the brown plains of the Iberian plateau, Otto and his younger brother suffered so with thirst that they drank the holy water. Their father filled the bottle from a tap, gave it to the housekeeper, and the dog was cured. The boys were thrashed about once a week—their mother's riding crop, their father's hand. There was no cruelty in it, merely custom. Otto calls his parents "permissive," and cites his father's reaction to his experiments with hash. Otto had an underwater-diving companion named Pepe el Moro who would sniff kif before diving in order to clear his sinuses and increase the depth of the dives. Otto sniffed, too. When his father learned that his son was using narcotics, he said only, "Stop that. It's unhealthy." When the *cuadrillas* were in town, the great matadors stayed at the Reina Cristina. Otto as a child knew Belmonte, and later Litri, Ordoñez, Miguelín. Their craft so appealed to him that he knew every moment of their ritual, from the praying in the chapel to the profiling over the sword. In the album is a snapshot of Otto with Ernest Hemingway on the veranda outside the Cristina's bar. Otto marvels at "the incredible patience" Hemingway displayed toward "a callow youth" in his teens. Otto's family had a farm in the mountains with an irrigation system that he still thinks of as nothing less than lyrical—its pools and rivulets descending among terraced beds of kitchen plants. His father also managed the Hotel Reina Victoria, in Ronda. Otto would go there on horseback, the more to be involved in the beautiful country—the Serranía de Ronda—and he paid for all his needs with Chesterfield cigarettes. He went slowly when he went back to school.

His mother's parents lived in Oxford, and he moved on from Tre-Arddur to St. Edward's because St. Edward's was there. It was a distinguished public school, distinguished for having been repugnant to young Laurence Olivier some decades before. Otto was hungry there, not caring for the food. With his air rifle, he killed sparrows and thrushes in his grandparents' garden and roasted them on spits over open fires. In his form, he won the St. Edward's general-knowledge prize in all the years he was there. He was very fond of his grandparents. His grandfather was J. O. Boving, an engineer known for a proposal to harness the Severn bore. He gave his grandson a copy of the Boving family tree, which is fruited, for the most part, with farmers. Its mighty trunk, emerging from the soil, has cracked to pieces a Corinthian temple, thus implying the family's durability relative to the artifacts of the earth. Anne, absorbed, now looks up from the picture. She says, "Most of my family should hang from a tree."

She pours cream from a cup into a bowl, and the cream is so thick that it clings to the cupside like mayonnaise. In bottles, it will not pour at all. To have such cream, she drives many miles each week to a farm in another state. Between layers of pecan cake, she is about to establish three concentric circles of royale chocolate and whipped cream. She has turned to this project after finishing another, in which a layer of meringued hazelnut was covered with a second story of hazelnut Bavarian cream that was in turn covered, top and sides, by a half-inch layer of chocolate cake that had been formed upon an overturned pie plate. Atop this structure was a penthouse confected of chocolate, butter, egg yolks, and brandy. "It looks simple, but it takes so bloody long," she said as she finished. "To admit you eat something like that, these days, is almost like confessing to incest. I was a size twelve before I met Otto. Now I'm size eighteen." Her height saves her. One might well say that she is grand, but she could not be described as fat. Her husband, for his part, works sixteen hours a day, is in constant motion, professes to eat almost nothing, and should be quite slim. By his account, "a couple of cucumbers" is about all he consumes in a day. Somehow, though, he has acquired at least twenty-five pounds that he would like to do without.

Now and again, he will stop to hold a pastry sleeve for her or hammer a dented cake pan back into form, but in the main they work separately, and rapidly, at spaced stations of the table, he slicing some salmon, completing a brioche to enclose it, she making puff paste, or a cake from yogurt cheese. (It takes a couple of days to drip, through cloth, the whey out of a gallon of yogurt. The yield is a quart of cheese.) She makes two, three, four, even five new desserts in a day. A light almond dacquoise is—as much as anything—the standard, the set piece, from which her work takes off on its travels through the stars. The dacquoise resembles cake and puts up a slight crunchy resistance before it effects a melting disappearance between tongue and palate and a swift transduction through the bloodstream to alight in the brain as a poem.

For all his rampant eclecticism—and the wide demands of his French-based, Continentally expanded, and sometimes Asian varietal fare—he knows where the resources of his trade are virtually unlimited. Mondays, when the inn is dark, he leaves his Herman boots in his bedroom—his terry-cloth hat, his seam-split dungarees—and in a dark-blue suit like a Barclays banker he heads for New York City. "In a few square blocks of this town are more consumer goods than in the whole of Soviet Russia," he remarked one time as he walked up Ninth Avenue and into the Salumeria Manganaro, where he bought a pound of taleggio ("It's like a soft fontina") and was pleased to find white truffles. "They're from Piedmont. Grate them on pasta and they make it explode." At Fresh Fish (498 Ninth), he bought river shrimp from Bangladesh weighing up to a quarter of a pound each. He bought sausage flavored with provolone and parsley at Giovanni Esposito (500), and at Bosco Brothers (520) he stopped to admire but not to purchase a pyramid of pigs' testicles, which he said were delicious in salad. "Texas strawberries, you know. They're wonderful. They're every bit as good as sweetbreads. Boil them tender. Dry them. Dredge them in flour. Pan-fry them." At Simitsis International Groceries & Meat (529), he bought a big hunk of citron in a room full of open bins of loose pasta, of big bags and buckets full of nuts and peppers, of great open cannisters of spices and sacks full of cornmeal, hominy grits, new pink beans, pigeon peas, split peas, red lentils, semolina, fava beans, buckwheat kasha, pearl barley, Roman beans, mung beans. "This place is fabulous. If I had a restaurant in New York—oh, boy! New York has everything you could possibly want in food. If you look hard enough, you'll find it all." At Citarella (2135 Broadway, at Seventy-fifth), he admired but did not buy a twenty-pound skate. He had walked the thirty-five blocks from Simitsis to Citarella. He prefers to walk when he's in town. I have seen him on the street with a full side of smoked salmon, wrapped in a towel, tied to a suitcase like a tennis racquet. If Anne is with him, he rides. "You poach skate and serve it with capers and black butter," he said. "It's a wonderful fish, completely underrated. I shot a big electric one in the Caymans." Citarella had flounder roe for eighty-five cents a pound. "You pay four dollars a pound for shad roe," said Otto. "Flounder roe is every bit as good. Shad roe has the name." He stopped for tea, ordering two cups, which he drank simultaneously. At Zabar's (Eightieth and Broadway), he bought thin slices of white-and-burgundy Volpi ham. "It's from St. Louis and it's as good as the best jamón serrano." At Japanese Food Land (Ninety-ninth and Broadway), he bought a couple of pounds of bean threads and four ounces of black fungus. On the sidewalks and having a snack, he ate twelve dried bananas. "That's, actually, nothing," he remarked. "I once et thirty-six sparrows in a bar in Spain. Gorriones, you know—spitted and roasted."

He tried to prove to himself not long ago that with United States ingredients he could duplicate the taste of chorizo, a hard Spanish sausage. He had to throw a good part of it away, because he failed to pack it tight enough and "fur grew inside." Casa Moneo, on Fourteenth Street between Seventh and Eighth, "is the best place for chorizos," he says. "They're made in Newark. They're as good as you can get in Spain."

He also buys chorizos at La Marqueta—a series of concession stalls housed below the railroad tracks on Park Avenue in Spanish Harlem. Chorizos. Jamón serrano. Giant green bananas—four for a dollar. Dried Irish moss. Linseed. Custard apples. "When they're very ripe they get slightly fermented. Mmm." He will buy a couple of pounds of ginger, a bunch of fresh coriander, a couple of pounds of unbleached, unpolished rice—letting go the dried crayfish and the green peanuts, the Congo oil and the pots of rue, letting go the various essences, which are in bottles labelled in Spanish: Essence of Disinvolvement, Essence of Envy and Hate. Breadfruit. Loin goat chops. "OHIO STATE UNIVERSITY" shopping bags. "Goat is milk-white when it's young. I don't want to get into an argument with these people, but that is not kid, it's lamb." Seeing a tray of pigs' tongues, he calls them "beautiful." And high-piled pigs' ears: "You slice them thin."

He drops in at the Bridge Kitchenware Corporation, 212 East Fifty-second Street, nods at Fred Bridge, and says, "I'm looking for a whip for crème fouettée. I have never seen one in America that's any good." Bridge hasn't either. Bridge has overcome the problem, however, by having a supply of stainless ones made for him in France. Otto looks over several as if he were choosing a new squash racquet. "Perfect," he says, eventually, to Bridge.

"Very beautiful. Flexible." He buys a quenelle scoop. Rummaging in the back of the store, he picks up a tin sieve. A clerk frankly tells him not to take it because it is no good. "That's why I want it," he says. "I've never seen one that was any good. The best of them won't last six months." He asks for parchment paper. To "make stuff *en papillote*," he sometimes uses, instead of parchment, narrow bags from liquor stores. "Tied at each end and oiled, they are perfect *en papillote* bags, as long as the paper has not been recycled. You can't make things *en papillote* in recycled paper because of the chemicals involved. Some restaurants use aluminum foil for *en papillote*. Contemptible."

He has lieutenants—certain fish merchants from his general neighborhood—who shop for him at the Fulton Market. But often enough he goes there himself, his body, at 4 A.M., feeling what he calls the *resaca*—"when the tide goes out and leaves the dry sand." He loves this world of rubber boots and bonfires, wet pavement and cracked ice, and just to enter it—to catch the bright eye of a fresh red snapper—is enough to cause his tides to rise. "There is no soul behind that eye," he says. "That is why shooting fish is such fun." Under the great illuminated sheds he checks everything (every aisle, bin, and stall), moving among the hills of porgies and the swordfish laid out like logs of copper beech, the sudden liveliness in his own eyes tempered only by the contrast he feels between the nonchalance of this New York scene and the careful constructions of the Algeciras wholesale fish market, where "they display the food with a lot more love."

"You never know what is going to be good. You have to look at everything," he says, and he looks at bushels of mussels, a ton of squid, bay scallops still in their shells. "Make sure they're not Maine mussels," he remarks, almost to himself. "If they are, forget it. Maine mussels are very clean, but they're small and awfully tough. You just want the big squid. The New Jersey squid." He looks at a crate of lobsters. They are dragons—up into their salad years—and three of them fill the crate, their heads seeming to rest on claws the size of pillows. "People think they're dragons because they look like dragons, but they're called that because they are caught in dragnets," he says, picking one up and turning it over, then the second, and the third. The third lobster has many hundreds of green pellets clinging like burrs to its ventral plates. "Eggs. They're better than caviar," says Otto. "They're so crunchy and so fresh-tasting—with lemon juice, and just enough bland vegetable oil to make them shine. You remove them from the lobster with a comb."

Baskets of urchins disappoint him. "See all the white spots? The freckles? See how the spines are flat? If the spines are standing, the creature is very much alive." For many months, he and his legates have been on the watch for urchins that are up to his standards. They must be very much alive because their roe, which is what he wants, is so rich and fragile that it soon goes bad.

He views with equal scorn a table of thin fresh herrings. He serves herring fillets in February, and this is not February. "That's the only time of year when we can get big fat herrings. They're sensational then, maybe a day or two out of the sea. You have et bottled herring, have you? Awful. Herring, or salmon, in sour cream. They don't use crème fraîche. They use a sauce with dubious taste but with better keeping qualities." Otto never prepares herring the same way twice, but his goal is the same if his ingredients are not. He uses, say, vinegar and dill with peppercorns and onions, and his goal is to give the herring "a taste so clean it's lovely."

He feels the slender flanks of sand lances, and he says, "You dredge them with flour, drop them into deep fat, and eat them like French fries." He presses the columnar flank of a swordfish, pleased to have it back in the market. He quotes Ted Williams. It is Williams' opinion that the surest way to save the Atlantic salmon is to declare the species full of mercury and spread the false word. "Swordfish is a bummer in the freezer," Otto says. "But there are all sorts of fish you *can* freeze. Shrimp are better frozen properly on a ship than carried for days to market unfrozen. In properly frozen shrimp there's never a hint of ammonia. Scallops freeze well, too—and crabmeat, octopus, striped bass, flounder, conch, tilefish, grouper. Red snapper frozen is no good. It gets watery, waterlogged. A soft-fleshed fish like a sea trout is no good frozen. Freezing tuna or bluefish precipitates the oily taste. No frozen fish is better than fresh, but well-frozen fish is better than fish a week old."

Groupers—weighing thirty, forty pounds—face him in a row, like used cars. "You can split those big heads," he says. "Dredge them in flour and pan-fry them. Then you just pick at them—take the cheeks, the tongue."

There are conger eels the size of big Southern rattlesnakes. "With those I make jellied eel, cooked first with parsley, white wine, and onions. Almost no one orders it. I eat it myself."

As he quits the market, he ritually buys a pile of smoked chub, their skins loose and golden. "Smoked chub are so good," he says. "They just melt like butter. You can eat half a dozen quite happily on the way home in the car."

Now the inn is quiet, Anne up and working while her family sleeps. She says she believes in guardian angels. She says her good luck is so pervasive that she pulls into gas stations and has flat tires there. She had luck today. When the sea urchins came, she had made enough trifle and baked enough cake to cover her desserts. She works on urchins now—cracking, scooping, separating out the roe. The column of gold is rising in the jar. She says of their move to another place that they are not going far, not far from New York, no telling where. "He has to feel comfortable. I trust in his paranoia to tell us where to go. What is certain is that we'll be between nowhere and no place, and things will be the same. For all those people who want flames and white gloves, there will be no flames or white gloves. What we have is simple food. Simple food if it is good is great. If you understand that, you understand him."

[*93*]

Her hair has come out of its knot, and a long strand crosses one eye. She puts down her work, dries her hands, and runs them backward from her temples. She speaks on, slowly. "You may have grasped this, but I don't know him very well. If you're close to a screen you can't see through it. He doesn't know me, either. We're just together. People are unknowable. They show you what they want you to see. He is a very honest person. Basically. In his bones. And that is what the food is all about. He is so good with flavor because he looks for arrows to point to the essence of the material. His tastes are very fresh and bouncy. He has honor, idealism, a lack of guile. I don't know how he puts them together. I don't know his likes and dislikes. I can't even buy him a birthday present. He has intelligence. He has education. He has character. He has integrity. He applies all these to this manual task. His hands follow what he is."

F R O M

BASIN AND

RANGE

(1 9 8 1)

[Basin and Range *is the opening volume in a tetralogy which describes the*
composition of North America at about the fortieth parallel, narrated as
journeys with various geologists. The title refers to the physiographic province
that extends from the Great Salt Lake to the Sierra Nevada, and southward.
The project took fifteen years, and the three other books are In Suspect Terrain,
Rising from the Plains, *and* Assembling California. *Their overall structure*
is not linear—east to west—but moves about geographically in its primary
absorption with the theory of plate tectonics and the theory's North American
expression. For example, New Jersey and Nevada are tectonically so similar
that they are presented in the text consecutively. The four books are free-
standing and can be read singly, but there is a pattern in the whole. The
opening passages of Basin and Range *are reproduced here.*]

The poles of the earth have wandered. The equator has apparently moved. The continents, perched on their plates, are thought to have been carried so very far and to be going in so many directions that it seems an act of almost pure hubris to assert that some landmark of our world is fixed at 73 degrees 57 minutes and 53 seconds west longitude and 40 degrees 51 minutes and 14 seconds north latitude—a temporary description, at any rate, as if for a boat on the sea. Nevertheless, these coordinates will, for what is generally described as the foreseeable future, bring you with absolute precision to the west apron of the George Washington Bridge. Nine A.M. A weekday morning. The traffic is some gross demonstration in particle physics. It bursts from its confining source, aimed at Chicago, Cheyenne, Sacramento, through the high dark roadcuts of the Palisades Sill. A young woman, on foot, is being pressed up against the rockwall by the wind booms of the big semis—Con Weimar Bulk Transportation, Fruehauf Long Ranger. Her face is Nordic, her eyes dark brown and Latin—the bequests of grandparents from the extremes of Europe. She wears mountain boots, bluejeans. She carries a single-jack sledgehammer. What the truckers seem to notice, though, is her youth, her long bright Norwegian hair; and they

flirt by air horn, driving needles into her ears. Her name is Karen
Kleinspehn. She is a geologist, a graduate student nearing her
Ph.D., and there is little doubt in her mind that she and the road
and the rock before her, and the big bridge and its awesome
city—in fact, nearly the whole of the continental United States
and Canada and Mexico to boot—are in stately manner moving
in the direction of the trucks. She has not come here, however,
to ponder global tectonics, although goodness knows she could,
the sill being, in theory, a signature of the events that created
the Atlantic. In the Triassic, when New Jersey and Mauretania
were of a piece, the region is said to have begun literally to pull
itself apart, straining to spread out, to break into great crustal
blocks. Valleys in effect competed. One of them would open
deep enough to admit ocean water, and so for some years would
resemble the present Red Sea. The mantle below the crust—
exciting and excited by these events—would send up fillings of
fluid rock, and with such pressure behind them that they could
intrude between horizontal layers of, say, shale and sandstone
and lift the country a thousand feet. The intrusion could spread
laterally through hundreds of square miles, becoming a broad
new layer—a sill—within the country rock.

This particular sill came into the earth about two miles below
the surface, Kleinspehn remarks, and she smacks it with the
sledge. An air horn blasts. The passing tires, in their numbers,
sound like heavy surf. She has to shout to be heard. She pounds
again. The rock is competent. The wall of the cut is sheer. She
hits it again and again—until a chunk of some poundage falls
free. Its fresh surface is asparkle with crystals—free-form, asym-
metrical, improvisational plagioclase crystals, bestrewn against a
field of dark pyroxene. The rock as a whole is called diabase. It
is salt-and-peppery charcoal-tweed savings-bank rock. It came to
be that way by cooling slowly, at depth, and forming these beautiful crystals.

"It pays to put your nose on the outcrop," she says, turning
the sample in her hand. With a smaller hammer, she tidies it
up, like a butcher trimming a roast. With a felt-tip pen, she marks

it "1." Moving along the cut, she points out xenoliths—blobs of the country rock that fell into the magma and became encased there like raisins in bread. She points to flow patterns, to swirls in the diabase where solidifying segments were rolled over, to layers of coarse-grained crystals that settled, like sediments, in beds. The Palisades Sill—in its chemistry and its texture—is a standard example of homogeneous magma resulting in multiple expressions of rock. It tilts westward. The sill came into a crustal block whose western extremity—known in New Jersey as the Border Fault—is thirty miles away. As the block's western end went down, it formed the Newark Basin. The high eastern end gradually eroded, shedding sediments into the basin, and the sill was ultimately revealed—a process assisted by the creation and development of the Hudson, which eventually cut out the cliffside panorama of New Jersey as seen across the river from Manhattan: the broad sill, which had cracked, while cooling, into slender columns so upright and uniform that inevitably they would be likened to palisades.

In the many fractures of these big roadcuts, there is some suggestion of columns, but actually the cracks running through the cuts are too various to be explained by columnar jointing, let alone by the impudence of dynamite. The sill may have been stressed pretty severely by the tilting of the fault block, Kleinspehn says, or it may have cracked in response to the release of weight as the load above it was eroded away. Solid-earth tides could break it up, too. The sea is not all that responds to the moon. Twice a day the solid earth bobs up and down, as much as a foot. That kind of force and that kind of distance are more than enough to break hard rock. Wells will flow faster during lunar high tides.

For that matter, geologists have done their share to bust up these roadcuts. "They've really been *through* here!" They have fungoed so much rock off the walls they may have set them back a foot. And everywhere, in profusion along this half mile of diabase, there are small, neatly cored holes, in no way resembling the shot holes and guide holes of the roadblasters, which are larger and vertical, but small horizontal borings that would be snug to a roll of coins. They were made by geologists taking paleomagnetic samples. As the magma crystallized and turned solid, certain iron minerals within it lined themselves up like compasses, pointing toward the magnetic pole. As it happened, the direction in those years was northerly. The earth's magnetic field has reversed itself a number of hundreds of times, switching from north to south, south to north, at intervals that have varied in length. Geologists have figured out just when the reversals occurred, and have thus developed a distinct arrhythmic yardstick through time. There are many other chronological frames, of course, and if from other indicators, such as fossils, one knows the age of a rock unit within several million years, a look at the mineral compasses inside it can narrow the age toward precision. Paleomagnetic insights have contributed greatly to the study of the travels of the continents, helping to show where they may have been with respect to one another. In the argot of geology, paleomagnetic specialists are sometimes called paleomagicians. Enough paleomagicians have been up and down the big roadcuts of the Palisades Sill to prepare what appears to be a Hilton for wrens and purple martins. Birds have shown no interest.

Near the end of the highway's groove in the sill, there opens a broad, forgettable view of the valley of the Hackensack. The road is descending toward the river. At an even greater angle, the sill—tilting westward—dives into the earth. Accordingly, as Karen Kleinspehn continues to move downhill she is going "up-section" through the diabase toward the top of the tilting sill. The texture of the rock becomes smoother, the crystals smaller, and soon she finds the contact where the magma—at 2000 degrees Fahrenheit—touched the country rock. The country rock was a shale, which had earlier been the deep muck of some Triassic lake, where the labyrinthodont amphibians lived, and paleoniscid fish. The diabase below the contact now is a smooth and uniform hard dark rock, no tweed—its crystals too small to be discernible, having had so little time to grow in the chill zone. The contact is a straight, clear line. She rests her hand across it. The heat of the magma penetrated about a hundred feet into the shale, enough to cook it, to metamorphose it, to turn it into spotted slate. Sampling the slate with her sledgehammer, she has to pound with even more persistence than before. "Some weird, wild minerals turn up in this stuff," she comments between swings. "The metamorphic aureole of this formation is about the hardest rock in New Jersey."

She moves a few hundred feet farther on, near the end of the series of cuts. Pin oaks, sycamores, aspens, cottonwoods have come in on the wind with milkweed and wisteria to seize living space between the rock and the road, although the environment appears to be less welcoming than the center of Carson Sink. There are fossil burrows in the slate—long stringers where Triassic animals travelled through the quiet mud, not far below the surface of the shallow lake. There is a huge rubber sandal by the road, a crate of broken eggs, three golf balls. Two are very cheap but one is an Acushnet Titleist. A soda can comes clinking down the interstate, moving ten miles an hour before the easterly winds of the traffic. The screen of trees damps the truck noise. Karen sits down to rest, to talk, with her back against a cottonwood. "Road-cuts can be a godsend. There's a series of roadcuts near Pikeville, Kentucky—very big ones—where you can see distributary channels in a river-delta system, with natural levees, and with splay deposits going out from the levees into overbank deposits of shales and coal. It's a face-on view of the fingers of a delta, coming at you—the Pocahontas delta system, shed off the Appalachians in Mississippian-Pennsylvanian time. You see river channels that migrated back and forth across a valley and were superposed vertically on one another through time. You see it all there in one series of exposures, instead of having to fit together many smaller pieces of the puzzle."

Geologists on the whole are inconsistent drivers. When a road-cut presents itself, they tend to lurch and weave. To them, the roadcut is a portal, a fragment of a regional story, a proscenium arch that leads their imaginations into the earth and through the surrounding terrain. In the rock itself are the essential clues to the scenes in which the rock began to form—a lake in Wyoming, about as large as Huron; a shallow ocean reaching westward from Washington Crossing; big rivers that rose in Nevada and fell through California to the sea. Unfortunately, highway departments tend to obscure such scenes. They scatter seed wherever they think it will grow. They "hair everything over"—as geologists around the country will typically complain.

"We think rocks are beautiful. Highway departments think rocks are obscene."

"In the North it's vetch."

"In the South it's the god-damned kudzu. You need a howitzer to blast through it. It covers the mountainsides, too."

"Almost all our stops on field trips are at roadcuts. In areas where structure is not well exposed, roadcuts are essential to do geology."

"Without some roadcuts, all you could do is drill a hole, or find natural streamcuts, which are few and far between."

"We as geologists are fortunate to live in a period of great road building."

"It's a way of sampling fresh rock. The road builders slice through indiscriminately, and no little rocks, no softer units are allowed to hide."

"A roadcut is to a geologist as a stethoscope is to a doctor."

"An X-ray to a dentist."

"The Rosetta Stone to an Egyptologist."

"A twenty-dollar bill to a hungry man."

"If I'm going to drive safely, I can't do geology."

In moist climates, where vegetation veils the earth, streamcuts are about the only natural places where geologists can see exposures of rock, and geologists have walked hundreds of thousands of miles in and beside streams. If roadcuts in the moist world are a kind of gift, they are equally so in other places. Rocks are not easy to read where natural outcrops are so deeply weathered that a hammer will virtually sink out of sight—for example, in piedmont Georgia. Make a fresh roadcut almost anywhere at all and geologists will close in swiftly, like missionaries racing anthropologists to a tribe just discovered up the Xingu.

"I studied roadcuts and outcrops as a kid, on long trips with my family," Karen says. "I was probably doomed to be a geologist from the beginning." She grew up in the Genesee Valley, and most of the long trips were down through Pennsylvania and the Virginias to see her father's parents, in North Carolina. On such a journey, it would have been difficult not to notice all the sheets of rock that had been bent, tortured, folded, faulted, crumpled —and to wonder how that happened, since the sheets of rock would have started out as flat as a pad of paper. "I am mainly interested in sedimentology, in sedimentary structures. It allows me to do a lot of field work. I'm not too interested in theories of what happens x kilometres down in the earth at certain temperatures and pressures. You seldom do field work if you're interested in the mantle. There's a little bit of the humanities that creeps into geology, and that's why I am in it. You can't prove things as rigorously as physicists or chemists do. There are no white coats in a geology lab, although geology is going that way. Under the Newark Basin are worn-down remains of the Appalachians —below us here, and under that valley, and so on over to the Border Fault. In the West, for my thesis, I am working on a basin that also formed on top of a preexisting deformed belt. I can't say that the basin formed just like this one, but what absorbs me are the mechanics of these successor basins, superposed on mountain belts. The Great Valley in California is probably an example of a late-stage compressional basin—formed as plates came together. We think the Newark Basin is an extensional basin—formed as plates moved apart. In the geologic record, how do we recognize the differences between the two? I am trying to get the picture of the basin as a whole, and what is the history that you can read in these cuts. I can't synthesize all this in one morning on a field trip, but I can look at the rock here and then evaluate someone else's interpretation." She pauses. She looks back along the rockwall. "This interstate is like a knife wound all across the country," she remarks. "Sure—you could do this sort of thing from here to California. Anyone who wants to, though, had better hurry. Before long, to go all the way across by yourself will be a fossil experience. A person or two. One car. Coast to coast. People do it now without thinking much about it. Yet it's a most unusual kind of personal freedom—particular to this time span, the one we happen to be in. It's an amazing, temporary phenomenon that will end. We have the best highway system in the world. It lets us do what people in no other country can do. And it is also an ecological disaster."

In June, every year, students and professors from Eastern colleges—with their hydrochloric-acid phials and their hammers and their Brunton compasses—head West. To be sure, there is plenty of absorbing geology under the shag of Eastern America, galvanic conundrums in Appalachian structure and intricate puzzles in history and stratigraphy. In no manner would one wish to mitigate the importance of the Eastern scene. Undeniably, though, the West is where the rocks are—"where it all hangs out," as someone in the United States Geological Survey has put it—and of Eastern geologists who do any kind of summer field work about seventy-five per cent go West. They carry state geological maps and the regional geological highway maps that have been published by the American Association of Petroleum Geologists—maps as prodigally colored as drip paintings and equally formless in their worm-trail-and-paramecium depictions of the country's uppermost rock. The maps give two dimensions but more than suggest the third. They tell the general age and story of the banks of the asphalt stream. Kleinspehn has been doing this for some years, getting into her Minibago, old and overloaded, a two-door Ford, heavy-duty springs, with odd pieces of the Rockies under the front seat and a mountain tent in the gear behind, to cross the Triassic lowlands and the Border Fault and to rise into the Ridge and Valley Province, the folded-and-faulted, deformed Appalachians—the beginnings of a journey that above all else is physiographic, a journey that tends to mock the idea of a nation, of a political state, as an unnatural subdivision of the globe, as a metaphor of the human ego sketched on paper and framed in straight lines and in riparian boundaries between unalterable coasts. The United States: really a quartering of a continent, a drawer in North America. Pull it out and prairie dogs would spill off one side, alligators off the other—a terrain crisscrossed with geological boundaries, mammalian boundaries, amphibian boundaries: the limits of the world of the river frog, the extent of the Nugget Formation, the range of the mountain cougar. The range of the cougar is the cougar's natural state, overlying segments of tens of thousands of other states, a few of them proclaimed a nation. The United States of America, with its capital city on the Atlantic Coastal Plain. The change is generally dramatic as one province gives way to another; and halfway across Pennsylvania, as you leave the quartzite ridges and carbonate valleys of the folded-and-faulted mountains, you drop for a moment into Cambrian rock near the base of a long climb, a ten-mile gradient upsection in time from the Cambrian into the Ordovician into the Silurian into the Devonian into the Mississippian (generally through the same chapters of the earth represented in the walls of the Grand Canyon) and finally out onto the Pennsylvanian itself, the upper deck, the capstone rock, of the Allegheny Plateau. Now even the Exxon map shows a new geology, roads running every which way like shatter lines in glass, following the crazed geometries of this deeply dissected country, whereas, before, the roads had no choice but to run northeast-southwest among the long ropy trends of the deformed mountains, following the endless ridges. On these transcontinental trips, Karen has driven as much as a thousand miles in a day at speeds that she has come to regard as dangerous and no less emphatically immoral. She has almost never slept under a roof, nor can she imagine why anyone on such a journey would want or need to; she "scopes out" her campsites in the late-failing light with strong affection for national forests and less for the three-dollar campgrounds where you roll out your Ensolite between two trailers, where gregarious trains honk like Buicks, and Yamahas on instruments climb escarpments in the night. The physiographic boundary is indistinct where you shade off the Allegheny Plateau and onto the stable craton, the continent's enduring core, its heartland, immemorially unstrained, the steady, predictable hedreocraton—the Stable Interior Craton. There are old mountains to the east, maturing mountains to the west, adolescent mountains beyond. The craton has participated on its edges in the violent creation of the mountains. But it remains intact within, and half a nation wide—the lasting, stolid craton, slowly, slowly downwasting. It has lost five centimetres since the birth of Christ. In much of Canada and parts of Minnesota and Wisconsin, the surface of the craton is Precambrian—earth-basement rock, the continental shield. Ohio, Indiana, Illinois, and so forth, the whole of what used to be called the Middle West, is shield rock covered with a sedimentary veneer that has never been metamorphosed, never been ground into tectonic hash—sandstones, siltstones, limestones, dolomites, flatter than the ground above them, the silent floors of departed oceans, of epicratonic seas. Iowa. Nebraska. Now with each westward township the country thickens, rises—a thousand, two thousand, five thousand feet—on crumbs shed off the Rockies and generously served to the craton. At last the Front Range comes to view—the chevroned mural of the mountains, sparkling white on gray, and on its outfanning sediments you are lifted into the Rockies and you plunge through a canyon to the Laramie Plains. "You go from one major geologic province to another and—whoa!—you really know you're doing it." There are mountains now behind you, mountains before you, mountains that are set on top of mountains, a complex score of underthrust, upthrust, overthrust mountains, at the conclusion of which, through another canyon, you come into the Basin and Range. Brigham Young, when he came through a neighboring canyon and saw rivers flowing out on alluvial fans from the wall of the Wasatch to the flats beyond, made a quick decision and said, "This is the place." The scene suggested settling for it. The alternative was to press on beside a saline sea and then across salt barrens so vast and flat that when microwave relays would be set there they would not require towers. There are mountains, to be sure—off to one side and the other: the Oquirrhs, the Stansburys, the Promontories, the Silver Island Mountains. And with Nevada these high, discrete, austere new ranges begin to come in waves, range after range after north-south range, consistently in rhythm with wide flat valleys: basin, range; basin, range; a mile of height between basin and range. Beside the Humboldt you wind around the noses of the mountains, the Humboldt, framed in cottonwood—a sound, substantial, year-round-flowing river, among the largest in the world that fail to reach the sea. It sinks, it disappears, in an evaporite plain, near the bottom of a series of fault blocks that have broken out to form a kind of stairway that you climb to go out of the Basin and Range. On one step is Reno, and at the top is Donner Summit of the uplifting Sierra Nevada, which has gone above fourteen thousand feet but seems by no means to have finished its invasion of the sky. The Sierra is rising on its east side and is hinged on the west, so the slope is long to the Sacramento Valley—the physiographic province of the Great Valley—flat and sea-level and utterly incongruous within its flanking mountains. It was not eroded out in the normal way of valleys. Mountains came up around it. Across the fertile flatland, beyond the avocados, stand the Coast Ranges, the ultimate province of the present, the berm of the ocean—the Coast Ranges, with their dry and straw-brown Spanish demeanor, their shadows of the live oaks on the ground.

If you were to make that trip in the Triassic—New York to San Francisco, Interstate 80, say roughly at the end of Triassic time—you would move west from the nonexistent Hudson River with the Palisades Sill ten thousand feet down. The motions that will open the Atlantic are well under way (as things appear in present theory), but the brine has not yet come in. Behind you, in fact, where the ocean will be, are several thousand miles of land—a contiguous landmass, fragments of which will be Africa, Antarctica, India, Australia. You cross the Newark Basin. It is for the most part filled with red mud. In the mud are tracks that seem to have been made by a two-ton newt. You come to a long, low, north-south-trending, black, steaming hill. It is a flow of lava that has come out over the mud and has cooled quickly in the air to form the dense smooth textures of basalt. Someday, towns and landmarks of this extruded hill will in one way or another take from it their names: Montclair, Mountainside, Great

Notch, Glen Ridge. You top the rise, and now you can see across
the rest of the basin to the Border Fault, and—where Whippany
and Parsippany will be, some thirty miles west of New York—
there is a mountain front perhaps seven thousand feet high. You
climb this range and see more and more mountains beyond, and
they are the folded-and-faulted Appalachians, but middle-aged
and a little rough still at the edges, not caterpillar furry and worn-
down smooth. Numbers do not seem to work well with regard to
deep time. Any number above a couple of thousand years—fifty
thousand, fifty million—will with nearly equal effect awe the
imagination to the point of paralysis. This Triassic journey, anyway, is happening close to two hundred million years ago, or five
per cent back into the existence of the earth. From the subalpine
peaks of New Jersey, the descent is long and gradual to the lowlands of western Pennsylvania, where flat-lying sedimentary rocks
begin to reach out across the craton—coals and sandstones, shales
and limestones, slowly downwasting, Ohio, Indiana, Illinois,
Iowa, erosionally losing an inch every thousand years. Where the
Missouri will flow, past Council Bluffs, you come into a world
of ruddy hills, Permian red, that continue to the far end of Nebraska, where you descend to the Wyoming flats. Sandy in places,
silty, muddy, they run on and on, near sea level, all the way
across Wyoming and into Utah. They are as red as brick. They
will become the red cliffs and red canyons of Wyoming, the walls
of Flaming Gorge. Triassic rock is not exclusively red, but much
of it is red all over the world—red in the shales of New Jersey,
red in the sandstones of Yunan, red in the banks of the Volga,
red by the Solway Firth. Triassic redbeds, as they are called, are
in the dry valleys of Antarctica, the red marls of Worcestershire,
the hills of Alsace-Lorraine. The Petrified Forest. The Painted
Desert. The South African redbeds of the Great Karroo. Triassic
red rock is red through and through, and not merely weathered
red on the surface, like the great Redwall Limestone of the Grand
Canyon, which is actually gray. There may have been a super-
abundance of oxygen in the atmosphere from late Pennsylvanian
through Permian and Triassic time. As sea level changed and

[*108*]

changed again all through the Pennsylvanian, tremendous quantities of vegetation grew and then were drowned and buried, grew and then were drowned and buried—to become, eventually, seam upon seam of coal, interlayered with sandstones and shales. Living plants take in carbon dioxide, keep the carbon in their carbohydrates, and give up the oxygen to the atmosphere. Animals, from bacteria upward, then eat the plants and reoxidize the carbon. This cycle would go awry if a great many plants were buried. Their carbon would be buried with them—isolated in rock—and so the amount of oxygen in the atmosphere would build up. All over the world, so much carbon was buried in Pennsylvanian time that the oxygen pressure in the atmosphere quite possibly doubled. There is more speculation than hypothesis in this, but what could the oxygen do? Where could it go? After carbon, the one other thing it could oxidize in great quantity was iron—abundant, pale-green ferrous iron, which exists everywhere, in fully five per cent of crustal rock; and when ferrous iron takes on oxygen, it turns a ferric red. That may have been what happened—in time that followed the Pennsylvanian. Permian rock is generally red. Redbeds on an epic scale are the signs of the Triassic, when the earth in its rutilance may have outdone Mars.

As you come off the red flats to cross western Utah, nearly two hundred million years before the present, you travel in the dark, there being not one grain of evidence to suggest its Triassic appearance, no paleoenvironmental clue. Ahead, though, in eastern Nevada, is a line of mountains that are much of an age with the peaks of New Jersey—a little rounded, beginning to show age—and after you climb them and go down off their western slopes you discern before you the white summits of alpine fresh terrain, of new rough mountains rammed into thin air, with snow banners flying off the matterhorns, ridges, crests, and spurs. You are in central Nevada, about four hundred miles east of San Francisco, and after you have climbed these mountains you look out upon (as it appears in present theory) open sea. You drop swiftly to the coast, and then move on across moderately profound water full of pelagic squid, water that is quietly accumulating the sediments which—ages in the future—will become the roof rock of the rising Sierra. Tall volcanoes are standing in the sea. Then, at roughly the point where the Sierran foothills will end and the Great Valley will begin—at Auburn, California—you move beyond the shelf and over deep ocean. There are probably some islands out there somewhere, but fundamentally you are crossing above ocean crustal floor that reaches to the China Sea. Below you there is no hint of North America, no hint of the valley or the hills where Sacramento and San Francisco will be.

I used to sit in class and listen to the terms come floating down the room like paper airplanes. Geology was called a descriptive science, and with its pitted outwash plains and drowned rivers, its hanging tributaries and starved coastlines, it was nothing if not descriptive. It was a fountain of metaphor—of isostatic adjustments and degraded channels, of angular unconformities and shifting divides, of rootless mountains and bitter lakes. Streams eroded headward, digging from two sides into mountain or hill, avidly struggling toward each other until the divide between them broke down, and the two rivers that did the breaking now became confluent (one yielding to the other, giving up its direction of flow and going the opposite way) to become a single stream. Stream capture. In the Sierra Nevada, the Yuba had captured the Bear. The Macho member of a formation in New Mexico was derived in large part from the solution and collapse of another formation. There was fatigued rock and incompetent rock and inequigranular fabric in rock. If you bent or folded rock, the inside of the curve was in a state of compression, the outside of the curve was under great tension, and somewhere in the middle was the surface of no strain. Thrust fault, reverse fault, normal fault—the two sides were active in every fault. The inclination of a slope on which boulders would stay put was the angle of repose. There seemed, indeed, to be more than a little of the humanities in this subject. Geologists communicated in English; and they could name things in a manner that sent shivers through the bones. They had roof pendants in their discordant batholiths, mosaic conglomerates in desert pavement. There was ultrabasic, deep-ocean, mottled green-and-black rock—or serpentine. There was the slip face of the barchan dune. In 1841, a paleontologist had decided that the big creatures of the Mesozoic were "fearfully great lizards," and had therefore named them dinosaurs. There were festooned crossbeds and limestone sinks, pillow lavas and petrified trees, incised meanders and defeated streams. There were dike swarms and slickensides, explosion pits, volcanic bombs. Pulsating glaciers. Hogbacks. Radiolarian ooze. There was almost enough resonance in some terms to stir the adolescent groin. The swelling up of mountains was described as an orogeny. Ontogeny, phylogeny, orogeny—accent syllable two. The Antler Orogeny, the Avalonian Orogeny, the Taconic, Acadian, Alleghenian Orogenies. The Laramide Orogeny. The center of the United States had had a dull geologic history—nothing much being accumulated, nothing much being eroded away. It was just sitting there conservatively. The East had once been radical—had been unstable, reformist, revolutionary, in the Paleozoic pulses of three or four orogenies. Now, for the last hundred and fifty million years, the East had been stable and conservative. The far-out stuff was in the Far West of the country—wild, weirdsma, a leather-jacket geology in mirrored shades, with its welded tuffs and Franciscan mélange (internally deformed, complex beyond analysis), its strike-slip faults and falling buildings, its boiling springs and fresh volcanics, its extensional disassembling of the earth.

There was, to be sure, another side of the page—full of geological language of the sort that would have attracted Gilbert and Sullivan. Rock that stayed put was called autochthonous, and if it had moved it was allochthonous. "Normal" meant "at right angles." "Normal" also meant a fault with a depressed hanging wall. There was a Green River Basin in Wyoming that was not to be confused with the Green River Basin in Wyoming. One was topographical and was *on* Wyoming. The other was structural and was *under* Wyoming. The Great Basin, which is centered in Utah and Nevada, was not to be confused with the Basin and

Range, which is centered in Utah and Nevada. The Great Basin was topographical, and extraordinary in the world as a vastness of land that had no drainage to the sea. The Basin and Range was a realm of related mountains that coincided with the Great Basin, spilling over slightly to the north and considerably to the south. To anyone with a smoothly functioning bifocal mind, there was no lack of clarity about Iowa in the Pennsylvanian, Missouri in the Mississippian, Nevada in Nebraskan, Indiana in Illinoian, Vermont in Kansan, Texas in Wisconsinan time. Meteoric water, with study, turned out to be rain. It ran downhill in consequent, subsequent, obsequent, resequent, and not a few insequent streams.

As years went by, such verbal deposits would thicken. Someone developed enough effrontery to call a piece of our earth an epieugeosyncline. There were those who said interfluve when they meant between two streams, and a perfectly good word like mesopotamian would do. A cactolith, according to the American Geological Institute's *Glossary of Geology and Related Sciences*, was "a quasi-horizontal chonolith composed of anastomosing ductoliths, whose distal ends curl like a harpolith, thin like a sphenolith, or bulge discordantly like an akmolith or ethmolith." The same class of people who called one rock serpentine called another jacupirangite. Clinoptilolite, eclogite, migmatite, tincalconite, szaibelyite, pumpellyite. Meyerhofferite. The same class of people who called one rock paracelsian called another despujolsite. Metakirchheimerite, phlogopite, katzenbuckelite, mboziite, noselite, neighborite, samsonite, pigeonite, muskoxite, pabstite, aenigmatite. Joesmithite. With the X-ray diffractometer and the X-ray fluorescence spectrometer, which came into general use in geology laboratories in the late nineteen-fifties, and then with the electron probe (around 1970), geologists obtained ever closer examinations of the components of rock. What they had long seen through magnifying lenses as specimens held in the hand—or in thin slices under microscopes—did not always register identically in the eyes of these machines. Andesite, for example, had been given its name for being the predominant rock of the high mountains of South America. According to the machines, there is surprisingly little andesite in the Andes. The Sierra Nevada is renowned throughout the world for its relatively young and absolutely beautiful granite. There is precious little granite in the Sierra. Yosemite Falls, Half Dome, El Capitan—for the most part the "granite" of the Sierra is granodiorite. It has always been difficult enough to hold in the mind that a magma which hardens in the earth as granite will—if it should flow out upon the earth—harden as rhyolite, that what hardens within the earth as diorite will harden upon the earth as andesite, that what hardens within the earth as gabbro will harden upon the earth as basalt, the difference from pair to pair being a matter of chemical composition and the differences within each pair being a matter of texture and of crystalline form, with the darker rock at the gabbro end and the lighter rock the granite. All of that—not to mention such wee appendixes as the fact that diabase is a special texture of gabbro—was difficult enough for the layman to remember before the diffractometers and the spectrometers and the electron probes came along to present their multiplex cavils. What had previously been described as the granite of the world turned out to be a large family of rock that included granodiorite, monzonite, syenite, adamellite, trondhjemite, alaskite, and a modest amount of true granite. A great deal of rhyolite, under scrutiny, became dacite, rhyodacite, quartz latite. Andesite was found to contain enough silica, potassium, sodium, and aluminum to be the fraternal twin of granodiorite. These points are pretty fine. The home terms still apply. The enthusiasm geologists show for adding new words to their conversation is, if anything, exceeded by their affection for the old. They are not about to drop granite. They say granodiorite when they are in church and granite the rest of the week.

When I was seventeen and staring up the skirts of Eastern valleys, I was taught the rudiments of what is now referred to as the Old Geology. The New Geology is the package phrase for the effects of the revolution that occurred in earth science in the nineteen-sixties, when geologists clambered onto seafloor spreading, when people began to discuss continents in terms of their velocities, and when the interactions of some twenty parts of the globe became known as plate tectonics. There were few hints of all that when I was seventeen, and now, a shake later, middle-aged and fading, I wanted to learn some geology again, to feel the difference between the Old and the New, to sense if possible how the science had settled down a decade after its great upheaval, but less in megapictures than in day-to-day contact with country rock, seeing what had not changed as well as what had changed. The thought occurred to me that if you were to walk a series of roadcuts with a geologist something illuminating would in all likelihood occur. This was long before I met Karen Kleinspehn, or, for that matter, David Love, of the United States Geological Survey, or Anita Harris, also of the Survey, or Eldridge Moores, of the University of California at Davis, all of whom would eventually take me with them through various stretches of the continent. What I did first off was what anyone would do. I called my local geologist. I live in Princeton, New Jersey, and the man I got in touch with was Kenneth Deffeyes, a senior professor who teaches introductory geology at Princeton University. It is an assignment that is angled wide. Students who have little aptitude for the sciences are required to take a course or two in the sciences en route to some cerebral Valhalla dangled high by the designers of curriculum. Deffeyes' course is one that such students are drawn to select. He calls it Earth and Its Resources. They call it Rocks for Jocks.

Deffeyes is a big man with a tenured waistline. His hair flies behind him like Ludwig van Beethoven's. He lectures in sneakers. His voice is syllabic, elocutionary, operatic. He has been described by a colleague as "an intellectual roving shortstop, with more ideas per square metre than anyone else in the department—they just tumble out." His surname rhymes with "the maze." He has been a geological engineer, a chemical ocean-ographer, a sedimentary petrologist. As he lectures, his eyes search the hall. He is careful to be clear but also to bring forth the full promise of his topic, for he knows that while the odd jock and the pale poet are the white of his target the bull's-eye is the future geologist. Undergraduates do not come to Princeton intending to study geology. When freshmen fill out cards stating their three principal interests, no one includes rocks. Those who will make the subject their field of major study become interested after they arrive. It is up to Deffeyes to interest them—and not a few of them—or his department goes into a subduction zone. So his eyes search the hall. People out of his course have been drafted by the Sacramento Kings and have set records in distance running. They have also become professors of geological geophysics at Caltech and of petrology at Harvard.

FROM

IN SUSPECT

TERRAIN

(1 9 8 3)

[*The central figure in this second geology book is Anita Harris, of the United States Geological Survey, who grew up in a tenement in the Williamsburg section of Brooklyn, graduated from Brooklyn College at the age of nineteen, and went into geology with the frank purpose of escaping the ghetto by earning a living "walking around in mountains." In time, her discoveries in conodont paleontology would cause exploration geologists from all over the world to seek her out. Her travels with John McPhee traversed the deformed Appalachians. The selection that follows is a set piece about a fragment of Appalachian landscape in illuminating counterpoint to the human history there.*]

Absorbing the valley scene, the gapped and distant ridgeline, the newly plowed fields where arrowheads appear in the spring, I remarked that we had entered the dominion of the Minsi, the northernmost band of the Lenape. They came into the region toward the dawn of Holocene time and lost claim to it in the beginnings of the Age of Washington. Like index fossils, they now represent this distinct historical stratum. Their home and prime hunting ground was the Minisink—over the mountain, beside the river, the country upstream from the gap. The name Delaware meant nothing to them. It belonged to a family of English peers. The Lenape named the river for themselves. I knew some of this from my grade-school days, not many miles away. The Minisink is a world of corn shocks and islands and valley mists, of trout streams and bears, today. Especially in New Jersey, it has not been mistreated, and, with respect to the epoch of the Minsi, geologically it is the same. The Indians of the Minisink were good geologists. Their trails ran great distances, not only to other hunting parks and shell-mounded beach camps but also to their quarries. They set up camps at the quarries. They cooked in vessels made of soapstone, which they cut from the ground in what is now London Britain Township, Chester

County, Pennsylvania. They made adzes of granite, basalt, argillite, even siltstone, from sources closer to home. They went to Berks County, in Pennsylvania, for gray chalcedony and brown jasper. They used glacial-erratic hornfels. They made arrowheads and spear points of Deepkill flint. They made drills and scrapers of Onondaga chert. Flint, chert, and jasper are daughters of chalcedony, which in turn is a variety of quartz. The Eastern flint belt runs from Ontario across New York State and then south to the Minisink. The Indians did not have to attend the Freiberg Mining Academy to be able to tell you that. They understood empirically the uniform bonding of cryptocrystalline quartz, which cannot be separated along flat planes but fractures conchoidally, by percussion, and makes a razor's edge. The forests were alive with game on the sides of what the Lenape called the Endless Mountain. There were eels, shad, sturgeon in the river. The people lived among maize fields in osier cabins. They worshipped light and the four winds—all the elements of nature, orchestrated by the Great Manito. The burial grounds of the Minsi display the finest vistas in the Minisink. As the dead were placed in the earth, they began their final journey, through the Milky Way.

Indians first appeared in the Minisink about a hundredth of a million years ago. The carbonate rocks in the valley before us were five hundred million years old. They were one-ninth as old as the earth itself. For their contained conodonts, they were of special interest to Anita, and after the interstate dropped to the valley floor we stopped at roadcuts to collect them. The roadcuts suggested the ruins of blocky walls built by Hellenic masons. They were on both sides of the interstate and in the median, too. There were bluish-white and pale-gray limestones, dolomites weathered buff. Rock will respond to weather with varieties of color—rusting red in its own magnetite, turning green from trace copper. Its appearance can be deceiving. Geologists are slow to identify exposures they have not seen before. They don't just cruise around ticking off names at distances that would impress a hunter. They go up to outcrops, hit them with hammers, and look at the rock through ten-power lenses. If the possibilities include the carbonates, they try a few drops of hydrochloric acid. Limestone with hydrochloric acid on it immediately forms a head, like beer. Dolomite is less responsive to acid. With her sledgehammer, Anita took many pounds of roadcut, and not without effort. Again and again, she really had to slam the wall. Looking at the fresh surface of a piece she removed, she said she'd give odds it was dolomite. It was not responsive to acid. She scraped it with a knife and made powder. Acid on the powder foamed. "This dolomite is clean enough to produce beautiful white marble if it were heated up and recrystallized," she said. "When it became involved in the mountain-building, if it had got up to five hundred degrees it would have turned into marble, like the Dolomites, in Italy. There is not a lot of dolomite in the Dolomites. Most of the rock there is marble." She pointed in the roadcut to the domal structures of algal stromatolites—fossil colonies of microorganisms that had lived in the Cambrian seas. "You know the water was shallow, because those things grew only near the light," she said. "You can see there was no mud around. The rock is so clean. And you know the water was warm, because you do not get massive carbonate deposition in cold water. The colder the water, the more soluble carbonates are. So you look at this roadcut and you know you are looking into a clear, shallow, tropical sea."

With dry land adrift and the earth prone to rolling, that Cambrian sea and New Jersey below it would have been about twenty degrees from the equator—the present latitude of Yucatán, where snorkelers kick along in transparent waters looking through their masks at limestones to be. The Yucatán peninsula is almost all carbonate and grew in its own sea. As did Florida. Under the shallow waters of the Bahamas are wave-washed carbonate dunes, their latitude between twenty and twenty-six degrees. At the end of Cambrian time, the equator crossed what is now the North American continent in a direction that has become north-south. The equator came in through the Big Bend country in Texas and ran up through the Oklahoma panhandle, Nebraska, and the Dakotas. If in late Cambrian time you had followed the present route of Interstate 80, you would have crossed the equator near Kearney, Nebraska. In New Jersey, you would have been in water scarcely above your hips, wading among algal mounds and grazing gastropods. You could have waded to the equator. West of Chicago and through most of Illinois, you would have been wading on clean sand, the quiet margin of the Canadian craton, which remained above the sea. The limy bottom apparently resumed in Iowa and went on into eastern Nebraska, and then, more or less at Kearney, you would have moved up onto a blistering-hot equatorial beach and into low terrain, subdued hills, rock that had been there a thousand million years. It was barren to a vengeance with a hint of life, possibly a hint of life—rocks stained green, stained red by algae. Wyoming. Past Laramie, you would have come to a west-facing beach and, after it, tidal mudflats all the way to Utah. The waters of the shelf would now begin to deepen. A hundred miles into Nevada was the continental slope and beyond it the blue ocean.

If you had turned around and gone back after fifty million years—well into Ordovician time, say four hundred and sixty million years ago—the shelf edge would still have been near Elko, Nevada, and the gradually rising clean-lime seafloor would have reached at least to Salt Lake City. Across Wyoming, there may have been low dry land or possibly continuing sea. The evidence has almost wholly worn away, but there is one clue. In southeastern Wyoming, a diamond pipe came up about a hundred million years ago, and, in the tumult that followed the explosion, marine limestone of late Ordovician age fell into the kimberlite and was preserved. In western Nebraska, you would have crossed dry and barren Precambrian terrain and by Lincoln have reached another sea. Iowa, Illinois, Indiana. The water was clear, the bottom uneven—many shallows and deeps upon the craton. In Ohio, the sea would have begun to cloud, increasingly so as you moved on east, silts slowly falling onto the lime. In Pennsylvania, as you approached the site of the future Delaware Water Gap, the bottom would have fallen away below you, and where it had earlier been close to the surface it would now be many tens of fathoms down.

"The carbonate platform collapsed," Anita said. "The continental shelf went down and formed a big depression. Sediments poured in." Much in the way that a sheet of paper bends downward if you move its two ends toward each other in your hands, the limestones and dolomites and the basement rock beneath them had subsided, forming a trough, which rapidly filled with dark mud. The mud became shale, and when the shale was drawn into the heat and pressure of the making of mountains its minerals realigned themselves and it turned into slate. We moved on west a couple of miles and stopped at a roadcut of ebony slate. Anita said, "Twelve thousand feet of this black mud was deposited in twelve million years. That's a big pile of rock." The formation was called Martinsburg. It had been folded and cleaved in orogenic violence following its deposition in the sea. As a result, it resembled stacks of black folios, each of a thousand leaves. Just to tap at such rock and remove a piece of it is to create something so beautiful in its curving shape and tiered laminations that it would surely be attractive to a bonsai gardener's eye. It seems a proper setting for a six-inch tree. I put a few pieces in the car, as I am wont to do when I see some Martinsburg. Across the Delaware, in Pennsylvania, the formation presents itself in large sections that are without joints and veins, the minerals line up finely in dense flat sheets, and the foliation planes are so extensive and straight that slabs of great size can be sawed from the earth. The rock there is described as "blue-gray true unfading slate." It is strong but "soft," and will accept a polishing that makes it smoother than glass. From Memphis to St. Joe, from Joplin to River City, there is scarcely a hustler in the history of pool who has not racked up his runs over Martinsburg slate. For anybody alive who still hears corruption in the click of pocket billiards, it is worth a moment of reflection that not only did all those pool tables accumulate on the ocean floor as Ordovician guck but so did the blackboards in the schools of all America.

The accumulation of the Martinsburg—the collapsing platform, the inpouring sediments—was the first great sign of a gathering storm. Geological revolution, crustal deformation, tectonic upheaval would follow. Waves of mountains would rise. Martinsburg time in earth history is analogous to the moment in human history when Henry Hudson, of the Dutch East India Company, sailed into the bay of the Lenape River.

Completing the crossing of the Great Valley of the Appalachians, Anita and I passed more limestones, more slate. Their original bedding planes, where we could discern them, were variously atilt, vertical, and overturned, so intricate had the formations become in the thrusting and folding of the long-gone primal massifs. The road came to the river, turned north to run beside it, and presented a full view of the break in the Kittatinny ridge, still far enough away to be comprehended in context but close enough to be seen as the phenomenon it is: a mountain severed, its folds and strata and cliffs symmetrical, thirteen hundred feet of rock in close fraternal image from the skyline to the boulders of a blue-and-white river. Small wonder that painters of the Hudson River School had come to the Delaware to do their best work. George Inness painted the Delaware Water Gap many times, and he chose this perspective—downriver about four miles—more than any other. I have often thought of those canvases—with their Durham boats on the water and cows in the meadows and chuffing locomotives on the Pennsylvania side—in the light of Anita's comment that you would understand a great deal of the history of the eastern continent if you understood all that had made possible one such picture. She was suggesting, it seemed to me, a sense of total composition—not merely one surface composition visible to the eye but a whole series of preceding compositions which in the later one fragmentarily endure and are incorporated into its substance—with materials of vastly differing age drawn together in a single scene, a composite canvas not only from the Hudson River School but including everything else that had been a part of the zones of time represented by the boats, gravels, steeples, cows, trains, talus, cutbanks, and kames, below a mountain broken open by a river half its age.

The mountain touched the Martinsburg, and its rock was the younger by at least ten million years. Kittatinny Mountain is largely quartzite, the primary component of the hubs of Hell. In the post-tectonic, profoundly eroded East, quartzite has tended to stand up high. The Martinsburg is soft, and is therefore valley. There is nothing but time between the two. Where the formations meet, a touch of a finger will cover both the beginning and the end of the ten million years, which are dated at about 440 and 430 million years before the present—from latest Ordovician time to a point in the early Silurian. During that time, something apparently lifted the Martinsburg out of its depositional pit and held it above sea level until weathers wore it low enough to be ready to accept whatever might spread over it from higher ground. The quartzite—as sand—spread over it, coming down from Taconic mountains. The sand became sandstone. Upward of fifty million years later, the sand grains fused and turned into quartzite in the heat and the crush of new rising mountains, or possibly a hundred million years after that, in the heat and the crush of more mountains. The Delaware River at that time was not even a cloud in the sky. Rivers of greater size were flowing the other way, crossing at wild angles the present route of the Delaware. Rivers go wherever the country tells them to, if the country is in vertical motion. The country would not be right for the Delaware for roughly a hundred million more years, and still another hundred million years would go by before the river achieved its present relationship with Kittatinny Mountain. No one knows how the river cut through. Did it cut from above through country now gone and lying as mud in the sea? Did it work its way through the mountain as two streams, eroding headward from either side, the one finally capturing the other? Was there once a great lake spilling over the mountain and creating the gap as its outlet? The big-lake idea has attracted no support. It is looked upon less as a hypothesis than as a theoretically possible but essentially foolish guess. There was for a time an ice-defended lake between the mountain and the Wisconsinan glacier. When the ice melted, the lake ran out through the Water Gap, leaving in evidence its stream deltas and seasonally banded bottom deposits. However, Glacial Lake Sciota, as it is called, was eight miles long and two hundred feet deep and could not have cut a gap through much of anything but sugar.

The ice arrived twenty-three thousand years before the present. The terminal moraine is only ten miles south of the gap. Nonetheless, the ice front was something like two thousand feet thick, for it went over the top of the mountain. It totally plugged and must have widened the Water Gap. It gouged out the riverbed and left there afterward two hundred feet of gravel. Indians were in the Minisink when the vegetation was tundra. Ten thousand years ago, when the vegetation changed from tundra to forest, Indians in the Minisink experienced the change. The styles in which they fractured their flint—their jasper, chert, chalcedony—can be correlated to Anatolian, Sumerian, Mosaic, and Byzantine time. Henry Hudson arrived in the New World about four hundred years before the present. He was followed by Dutch traders, Dutch colonists, Dutch miners. They discovered ore-grade copper in the Minisink, or thought they did. Part fact, part folklore, it is a tradition of the region that a man named Hendrik Van Allen assessed Kittatinny Mountain and decided it was half copper. The Dutch crown ordered him to establish a mine, and to build a road on which the ore could be removed. The road ran up the Minisink and through level country to the Hudson River at Esopus Creek (Kingston, New York). A hundred miles long, it was the first constructed highway in the New World to cover so much distance. It covers it still, and is in many places scarcely changed. When Van Allen was not busy supervising the road builders, he carried on an élite flirtational minuet with the daughter of a Lenape chief. The chief was Wissinoming, his daughter Winona. One day, Van Allen went alone to hunt in the woods near the river islands of the Minisink, and he discharged his piece in the direction of a squirrel. The creature scurried through the branches of trees. Van Allen shot again. The creature scurried through the branches of other trees. Van Allen reloaded, stalked the little bugger, and, pointing his rifle upward, sighted with exceptional care. He fired. The squirrel fell to the ground. Van Allen retrieved it, and found an arrow through its heart. By the edge of the river, Winona threw him a smile from her red canoe. They fell in love. In the Minisink, there was no copper worth mentioning. Van Allen didn't care. Winona rewrote the country for him, told him the traditions of the river, told him the story of the Endless Mountain. In the words of Winona's legend as it was eventually set down, "she spoke of the old tradition of this beautiful valley having once been a deep sea of water, and the bursting asunder of the mountains at the will of the Great Spirit, to uncover for the home of her people the vale of the Minisink." In 1664, Peter Stuyvesant, without a shot, surrendered New Amsterdam and all that went with it to naval representatives of Charles, King of England. Word was sent to Hendrik Van Allen to close his mines and go home. It was not in him to take an Indian wife to Europe. He explained these matters to Winona in a scene played out on the cliffs high above the Water Gap. She jumped to her death and he followed.

On foot at the base of the cliffs—in the gusts and shattering noise of the big tractor-trailers passing almost close enough to touch—we walked the narrow space between a concrete guard wall and the rock. Like the river, we were moving through the mountain, but in the reverse direction. Between the mirroring faces of rock, rising thirteen hundred feet above the water, the gap was so narrow that the interstate had been squeezed in without a shoulder. There was a parking lot nearby, where we had left the car—a Delaware Water Gap National Recreation Area parking lot, conveniently placed so that the citizen-traveller could see at point-blank range this celebrated natural passage through a mountain wall, never mind that it was now so full of interstate, so full of railroad track and other roadways that it suggested a convergence of tubes leading to a patient in Intensive Care. We saw painted on a storm sewer a white blaze of the Appalachian Trail, which came down from the mountain in New Jersey, crossed the river on the interstate, and returned to the ridgetop on the Pennsylvania side. There were local names for the sides of the gap in the mountain. The Pennsylvania side was Mt. Minsi, the New Jersey side Mt. Tammany. The rock of the cliffs above us was cleanly bedded, stratified, and had been not only deposited but also deformed in the course of the eastern orogenies. Regionally, it had been pushed together like cloth on a table. The particular fragment of the particular fold that erosion had left as the sustaining rock of the mountain happened to be dipping to the northwest at an angle of some forty-five degrees. As we walked in that general direction, each upended layer was somewhat younger than the last, and each, in the evidence it held, did not so much suggest as record progressive changes in Silurian worlds. "The dip always points upsection, always points toward younger rocks," Anita said. "You learn that the first day in Geology I."

"Do you ever get tired of teaching ignoramuses?" I asked her.

She said, "I haven't worked on this level since I don't know when."

Near the road and the river, at the beginning of the outcrop, great boulders of talus had obscured the contact between the mountain quartzite and the underlying slate. To move on through the gap, traversing the interior of the mountain, was to walk from early to late Silurian time, to examine an assembly of rock that had formed between 430 and 400 million years before the present. The first and oldest quartzite was conglomeratic. Its ingredients had lithified as pebbles and sand. Shouting to be heard, Anita said, "In those pebbles you can see a mountain storm. You can see the pebbles coming into a sandbar in a braided river. There is very little mud in this rock. The streams had a high enough gradient to be running fast and to carry the mud away. These sands and pebbles were coming off a mountain range, and it was young and high."

A braided river carries such an enormous burden of sand and gravel that it does not meander through its valley like most streams, making cutbanks to one side and point bars opposite. Instead, it runs in braided channels through its own broad bed. Looking at those Silurian conglomerates, I could all but hear the big braided rivers I had seen coming down from the Alaska Range, with gravels a mile wide, caribou and bears on the gravel, and channels flowing in silver plaits. If those rivers testify, as they do, to the erosional disassembling of raw young mountains, then so did the rock before us, with its clean river gravels preserved in river sand. "Geology repeats itself," Anita said, and we moved along, touching, picking at the rock. She pointed out the horse-belly curves of channel-fill deposits, and the fact that none was deeper than five feet—a result of the braiding and the shifting of the channels. Evidently, the calm earth and quiet seas that were described by the older rock we had collected up the road had been utterly revolutionized in the event that built the ancient mountains, which, bald as the djebels of Arabia, had stood to the east and shed the sand and gravel this way. In the ripple marks, the crossbedding, the manner in which the sands had come to rest, Anita could see the westerly direction of the braided-river currents more than four hundred million years ago.

Three hundred years ago, William Penn arrived in this country and decided almost at once that the Lenape were Jews. "Their eye is little and black, not unlike a straight-look't Jew," he wrote home. "I am ready to believe them of the Jewish race. . . . A man would think himself in Dukes-place or Berry-street in London, when he seeth them." They were "generally tall, straight, well-built" people "of singular proportion." They greased themselves with clarified bear fat. Penn studied their language—the better to know them, the better to work out his treaties. "Their language is lofty, yet narrow, but like the Hebrew. . . . One word serveth in the place of three. . . . I must say that I know not a language spoken in Europe that hath words of more sweetness or greatness, in accent or emphasis, than theirs." Penn heard "grandeur" in their tribal proper names. He listed them: Tammany, Poquessin, Rancocas, Shakamaxon. He could have added Wyomissing, Wissinoming, Wyoming. He made treaties with the Lenape under the elms of Shakamaxon. Tammany was present. He was to become the most renowned chief in the history of the tribe. Many years after his death, American whites in Eastern cities formed societies in his name, and called him St. Tammany, the nation's patron saint. Penn's fondness for the Lenape was the product of his admiration. Getting along with the Lenape was not difficult. They were accommodating, intelligent, and peaceful. The Indians revered Penn as well. He kept his promises, paid his way, and was fair.

Under the elms of Shakamaxon, the pledge was made that Pennsylvania and the Lenape would be friends "as long as the sun will shine and the rivers flow with water." Penn outlined his needs for land. It was agreed that he should have some country west of the Lenape River. The tracts were to be defined by the distance a man could walk in a prescribed time—typically one day, or two—at an easygoing pace, stopping for lunch, for the odd smoke, as was the Lenape manner. In camaraderie, the Penn party and the Indians gave it up somewhere in Bucks County. Penn went home to England. He died in 1718.

About fifteen years later, Penn's son Thomas, a businessman who had a lawyer's grasp of grasping, appeared from England with a copy of a deed he said his father had transacted, extending his lands to the north by a day and a half's walk. He made it known to a new generation of Lenape, who had never heard of it, and demanded that they acquiesce in the completion of—as it came to be called—the Walking Purchase. With his brothers, John and Richard, he advertised for participants. He offered five hundred acres of land for the fleetest feet in Pennsylvania. In effect, he hired three marathon runners. When the day came—September 19, 1737—the Lenape complained. They could not keep up. But they followed. Their forebears had made a bargain. The white men "walked" sixty-five miles, well into the Poconos. Even so blatant an affront might in time have been accepted by the compliant tribe. But now the brothers made an explosive mistake. Their new terrain logically required a northern boundary. Illogically, the one they drew did not run east to a point on the river close to the Water Gap but northeast on a vector that encompassed and annexed the Minisink. Massacres ensued. Buildings were burned. Up and down the river, white scalps were cut. The Lenape reached for "the French hatchet." Peaceful, accommodating they once had been, but now they were participants in the French and Indian Wars. Where they had tolerated whites in the Minisink, they burned whole settlements and destroyed the occupants. They killed John Rush. They killed his wife, his son and daughter. They killed seventeen Vanakens and Vancamps. They pursued people on the river and killed them in their boats. They killed Hans Vanfleara and Lambert Brink, Piercewell Goulding and Matthew Rue. They could not, however, kill their way backward through time. They never would regain the Minisink.

As we moved along beside the screaming trucks, we were averaging about ten thousand years per step. The progression was not uniform, of course. There might be two million years in one fossil streambed, and then the next lamination in the rock would record a single season, or a single storm—on one flaky surface, a single drop of rain. We looked above our heads at the projecting underside of a layer of sandstone patterned with polygons, impressions made as the sand came pouring down in storm-flood waters over mud cracks that had baked in the sun. From a layer of conglomerate, Anita removed a pebble with the pick end of her rock hammer. "Milky quartz," she said. "Bull quartz. We saw this rock back up the road in the Precambrian highlands. When the Taconic Orogeny came, it lifted the older rock, and erosion turned it into pebbles and sand, which is what is here in this conglomerate. It's an example of how the whole Appalachian system continually fed upon itself. These are Precambrian pebbles, in Silurian rock. You'll see Silurian pebbles in Devonian rock, Devonian pebbles in Mississippian rock. Geology repeats itself." Now and again, we came to small numbers that had been painted long ago on the outcrops. Anita said she had painted the numbers when she and Jack Epstein were working on the geology of the Water Gap. She said, "I'd hate to tell you how many months I've spent here measuring every foot of rock." Among the quartzites were occasional bands not only of sandstone but of shale. The shales were muds that had settled in a matter of days or hours and had filled in the lovely periodicity of the underlying ripples in the ancient river sand. For each picture before us in the rock, there was a corresponding picture in her mind: scenes of the early Silurian barren ground, scenes of the rivers miles wide, and, over all, a series of pictures of the big Taconic mountains to the east gradually losing their competition with erosion in the wash of Silurian rain—a general rounding down of things, with river gradients declining. There were pictures of subsiding country, pictures of rising seas. She found shale that had been the mud of an estuary, and fossil shellfish, fossil jellyfish, which had lived in the estuary. In thin dark flakes nearby she saw "a little black lagoon behind a beach." And in a massive layer of clear white lithified sand she saw the beach. "You don't see sand that light except in beaches," she said. "That is beach sand. You would have looked westward over the sea."

To travel then along the present route of Interstate 80, you would have been in need of a seaworthy shallow-draft boat. The journey could have started in mountain rapids, for the future site of the George Washington Bridge was under thousands of feet of rock. Down the huge fans of boulders and gravel that leaned against the mountains, the west-running rivers raced toward the epicontinental sea. They projected their alluvium into the water and spread it so extensively that up and down the long flanks of the Taconic sierra the alluvium coalesced, gradually building westward as an enormous collection of sediment—a deltaic complex. At the future site of the Water Gap, you would have shoved off the white beach and set a westerly course across the sea—looking back from time to time up the V-shaped creases of steep mountain valleys. That was the world in which the older rock of the Water Gap had been forming—the braided-river conglomerates, the estuary mud, the beach sand. In the Holocene epoch, the Andes would look like that, with immense fans of gravel coming off their eastern slopes—the essential difference being vegetation, of which there was virtually none in the early Silurian. The sea was shallow, with a sandy bottom, in Pennsylvania. The equator had shifted some and was running in the direction that is now northeast-southwest, through Minneapolis and Denver. There were muds of dark lime in the seafloors of Ohio, and from Indiana westward there were white-lime sands only a few feet under clear water.

If you had turned around and come back thirty million years later, in all likelihood you would still have been riding the sparkling waves of the limestone-platform sea, but its extent in the late Silurian is not well reported. Most of the rock is gone. There are widely scattered clues. Among the marine limestones that fell into the diamond pipe near Laramie, some are late Silurian in age. From Wyoming toward the east, there seems to have existed a vastly extrapolated sea. The extrapolation stops in Chicago. You would have come upon a huge coral reef, which is still there, which grew in Silurian time, and did not grow in a desert. It was a wave-washed atoll then, a Kwajalein, an Eniwetok, and in time it would become sugary blue dolomite packed with Silurian shells. After standing there almost four hundred million years, the dolomite would be quarried to become for many miles the concrete surface of Interstate 80 and to become as well the foundations of most of the tall buildings that now proclaim Chicago, as the atoll did in Silurian time. Interstate 80 actually crosses the atoll on bridges above the quarry, which is as close an approximation to the Grand Canyon as Chicago is likely to see, and is arguably its foremost attraction. Beyond the atoll, you would have come to other atolls and hypersaline seas. When water is about three times as salty as the ocean, gypsum will crystallize out. Sticking up from the bottom in central Ohio were dagger-length blades of gypsum crystal. You would have been bucking hot tropical trade winds then, blowing toward the equator, evaporating the knee-deep sea. East of Youngstown, red muds clouded the water—muds coming off the approaching shore. The beach was in central Pennsylvania now, near the future site of Bloomsburg, near the forks of the Susquehanna. The great sedimentary wedge of the delta complex had grown a hundred miles. The Taconic mountains were of humble size. The steep braided rivers were gone, their wild conglomerates buried under meandering mudbanked streams moving serenely through a low and quiet country—a rose-and-burgundy country. There were green plants in the red earth, for the first time ever.

Walking forward through time and past the tilted strata of the

Water Gap, we had come to sandstones, siltstones, and shales, in various hues of burgundy and rose. In the irregular laminations of the rock—in its worm burrows, ripples, and crossbeds—Anita saw and described tidal channels, tidal flats, a river coming into an estuary, a barrier bar, a littoral sea. She saw the delta, spread out low and red, the Taconic mountains reduced to hills. We had left behind us the rough conglomerates and hard gray quartzites that had come off the Taconic mountains when they were high—the formation, known as Shawangunk, that forms the mural cliffs above the Delaware River. (The quartzites are paradisal to rappeling climbers, who refer in their vernacular to "the gap rap," a choice part of "the Gunks.") And now, half a mile up the highway and twenty million years up the time scale, we were looking at the younger of the two formations of which Kittatinny Mountain is locally composed. Generally red, the rock is named for Bloomsburg, outer reach of the deltaic plain in late Silurian time, four hundred million years before the present.

Less than two hundred years before the present, when the United States was twenty-four years old, the first wagon road was achieved through the Water Gap. The dark narrow passage in rattlesnake-defended rock had seemed formidable to Colonial people, and the Water Gap had not served them as a transportational gateway but had been left aloof, mysterious, frightening, and natural.

In the hundred feet or so of transition rocks between the gray Shawangunk and the red Bloomsburg, we had seen the Silurian picture change from sea and seashore to a low alluviated coastal plain; and if we had a microscope, Anita said, we would see a few fish scales in the Bloomsburg river sands—from fish that looked like pancake spatulas, with eyes in the front corners.

In 1820, the Water Gap was discovered by tourists. They were Philadelphians with names like Binney.

Breaking away some red sandstone, Anita remarked that it was telling a story of cut-and-fill—the classic story of a meandering stream. The stream cuts on one side while it fills in on the other. Where bits and hunks of mudstone were included in the sandstone, the stream had cut into a bank so vigorously that it undermined the muddy soil above and caused it to fall. Meanwhile, from the opposite bank—from the inside of the bend in the river—a point bar had been building outward, protruding into the channel, and the point bar was preserved in clean sandstones, where curvilinear layers, the crossbeds, seemed to have been woven of rushes.

Confronted with a mountain sawed in half, a traveller would naturally speculate about how that might have happened—as had the Indians before, when they supposedly concluded that the Minisink had once been "a deep sea of water." Samuel Preston agreed with the Indians. In 1828, in a letter to *Hazard's Register of Pennsylvania*, Preston referred to the Water Gap as "the greatest natural curiosity in any part of the State." He went on to hypothesize that "from the appearance of so much alluvial or made land above the mountain, there must, in some former period of the world, have been a great dam against the mountain that formed all the settlements called Minisink into a lake, which extended and backed the water at least fifty miles." And therefore, he worked out, "from the water-made land, and distance that it appears to have backed over the falls in the river, the height must, on a moderate calculation, have been between one hundred and fifty and two hundred feet, which would have formed a cataract, in proportion to the quantity of water, similar to Niagara." Preston was a tourist, not a geologist. The first volume of Charles Lyell's "Principles of Geology," the textbook that most adroitly explained the new science to people of the nineteenth century, would not be published for another two years, let alone cross the sea from London. All the more remarkable was Preston's Hypothesis. Like many an accomplished geologist who would follow, Preston made excellent sense even if he was wrong. Withal, he had the courage of his geology. "If any persons think my hypothesis erroneous," he concluded, "they may go and examine for themselves. . . . The Water Gap will not run away."

While sediments accumulated slowly in the easygoing lowlands of the late Silurian world, iron in the rock was oxidized, and therefore the rock turned red. Alternatively, it could have been red in the first place, if it weathered from a red rock source. There were dark-hued muds and light silts in the outcrop, settled from Silurian floods. There were balls and pillows, climbing ripples, flow rolls, and mini-dunes—multihued structures in the river sands. Maroon. Damask. Carmine. Rouge.

Artists were the Delaware Water Gap's most effective discoverers. Inadvertently, they publicized it. They almost literally put it on the map. Arrested by the symmetries of this geomorphological phenomenon, they sketched, painted, and engraved it. The earliest dated work is the Strickland Aquatint, 1830, with a long and narrow flat-bottomed Durham boat in the foreground on the river, four crewmen standing at their oars, a steersman (also standing) in the stern, and in the background the wildwoods rising up the mountain with its deep, improbable incision.

Cutting and filling, a stream would cross its own valley, gradationally leaving gravels under sands under silts under muds under fine grains that settled in overbank floods. With nothing missing, the sequence was before us now, and was many times reiterated in the rock—a history of the migrations of the stream as it spread layer upon layer through its subsiding valley, 404, 403, 402 million years ago.

In 1832, Asher B. Durand came upon the scene. Durand was one of the founders of what in time would be labelled the Hudson River School. The term was a pejorative laid by a critic on painters who went outdoors to vent their romantic spirits. They went up the Hudson, they went up the Rockies, and they went into the Water Gap unafraid. Durand painted another Durham boat. His trees looked Japanese. The picture was published after Durand himself made a copper engraving. It contributed to the axiom that where an easel had stood a hotel would follow. Kittatinny House was established in 1833, sleeping twenty-five.

Anita chipped out a piece of Bloomsburg conglomerate—evidence in itself that the stream which had made it was by no means spent. The rolling Silurian countryside must have been lovely— its river valleys velvet green. There were highland jaspers among the pebbles in the sand.

The early geologists began arriving in 1836, led by Henry Darwin Rogers. They were conducting Pennsylvania's first geological survey. In the deep marine Martinsburg slate and in the mountain strata that stood above it—in the "plication" and the "corrugation" of the sediments—Rogers saw "stupendous crust-movement and revolution," the "most momentous" of ancient times, and reported to Harrisburg what would eventually become known as the Taconic and Alleghenian Orogenies. He decided that something had wrenched the mountain in New Jersey several hundred feet out of line with its counterpart in Pennsylvania. "I conceive these transverse dislocations to pervade all the great ridges and valleys of our Appalachian region," he wrote, "and to be a primary cause of most, if not all, of those deep notches which are known by the name of Water Gaps, and which cleave so many of our high mountain ridges to their very bases."

There were some thin green beds among the Bloomsburg reds. Anita said they were the *Kupferschiefer* greens that had given false hope to the Dutch. Whatever else there might be in the Bloomsburg Delta, there was not a great deal of copper. In the eighteen-forties, the mines of the Minisink were started up anew. They bankrupted out in a season. The Reverend F. F. Ellinwood delivered the "Dedication Sermon" in the Church of the Mountain, village of Delaware Water Gap, Pennsylvania, August 29, 1854, a year that Ellinwood placed in the sixth millennium after Creation. "The rude blasts of six thousand winters have howled in undaunted wildness over the consecrated spot, while yet its predicted destiny was not fulfilled," he told the congregation. "But here, at length, stands, in very deed the church firmly built upon the rock, and it is our hope and prayer that the gates of Hell shall not prevail against it. . . . For many centuries past, has Jehovah dwelt in the rocky fastnesses of this mountain. Ere there was a human ear to listen, His voice was uttered here in the sighing of the breeze and the thunder of the storms, which even then were wont to writhe in the close grapple of this narrow gorge. Ere one human footstep had invaded the wildness of the place, or the hand of art had applied the drill and blast to the silent rock, God's hand was working here alone—delving out its deep, rugged pathway for yonder river, and clothing those gigantic bluffs and terraces with undying verdure, and the far gleaming brightness of their laurel bloom." The hand of art, that very summer, was blasting the Delaware, Lackawanna & Western Railroad into the silent rock. Stagecoaches would soon leave the scene. A pathway by the river was replaced with rails. The sycamores that shaded it were felled. A telegraph wire was strung through the gap. Given a choice between utility and grandeur, people apparently wanted to have it both ways. Trains would travel in one direction carrying aristocrats and in the other carrying coal.

Anita put her fingers on fossil mud cracks, evidence not only of hours and seasons in the sun but of tranquillity in the environment in which the rock had formed. She also moved her fingers down the smooth friction streaks of slickensides (tectonic scars made by block sliding upon block, in the deforming turbulence of later times).

In the Ecological epoch, the Backpackerhaus School of photography will not so much as glance at anything within twenty-five miles of a railhead, let alone commit it to film, but in the eighteen-fifties George Inness came to the Water Gap and set up his easel in sight of the trains. The canvases would eventually hang in the Metropolitan Museum, the Tate Gallery, the National Gallery (London). Meanwhile, in 1860, Currier & Ives made a lithograph from one of them and published it far and wide. By 1866, there were two hundred and fifty beds in Kittatinny House alone, notwithstanding that the manager had killed a huge and ferocious catamount not far from the lobby. That scarcely mattered, for this was the New World, and out in the laurel there were also wolves and bears. The gap was on its way to becoming a first-class, busy summer resort.

"Note the fining-upward cycles," Anita said. "Those are crossbedded sandstones with mud clasts at the base, rippled to unevenly bedded shaly siltstones and sandstones in the middle, and indistinctly mud-cracked bioturbated shaly siltstones with dolomite concretions at the top."

It was a lady visiting the Water Gap in the eighteen-sixties who made the once famous remark "What a most wonderful place would be the Delaware Water Gap if Niagara Falls were here."

The Aldine, in 1875, presented three wood engravings of the Water Gap featuring in the foreground gentlemen with walking sticks and ladies with parasols, their long full dresses sweeping the quartzite. The accompanying text awarded the Delaware Water Gap an aesthetic edge over most of the alpine passes of Europe. *The Aldine* subtitled itself "The Art Journal of America" but was not shy to make dashes into other fields. "The mountains of Pennsylvania are far less known and visited than many of the American ranges at much greater distance, and even less than many of the European ranges, while they may be said to vie in beauty with any others upon earth, and to have, in many sections, features of grandeur entitling them to eminent rank," the magazine told its readers. "Not only the nature lover, by the way, has his scope for observation and thought in the Water Gap. The scientist has something to do, and is almost certain to do it, if he lingers there for any considerable period. He may not have quite decided how Niagara comes to be where it is—whether it was originally in the same place, or down at the mouth of the St. Lawrence; but he will find himself joining in the scientific speculations of the past half-century, as to whether the Water Gap changed to be what it is at the Flood; or whether some immense freshet broke through the barriers once standing across the way and let out what had been the waters of an immense inland lake."

By 1877, Kittatinny House was five stories high. *Harper's Weekly*, at the end of the season, ran a wood engraving of the Water Gap in color by Granville Perkins, who had taken enough vertical license to outstretch El Greco. Under the enlofted mountain, a woman reclined on the riverbank with a pink parasol in her hand. A man in a straw boater, dark suit, was stretched beside her like a snake in the grass.

In the crossbedding and planar bedding of the Bloomsburg rocks, as we slowly traced them forward through time, there had been evidence of what geologists call the "lower upper flow regime." That was now becoming an "upper lower flow regime."

When people were bored with the river, there were orchestras, magicians, lecturers, masquerade balls. They could read one another's blank verse:

> Huge pile of Nature's majesty! how oft
> The mind, in contemplation wrapt, has scann'd
> Thy form serene and naked; if to tell,
> That when creation from old chaos rose,
> Thou wert as now thou art; or if some cause,
> Some secret cause, has rent thy rocky mantle,
> And hurl'd thy fragments o'er the plain below.
> The pride of man may form conceptions vast,
> Of all the fearful might of giant power
> That rent the rampart to its very base,
> Giving an exit to Lenape's stream,
> And wildly mixing with woods and waters.
> A mighty scene to set enchantment free,
> Burst the firm barrier of eternal rock,
> If by the howling of volcanic rage,
> Or foaming terror of Noachian floods.
> Let fancy take her strongest flight. . . .
> But, as for us, let speculations go,
> And be the food of geologic sons;
> Who from the pebble judge the mountain's form . . .

Anita said the rock had been weakened here in this part of the mountain. The river, cutting through the formations, had found the weakness and exploited it. "Wherever a water gap or a wind gap exists, there is generally tectonic weakness in the bedrock," she went on. "The rock was very much fractured and shattered. There is particularly tight folding here."

The hotels were in Pennsylvania, and were so numerous in the eighteen-eighties and eighteen-nineties that they all but jostled one another, and suffered from the competition. Up the slope from Kittatinny House, as in a game of king-of-the-mountain, stood Water Gap House, elongate and white, with several decks of circumambient veranda under cupolas that appeared to be mansard smokestacks. All it lacked was a stern wheel. There was a fine view. On the narrow floodplain and river terraces of New Jersey, where I-80 would be, there were cultivated fields and split-rail fences, corn shocks in autumn, fresh furrows in spring.

Anita and I came to the end of the Bloomsburg, or as far as it went in the outcrops of the gap. "These are coarse basal sands," she said of one final layer. "They were deposited in channels and point bars through lateral accretion as the stream meandered." In all, there were fifteen hundred feet of the formation, reporting the disintegration of high Silurian worlds.

Ten or twelve years after the turn of the century, a Bergdoll touring car pulled into the porte cochère of Water Gap House and the chauffeur stepped out, leaving Theodore Roosevelt alone in the open back while a photograph arrested his inscrutable face, his light linen suit, his ten-gallon paunch and matching hat. This must have been a high moment for the resort community, but just as Teddy (1858–1919) was in his emeritus years, so, in a sense, was the Water Gap. A fickling clientele preferred Niagaras with falls. An intercity trolley had been added to the scene. Two miles downstream—in what had been George Inness's favorite foreground—was a new railroad bridge that looked like a Roman aqueduct. Rails penetrated the gap on both sides of the river. There was a golf course—dramatic in its glacial variations on precipitous tills pushed by the ice up the side of the broken mountain—where Walter Hagen, in 1926, won the Eastern Open Championship. Soon thereafter, the tournament was played for the last time. Walter Hagen was not coming back, and neither was the nineteenth century. The perennial Philadelphians were now in Maine. In 1931, Kittatinny House burned up like a signal fire. Freight trains wailed as they rumbled past the embers. In 1960 came the interstate—a hundred and sixty years after the first wagon road. As a unit of earth history, a hundred and sixty years could not be said to be exactly nothing—although, in the gradually accumulated red rock beside the river, ninety-four thousand such units were represented. To put it another way, in the fifteen-hundred-foot thickness of the Bloomsburg formation, there were five millimetres for each hundred and sixty years. The interstate, with its keloid configuration, was blasted into the Shawangunk quartzites, blasted into the redbeds of the Bloomsburg, along the New Jersey side. As if that was not enough for one water gap, it turned and crossed the river.

In all the rock we had walked by, the rivers and streams that carried the material had been flowing west and northwest. I looked over the bank at the inventive Delaware, going the other way. "When did the Delaware River come into existence?" I asked Anita.

She shrugged, and said, "Long ago."

I said, "Really."

She turned and looked back toward the great slot in the mountain, and said, "In the late Jurassic, maybe. Possibly the early Cretaceous. I can look it up. I didn't pay much attention to that part of geology."

In round numbers, then, the age of the river was a hundred and fifty million years. The age of the Water Gap rock was four hundred million years. Another fifty million years before that, the Taconic mountains appeared. The river 150, the rock 400, the first ancestral mountains 450 million years before the present—these dates are so unwieldy that they might as well be off a Manchu calendar unless you sense the pace of geologic change and draw an analogy between, say, a hundred million years of geology and one human century, with its upward-fining sequences, its laminations of events, its slow deteriorations and instant catastrophes. You see the rivers running east. Then you see mountains rise. Rivers run off them to the west. Mountains come up like waves. They crest, break, and spread themselves westward. When they are spent, there is an interval of time, and then again you see the rivers running eastward. You look over the shoulder of the painter and you see all that in the landscape. You see it if first you have seen it in the rock. The composition is almost infinitely less than the sum of its parts, the flickers and glimpses of a thousand million years.

FROM

LA PLACE

DE LA CONCORDE

SUISSE

(1 9 8 4)

[*You cannot separate the Swiss society from the Swiss Army. The society is
an army, the Army is the society. A president of a Swiss bank will also be
a colonel in the Swiss Army. On low and high ground in the Canton de
Valais, the author was for a time attached to the Section de Renseignements
of the Eighth Battalion of the Fifth Regiment of the Tenth Mountain Division. The corporal who led the Section de Renseignements was Luc Massy,
a master winemaker from the Canton de Vaud, who could take the army or
leave it alone. Over the years, the irreverent Massy had put in various days
in le trou—the army's term for military jail. Now, clandestinely, he carried
a pack of his own wine on his back, sparing his companions the ordinary
Fendant of Valais.*]

The Swiss have not fought a war for nearly five hundred years, and are determined to know how so as not to.

In Italy, it has been said of the Swiss Army, "I didn't know they had one." When the Italian learns that the Swiss Army vastly outnumbers Italy's, the Italian says, "That is not difficult."

The Swiss Army has served as a model for less languid nations. The Israeli Army is a copy of the Swiss Army.

Switzerland is two times the size of New Jersey. New Jersey, by far, has the larger population. Nonetheless, there are six hundred and fifty thousand people in the Swiss Army. At any given time, most of them are walking around in street clothes or in blue from the collar down. They are a civilian army, a trained and practiced militia, ever ready to mobilize. They serve for thirty years. All six hundred and fifty thousand are prepared to be present at mobilization points and battle stations in considerably less than forty-eight hours.

If you understand the New York Yacht Club, the Cosmos Club, the Metropolitan Club, the Century Club, the Piedmont Driving Club, you would understand the Swiss Army.

Some of these thoughts run through my mind as the Section de Renseignements—of the Eighth Battalion of the Fifth Regi-

ment of the Tenth Mountain Division—gets ready to patrol a
sector of the uppermost Rhone. The battalion has been told to
move, and it is the business of these soldiers to learn as thoroughly
and as rapidly as they can what their major needs to know about
the new sector; for example, how many troops will fit in a cable
car to the Riederalp? Where is a good site for a command post
on the lower declivities of the alp above Lax? How many soldiers
could sleep in the Schwarzenbach barn? Would that be all right
with Schwarzenbach? Have explosives already been installed—
as is the case at thousands of strategic points in Switzerland—to
blow up the Nussbaum bridge?

With notebooks and pencils, the patrols of the Section de
Renseignements go from place to place exploring, asking questions, collecting particulars, scribbling information, character-
izing and describing people and scenes, doing reconnaissance of
various terrains, doing surveillance of present activity, and track-
ing events of the recent past. Afterward, they trudge back and,
under pressure of time, compress, arrange, and present what they
have heard and seen. All of that is incorporated into the substance
of the word "renseignements."

I have limitless empathy for the Section de Renseignements.
The leader of the second patrol today is Luc Massy, who entered
the army ten years ago with essentially his present status. He is
five feet eleven inches tall, with blond hair and an aquiline
nose—trim, irreverent, thirty years old. The others are Jean-
Bruno Wettstein, Denis Schyrr, Pierre Pera, Jean Reidenbach.
Each wears boots, gaiters, a mountain jacket, and a woolly-earflap
Finnish hat, and carries a fusil d'assaut, which can fire twenty-
four bullets in eight seconds and, with added onomatopoeia, is
also know as a Sturmgewehr. Massy wears hobnailed boots. Most
of the other soldiers are younger, and when they came into the
army were issued boots with rubber soles—Swiss crosses protruding from the soles in lieu of hobnails. Massy says he feels
the north wind, and therefore the weather will be stable for three,
six, or nine days. The air seems still to me—a clear and frosted
morning at the end of October in a deep valley under Alps freshly

dusted with snow. Using pocket calculators and topographic maps, the patrol has charted its assignments—uphill, down, up, down—figuring that eleven hours will be required to complete them. Accordingly, each man puts in his pack a plastic sack of lunch and a plastic sack of dinner—dried fruit, fresh fruit, bread, cheese, pâté, sausage, and bars that are labelled "Militärschokolade, Chocolat Militaire."

This is the Valais, the Swiss canton with the country's highest mountains—a canton divided by the west-running Rhone, which once flowed as ice five thousand feet deep to cut among the mountains its otherwise irrational groove. The Alps crowd the great chasm—off the left bank the Pennines, off the right bank the Bernese Oberland. The canton is divided in language as well, part French, part German, and not in a mixed-up manner, which would be utterly un-Swiss, but with a break that is clear in the march of towns—Champéry, Martigny, Sion, Sierre, Salgesch, Turtmann, Ausserberg, Brig—and clearer still in the names of the hanging valleys that come down among the peaks and plummet to the Rhone: Val de Bagnes, Val d'Hérens, Val d'Anniviers, Turtmanntal, Lötschental, Mattertal. The Tenth Mountain Division consists almost wholly of Suisses romands, as French-speaking Swiss are known. In their present exercises, they are well spread out through French and German Valais. In the German-speaking villages, soldiers puzzle at the names of streets and shops and understand nothing of the talk they overhear.

The Divisionnaire of the Tenth Mountain Division is, of course, from French Switzerland—La Suisse Romande, also known as La Romandie. His name is Adrien Tschumy. On his shoulders—and nested in the fleece of his Finnish hat—are pairs of stars. There is a Swiss cross in the center of each star. The Divisionnaire is tall, trim, contemplative, with dark hair, a narrow face, and a manner that is quietly convincing. In military roles, the film actor Gregory Peck has resembled Tschumy, who resembles General MacArthur.

Tschumy must go to remote places to see his men in action.

In Switzerland, there are no Fort Hoods, Fort Irwins, no vast terrains set aside for explosive games. There are few barracks. Troops on active duty for refresher courses (also known as repetition courses) are quartered for the most part in villages and towns, and if they are using live ammunition they must walk to far places to shoot. Here, for instance, Tschumy visits a company of grenadiers in the morning shadow of the Torrenthorn, six thousand feet above the Rhone. The Swiss Army grenadiers look upon themselves in the way that the United States Marines look upon themselves. The Swiss Army grenadiers specialize in events that take place at two thousand metres and skyward. They are technical climbers, schussbooming skiers, demolition experts, and crack shots, who sleep on granite mattresses and eat chocolate-coated nails. Some of them are bankers. Others are chauffeurs, dental technicians, civil engineers, alpine guides. They have discovered an enemy command post and are moving in its direction under the covering fire of automatic rifles. The bullets are bullets. Signal flags, understood all over Switzerland, have been set out to advertise the danger to passing promeneurs. Moving uphill, up a small cirque valley, the soldiers advance behind exploding grenades. Officers observe. One lieutenant works for I.B.M. in White Plains, New York, and has taken three weeks off to do his service. Crawling through snow under more bullets, the grenadiers reach the wall of the command post, a dotted line in their minds, and lay beside it a high-explosive plastic. They run. Chunks of broken rock rise out of the snow and fly in all directions, as much as three hundred metres—some above the head of the Divisionnaire. Like a theatre, the reverberant cirque enhances the explosion.

Meanwhile, certain boulders across a ravine have been identified as enemy helicopters that have just landed. For seven hundred years, Swiss soldiers have been masters of the mountain pass, and have looked upon the high divides not only as standpoints of invincible defense but as virtual weapons in themselves—terrain where the alien was disadvantaged and the Swiss could win battles even with falling rocks. Helicopters flout

[*148*]

the mountain pass. The flying horses, as they are regarded, can appear from anywhere, come whirling over some unlikely arête, and with machine guns firing drop soldiers in the snow. The defense adapts. Men with bazookas on their backs run toward the helicopters and fall prone while their partners aim the tubes and fire. Explosions turn the choppers into scree.

Now the grenadiers discover the existence of an enemy radio shack farther up the valley. They go after it with a blend of automatic rifles and grenades, crawling under the rifle fire to heave the grenades. The noise is loud to the point of pain, and the observing officers have fingers in their ears. Bullets rain on the mountain wall. The soldiers run forward, hide behind rocks. Grenades explode. As the soldiers move up the valley—now running low, now crawling, now inching along on their chests—a corporal walks upright behind them, like a football coach following the progress of a scrimmage. Wooden silhouettes representing enemy soldiers are blown and shot to bits. The objective is reached, and, with a final rush—with an explosion louder than any that has come before—the radio shack is taken without prisoners.

Walking back to lower ground, the Divisionnaire has many points to teach. Characteristically, he taps one index finger on the other as he talks. His primary point seems to be that the officers' preparation should have been more thorough. Intent on what he is saying, he does not look up. If he did, he could see out of Switzerland. He could see Mont Blanc, twice his altitude, bright in the morning light, and in Swiss terrain the Grand Combin, the Dent Blanche, the Weisshorn—a freshened sea of peaks beyond the deep airspace of the invisible Rhone. Resting level on rock and snow, a table has been set, with a red tablecloth; and the sun—at half past nine—has come over the Torrenthorn to shine on silver platters of rolled shaved beef, bacon, sausages, wedges of tomato, half-sliced pickles in the shape of fans. Officers stand around the table. There is a company of teacups in close ranks, another of stemmed glassware. There are baskets of bread. The wines are of the Valais. The red is Chapelle de Salquenen.

The rosé is Œil de Perdrix, in a bucket full of snow. Tschumy drinks a cup of tea. A promeneur happens by—a citizen in knickers, boots, heavy socks, a mountain hat—on his way from who knows to where. He just appears, like a genie. His appearance suggests that he is above fifty and done with the army. He absorbs the scene: the festive table, the officers sipping and nibbling and quietly debriefing, the soldiers at a distance sitting in clusters on their packs, the charcoal streaks on the exploded snow. "Gut," he says, and he waves and walks on.

"Wiedersehen," the Divisionnaire calls after him, and the Divisionnaire is himself soon away—rising into the air in his Alouette III, his French six-seat jet-powered chopper, ascending among walls of red rock to cross into the Lötschental. Trending northeast, the valley rises toward the center of the Bernese Oberland. It is possible in Switzerland to be so far above and away from the Mittelland—the smooth perfected country that runs from Lake Geneva through Bern and Zurich —that even a Swiss valley, like the rough young mountains surrounding it, may seem penarctic and remote. The Lötschental is such a valley. The people of the Lötschental live in small, dark-cabin towns. A stream flows among them, pushing boulders. High serrated mountains are lined up in rows on either side, and the valley floor rises between them into fields of perennial snow. There are charcoal streaks on the snow. In the last five miles of the Lötschental, moving glacier ice is packed between the summits and leads to a gap where the converging mountains all but close. Twenty-five, twenty-six, twenty-seven hundred metres, the ice bends upward like the tip of a ski. Passing three thousand metres, the helicopter floats up a face of rock and moves through the gap into a world too bright for unshielded eyes. It is the top of the Bernese Oberland, where ice fields and snowfields are the white diammeters of circumvallate arêtes, where all horizons are violent. The granite Jungfrau, the Mönch, the Eiger, the Fiescherhorn, the Aletschhorn, the Fiescher Gabelhorn conduct the eye across the glaciers to the gneisses of the Aar massif, to the obeliscal

Finsteraarhorn, four thousand two hundred and seventy-three metres, the highest mountain north of the Rhone. Crystallizing and recrystallizing, the ice among the peaks collects and compacts itself into the Grosser Aletschgletscher, the supreme glacier of Europe, with avenues of ice coming in from six or eight directions to conjoin in a frozen intersection officially identified on maps as Konkordiaplatz, La Place de la Concorde Suisse. The Divisionnaire looks about him with a thoughtful smile. This place that will never need defending represents what the Swiss defend. In surroundings quieter than a jet-driven helicopter, I have heard him say that he is without reservation "persuadé de la valeur de l'effort de défense"—so thoroughly persuaded, in fact, that he gave up a career as a hydroelectric engineer to devote full time to the army. When he was a part-time artillery officer, rising to colonel, he was a civilian concerned primarily with the efficiency of turbines, which he understood so well that he practiced his trade not only in all parts of Switzerland but also from China to Chile to Hydro-Quebec. A couple of years ago, when he was fifty, he was invited to become an army professional. The professionals are less than half of one per cent of the Swiss Army. They are not only officers but people of almost all ranks and specialties, who teach the militia the ways of war and help make the militia cohesive. Tschumy was given two stars for his hat and his epaulets, and responsibility for the Tenth Mountain Division. One star signifies a brigadier, and three stars a commandant de corps. There are seven commandants de corps, the highest-ranking officers in the army. The word "general" is not used except in situations of extreme emergency, when a fourth star is presented to one leader, chosen by the Federal Assembly.

In five centuries of neutrality, Switzerland has had four generals. The first was Guillaume-Henri Dufour, who was appointed in 1847 to suppress a rebellion of seven Catholic cantons: Lucerne, Uri, Schwyz, Unterwalden, Zug, Fribourg, and Valais. Neutrality does not exclude civil war. Dufour pounded the Catholics, who gave up after twenty-seven days. With paradoxical obscurity, his name rests on Dufourspitze, one of the least-known summits in the world, although it is the highest in Switzerland. Never mind that like the Matterhorn it is half Italian. Switzerland's other generals were appointed at times of nervous mobilization at the borders, of fearing what might happen as a result of proximate wars. General Hans Herzog became a national hero as the principal spectator of the Franco-Prussian War. In the First World War, General Ulrich Wille led the Swiss to victory. Victory consisted of successfully avoiding the conflict. As someone put it, "we won by having no war." In the Second World War, the victorious Swiss general was Henri Guisan, of the Canton de Vaud. There is a General Guisan Quai in Zurich, a Quai Général Guisan in Geneva. In every part of Switzerland, there are streets and plazas and equestrian statues—there are busts on plinths overhung with banners and flags—doing honor to the general of an army that did not fight. Switzerland defends itself on what it calls the Porcupine Principle. You roll up into a ball and brandish your quills. In the words of Divisionnaire Tschumy, "The foremost battle is to prevent war with a price of entry that is too high. You must understand that there is no difference between the Swiss people and the Swiss Army. There is no difference in will. Economic, military—it's the same thing. For seven hundred years, freedom has been the fundamental story of Switzerland, and we are not prepared to give it up now. We want to defend ourselves, which is not the same as fighting abroad. We want peace, but not under someone else's conditions. We will fight from the border. In response to a ground attack, which would in all likelihood come from the northeast, we intend to keep a maximum proportion of our land free. There are those who think we should train only for guerrilla warfare. That would be a form of giving up. Another possibility is that someone might use Switzerland by going through a corner or two, or to get to the north by the Simplon Pass or the pass of Grand-Saint-Bernard. We must stop that, too. We can really do something. We haven't enough tanks, but, given the nature of our terrain, we can fight with infantry. The first days of fighting would be dangerous for us. We would lose many people. But I am confident of our defenses. If I were not confident, I would not be a divisionnaire."

Like a fly inside a chandelier, the helicopter crosses La Place de la Concorde Suisse. Making a shortcut to Alte Pür, it goes up the side of an arête, over the knife-edged rock, and crosses another glacier—the Fieschergletscher—under the spire of the Finster-aarhorn. It was below the Finsteraarhorn that the Swiss first fig-ured out the movements and the sweeping implications of glacier ice, dominating a world that looked something like this. Wasen-horn, Firehorn, Chastelhorn—the mountains decline in alti-tude, the terrain falls toward the Rhone, whose valley, near its beginnings, is as narrow as the Lötschental and seems as remote. It contains two paved airstrips—but no airport, no evident hang-ars, no evident airplanes, no fuelling trucks, not even a wind sock. One sees such airstrips in many mountain valleys. Near the older ones are hangars that are rises in the ground. They are painted in camouflage and covered with living grass. Other strips are more enigmatic, since no apparent structures exist. If one just happens to be looking, though, one might see a mountain open—might see something like an enormous mousehole appear chimerically at the base of an alp. Out of the mountain comes a supersonic aircraft—a Tiger, a Mirage—bearing on its wings the national white cross. In a matter of seconds, it is climbing the air. Pilots sit inside the mountains waiting, night and day. On topographic maps revised and printed since the airstrips were built, the airstrips do not appear. The maps are sold in bookstores all over Switzerland, but those who wish to fill in the airstrips need their own renseignements. Even the map on the Division-naire's lap does not show the airstrips below. The Alouette crosses the Rhone, and goes south into the small, steep-sided Blinnental. It drops into the exact center of the V of the valley, and gradually to the floor, not much shy of the Blinnengletscher and the in-ternational divide. The Blinnental is essentially uninhabited, and utterly so at Alte Pür—an alpine meadow, grazed some in sum-mer, perhaps, but not extensively, and barren-looking now. It is a good place for artillery—a good place for forward observers to practice their art of defining the targets of the guns. Somewhere up a small valley on the north side of the Rhone is an obusier 46, which can throw fifteen kilograms ten kilometres and is practicing close to the limits of its range. The target is a cliff off the shoulder of an alp almost due south of the distant gun. Above the observers' heads, there is an occasional high hum, a soft whistle, as fifteen kilograms complete their parabola and zap the hapless alp. There is no concern whatever that if the shell should miss the alp it might go whistling into Italy. The shell is not going to miss. The observers are under camouflage nets with their field telephones and other equipment. Four such groups are in the meadow, practicing together on the same situation. Their major is Jacques Hentsch, and he says the shells are taking thirty seconds to reach the target from the gun. The observers compute the difference between the intended and the actual hit. On their telephones, they present the results to the artillerymen at the gun, who make the necessary adjustments and fire again. "No problem," says Major Hentsch. There is a problem, though. The calculations and the phone calls and the adjustments at the gun are supposed to take forty seconds, to which is added the thirty seconds of travel time for the ensuing shell. Now and again, a shell goes overhead and flame and thunder erupt from the alp, but not at anything approximating one-minute-and-ten-second intervals, and while the Divisionnaire—one index finger tapping against the other—speaks tensely to the observers Major Hentsch has leisure to remark that people in New York are indulging in pure hokum when they say that interest rates will continue to fall and thus the stock market is certain to go on rising. Nevertheless, he adds, New York is still one of the few places in the world where you can make money. Hentsch belongs to one of the most august and ancient private-banking families in Geneva. On his own, he has become well known for his resourceful development of new accounts. He manages portfolios. He says that he is like a priest, in that he must know his customers well in order to serve them. Less than a week ago, he was in Portland, Maine, buying lobsters. Last year, he bought twenty-five thousand lobsters, importing them through Zurich into Sweden. Of service in the Swiss Army, he says, "It belongs to the passport." And apropos of nothing at all he adds, "We are nice people. Not everyone understands that."

Why is the Divisionnaire so unhappy? With Swiss precision, every shell has exploded in an area smaller than the courtyard of the Pentagon, and the area is the target.

A communications problem, Hentsch explains, is causing the shells to come so slowly. The artillerymen at the gun are Suisses allemands, there being a shortage of artillery officers in La Suisse Romande. The forward observers are feeding back their data in French, which the people at the gun only poorly understand. The observers, for their part, observe nothing in German. The shells continue to come slowly. The shooting ends badly. A black soldier comes up to the Divisionnaire and offers him raclette for lunch. With grace, the invitation is declined.

The patrol has walked several kilometres on the high ground above the Rhone and now looks down on the Nussbaum bridge. The drop is steep at first, through a meadowful of agile cows, and then considerably steeper. Massy, chef de patrouille, cannot see a way to go down, and neither can anyone else. Massy looks west, studying possibilities. Massy looks east. Massy looks down at his boots and past his toes to the Nussbaum bridge. What to do? The hour is somewhat past noon. The sun at last is bathing the deep narrow valley. The breeze is becoming warm. The larches are bright gold. The meadow is dry. The bridge can wait. When in doubt, eat lunch.

We sit down and break out our Valais bread and cheese. Across the valley, a waterfall erupts from dark wooded slopes of the Bettmeralp, which is treeless and white far above. Near the waterfall, a dark-brown village clings to the alp. Over our heads, an eagle is sliding through the sky. Massy removes from his pack a bulky towel and unrolls it to reveal a bottle of wine. In his battle jacket he keeps a tire-bouchon, always ready, like a grenade. He opens its knife blade and deroofs the leaded wine. He erects the corkscrew and revolves it into the cork. He sets the lever arm on the lip of the bottle. We hear the sound of a tennis ball, well hit. Massy runs the cork by his nose. In his breast pocket, at all times, is a small plastic cylinder that resembles a dice cup. It protects a drinking glass so small that even in its sheath it does not create a bulge in the jacket. With straight, converging sides, it has the simple shape of a peach basket, if not the size. It holds six centilitres and is a verre de cave, a winemaker's glass, whose proportions any Swiss winemaker could identify as the glass of the Canton de Vaud.

Massy fills the glass, holds it up to his eye. "Santé," he says, with a nod to the rest of us, and—thoughtfully, unhurriedly— drinks it himself. Because I happen to be sitting beside him on his left, he says, "John, you are not very well placed. In my town, we drink counterclockwise." After finishing the glass, he fills it again and hands it to his right—to Jean Reidenbach. The background music is a dissonance of cattle bells. We count nineteen Brown Swiss in the meadow just below us, and they sound like the Salvation Army. A narrow red train appears far below. Coming out of a tunnel, it crosses a bridge, whistling—three cars in all, the Furka-Oberalp. The train will go up the Rhone until there is no more Rhone, and then climb on cogs to the Furka Pass, and the Oberalp Pass, to finish its journey descending the nascent Rhine, pool to cascade pool, pastel green with glacial flour. The railroad bridge is a beautiful stonework that looks like a piece of a cloister. In all respects but width, it shames the Nussbaum bridge, the latter being wide enough for two automobiles or possibly one red tank. A téléphérique is down there as well. Wires go up the Bettmeralp. Denis Schyrr volunteers to get the necessary facts at the téléphérique station later on, but he adds, "Do you suppose they speak French?"

Massy shrugs. He takes the glass from Reidenbach, refills it, and hands it to Schyrr. "This is a good way to drink," Massy remarks. "A good way to avoid getting—you know—drunk." Six centilitres is about two ounces. If the glass were filled with whiskey, you would know you'd had a drink. The apples and sausages are fresh and good, less so the pâté in the can. The sunlight is delicious. The packs are supportive. The rifles lean against a tree. After Pierre Pera, it is my turn to drink, and then Massy's, Reidenbach's, Schyrr's, Wettstein's, Pera's, mine, and Massy's. Pera is a plumber in Montreux. Denis Schyrr, blond and scholarly with his metal-rimmed spectacles, is a landscape gardener, a paysagiste-horticulteur, in La Tour de Peilz, near Vevey. Jean Reidenbach, with his tall rustic frame and unruly hair, looks like some sort of paysagiste himself, but is in fact a receptionist at the Ramada in Geneva. The wine is light and pleasant, not to say elegant. Massy pours himself another measure and contemplates it against the Bettmeralp, gold on white. From the one bottle, it is amazing how many times the glass will go around. It stops where it stops—even if the ritual ends, as it always begins, with Massy. Fraternité—yes. Égalité—no. Last month in Lausanne, at the Concours de Jean-Louis, Massy placed sixth in a field of ten thousand wine tasters. Here in this Valais meadow, the label on the bottle in his hand says "Clos du Boux, Epesses. J.-F. Massy, Propriétaire." J.-F. is Massy's father, now his partner, who is trim, compact, has an aquiline nose, and—including the bemused smile—looks exactly like Massy. Also on the label is a line drawing of a two-story house with a Bernese roof, Lombardy poplars at each end. It is completely surrounded by the vines of the Clos du Boux. The house consists of two ground floors, affixed to the slanting vineyard. Massy lives downstairs with his wife and infant son. His father and his mother live above. He leans on his pack and in the balmy sunlight closes his eyes. Three days ago, he was in Epesses making wine.

[*What follows is from a flashback to the first day, when the division assembled in Brig to begin its annual three weeks of military duty.*]

The soldiers were dressed now in their gaiters, their mountain jackets, their Finnish hats. Packs on their backs, rifles across their chests, they walked half a mile through the quiet streets of Brig. They were on their way to La Prise du Drapeau, a ceremony in which the battalion would bring forth from storage its hallowed flag, to be carried into putative battle.

"It symbolizes our fighting spirit," someone remarked.

And Wettstein said, "Fighting spirit is very important in football games."

Wettstein, once a long-distance runner, continues to be in fine condition through his work as an agronomist in the Alpine meadows known as alpages. With amiable brown eyes and a ready smile, he softens the bite of his words. Straight brown hair lightly touches his shoulders. He is the son of a radiologist, and he grew up in Geneva, a city that, in his words, is full of "bad Swiss." One year, as an exchange student, he went to Linn-Mar High School, in Marion, Iowa, where he won his "L-M" in track. "The Republic and Canton of Geneva has been in the confederation only since 1815," he said, explaining his remark about his home town. "It is an international city with no strong Swiss traditions." Genevans sometimes say that it is not necessary to be stupid to be a colonel but it helps.

Passing German street signs and German shop signs, the soldiers walked through town to hear a speech in French.

"Who will speak?"

"The major."

"What will he say?"

"He will say, 'The purpose of the army is to keep Switzerland free. The Russians are not very far away. Have a good three weeks. Dismissed.' "

The soldiers left their packs in a small meadow and formed ranks on a green beside a school. In various directions, there was little to see but light industry, a church steeple, small apartment buildings, sheep, cattle, and fruit trees—until you looked up. Everywhere above were Alps—gold, red, and green on the lower slopes, white beyond the timberline: Glishorn, Hübschhorn,

Klenenhorn, the framing peaks of Simplon; Riederhorn, Hohstock, Sparrhorn, ascending the Bernese Oberland. Clouds were streaming up the mountainsides, running through the conifers like smoke. All five companies of the Eighth Battalion were assembled at parade rest and waiting. The Divisionnaire arrived, and the regimental colonel, Chaudet—the Divisionnaire in a white Mercedes, the Colonel in his gray one. Lesser officers lined up flanking Tschumy and Chaudet, including Captain François Rumpf, of the Bankverein; Major Peter Keller, of Hoffmann–La Roche; Colonel Louis Gilliéron, of La Suisse Assurances; and Major Jean-Daniel Favre, of the Schweizerische Industrie Gesellschaft.

The five companies stood and silently waited. The Divisionnaire, the Colonel, and the lesser officers waited. The Alps waited. Time came and went forever while they waited for the band. It is a tradition among Swiss Army musicians that Swiss Army musicians are unique and special and deserve to be treated as such, in a class by themselves, above schedules and—like nothing else in Switzerland—beyond the clock.

Captain Rumpf whispered, "They are prima donnas."

Thirty minutes after the Divisionnaire had appeared, the band showed up, wearing old steel combat helmets of the sort that faced west across the Western Front. They puffed with effort on their tubas and bassoons, and—unlike the waiting soldiers—could in no sense be described as élite. They were middle-aged, for the most part, with beards of assorted lengths and paunches as prominent as drums. They appeared to have come out of an American Legion hall on the edge of River City. They might have been holding their thirty-fifth reunion. With emotion, elegance, stateliness, they played the national anthem.

The flag was carried forth, and Major Jacques-Henri Beausire stood in a jeep and addressed his battalion. "Officiers, sous-officiers, soldats . . ."

Major Beausire, an independent economic entrepreneur, is a former banker, whose brush-cut hair and firm heavy build more readily suggested an emeritus fullback.

"Ce matin, vous avez déjà accompli un des moments difficiles. . . ."

The speech was inconvenienced by a Toyota forklift in a marble yard next door.

". . . laisser les siens pour une période de trois semaines . . ."

The machine sporadically burped, and only fragments of the speech came through.

". . . quitter son activité professionelle malgré les soucis de la période économique que nous traversons. . . ."

Seven tons of rock fell off the fork.

"Je sais que vous aurez à cœur de démontrer que les gens de votre âge ne correspondent pas forcément à l'image de la minorité qui nous est abondamment rapportée et décrite par les moyens d'information. . . ."

As the soldiers left the ceremony, Wettstein parroted the Major, saying, " 'You are here now and have made a great sacrifice to leave your homes and jobs. You are representing the nation and not a discontented minority of youth. . . .' It is the same speech always," he said. "It is the same speech as in the States."

Massy said, "It is written by the same person."

"**F**ermez les bouteilles!" barked Massy, in his voice of mock command. After the flag ceremony, he and his company were served stew in the meadow where they had left their packs, and now it was time to move—to climb about a thousand feet to their quarters, in Ried, a village said by Lieutenant Wyssa to be a ninety-minute walk from Brig. Massy was by no means the only soldier who had brought wine for the noonday meal, but he alone had brought a glass. The others drank from their bottles. A hundred and thirty speckled gray packs were lined up in neat rows, like granite tombstones, near the joking, reuniting soldiers, whose automatic rifles were resting on their bipods by the packs. A soldier with an apple in his hand was sleeping on the ground. For a time, he went on sleeping while the rest of the company stirred.

Before long, Lieutenant Wyssa gave an order a good deal more official than "Fermez les bouteilles." The Section de Renseignements, moving out past the marble yard and the remorseless Toyota forklift, ambled in a southerly direction through the fringes of the town. As before, they did not march; they walked—single file or double or triple, at the soldiers' choice. "Serrez! Serrez!" Wyssa called out, trying to keep them together, for they tended to be vague, like strollers on an evening paseo instead of a typical Swiss infantry unit demonstrating its precision and anticipatory responses to command. "Serrez! Serrez!"

Even within the limits of Brig, there were Brown Swiss cows and black-nosed Valais sheep. There were stone barns. I asked the agronomist Jean-Bruno Wettstein if—as in the high alpages —the little barns were called écuries.

"In the French part of Switzerland, we don't speak French very well," he said. "Actually, an écurie is for horses, and an étable is for cows. The Swiss mix the terms. They use them interchangeably. If a place has room for animals and people, it is called a chalet d'alpage."

We moved under a road sign that said "SIMPLON ITALIA," and soon left the road to walk beside a stream. It was called the Saltina, and it came from the mountains around Simplon Pass. Rushing white, it was having a last word before expiring into the Rhone. The soldier walking in front of me could not hear the noisy water. He had earphones in his ears, and the wires ran inside his mountain jacket. "In the Section de Renseignements, we try to decide what is the intention of the enemy," Lieutenant Wyssa said to me, in a voice pitched high to ride over the sound of the stream. "We seek information, and sometimes it seeks us. Before we can use it, we must decide if it is true, probable, or false." I asked him what he had studied at Penn, and he said, "Anti-trust and tax law."

[*161*]

Leaving the Saltina, the soldiers climbed a short, steep trail through woods and reached a road that doubled back to a high stone bridge across the stream. It was called Napoleon's Bridge, and Napoleon was said to have crossed it with an army at some point on the road to Elba. The soldiers were quoting Napoleon: "Les meilleures troupes, celles auxquelles vous pouvez faire le plus confiance, ce sont les Suisses!" A Valais mercenary battalion worked for Napoleon in Spain and Russia.

"The French people are not rid of him yet," said Jean-Bruno Wettstein.

The bridge spanned a gorge that no terrestrial vehicle could cross on its own. Small steel doors in one pier hinted that Napoleonsbrücke was ready to blow. It had been superseded, however, by an even higher bridge, which leaped through the sky above—a part of the new road to Simplon. In an extreme emergency, the midspan of the new bridge would no doubt drop on the old one.

Set back on the flaring lip of the gorge was a spread of numbered squares: 1, 2, 3, 4, 5, 6—a three-hundred-metre target range. One sees such ranges near every village and town: against rock outcrops, across meadows as smooth and green as cricket pitches, halfway up hillsides backstopped with forest. Shooting rifles is a national sport. It is also compulsory. The national shooting contests—the Knabenschiessen, the Wyberschiessen, the Rütlischiessen—are major annual events, even more important than the Steinstossen, in which the object is to heave as far as possible a rock that weighs a hundred and eighty-four pounds. (The Swiss—and therefore world—record is three and a half metres.) Meanwhile, soldiers in all age groups practice at their local shooting ranges and must demonstrate adequate competence once a year. Massy goes to the range up the hill behind Epesses; Wettstein goes down the road from Nyon to targets set up close to the French frontier. In their annual test, they fire twenty-four shots, some rapidly, some at will, against plain and camouflaged targets. There is a point system, with a perfect score of a hundred and twelve. If they fail to score fifty-two, they have to put on their uniforms and report to Lausanne for two days of shooting under instructive supervision.

Wettstein said, "I score in the sixties. I'm not a very good shooter, even if I try. Once, I did well. I had a ninety-one."

"You closed your eyes and had a lucky day."

"No. My brother went for me."

"Serrez! Serrez!"

One of Wettstein's childhood heroes was the runner Jean-François Pahud. When Wettstein spent his year at Linn-Mar High School, in Marion, Iowa, he was a middle- and long-distance running star. So impressed are the Swiss with the accomplishments of Swiss in the United States that the entire top floor of the Musée des Suisses à l'Étranger, outside Geneva, is given over to the subject. There is a lovingly framed photograph of the basketball team of Berne High School, in Indiana. There are snapshots, newspaper pages, and so forth from Switzerland County, Indiana; Tell City, Indiana; New Bern, North Carolina; East Bernstadt, Kentucky; New Glarus, Wisconsin. There are testimonials to the families from Ticino who emigrated to Asti, California, and made Italian Swiss Colony wine.

An oil portrait of General Johann Augustus Sutter, of Basel, presents him with a broad-brimmed flat-topped hat above crafty blue eyes and a gray handlebar mustache—looking much like, and even less military than, Harland Sanders, of Kentucky, the chicken colonel. Sutter, of course, was a general nowhere, least of all in Switzerland—but he founded New Helvetia, California, whose name became Sacramento after gold was discovered there, in 1848.

Portraits and paraphernalia of the most major figures march down the walls of the museum's attic rooms.

Albert Gallatin, of Geneva, instructor in French at Harvard, United States representative, United States senator, Secretary of the Treasury at the time of the Louisiana Purchase.

Louis Agassiz, of Neuchâtel, one of the most celebrated professors Harvard has ever had, who convinced the world of the validity of his theory that ice two miles thick had once spread widely over Europe and North America.

William Wyler, of Oberehrendingen, in the Canton d'Argovie, director of "Wuthering Heights," director of "Friendly Persuasion," director of "The Big Country," director of "Ben Hur."

Louis Chevrolet, of La Chaux-de-Fonds, Canton de Neuchâtel, who emigrated to the United States at the age of twenty-one, undertook to make motor vehicles, and placed on the front end of each of them the enduring emblem that "n'est pas sans rappeler, de façon stylisée, le pays d'origine du constructeur"—that is, the map of Switzerland.

Othmar-Hermann Ammann, of Schaffhausen, civil engineer, variously designer or builder of the Golden Gate Bridge, the Verrazano-Narrows Bridge, the Hell Gate Bridge, the Queensboro Bridge, the Triborough Bridge, the Throgs Neck Bridge, the Bronx-Whitestone Bridge, the Goethals Bridge, the Bayonne Bridge, the George Washington Bridge, the Lincoln Tunnel.

So proud is Switzerland of its progeny in America that mention is made even of Solomon Guggenheim, who was born in Philadelphia to parents born in Switzerland.

"Serrez! Serrez!"

The stragglers coalesced beyond Napoleon's Bridge.

Soon we were looking far down on Brig from high rural ground, a breeze in our faces, the Saltina delta and the Rhone Valley deep in the lee of the Bernese Oberland. Turning the other way, we faced the Hübschhorn, all white and half in sunlight up the pass. Wettstein said that while the Simplon Tunnel was being built, before the First World War, the army attacked striking workers. In 1932, when there were political riots in Geneva, the army killed thirteen civilians and wounded eighty. "The army defends against the enemy and preserves internal peace." He also said that the public rampage of recent times by discontented youth had become "minor, small scale," and was "not representative of Switzerland; young Swiss today have become conservative and less absorbed with politics, as they have in the States."

We went by small farms with block-lettered messages on the farmhouse walls beseeching God to guard them. We passed cherry trees that were now as orange as maples. There were more black-nosed sheep, and, at every turn, the universal cattle, with the tintinnabulation of their bells, bells, bells—the clink and clank and clangor of the bells.

A chalet under construction irritated Wettstein. "These are hay meadows," he said. "And there is a problem if they are used for construction. In the mountains, there is plenty of room for grazing but not enough for hay." Since the Second World War, in a steady attrition, Switzerland has lost to development nearly forty per cent of its productive agricultural land. When Wettstein was ten years old, he decided he wanted to be a farmer; but in Switzerland—as an expression goes—it is more difficult to become a farmer than to become President of the Confederation. A farm of, say, sixty acres would cost more than a million dollars if it were available, and that is unlikely. Wettstein settled for agronomy. To the south of us, beyond the Hübschhorn, he had worked not long before at a chalet d'alpage that sends milk plunging by pipeline three kilometres to the village of Simplon, where it is made into cheese—assuming it is not butter when it arrives. Describing the operation, Wettstein quoted J. Robert Oppenheimer on the development of the fission bomb, saying it was one per cent genius and ninety-nine per cent hard work. Wettstein has also put in some months trying to improve the deteriorating chalets and bad grass of Bourg-Saint-Pierre, near the Grand-Saint-Bernard Pass. At Vernamiège, high up the side of the Val d'Hérens, he cleaned up the overgrowth on abandoned agricultural terraces—restoring the land, removing the fire danger, and kicking out the vipers.

"The . . . ?"

"Snakes. They are poisonous adders. They are all over Switzerland. They are not good for tourists. There are many in Valais—everywhere up to two thousand metres."

"What is our present altitude?"

"Eight hundred metres. They don't bite much. You have to step on them. No one is killed by them. They are mostly dangerous to children."

We walked by small perfect squares of standing corn, tan now and dry, stiff as hairbrushes among the grazed meadows. We walked by huge cabbages. Wettstein said, "Children in Switzerland are born in cabbages, so the cabbages must be large."

And eighty-nine minutes after the climb to Ried began, the Section de Renseignements arrived in the center of the village. "Eighty-nine minutes," said Massy. "Lieutenant Wyssa told us ninety. He doesn't lie too much."

It was a village of small homes and a few granaries standing on posts interrupted by broad disks of rock, keeping rodents away from the grain—a simple mountain town no larger than Epesses, and not nearly as compact and ornate. Incongruous in its center was a dark-wood-and-concrete modern school. It sat on a foundation so generously poured that the building seemed to be about two-thirds basement. A large L-shaped entryway led into the basement. A sentry with rifle stood at the bend in the L. Most of the soldiers waited outside—waited to be issued more clothing, extra gear. A swarm of farmers in uniform—who are known as soldats du train because they deal with horses—were singing and swilling in groups. One after another, the Vaudois soldiers went up to the village bulletin board and squinted at a language they could not read. "They discover the geography of Switzerland," said Corporal Philip Müheim, who works in an import-export office in Vevey. "This army is more human than military. We are militarily ten or fifteen years behind, but the army is a tradition." The Swiss school system tends to separate people from the age of twelve according to background, intelligence, and future profession. In the vital way that the American public high school draws together the skeins of American society, the Swiss Army knits Switzerland.

Wettstein said, "If an enemy comes, the whole thing will be over blitzkrieg fast."

Dark was coming on, and the air was cold. When at last it was time to go inside, Massy and the others carried their gear past the sentry in the doorway and went in under the school. The basement door, standing open, was nearly two feet thick and was made of concrete framed with steel. Its hinges were like cannon barrels. Inside were rooms enough—room after room after room—to contain the population of the town. Latrine, showers, kitchen—all of it was under a concrete ceiling three feet thick. It was not the fate of the Section de Renseignements to sleep in a room near the door—to have whatever advantage such propinquity might provide. They had been assigned to a room beyond a room—blank-walled, with sixteen double bunks filling up most of the space, foam mattresses on the bunks. Massy climbed to an upper bunk and sat there looking depressed, with his legs dangling. In bunks around and below him were Pillard, Wettstein, Tanniger, Layaz, Schyrr, Pera. After unrolling a towel, Massy slowly elevated the cork in a bottle of Clos du Boux, Epesses. He looked dismally around the gray walls of the village bomb shelter. His glance was arrested by a long galvanized tube suspended like stovepipe from the ceiling and designed to bring in fresh air. Lugubriously, he said, "La fenêtre."

[*McPhee went off to Oberarth for a while to visit other units of the army and returned some days later to the Section de Renseignements of the Eighth Battalion of the Fifth Regiment of the Tenth Mountain Division.*]

It is five hours after midnight, and in absolute darkness the Section de Renseignements sleeps—a deep agglomerate sleep, without a stir. The door opens at one end of the room. Light falls on the nearer bunks. A corporal with a bullhorn voice calls out, "Messieurs, bonjour!"

Reveille is not known by that name here. Here it is called la diane. Call it what you will, the response is complete silence.

Ten minutes later, the corporal tries again. In the continuing silence, Massy alone concedes that he is conscious. Staring upward into the black, he says, "Il fait beau."

[*167*]

Minutes later, the corporal reappears in the doorway and sternly orders everyone up. When the corporal is gone, Massy remarks, "He is thinking that he is a general."

No one else has complained, moaned, stretched, turned over, lifted his head, sat up—or, in fact, moved. When Lieutenant Wyssa arrives, he says exactly nothing, and they begin to stir. They dress, fill their packs. They breakfast on bread and fruit confections. They receive their assignments, calculate itineraries, and prepare for an arduous day. The enemy is everywhere—threatening passes, threatening the hanging valleys, threatening the riparian landscapes of the Rhone. A command post has been established in a small garage in a private home. In addition to the usual note-taking and sketchmaking and assessments of bridges and barns, the patrol today will carry a transceiver and report to the command post coded descriptions of activity in the Valais.

The sky is heavy, but there is brightness at the southern edge. With their packs and assault rifles, the patrol sets out. Walking downhill—among cattle and barns and apple trees in fruit—Jean-Bruno Wettstein tells me that during my absence the Section de Renseignements was visited by Divisionnaire Tschumy. "He said he believed that Switzerland must be defended from the borders by the army. He said a lot of young people, basing their views on Che Guevara and the French Maquis, think guerrilla warfare is the answer, but actually to depend from the outset on guerrilla warfare is to permit your cities to be occupied, and therefore to capitulate. He said, 'We don't want to be occupied. The army must be prepared to meet an invader head-on, because guerrilla warfare is particularly hard on civilians.' The Swiss remember Oradour, the French village that was almost totally murdered—and many similar examples. I believe Tschumy is right. Tschumy is realistic. The Maquis may have been somewhat effective, but their country was already occupied."

A light rain begins to fall. Taking shelter under the tall concrete pillars of the elevated Simplon road, the soldiers put on rain gear, and turn on the transceiver to send their first coded message: "THE REDS ARE USING POISON GAS AT GRIMSELPASS."

The code consists of three-digit numbers, which represent

phrases that are recorded in a top-secret book. An infantry battalion, for example, is a 200. A message might read, "200 206 195 495 202 322 999." One does not easily learn to compose such tight prose, and in the Section de Renseignements there is particular need for practice.

"ROUGE A PARACHUTÉ SUR GRIMSELPASS."

"We are Boy Scouts," Wettstein comments as the message goes out.

They are, at any rate, four today—Massy, Wettstein, Pillard, and Pierre Gabus, a Geneva lawyer. They are descending into Brig—Roman Brig, staging point for travellers preparing to cross the Simplon, a historically imbricate town. To walk to its center from the outside is to go from basketball courts and light industry into neighborhoods of the nineteenth and eighteenth centuries and on into Renaissance vestiges and cobblestoned medieval streets. In the covered Metzgergasse, the soldiers step out of the rain and transmit another message: "RED ARTILLERY IS HITTING THE NUFENENPASS."

They have leaned their rifles against the window of a textile shop, in front of a display of cotton sweatshirts, on one of which is lettered "U.S. BASEBALL NEW YORK."

"U.S. cultural infiltration," Wettstein remarks. "That is a typical Swiss shirt."

It is true. In all parts of Switzerland, people wear shirts that say "CALIFORNIA UNIVERSITY" or "FLORIDA UNIVERSITY" or "NEW YORK UNIVERSITY." One afternoon among the walking rich on the Bahnhofstrasse in Zurich, I saw a tall young woman roasting and selling chestnuts, her ocean-swell breasts filling a Harvard sweatshirt.

The rain stops. The patrol moves on, and passes a Bridge of Sighs connecting two parts of a seventeenth-century palace. Wettstein says, "Now forget the army for a minute and look at that."

In Sebastiansplatz, everyone stops to drink at the fountain commemorating George Chávez, the first man to fly out of Switzerland and cross the Alps in an airplane. He crashed and died on the other side.

On the Bahnhofstrasse of Brig are many shoppers, none of

whom shows any surprise on seeing a patrol of soldiers with assault rifles coming down the street, just as the citizens of Oberarth were not surprised to find a battle taking place in their town. Massy's attention is arrested by a Prontophot booth in the foyer of a Jelmoli store opposite the Walliser Kantonalbank. For a coin or two, the booth will produce a passport-size photograph. The soldiers stack their rifles against a table of dry flowers, for sale in bunches, two francs a bunch. All five of us, stacked one on another, under Massy's direction assemble in the booth. We freeze before the lens. While we wait for the picture, a message goes out, Prontophot booth to command post, now hear this: "ONE COMPANY OF MOTORIZED ENEMY FUSILIERS HAS LANDED IN HELICOPTERS BETWEEN MÜNSTER AND THE RHONE. AN ENEMY SECTION DE RENSEIGNEMENTS HAS CROSSED THE NIEDERWALD." It appears that we have a red rival.

Having traversed the city, the patrol reaches the Rhone—here a green running river with frequent patches of white. There are two bridges not far apart. Massy sketches them and records data on their structures and dimensions. The soldiers cross the river, walk downstream along the right bank, and stop to admire a big steel bucket that slides several hundred metres down a cable, splashes into the rapids, picks up a few tons of gravel, and emerges from the river to ascend to a cement plant. After the big steel bucket has made six round trips, they turn and face the Bernese Oberland. It begins only a few feet away, as the terrain rises sharply from the river.

According to instructions, the patrol is to climb some distance and check out possibilities. The first possibility is that we will fall off the cliffside into the Rhone. The climb is efficient, in the sense that almost every step is up. Where the going is particularly steep, there are cables to hang on to—put here, says Massy, by farmers. It is a trail of short switchbacks, now among scattered trees, now across rock face. Astonishingly soon, the view expands. The Rhone seems a long plunge below. In Brig, over the river, we can see the green where the battalion held its Prise du Drapeau, the marble yard, the Saltina coming down from Simplon, the twin dark holes of the railway tunnels to Italy. In the long perspective to the west, the walls of the Rhone Valley seem to come together and close. In the middle ground is the jet strip at Turtmann. Massy is reciting numbers into the walkie-talkie: "A COMPANY OF SWISS FUSILIERS IS WITH DIFFICULTY HOLDING TURTMANN." The sun comes and goes in a sky of breaking cloud.

In all, we climb about fourteen hundred feet before the terrain leans back—as a pronouncedly inclined alpage. The view is now panoptic—over the deep-set river to the white summits, the long front line of the Pennines leading the eye west. Twenty miles downstream, the valley bends slightly and cuts the view. Above the river, avalanche tracks stripe the mountainsides between dark gorges no machine could pass. The floor of the valley is groomed and industrial. There are rows of Lombardy poplars along airstrips that serve no city. This centerland of the Valais, with its vegetable fields and orchards, too—its apples and asparagus, tomatoes and pears—would appear to be an ultimate citadel for the democracy, where the nation could attempt an impregnable stand. As if the mountains were not barrier enough, ancient landslides have left their natural barricades at intervals down the valley.

A farmhouse near the alpage is checked out for water and habitation. There is enough of both for one company. We make our way on upward and—with some surprise, as always—climb onto a curving mountain road.

"A COMPANY OF FUSILIERS HAS PARACHUTED INTO THE NUFENENPASS."

We walk west about a kilometre, with the Pennine Alps to our left, the Rhone deep below, and come into a vertical village, stacked up facing the sun. There is a restaurant called Restaurant. Inside is a long table by a window looking at the mountains. In the restaurant's umbrella stand the patrol stands four assault rifles. Half-litre glasses of beer are soon on the table by the window. The prospect is giddy—a long fall down the mountainside and deep into le trou. I remember Lieutenant Strub saying, "Basically, with age, you become sly in the army, and you know in which restaurant you will find the soldiers, and the slyness is a military advantage if an enemy comes."

The walkie-talkie is set up on the table, its antenna inclining toward the light. Massy strings numbers with a pencil on a pad. He reports to the command post, "A COMPANY OF MOTORIZED RED FUSILIERS HAS DESCENDED FROM THE NUFENENPASS AND HAS REACHED ULRICHEN."

From Birgisch, as this village is called, the patrol is to return with an aerial sketch of the valley environs of Brig. Pierre Gabus looks out the window and draws one, deftly.

Fondue arrives—authoritative with kirsch and bubbling with the Fendant of Valais. An alcohol flame spreads flat on the bottom of the pot, browning the edges of the cheese inside. There is a transition from beer to wine. Massy pours. Wettstein says, "The army needs marginal people. They know that in an emergency if there's a job to be done we'll do it. That's why they leave us alone. We agree to walk and to shoot, but for us it is difficult to submit to discipline."

Long forks are flying. The fondue is surpassingly good. Four new customers have taken seats at a nearby table. They see the situation and are obviously amused. They are men, dressed in wool shirts, and are stopping in from work—farmers probably, at any rate civilians, but, of course, they are also in the army. They laugh. They jeer. They exhibit a mixture of mockery and empathy. When Massy lifts the transceiver and reads off a set of numbers, they moo in unison, helping the command post to imagine a bucolic scene.

"Moooo."

"LA GARE DE BRIGUE A ÉTÉ DÉTRUITE PAR LES SABOTEURS."

"Moooo."

"A BATTALION OF ENEMY MOTORIZED FUSILIERS HAS LANDED IN HELICOPTERS IN THE PLAIN OF THE RHONE BETWEEN TURTMANN AND THE RIVER."

"Compris! Compris! Moooo."

Massy holds the transceiver even higher, turns it upside down, and stirs the fondue with the antenna. He wipes it off and calls in another message: "A PEASANT IN OBERWALD HAS SEEN FOUR ARMORED CARS COMING OUT OF ST. NIKLAUS AND HEADING FOR THE VALLEY."

As the alcohol burns on, the golden crust is ever more delicious, scraped from the edge of the fondue. Dessert is coupe Danemark—four and a half francs' worth of whipped cream over ice cream under ductile chocolate. There are five wee glasses of kirsch.

Wettstein waxes declarative, saying, "This is the best day I have spent in the Swiss Army."

On winter marches in the time of the Borgias, it was thought that Swiss soldiers, in their cold armor, might lose too much body heat. Accordingly, they were given orders never to drink water but to quench all thirst with schnapps.

"TWO COMPANIES OF ENEMY MOTORIZED FUSILIERS HAVE REACHED RARON. ABOUT FIFTEEN ARMORED VEHICLES HAVE BEEN DESTROYED."

Massy signals for a check and knocks back the last of the kirsch. Again he lifts the transceiver. There is more to report before we go.

"AN ATOMIC BOMB OF PETITE SIZE HAS BEEN DROPPED ON SIERRE. OUR BARRICADES AT VISP STILL HOLD. THE BRIDGES OF GRENGIOLS ARE SECURE. WE ARE IN CONTACT WITH THE ENEMY."

TABLE

OF CONTENTS

(1 9 8 5)

[A collection of eight, including a profile of a flying game warden in northern Maine whose name is John McPhee; a profile of a director of the National Park Service; essays on small-scale hydropower, ice ponds, telephones in Arctic Alaska, bears in New Jersey, bear cubs in Pennsylvania; and a long piece on young doctors in communities in rural Maine. The bear cubs open the book.]

Under the Snow

When my third daughter was an infant, I could place her against my shoulder and she would stick there like velvet. Only her eyes jumped from place to place. In a breeze, her bright-red hair might stir, but she would not. Even then, there was profundity in her repose.

When my fourth daughter was an infant, I wondered if her veins were full of ants. Placing her against a shoulder was a risk both to her and to the shoulder. Impulsively, constantly, everything about her moved. Her head seemed about to revolve as it followed the bestirring world.

These memories became very much alive some months ago when—one after another—I had bear cubs under my vest. Weighing three, four, 5.6 pounds, they were wild bears, and for an hour or so had been taken from their dens in Pennsylvania. They were about two months old, with fine short brown hair. When they were made to stand alone, to be photographed in the mouth of a den, they shivered. Instinctively, a person would be moved to hold them. Picked up by the scruff of the neck, they splayed their paws like kittens and screamed like baby bears. The cry of a baby bear is muted, like a human infant's heard from her crib down the hall. The first cub I placed on my shoulder stayed there like a piece of velvet. The shivering stopped. Her bright-blue eyes looked about, not seeing much of anything. My hand, cupped against her back, all but encompassed her rib cage, which was warm and calm. I covered her to the shoulders with a flap of down vest and zipped up my parka to hold her in place.

I was there by invitation, an indirect result of work I had been doing nearby. Would I be busy on March 14th? If there had been a conflict—if, say, I had been invited to lunch on that day with the Queen of Scotland and the King of Spain—I would have gone to the cubs. The first den was a rock cavity in a lichen-covered sandstone outcrop near the top of a slope, a couple of hundred yards from a road in Hawley. It was on posted property of the Scrub Oak Hunting Club—dry hardwood forest underlain by laurel and patches of snow—in the northern Pocono woods. Up in the sky was Buck Alt. Not long ago, he was a dairy farmer, and now he was working for the Keystone State, with directional antennae on his wing struts angled in the direction of bears. Many bears in Pennsylvania have radios around their necks as a result of the summer trapping work of Alt's son Gary, who is a wildlife biologist. In winter, Buck Alt flies the country listening to the radio, crissing and crossing until the bears come on. They come on stronger the closer to them he flies. The transmitters are not omnidirectional. Suddenly, the sound cuts out. Buck looks down, chooses a landmark, approaches it again, on another vector. Gradually, he works his way in, until he is flying in ever tighter circles above the bear. He marks a map. He is accurate within two acres. The plane he flies is a Super Cub.

The den could have served as a set for a Passion play. It was a small chamber, open on one side, with a rock across its entrance. Between the freestanding rock and the back of the cave was room for one large bear, and she was curled in a corner on a bed of leaves, her broad head plainly visible from the outside, her cubs invisible between the rock and a soft place, chuckling, suckling, in the wintertime tropics of their own mammalian heaven. Invisible they were, yes, but by no means inaudible. What biologists call chuckling sounded like starlings in a tree.

[*178*]

People walking in woods sometimes come close enough to a den to cause the mother to get up and run off, unmindful of her reputation as a fearless defender of cubs. The cubs stop chuckling and begin to cry: possibly three, four cubs—a ward of mewling bears. The people hear the crying. They find the den and see the cubs. Sometimes they pick them up and carry them away, reporting to the state that they have saved the lives of bear cubs abandoned by their mother. Wherever and whenever this occurs, Gary Alt collects the cubs. After ten years of bear trapping and biological study, Alt has equipped so many sows with radios that he has been able to conduct a foster-mother program with an amazingly high rate of success. A mother in hibernation will readily accept a foster cub. If the need to place an orphan arises somewhat later, when mothers and their cubs are out and around, a sow will kill an alien cub as soon as she smells it. Alt has overcome this problem by stuffing sows' noses with Vicks VapoRub. One way or another, he has found new families for forty-seven orphaned cubs. Forty-six have survived. The other, which had become accustomed over three weeks to feedings and caresses by human hands, was not content in a foster den, crawled outside, and died in the snow.

With a hypodermic jab stick, Alt now drugged the mother, putting her to sleep for the duration of the visit. From deeps of shining fur, he fished out cubs. One. Two. A third. A fourth. Five! The fifth was a foster daughter brought earlier in the winter from two hundred miles away. Three of the four others were male—a ratio consistent with the heavy preponderance of males that Alt's studies have shown through the years. To various on-lookers he handed the cubs for safekeeping while he and several assistants carried the mother into the open and weighed her with block and tackle. To protect her eyes, Alt had blindfolded her with a red bandanna. They carried her upside down, being extremely careful lest they scrape and damage her nipples. She weighed two hundred and nineteen pounds. Alt had caught her and weighed her some months before. In the den, she had lost ninety pounds. When she was four years old, she had had four cubs; two years later, four more cubs; and now, after two more years, four cubs. He knew all that about her, he had caught her so many times. He referred to her as Daisy. Daisy was as nothing compared with Vanessa, who was sleeping off the winter somewhere else. In ten seasons, Vanessa had given birth to twenty-three cubs and had lost none. The growth and reproductive rates of black bears are greater in Pennsylvania than anywhere else. Black bears in Pennsylvania grow more rapidly than grizzlies in Montana. Eastern black bears are generally much larger than Western ones. A seven-hundred-pound bear is unusual but not rare in Pennsylvania. Alt once caught a big boar like that who had a thirty-seven-inch neck and was a hair under seven feet long.

This bear, nose to tail, measured five feet five. Alt said, "That's a nice long sow." For weighing the cubs, he had a small nylon stuff sack. He stuffed it with bear and hung it on a scale. Two months before, when the cubs were born, each would have weighed approximately half a pound—less than a newborn porcupine. Now the cubs weighed 3.4, 4.1, 4.4, 4.6, 5.6—cute little numbers with soft tan noses and erectile pyramid ears. Bears have sex in June and July, but the mother's system holds the fertilized egg away from the uterus until November, when implantation occurs. Fetal development lasts scarcely six weeks. Therefore, the creatures who live upon the hibernating mother are so small that everyone survives.

The orphan, less winsome than the others, looked like a chocolate-covered possum. I kept her under my vest. She seemed content there and scarcely moved. In time, I exchanged her for 5.6—the big boy in the litter. Lifted by the scruff and held in the air, he bawled, flashed his claws, and curled his lips like a woofing boar. I stuffed him under the vest, where he shut up and nuzzled. His claws were already more than half an inch long. Alt said that the family would come out of the den in a few weeks but that much of the spring would go by before the cubs gained weight. The difference would be that they were no longer malleable and ductile. They would become pugnacious and scratchy, not to say vicious, and would chew up the hand that caressed them. He said, "If you have an enemy, give him a bear cub."

Six men carried the mother back to the den, the red bandanna still tied around her eyes. Alt repacked her into the rock. "We like to return her to the den as close as possible to the way we found her," he said. Someone remarked that one biologist can work a coon, while an army is needed to deal with a bear. An army seemed to be present. Twelve people had followed Alt to the den. Some days, the group around him is four times as large. Alt, who is in his thirties, was wearing a visored khaki cap with a blue-and-gold keystone on the forehead, and a khaki cardigan under a khaki jumpsuit. A lithe and light-bodied man with tinted glasses and a blond mustache, he looked like a lieutenant in the Ardennes Forest. Included in the retinue were two reporters and a news photographer. Alt encourages media attention, the better to soften the image of the bears. He says, "People fear bears more than they need to, and respect them not enough." Over the next twenty days, he had scheduled four hundred visitors—state senators, representatives, commissioners, television reporters, word processors, biologists, friends—to go along on his rounds of dens. Days before, he and the denned bears had been hosts to the BBC. The Brits wanted snow. God was having none of it. The BBC brought in the snow.

In the course of the day, we made a brief tour of dens that for the time being stood vacant. Most were rock cavities. They had been used before, and in all likelihood would be used again. Bears in winter in the Pocono Plateau are like chocolate chips in a cookie. The bears seldom go back to the same den two years running, and they often change dens in the course of a winter. In a forty-five-hundred-acre housing development called Hemlock Farms are twenty-three dens known to be in current use and countless others awaiting new tenants. Alt showed one that was within fifteen feet of the intersection of East Spur Court and Pommel Drive. He said that when a sow with two cubs was in there he had seen deer browsing by the outcrop and ignorant dogs stopping off to lift a leg. Hemlock Farms is expensive, and full of cantilevered cypress and unencumbered glass. Houses perch on high flat rock. Now and again, there are bears in the rock—in, say, a floor-through cavity just under the porch. The owners are from New York. Alt does not always tell them that their property is zoned for bears. Once, when he did so, a "FOR SALE" sign went up within two weeks.

Not far away is Interstate 84. Flying over it one day, Buck Alt heard an oddly intermittent signal. Instead of breaking off once and cleanly, it broke off many times. Crossing back over, he heard it again. Soon he was in a tight turn, now hearing something, now nothing, in a pattern that did not suggest anything he had heard before. It did, however, suggest the interstate. Where a big green sign says, "MILFORD 11, PORT JERVIS 20," Gary hunted around and found the bear. He took us now to see the den. We went down a steep slope at the side of the highway and, crouching, peered into a culvert. It was about fifty yards long. There was a disk of daylight at the opposite end. Thirty inches in diameter, it was a perfect place to stash a body, and that is what the bear thought, too. On Gary's first visit, the disk of daylight had not been visible. The bear had denned under the eastbound lanes. She had given birth to three cubs. Soon after he found her, heavy rains were predicted. He hauled the family out and off to a vacant den. The cubs weighed less than a pound. Two days later, water a foot deep was racing through the culvert.

Under High Knob, in remote undeveloped forest about six hundred metres above sea level, a slope falling away in an easterly direction contained a classic excavated den: a small entrance leading into an intimate ovate cavern, with a depression in the center for a bed—in all, about twenty-four cubic feet, the size of a refrigerator-freezer. The den had not been occupied in several seasons, but Rob Buss, a district game protector who works regularly with Gary Alt, had been around to check it three days before and had shined his flashlight into a darkness stuffed with fur. Meanwhile, six inches of fresh snow had fallen on High Knob, and now Alt and his team, making preparations a short distance from the den, scooped up snow in their arms and filled a big sack. They had nets of nylon mesh. There was a fifty-fifty likelihood of yearling bears in the den. Mothers keep cubs until their second spring. When a biologist comes along and provokes the occupants to emerge, there is no way to predict how many will appear. Sometimes they keep coming and coming, like clowns from a compact car. As a bear emerges, it walks into the nylon mesh. A drawstring closes. At the same time, the den entrance is stuffed with a bag of snow. That stops the others. After the first bear has been dealt with, Alt removes the sack of snow. Out comes another bear. A yearling weighs about eighty pounds, and may move so fast that it runs over someone on the biological team and stands on top of him sniffing at his ears. Or her ears. Janice Gruttadauria, a research assistant, is a part of the team. Bear after bear, the procedure is repeated until the bag of snow is pulled away and nothing comes out. That is when Alt asks Rob Buss to go inside and see if anything is there.

Now, moving close to the entrance, Alt spread a tarp on the snow, lay down on it, turned on a five-cell flashlight, and put his head inside the den. The beam played over thick black fur and came to rest on a tiny foot. The sack of snow would not be needed. After drugging the mother with a jab stick, he joined her in the den. The entrance was so narrow he had to shrug his shoulders to get in. He shoved the sleeping mother, head first, out of the darkness and into the light.

While she was away, I shrugged my own shoulders and had a look inside. The den smelled of earth but not of bear. The walls were dripping with roots. The water and protein metabolism of hibernating black bears has been explored by the Mayo Clinic as a research model for, among other things, human endurance on long flights through space and medical situations closer to home, such as the maintenance of anephric human beings who are awaiting kidney transplants.

Outside, each in turn, the cubs were put in the stuff sack—a male and a female. The female weighed four pounds. Greedily, I reached for her when Alt took her out of the bag. I planted her on my shoulder while I wrote down facts about her mother: weight, a hundred and ninety-two pounds; length, fifty-eight inches; some toes missing; severe frostbite from a bygone winter evidenced along the edges of the ears.

Eventually, with all weighing and tagging complete, it was time to go. Alt went into the den. Soon he called out that he was ready for the mother. It would be a tight fit. Feet first, she was shoved in, like a safe-deposit box. Inside, Alt tugged at her in close embrace, and the two of them gradually revolved until she was at the back and their positions had reversed. He shaped her like a doughnut—her accustomed den position. The cubs go in the center. The male was handed in to him. Now he was asking for the female. For a moment, I glanced around as if looking to see who had her. The thought crossed my mind that if I bolted and ran far enough and fast enough I could flag a passing car and keep her. Then I pulled her from under the flap of my vest and handed her away.

Alt and others covered the entrance with laurel boughs, and covered the boughs with snow. They camouflaged the den, but that was not the purpose. Practicing wildlife management to a fare-thee-well, Alt wanted the den to be even darker than it had been before; this would cause the family to stay longer inside and improve the cubs' chances when at last they faced the world.

In the evening, I drove down off the Pocono Plateau and over the folded mountains and across the Great Valley and up the New Jersey Highlands and down into the basin and home. No amount of intervening terrain, though—and no amount of distance—could remove from my mind the picture of the covered entrance in the Pennsylvania hillside, or the thought of what was up there under the snow.

F R O M

Heirs of General Practice

When Ann Dorney was seventeen years old, she thought she might decide to become a physician. Looking for advice, she arranged an interview at a university medical center, where she was asked what subspecialty she had in mind. Had she considered neonatology? Departing in confusion, she decided instead to expand her experience as a teacher of mathematics, which, in her precocity, she already was. She had tutored other students since she was fourteen years old, and she continued to do so as an undergraduate in college. She appeared to have her future framed, but then an opportunity came along to spend a four-month work term in the office of a small-town physician. He was a general practitioner, by training and definition, but the year was 1973 and the lettering on the door had changed to "FAMILY PRACTICE." She worked in his office, went with him on hospital rounds, and attended the delivery of babies. She saw each of the other Ages of Man and an exponential variety of cases. The math teacher began to fade again, and she applied to medical schools—nearly a dozen in all. Interviews were required, and she was short of funds on which to travel. For a hundred dollars, she bought an Ameripass, which was good on any Greyhound bus going anywhere at all within a single week. Thus, for something like a hundred and sixty-eight hours she rode from city to city, slept upright, checked her suitcase in coin lockers, took off her jeans in ladies' rooms, put on a dress and nylons, and carefully set her hair before catching a local bus to the medical school. "It was a scene," she says. "It was really a scene." She chose George Washington University. As a medical freshman, when she was asked to list her preferred specialties she wrote "family practice" and left the rest of the space blank. Professors attempted to dissuade her, but they were unsuccessful.

Sue Cochran entered Radcliffe College in 1969, and after two years felt a need to go away and develop a sense of purpose. She went to work for a rural doctor. Her brother, her brother's wife, her sister, and her sister's husband were all on their way to becoming specialists in internal medicine. Her father, a teacher at Harvard Medical School, was a neonatologist—in her words, "a high-tech physician." The rural doctor was her great-aunt, who was scornful of specialists of every kind. For decades, the aunt had looked after a large part of the population around two mountain towns, and she passed along to her grandniece not only a sense of what Sue Cochran calls "the psychosocial input into physical illness" but also a desire to practice medicine in a rural area and to concentrate on prevention at least as much as cure. Of her medical siblings and siblings-in-law, she says now, "They think I'm flaky." She goes on to say, "The one who's the most supportive is my father, and even he thinks I'm pretty crazy."

David Thanhauser also dropped out for a time—but, in his case, out of medical school. After graduating from Williams College, in 1969, he spent two years in medical study at Boston University before he quit, in what he now describes as "righteous adolescent anger"—angered by the world and by society in general but more specifically because he could not accept being inside what he calls "the heart of the beast of specialty medicine." In the cancer wards, for example, he felt that "technological medicine was being carried to its extreme while the feelings of people were getting no attention." In the gynecology clinic, women— many of them Hispanic or black—were given pelvic examinations before doors that kept opening and shutting. "You learn good medicine by practicing good medicine," he says. "We were learning by practicing bad medicine." In the same era, Boston revolutionaries his age were saying that while medical students were inside the hospital learning "Band-Aid medicine" a profound malaise was outside the walls. Thanhauser retreated to rural Maine, spent something under five thousand dollars (a legacy from a grandfather) to buy fifty acres of land, and, with hammer in hand, built a small house. He thought he would give up medicine and become a teacher, but meanwhile he found work as a paramedic with generalists in Bangor. Watching these family practitioners work, he saw that they were doing an excellent job, whereas the message at Boston University had been that after people have been treated by generalists in Maine the next stop is Boston, where the damage is repaired. Before long, Thanhauser went back to medical school, but with intent to enter a family-practice residency and return to rural Maine. If such a residency had not been an option for him, his sense of conflict would not have abated and he might have abandoned medicine altogether.

Sanders Burstein, who grew up in a New York suburb, was in medical school when he made his decision, forgoing urology, oncology, nephrology, gastroenterology to characterize his future as "family practice in a rural setting." Paul Forman made the same choice at a younger age: "I knew when I was in high school that I wanted to be a country doc." Terrence Flanagan, after finishing Harvard College, went to western Ireland for a time, and decided there that he wanted to become a doctor and practice in some remote settlement in his native Maine. After enrolling in the medical school of the University of Pennsylvania, he declared his interest in family practice. "Great," said William Penn, but almost no mention was made of the topic for the next four years. At the time of Flanagan's arrival, in 1975, the family-practice office at Penn was next door to the office of the dean; when Flanagan left, family practice was in the basement, and to get into the room you had to ask for the key. When Donna Conkling went into medicine, she had an M.A.T. in English literature from the University of Chicago. As a medical student, she was surprised one day by a resident's saying to her, "You're really smart. Why are you going into family practice?" The question seemed to her to contradict itself. Her opinion was that you had to be smart to go into family practice.

All these people—in the idiom of medical education—matched the same residency program. Specifically, they went on from medical school to complete their training at what is now called the Maine–Dartmouth Family Practice Residency, which functions principally in and close by the Kennebec Valley Medical Center, in Augusta. And so did David Jones, who knew much earlier than any of the others what he wanted to do in life. Jones is the third of five brothers. One is a nephrologist in California. Another is a cardiologist at Johns Hopkins. Their father was for many years an internist at Massachusetts General Hospital. Jones had his own idea, and he had it when he was seven. At that age, he began to say, "I am going to be a G.P. That's right, I am going to be a G.P., with a farm, a stream in my back yard, and one horse." Now, a couple of decades later, Dr. Jones has his farm, he has four horses, including an Appaloosa named Papoose, and the brooks on his land run into the Aroostook River.

Sanders Burstein goes to the emergency room because Tim Brewer has fallen off the monkey bars at the Fort Street School. Tim is seven, wears corduroy jeans and running shoes, and has a gash in the top of his head. A grandmother is present. Burstein works without hurry, conversing with Tim, whose fortitude deserves the compliments he receives. There are multiple pricks of lidocaine, splashes of hydrogen peroxide, followed by syringed water. The lad's chin is high. He sits rigidly upright. Burstein ties stitches like dry flies. When he is done, Barbara Smith, R.N., leans forward and carefully combs Tim's bright-blond hair.

The scene strongly brings to mind a stack of magazines tied up with string in an attic. It strongly brings to mind that medical superman of yesteryear, the old doc on the cover of *The Saturday Evening Post* with his stethoscope planted on the chest of a child's doll, the old doc who rode from house to house through deep snows with his black bag beside him and his roan gelding pulling the sleigh, the old doc who did appendectomies on the kitchen table, the old doc who worked nine days a week and rested on the tenth. If the social status of a urologist, a nephrologist, a gastroenterologist can send a wistful moment through the thoughts of a family practitioner, that is as nothing compared with this hovering ghost, this image afloat above the family practitioner's head: Superdoc, the Great American G.P., omniscient, ubiquitous. Who will ever forget his snowshoeing through the Blizzard of '88 to set Increase Flintcotton's broken leg? Never mind that despite old Superdoc's gruelling schedule he somehow had time to sit for Norman Rockwell while the artist did one portrait after another, from this angle and that. Never mind that old Superdoc saw three, and sometimes as many as five, patients a day. Never mind that in the course of his long career he saw so little medicine that his scientific knowledge steadily declined from new to nil. All of that is gone with the blizzards; and what is left behind is his mythic standard.

Fred Schmidt, thirty-three years old, is, among other things, a woodcutter, who gets forty-six dollars a cord, and works alone.

"Smoke?"

"I quit four years ago."

"Why did you quit?"

"The time had come."

Schmidt is in for a routine physical—Lovejoy Health Center, Albion, Maine. A muscular man with curly hair and a woodsman's ample mustache, he is so healthy that Paul Forman, the examining doctor, wonders if he has a hidden agenda. As they converse, however, there is no hint of trouble, and Forman begins to feel oddly guilty for not giving Schmidt his money's worth. Forman feels as if he is purloining half a cord of wood from this well-kept human landscape. Rummaging, he asks Schmidt if he uses hearing protection when he operates his chain saw. Schmidt says no. Forman's conscience is saved. He will give Schmidt some preventive medicine—sawed, split, and stacked.

Old-time pilots in open cockpits used to get something called aviator's notch, Forman says, and he draws on an audiogram pad a graph that shows a precipitous loss of hearing high in the frequency range of the engine of a Jenny or a Spad. The loss appears on the graph as a V-shaped notch. "The airplane engines gradually destroyed the ear's ability to pick up any sound in those frequencies," Forman continues. "If you don't protect your ears, you are in danger of getting aviator's notch from your chain saw. We see similar things with rock and roll." Partial deafness is only the beginning. In the literature on amplified sound, there appears this sentence: "Loud noise causes blood vessels to constrict, the skin to pale, muscles to tense, and the adrenal hormone to be injected into the bloodstream; thus, the heart and nervous system of the individual are profoundly affected; animals, forced to listen to noise, become sullen, unresponsive, erratic, or violent."

Has Schmidt ever heard of Iowa ear? The farmer on his tractor looks over his right shoulder, watching his planter or plow and sighting back down the row. This aims his left ear toward the tractor's engine. Iowa ear, always the left, is aviator's notch, grounded.

Schmidt hears all this amiably, perhaps even gratefully, giving no sign that he has developed a notch of his own with regard to doctors.

Forman changes the subject. He asks if Schmidt's wife, Terry, is having contractions.

"Not yet."

Forman will deliver this imminent baby. He also looks after

[*190*]

the Schmidts' existing child. Half a dozen years ago, before Forman and his partner, Forrest West, arrived in Albion, the Lovejoy Health Center was an overgrown field. "Before the clinic was here, I didn't have a doctor," Schmidt remarks. "When I needed a tetanus shot, I drove twenty miles to the Band-Aid station. They said come back tomorrow. I went to a doctor's office somewhere. They said forget it, you're not a regular customer."

Forrest West, in an adjacent examining room, talks with Seth Fuller, a farmer, born in 1904. Fuller is West's neighbor. Fuller remembers when West and Forman first came into the area and went to potluck suppers and casserole dinners, meeting people and asking about plans for a health center—in effect, applying to be its doctors. Six communities—China, Albion, Unity, Palermo, Thorndike, and Troy, which are separated by dairyland and forested hills—had been identified by the federal government as grossly underserved, and money had been raised locally for a modest wooden structure. Forman and West were, in Forman's words, on "the hippie wavelength," but their credentials were even longer than their hair. They were strongly recommended by the residency in Augusta. Fuller and the others voted them in.

Fuller's wife, Gladys, is in the exam room, too. She was West's first myocardial infarction in Albion. She has recovered long since. It is her husband who has now come in with the presenting complaint. He can describe it only as "a gradual weakening." He says he lies on the couch at home sleeping and when he wakes up is not interested in stirring. He has let the farm become inactive. He is trim, short, with a wiry frame and alert eyes— obviously, in his demeanor if not his present manner, a hard-working, life-loving man. His hair is steel gray and cut short— like his accent, which is pure Maine. "I suppose I could feel worse, but I don't know that it would make much difference," he says. He has had recent X-rays that looked normal, and a blood test as well. "There's an end to that dragging down," he tells West. "I can't go on losing weight forever." He weighs a hundred pounds. Two years ago, he weighed a hundred and four.

He removes his shirt. His biceps suggest considerable strength despite his frailty. West listens to his lungs and heart. What could be Seth Fuller's difficulty? An occult malignancy? Stomach not absorbing vitamins? He had a partial gastrectomy, West remembers, but that was some time ago. He tells Fuller that he would like to admit him to the Mid-Maine Medical Center, in Waterville. "O.K.?"

"I guess so."

Forrest West, in a green shirt and green hopsacking trousers with a broad leather belt, could be a forest ranger. He wears moccasins and no tie. He has tousled hair, a soothing mustache, dark eyes, and a speaking tone so calm and quiet it may occupy a frequency of its own. Paul Forman, tall and slim, is the more emotional and animated of the two. He comes to work wearing a short-sleeved shirt, a tie, a railroad engineer's cap, and, like West, puts on no white coat, no office paraphernalia to suggest his medical authority. On West's desk is an antique wooden box with gold scroll lettering that says, "West's Excelsior Veterinary Remedies." Forman could have stepped out of the cab of a train.

Forman and West have six thousand people in their catchment area. After five years, they include in their folders twenty-three hundred families. When they first approached the six towns, it was with some worry, although the situation in many ways appeared to fit their ideals. They listened to the people closely, trying to discern the extent to which they might be believers in the myth of the old Superdoc and be hoping for his return. With modern roads and modern populations, even in rural Maine a doctor could be overworked to the point of burning out. Forman and West found, to their relief, that the people of the towns were much aware of the difference, and were not expecting miracles —just a service the towns did not have.

Now Forman addresses a neighbor who has come in to discuss the results of a blood test. It shows an elevation in levels of serum glutamic-oxaloacetic transaminase, serum glutamic-pyruvic transaminase, lactic dehydrogenase. A question that has arisen in Forman's mind is not complicated by variable diagnosis. He says, "How much are you drinking?"

"Like I told you, I drink only ten beers a week."

"And how much hard stuff?"

"Don't touch it."

"How about carbon tetrachloride?"

"Don't touch it."

"Do you think you could give up alcohol?"

"I sure do. Wouldn't bother me a bit."

"Stay off alcohol for two months."

In Exam Room 3, Forrest West sets a Doppler microphone on the rising abdomen of Jane Glidden, whose second child is halfway along between conception and birth. She is twenty-three, works as a waitress, is married to a machinist, and lives in a house trailer in Palermo. Her mother, her father, her grandparents, and her year-old son are all patients of Dr. West's. A year ago, she came in to the clinic after two hours of labor, and—with time having run out for a trip to the hospital—her baby was born in Exam Room 3. The Doppler is turned on, and the new baby broadcasts loudly from the womb. It is the sound of a chorus of swamp frogs.

A mother brings in a child with a perforated eardrum. Forman asks her why she did not go to an otolaryngologist.

She says, "I figured you guys could do just as well as he could, and a lot cheaper."

The perforation is long-standing, not infected. Forman says, "I think you ought to see an ear specialist to follow that along."

Chris McMorrow next, thirty years old, a patient of Forman's who cannot eat lobster because afterward his throat always burns—an abysmal handicap in Maine. On this visit, McMorrow complains of a persistent headache and a crick in the neck. These symptoms may or may not be related to his eighteen-speed mountain bike, a leg-driven balloon-tired machine that is geared for roadless areas, including mountainsides. Last weekend, McMorrow went biking on Mt. Katahdin. Forman tells him that his trapezius muscle, in spasm, is producing the headaches by hauling on his scalp. The medical way to deal with the problem is with aspirin, or with stronger drugs—also by strengthening the muscle or by avoiding the use of it for purposes that tax it. Another approach is chiropractic—having to do with a possible pinched nerve in a vertebra—and Forman says that that helps some people. He says he is not as down on chiropractors as many doctors are, because he has friends that chiropractic has helped. Forman goes on to explain to McMorrow that osteopathy is a mixture of medical and manipulation techniques. Categorically, he will not cast aspersion on either profession. "Make an appointment if you wish."

Esten Peabody—white-bearded and fifty-one—comes in full of potato chips, which he professes to find irresistible. He is also full of good news: he has donated a pint of blood, and his blood pressure has dropped below the danger level.

Forman says, "We'll have to go back to using leeches." He also tells Peabody a thing or two about his diet, and reminds him of the silent progress of hypertension: "You don't feel bad until you have a stroke or your kidneys rot out. It's an asymptomatic disease."

Warren Harding, sixty-two, walks in slowly, sits down, and delivers to Forrest West a lecture on subverted justice—case after case dismissed because confessions were felt to be coerced. West listens. "We are throwing out the United States Constitution to protect criminals," Warren Harding tells him, and then asks, without a pause, "Will I get better? Will I ever get any strength back in my left arm?" Harding is an Albion farmer. For reasons unexplained, there is a closed safety pin hanging in the middle of his T-shirt.

West says to him, "When a stroke stabilizes for this length of time, things don't change."

West grew up in suburban Philadelphia, Forman in Pittsfield, Massachusetts. They went to small, northerly colleges (Williams and Hamilton) and to first-rate medical schools (Jefferson and Albany) on their way to Maine. When Forman was still in medical school, he wrote down his goals as a physician, and although he did not know Forrest West, he could have been speaking for him, too. He said he wanted "to develop a well-rounded understanding of medicine" so that he could "approach the patient as a whole person" whose physical problems often arise from emotional and social causes. He wished "to teach people about their own health, allay their fears about mild problems, counsel and guide them through seemingly complex treatment regimens when their problems are more serious"—all in a context of "compassionate, *high-quality* medicine." The italics were his. He wanted to seek a place where he was really needed, in order to "avoid being just another specialist competing for a limited number of cases," and he particularly hoped to find it "in an area with high mountains, cold white winters, and people who love and respect the natural resources available to them." He wrote that ten years ago, when he was twenty-five. Now he and his family live on a smoothly scraped dirt road and own twenty-three acres of high, forested land. From the deck of their house one can see long distances into some of the most beautiful country in Maine. Dari Forman, the doctor's wife, is a carpenter and custom furnituremaker, and she designed and built the house—a rhythmic geometry of heavy beams and bright glass composed with regard to the sun. Hemlock rafters, pine siding, elm-and-cherry stairway—she chose the rough lumber and had it milled. With dry pegs she joined green beams, which developed beauty as they checked. Insufficiently impressed by her wood stove and her passive-solar installations, the mortgagee bank—being a Maine bank, and not a Las Vegas drive-in—insisted on alternative electric-baseboard heat. Even with outside air at twenty below, the electric heat has never been needed.

Her husband repairs canoes, flies sailplanes, makes house calls. "Some families are suspicious of doctors," he says. "And especially of young whippersnappers. A house call can help persuade them to come in." As Forman and West drive through the countryside from one to another of the six towns, they connect patients' faces to a high percentage of the names on the mailboxes. They believe in "one-on-one doctor-patient relationships," and they believe in availability (to the maximum extent that the concerns of "the doctor's family and the doctor's mental health" will permit). Always, they leave open two morning and two afternoon appointments, so that no patient in difficulty will call their number and be given the classic American sentence "The next open appointment is in December." After five years, Forman and West are functioning near the extreme margins of these criteria, and they would be pleased to be joined by a third physician. It would have to be someone, though, who shares their "definition of emergency," which they give in the form of an example: a patient who calls up at midnight with sore throat. "Unless such patients are chronic abusers, you go and see them. They have been miserable enough to make the call."

Toward noon one day, West gets into his car to drive twelve miles to the hospital in Waterville and make a house call en route. He listens to cassettes as he makes these journeys, listens hundreds of hours per year. The cassette of the moment is called "Dermatology Update—Scabies, Anogenital Skin Disease, and Psoriasis." Forman listens to similar tapes in his car. To keep up with things, they also rely on conversations with specialists they know and trust. They read three or four medical journals and throw the rest out. Perhaps to a higher degree than on any other type of doctor, pressure is on the family practitioner to keep up with developing medical knowledge, for fear that one's capability quotient will drop below the multivalent stratum and into the dilettante zone. Various specialists and subspecialists who do not look upon family practitioners as people with a Renaissance range of application and knowledge will undercut them more on the matter of keeping up than on any other, saying, typically, that medical knowledge "explodes every five years" or "increases five per cent a year and therefore doubles every fourteen years," and that almost no one in any subspecialty can ingest enough of the new information, let alone a generalist whose pretense to competence spans many fields.

Disagreement being an apparent norm in medical dialogue, it is not difficult to find specialists who beg to differ:

"It *is* possible to know a broad swath of medicine."

"It's simply not true that medicine explodes every five years. You can generally get along on old practices."

"In terms of day-to-day care of people, quite frankly, you don't have to keep up. Diseases haven't changed that much. People's

[*196*]

emotions haven't changed that much. Except for status, family practitioners don't have to keep up with a good many things. Technology is the kudzu of medicine. It's choking all of us. There are so many technological things we don't need. If you look at hospital mortality rates—the number of patients who come in, the number who die, the number who go home—they have not really changed in thirty years."

Another way to keep up—and get a free meal at the same time—is to attend, say, a peritonitis conference in a hospital lunchroom. The atmosphere in such places tends to be smoky, collegial, and varied, involving large percentages of the staff. Tomorrow is phlebitis. Meanwhile, the peritonitis charts are barely legible through the smoke. That big gentleman in the green tunic and green cap—the man with the hacking cough, the chain Marlboros, and the Hawaiian paunch—is a thoracic surgeon.

West turns into the driveway of the old farmhouse of Franklin Whitman. West drapes his stethoscope around his neck, picks up his black leather medical bag, and goes into the house through the kitchen entrance. He greets Everett Whitman, who is about fifty, and Everett's mother, Florence, and walks through the kitchen into a parlor that is crowded with the accumulations of uncounted years. Deeply piled on tables and cabinets are stacks of magazines tied with string. There are many cardboard cartons, some open, and miscellaneously filled. Where the wallpaper is lesioned, plaster is loose upon the lath of the walls—over a sewing machine that was new before the first Ford. Stuffed chairs are slipcovered with blankets. On a central table, a cat rests at the apex of a pyramid of boxes and magazines. As West enters, the cat leaps away, knocking over a glass, and the beverage inside flows and drips off the magazines and table to the floor. The room is generously heated. Franklin Whitman, seventy-four years old, lies on a couch with blankets drawn over his chin. A bald head and horn-rimmed glasses are about all that can be seen of him, and an obvious shiver. He is pleased to see West, and says so, despite his acute discomfort—his classic erratic chills and fever, picket-fence in pattern, which overlie chronic suffering

[*197*]

from acute arthritis. As West listens to his heart, and listens to and notes his blood pressure, Whitman's wife and son stand in the doorway and watch. The blood pressure goes down when the patient sits up. Flu? Septicemia? West has been here several times in recent days. Whitman is on steroids, and they suppress the immune reaction. Has a bacterial infection developed in his blood? West decides to admit him, and explains to all three why the hospital at this point seems the place for the patient to be. As he leaves, Florence Whitman, who is elderly and fragile, too, says to him in a vibrant voice, "Thank you for coming, Doctor. Thank you for coming so soon."

West drives to Waterville—to the Mid-Maine Medical Center, and, within the complex, to a hospital of largely fresh construction, its sparkling corridors and heavy silent doors imparting a sense of order and, with it, an implication that this place is still on the innocent side of the creeping chaos that seems to advance with time on even the most impressively pedigreed of medical institutions. At a nurses' station, West looks over some charts, some radiological reports, preparing to see his patients. The first is Seth Fuller, whose X-rays now reveal the collapse of a small segment of lung—left and low. Possible causes include but are not limited to a swollen lymph node, a tumor, the aspiration of something or other. "Remember," he comments, "there is always a chance that it is something benign, with a good prognosis."

West goes to Fuller's bedside. Fuller is sitting up, eyes missing nothing, talking quietly with his wife, his daughter, and her husband. Now and again, he coughs—a low dry cough. The *Central Maine Morning Sentinel* is on the bed by his elbow: "WALESA WINS NOBEL PRIZE," "WHITE SOX, DODGERS WIN PLAYOFF GAMES." A bearded, barrel-chested man lies anonymously in the next bed, looking away from the Fuller tableau and out a wide window into a sunlighted October day, rock maples in blaze—a day as bright and crisp and indigenous as West's patient in bed. Fuller is active in the Grange. One year, when the state was offering fruit trees in Winslow, Fuller went over and picked up a load of trees for West. West tells him about the

[*198*]

X-rays and reviews the list of possibilities, his slow voice flat and calm. The two say nothing for a while—in a communicative and unawkward silence, each relying (with a confidence long since developed) on the other. Eventually, West says, "Sometimes, if you have a tumor and it's localized in a small area you can treat it by taking it out."

Fuller says nothing for a time, and then says, "Some fellows get along with just one lung. I had a neighbor had just one lung. He was awful short of breath. He couldn't walk uphill for nothin'."

Again, time passes gracefully while neither West nor Fuller speaks. Finally, West says, "O.K.?"

And Fuller says, "O.K. I'll be right here, then."

Referral is the fulcrum of the family practitioner's craft. From case to case—situation to situation, medical topic to medical topic—the exact position of the fulcrum varies with the doctor. One who too readily refers patients to assorted specialists is suffering a loss of science—giving up one chance after another to add experience in manageable situations. An ideal family practitioner works not just within but also up to the limits of her competence, his competence—knowing precisely where those limits are. Forman says, "You try to make the right scientific diagnosis with the least steps, try to make a good quick history that doesn't miss things. This is the real challenge of family practice. You know the health resources available to you. You don't hold on to patients too long out of pride or ignorance. The talent is in knowing when to give them up."

In some ways, a good family practitioner is not unlike a good bush pilot. There is no dearth of self-confident, highly skillful, bad bush pilots who cross the margins of heavy weather and whang into mountains. The good pilots know when to choose not to fly—know their own limitations and the limitations of their craft—and are unembarrassed by their decisions. "In the past year and a half, I have helped salvage six planes that were wrecked by *one* pilot," a very good bush pilot once said to me. "Why do passengers *go* with such pilots? Would they go to the moon with an astronaut who did not have round-trip fuel? If you were in San Francisco and the boat to Maui was leaking and the rats were leaving, even if you had a ticket you *would not go*. Safety in the air is where you find it. Proper navigation helps, but proper judgment takes care of all conditions. You say to yourself, 'I ain't going to go today. The situation is too much for me.' And you resist all pressure to the contrary."

When outpatients appear in the F.M.I. with problems that are beyond the competence of the residents, they are routinely referred to specialists and subspecialists on the staffs of Kennebec Valley and other hospitals. They can be referred up the system to Portland and beyond. When something perplexing suggests neurology, however, the residents can step to an intercom and call upstairs, asking for their director, Alexander McPhedran.

Here, for example, Tim Clifford, a second-year resident, sees a patient whose name is Elaine Ladd. She is twenty-two years old, small, slim, light on her feet, with uncorrected teeth, a sweeping and engaging smile. She wears a print dress. Her blond hair is gathered in a band. She reports what Clifford records as a six-month history of right-leg weakness. As she got out of bed one day, she fell to the floor. Another day, she fell, unaccountably, on a flight of stairs. There have been similar occasions, in all of which, when the leg collapsed, the knee did not buckle. At these times, her right foot and leg felt heavy, her toes tingled, and the sole of her right foot was numb. She has had some pain but has taken no medicines. She has minor curvature of the spine, Clifford notes. Three years ago, when she was nineteen, she gave birth to a baby—experiencing a normal delivery—and now this pretty and curly-haired child runs in the F.M.I. hallway and bounces in and out of the examining room while Tim Clifford examines her mother. The cranial nerves are intact. There is no arm drift. Her gait is normal. Her biceps and triceps are normal. Clifford excuses himself and, with the help of the intercom and the magic of beeperology, asks Alex McPhedran to join him. The two doctors meet in the first-floor hallway. Clifford says he can find nothing to suggest a problem. If it were not for the stories of the patient's repeated falling, he would call her absolutely normal.

McPhedran follows Clifford into the examining room and, with Elaine Ladd, is soon in a dialogue much encircled by her child.

"Three times I have fallen—once when I got up to chase my daughter."

"Do you exercise regularly?"

"No. I just walk."

"When you walk, how far do you go?"

"Ten miles."

"Does the tingling go away as you walk?"

"Yes."

"This has been going on for six months?"

"Yes."

"Why are you here now?"

"I'm scared. I'm scared when I have no feeling in my toes. I've never told this to anyone before: I paint. Sometimes, when I am doing something very delicate, my hand shakes. Also, I faint."

"Frequently?"

"Yes."

"Does your hand shake at other times—for example, when you are putting a pin in a diaper?"

Elaine Ladd contemplates Dr. McPhedran. Her look is quizzical. "A pin?" she says.

"Oh," says McPhedran, perceptibly taken aback. "I guess I am showing my age. People don't put pins in diapers anymore. Sorry about that."

McPhedran, in his fifties, is a large-framed, pleasant man with a long toss of hair, a bemused smile, and a look which suggests, correctly, that he rises early, works late, and worries on Sunday.

[*201*]

He asks to see Elaine Ladd's back and, with a broad-nibbed pen, draws a line down her spine. He says, "Is there someone who can clean this off for you?"

"No," she answers. "But I have a back-scrubber."

A nurse comes into the room and hands McPhedran a slip of paper. He looks at it and learns of the birth of his first grandchild. He sets aside his reactions, making no remark. He opens a safety pin and asks Elaine Ladd to say, as he presses it against this and that place on her feet and lower legs, whether the sensation is dull or sharp. In random choice, he turns the pin, as she says, "Dull, shop . . . Dull, shop . . . Shop, shop, dull, dull, shop."

He breaks a tongue depressor to obtain a short sharp stick, and with considerable pressure he scrapes the stick across the soles of her feet. "I'm sorry," he says. "I know it's sort of irritating."

She tells him not to be concerned.

When he scrapes the bottom of her right foot, her toes do not go down.

Soon McPhedran and Clifford withdraw to a porch at one end of the F.M.I. In the course of their conversation, McPhedran explores the case rhetorically, asking himself questions: "Is it in a peripheral nerve? Is it a cord lesion?"

And Clifford tells him, "I see no way to go further without involving her in your thinking."

McPhedran, for the moment, continues to think aloud. He says, "You can test sensory-evoked potentials without hurting the patient at all. This is what the space age has done for neurological physiology."

Clifford says, "I think the patient should hear right away what someone thinks. She can't just go home and sit around."

McPhedran agrees, but, returning to the examining room, follows his intuition. He mentions a lumbar puncture—a spinal tap—and tests of the eyes he would like her to have. "It's a good idea to find out about it," he goes on. "You wouldn't have come in if it weren't a nuisance. And I think we ought to pursue it."

Elaine Ladd meets his gaze brightly, agreeably, and seems not to be dissatisfied with the quantity of what he is saying. She frames no question. He has edged up to and around his thoughts, which, for the time being, he elects to keep to himself. This could be a meningioma of the spinal cord. He does not think so. It could be scoliosis—progressing, and affecting the nervous system. He does not think so. He thinks her problem is multiple sclerosis.

McPhedran is in many ways a walking microcosm of the family-practice movement, a man whose professional career is a CAT scan of the medicine of his time. He grew up in the Germantown section of Philadelphia, the son of a specialist in pulmonary diseases, and was educated at Harvard College and Harvard Medical School. As a medical student, he was interested principally in developing general competence, so he gravitated toward internal medicine. Even more, he was drawn to doing clinical teaching in a big city—this because he admired his teachers and the role they were playing in the medical system. The most interesting teachers, he thought, were the neurologists, probably because so much of what they did depended on interviewing, examining—activities that framed the whole patient. Under the influence of these academic neurologists, his interests gradually narrowed and deepened. Following two years of residency in internal medicine at Beth Israel in Boston, he added three years in neurology at Massachusetts General and one year in Harvard Medical School's laboratory of neurophysiology. Ready to teach, he was hired by Emory University, in Atlanta, as, in his words, "their neurophysiology person." He taught there for ten years. He taught medical residents, neurosurgical residents, and neurologists, meanwhile concentrating his own special interest ever more exclusively on electromyography—the study of electrical activity in muscles. As a member of the Department of Medicine, he was an attending physician on the medical floor; nonetheless, as he became increasingly subspecialized in neurology he saw a diminishing variety of patients. "Gradually, you get to know more and more about less and less," he comments. "Eventually, I realized that I could not even manage a person with hypertension. There were many medical problems I knew nothing about. I felt a slipping, or lost, competency in general medicine. Even in neurology, my competency was narrowing. I did no pediatric neurology, for example. I felt my general competence slipping away while I became ever more adept with oscilloscopes and amplifiers, measuring the electrical activity of nerves and muscles, diagnosing neuromuscular diseases or establishing that the nerves and muscles were healthy. An electromyographer has no patients of his own. An electromyographer does tests for someone else. On the economic side of it, the sad fact is that people who want to make a high income in medicine learn to do things like electromyography. More than science attracts people to such fields. In Maine, the present cost for an electromyogram is two hundred and forty dollars. The procedure takes about as long as a complete physical exam and costs at least three times as much. The money in medicine these days is in tests and procedures, and this leads to conflicts of interest—to tests that are not necessary. To be part of the system, an electromyographer does not say that an electromyogram is unnecessary and refuse to do one. Patients, for their part, never protest charges for tests. The public seems to value tests and procedures to an extent that is not justified by their relative scientific value. Good clinical judgment is more important than tests."

As doctors in increasing numbers went into tests and procedures, their vernacular changed, too, and they began to chat intensely about the "marketing of services." The phrase did not rest comfortably on Celtic sensibilities. When McPhedran heard metropolitan-hospital doctors saying things like "How can we market our services to the people upcountry so that they will send us patients?" he wondered who might actually be out there seeing the patients upcountry.

McPhedran was appointed to the National Advisory Council for Regional Medical Programs, went to Washington regularly, and made site visits all over the United States. On these journeys, what he discerned most immediately was that primary-care physicians were disappearing. He visited regions where there were no physicians at all. Elsewhere, everybody was a "consultant." Almost everyone was in a city, running tests. "In many places, there were specialists, but no one was responsible for continuing care of patients. While the O.B.-G.Y.N.s were taking care of women's procreative organs, many patients were without a regular doctor. Internists were doing it. But they were not around in sufficient numbers to take care of everyone. Also, they did just adults."

Back home, he often found himself asking someone, "Who is your doctor?"

The person would say something like "I had a doctor, but he moved away. Can you take care of me?"

And McPhedran would say, "No. I'm a consultant in neurology at the Emory Clinic."

On one of his federal assignments, he happened into Maine —a state with no medical school and a scarcity of rural doctors, a state attempting to set up a family-practice residency that would siphon new doctors out of the megalopolis and sprinkle them through the northern countryside. By teaching in such a residency, he decided, he could help train physicians for primary care, continue to do neurology, and possibly regain the medical perspective he felt that he had lost. In his strong reaction to the increased subspecialization of his own career, he gave up university teaching, abandoned the developing subtleties of electromyography, moved to Maine, and soon began preparing for family-practice board examinations. When he took them and passed, he became a family practitioner. Not a few people were saying that family practice was a fad. McPhedran saw it as a trend—a change in the profession's view of itself.

McPhedran's manner amuses his students, who regard his politeness as bordering on the eccentric—a man who apologizes to patients for scratching the bottoms of their feet, who says to patients, almost apologetically, "Did I answer your question? Did I tell you what you wanted? I'm grateful to you for asking questions. I'd rather have you ask them than go away wondering." For all his super-subspecialized neurological skills, he is the quintessential family doctor, listening closely, empathetic—out of the basements of neurology, into the world. To be sure, he still spends

[*205*]

a good deal of time reading electroencephalograms, and not a little reading music.

For the F.M.I.'s standard twenty-five-dollar office-visit fee, Alexander McPhedran now spends forty-five minutes with a woman who will leave him feeling as if he had been with her all day. The gulf between them is wide indeed. She wants—insists upon—neurosurgery. He suggests that she try Anacin instead. The neurologist in him knows that surgery is contraindicated for her type of facial pain. The neurologist could say that and be done with it. As a family practitioner, though, he will try to deal with the pain—and with a mind that is set in the direction of a surgical fix.

"When I go to a doctor, I expect to be given something, and I expect it to work," she says. "If I need surgery, I expect to have surgery. I have had this pain for two months, and I want it over with."

McPhedran tells her in a flat voice that no reputable neurosurgeon would operate on her. She looks doubtful. She says she will check that out. McPhedran admits the possibility that Anacin might fail her. In that eventuality, he says, he recommends Excedrin. After she leaves, he remarks, "The placebo effect of surgery is high. A sham operation might do it for her. But I have to protect her from such a procedure if I can."

Amy Hufnagel comes in, breezily says "Hi" to Dr. McPhedran, tells him she is a bit pressed to be on time for a field-hockey game, and sticks out her tongue. Amy Hufnagel is a robust, athletic, attractive teen-ager with long brunette hair, an overt sense of humor, and an ability to score goals. She wears a tartan shirt, a green corduroy skirt. There are two pearls in each ear. About her tongue she is not at all self-conscious. In the corridors of Winthrop High School, she enjoys cornering some unsuspecting friend and saying, "Look! Do you want to see something gross?" With which she sticks out her tongue. It is wrinkled up like a calf's brain. It has a caved-in side. It twitches. As she sticks it out now for McPhedran, a large part of the surface, on the left side, leaps and bubbles like boiling soup. A part of it has atrophied as well—a baylike indentation. The tongue dances. It humps. Amy laughs. Her speech is not affected. She has difficulty eating some foods but no additional inconvenience. McPhedran tests— as he has on other occasions—the nerves and muscles of her mouth, face, and eyes. All are normal. The pharynx nerve is normal. In recent months, there has been some clicking in her left ear. He has no idea what to make of that. He does not know what to make of the whole situation. She has been his patient for more than a year. He calls her condition hemiatrophy of the tongue, but that is merely a description. Something is apparently going on in the twelfth nerve on the left side, but he cannot say what it is. Could it be mononeuropathy multiplex? In nearly thirty years in neurology, he has not seen the like of it.

When to refer. If a capacity for making that decision is the supreme talent of the family practitioner, it is no less relevant from time to time in the experience of a subspecialist. This neurologist—of course—has long since referred this patient to higher authority. When McPhedran comes upon something that is beyond his range, his reading, his neurological comprehension, he sends the patient to his own incomparable mentor—Raymond D. Adams, of Harvard University and Massachusetts General Hospital, a master of clinical analysis. Adams is unfailingly accommodating. He knows he will see something interesting if it comes from Alex.

Amy, her mother, and her father went to Boston. They spent two days there and returned to Augusta. Afterward, Raymond D. Adams wrote to Alexander McPhedran, "The Hufnagels are a delightful family." That was the extent of his diagnosis. He had absolutely no idea what was wrong with Amy's tongue.

North of the C.P. Line

My other self—as he might have been called in a brief, ambiguous novel—was in this instance a bush pilot, several hundred feet above Third Matagamon Lake, face to face with a strong winter wind. The plane was a Super Cub, scarcely large enough for the two of us. We sat in tandem and talked through an intercom. There is a lot of identification, even transformation, in the work I do—moving along from place to place, person to person, as a reporter, a writer, repeatedly trying to sense another existence and in some ways to share it. Never had that been more true than now, in part because he was sitting there with my life in his hands while placing (in another way) his life in mine. He spoke with affection about the plane, calling it a sophisticated kite and admitting his amazement that it could take such a frontal battering when all it was made of, essentially, was cotton.

I said that was amazing, right enough—and how fast did he imagine the wind was blowing?

He said he could guess, with some help from the airspeed indicator, but one way to tell for sure was to stop the plane. Flying level, holding course, he slowed down, and slowed down more, and told me to watch the ground until the spruce did not move. A steady progression over the trees became a stately progression over the trees, and ultimately—like a frame of motion picture frozen on a screen—came to a dead stop. With respect to the earth, we were stock-still. Against the deep snow, the spruce made chevrons with their shadows. Nothing in the pattern moved. Mt. Katahdin, on our flank—sparkling white above its ruff of dark trees—did not move. The black forest reached to the horizon around the white paisley shapes of the Allagash Lakes—a scene preserved before us as if it were on canvas, while we hung there at ground speed zero.

"We're indicating forty-five miles per hour," he said. "There's your answer. That's how fast the wind is blowing."

There were snowshoes on the wing struts—two pairs. He said, "You never know when the airplane is going to refuse to go." He had skis and poles and an M-1 rifle. ("The sound of a revolver doesn't carry.") A five-foot steel ice chisel was mounted on the fuselage. There was some kero dust ("kerosene and sawdust, it burns for quite a while") and strike-anywhere matches in a waterproof steel case. There was some trail mix, but no regular stores of food. ("If I carry a lot of food in the airplane, I just eat it. I carry trail mix the way some people carry chewing tobacco.") There were goose-down warmup pants and extra down parkas that were supposedly good to seventy below zero. (They reminded me of a friend who, one Alaskan winter, took a mail-order parka to Anaktuvuk Pass and came back complaining that it didn't work.) By now, I had seen about all I wanted to of the underlying landscape without apparent motion, and I listened for the sound of an advancing throttle.

This pilot, as it happened, was an author as well, and he had written magazine pieces about the North Maine Woods—its terrain, its wildlife, and related subjects—as had I. In the spring of 1976, he wrote to *The New Yorker* and complained that I was using his name. He said, "For all practical purposes he is using my name (and I his)," and he went on to explain that the signature at the bottom of my pieces had from time to time embarrassed him in his principal occupation, as an employee of the State of Maine. He said he tended to agree with some of my thoughts—

[*209*]

for example, about the Army Corps of Engineers and its plans
to dam the St. John River—but he was not at liberty to do so in
open print, because he was under oath to be neutral on public
issues. And now his oath seemed to be hanging out like a wet
necktie, because right there in *The New Yorker* was a tirade worthy
of Rumpelstiltskin, ranting against the people who wished to flood
the North Maine Woods by building the twelfth-largest dam on
earth—in a piece of writing that many people he knew assumed
he had written, as well they might, for it was signed with his
exact name.

At that time, Maine had four game-warden pilots. This one
was the northernmost, with seven thousand square miles of forest
as his home range. In what was by then a decade of service there,
he had become known as the Flying Warden of the North Maine
Woods. Nonetheless, I had never heard of him. If we are cousins,
we are much removed. We are related only to the extent that we
descend from a clan that immemorially occupied one small island
in the Hebrides, where our surname developed. Yet for all practical purposes we are indeed using each other's names, and while
I had been making my own professional journeys on lakes and
streams through the woods of Maine I had in my ignorance felt
no twinge of encroachment and could not have imagined being
over myself in the air.

I had been to the Hebrides once, to live for a time on the clan
island and gather material for a piece of writing. Now *The New
Yorker*, at my request, sent that piece of writing to Maine. It was
not just a matter of the postage. I was in Alaska, far from home,
and a copy of his letter had been sent to me up there. In a cabin
near the Yukon River, I wrote a sympathetic response—a condensed autobiography, an *apologia pro nomine suo*, always en-
deavoring to match his graceful good humor—and soon thereafter
mailed it to Maine. The warden was not there to receive it. Taking
some time off, he had got into his own airplane with his father,
Malcolm, and headed northwest through Quebec in foul weather,
flying low up the Saguenay River, dodging wires. ("You have to
be alert. You have to watch out.") Conditions soon changed to
what he calls "severe clear," and remained almost cloudless from

Lac St. Jean to Moose Factory (on James Bay) to Churchill (on Hudson Bay) to Yellowknife to Great Bear Lake. Landing on floats, they were fishing all the way. They followed the Yukon River through interior Alaska, and—more or less while I was writing my letter—passed above my head on their way to the Bering Sea.

When he returned to Maine, he found my letter regretting the inconvenience I had caused him, and the story of the Scottish island, which established for him our remote kinship and common history. For a year or two, there was more correspondence, but we remained strangers. His mother told him that she could not distinguish my handwriting from his.

Then, just after breakup—or ice out, as they call it in Maine—a friend and I were on Allagash Lake when a blue-and-white floatplane came over the trees, went into a tight turn, and circled the canoe. Allagash Lake is one beautiful lake. Allagash Mountain stands beside it. There are forty-two hundred acres of water and a fleet of wooded islands. There are brook trout, lake trout. Allagash Lake has never been stocked. In its elevation, and among its circumvallate hills, it is the high coronet of the wilderness waterway, of the Allagash River system. Floatplanes are strictly forbidden to set down on Allagash Lake, but there is an official exception. I had mentioned in a letter the plans for that trip, and had described as well my dark-chocolate canoe. The airplane gave up its altitude, flared, and sent spray off the lake. It taxied toward the canoe. Then the propeller stopped, and the airplane drifted. We moved alongside and took hold of a pontoon. I was ninety-nine per cent certain that I knew who was inside. Even so, there was room for surprise. The door opened. The pilot stepped down and stood on the pontoon. About forty, weathered and slim, he looked like a North-West Mounted Policeman. His uniform jacket was bright red, trimmed with black flaps over the breast pockets, black epaulets. A badge above one pocket said "STATE OF MAINE WARDEN PILOT." Above the other pocket was a brass plate incised in block letters with his name: JOHN MCPHEE. I almost fell into the lake.

He was an appealing, friendly man, and he did not ask for my fishing license. We talked for at least an hour there, canoe and airplane about a mile offshore, on the calm surface of early evening. He had a quick smile, a pilot's alert, responsive eyes. He looked a lot like my cousin John and not a little like John's father, John. We talked of the backcountry—the Allagash and St. John lake-and-river country—and the creatures that live in its woods and waters. From anecdote to anecdote, unselfconsciously he poured forth his knowledge—of natural disasters and human intrusions, of isolated phenomena and recurrent events, of who was doing what to whom. I remember a wistful feeling—it has not diminished—imagining the life that had produced that knowledge. We asked if he would stay for dinner. He said he was always ready to eat. We pushed away from the pontoon and headed toward the stand of white pines below which we had pitched our tents. The warden followed, taxiing dead slow—the canoe leading the airplane, tandem, cutting three wakes across a mile of water. He tied it to one of the pines.

One evening, on the ground, we went into a small pond near the Allagash River and tried to call a moose. For all his deep and varied woodcraft, Jack is a novice at calling moose. We had even gone together for a lesson—into a township of Range 6 where moose were said to be as concentrated as anywhere in Maine. The person who said so was Perley Eastman, who has spent many hours in the air with Jack making population studies of wildlife. He is employed as a "wildlife technician," but he can be more accurately described as a trapper, a woodsman, an indigene of the unincorporated townships. Thirty years ago, when logs were still being driven down the Aroostook River in spring, Perley worked the drive. A man of considerable strength and endurance, he is now well along in middle age, and he has a list of medical problems ranging from hiatus hernia to hypertension and a pulse of a hundred and thirteen. Nonetheless, he participates in an annual long-distance canoe race on the river and to this date has never lost. He has his dreams. He senses that the country he prefers in Maine multiplied by a hundred is Alaska, and he has obtained an enormous photograph—eight feet high and thirteen feet long—of the Tanana terrain somewhere east of Fairbanks. The picture completely covers one of his bedroom walls. The day he put it up, he piled campfire ashes on the floor and slept that night in a down bag beside the ashes and the picture. Outside his bedroom window, the view is sweeping—across a meadow framed by the evergreen woods. The black things in motion in the meadow are bears.

With a rolled megaphone of birch bark, Perley calls moose. The call is a bovino-ungulate psychosexual grunt. Moose have pursued Perley and tried to get into his car. The call is scrapingly nasal, and is presented in metric components: two long, two short—which in American Morse code is the number seven, as any moose can tell you. On the night of our lesson, Perley had moose in cavalries circling the periphery of a bog. The rutting season was still some days away, and they lacked the lust to come get him.

And now, at sunset on the pond in the Allagash woods, moose were being called by two people who themselves were accustomed to answering to identical sounds. The horizon was orange and was broken by black jagged spruce. We stood side by side. His grunts and my grunts seemed to me to be indistinguishable and therefore equally inept. Not one moose responded. It seemed to me, as we called and called again, that a bagpiper was more likely to answer.

Hunting for moose, or for anything else, is forbidden on Sundays in Maine—a law that is frequently ignored. To deal with such violations, wardens have procedures that are known in their vernacular as "working Sunday hunters." Working Sunday hunters is how the Federal Bureau of Investigation might describe its approach to payoff-prone members of the United States Senate and House of Representatives. The warden pilot spots a hunters' camp, picks up a ground warden, and drops him off about a mile from the camp. The ground warden advances through the forest

[213]

with a sixty-power spotting scope and sets it up where he can observe the hunters. The warden pilot, who has returned to the air, now lands at the campsite, checks licenses, talks weather, drinks coffee, and flies away to look for other hunters while the ground warden, through the spotting scope, watches what happens next. The hunters go into their tents. They come out loading their guns. They head into the woods. The ground warden follows and makes arrests.

The symbiosis is complex between hunter and warden. Even with the tote roads, and the topographically guiding presence of lakes and streams, the Maine woods are so vast, the trackless areas so broad and numerous, that various people—hikers, campers, fishermen, and particularly hunters—frequently become lost. Even timber cruisers employed by the proprietary land companies sometimes get lost. An International Paper Company cruiser failed to return on the night of November 11, 1976. A skeleton discovered a few years later was thought to be his. In the autumn hunting seasons, Jack seeks and finds a lost hunter almost every day. Search-and-rescue is the most rewarding—and often, of course, the grimmest—aspect of his work. He seeks the corpses of people who drown in lakes and rivers—more than thirty in the past year. He has learned how to read a body under rapids. He is so accustomed to lost hunters—so used to their patterns of gradual disorientation—that he sometimes knows just where to go to find them. For example, there is some very good moose, beaver, trout, deer, and lost-hunter country in Township 16, Range 6. He often gets calls informing him that a Ten-Sixty— a lost hunter—is somewhere in that terrain. "It's a tangle down there," he said one day, flying over it. "There are so many beaver flowages, and no landmarks. Hunters get lost, and they head the wrong way. They almost always end up in the same place, though. The configuration of the woods gradually funnels them into it." He has found more than a dozen hunters there. "One purpose of the airplane is hardcore search-and-rescue," he went on. "If you save one life a year, it's worth it. If someone is lost, optimism rises when the airplane comes. We are ninety-nine per cent successful. If a lost person is out more than three nights, the success ratio goes down markedly."

On November 16, 1983, a deer hunter named Newton Sterling went into the woods in Township 15, Range 13, a little west of the St. John, between Seminary Brook and the Big Black River. Something like four inches of snow was on the ground. The walking was easy. Sterling, his brother, and two younger relatives had seen what appeared to be a trophy buck, and they were following a plan to take him. Their intent was to make this first early-morning foray a brief one. So Newt Sterling had contented himself with a cup of coffee, postponing the rest of his breakfast. He had also left behind his backpack, thermos, candy bars, and survival blanket. He established himself on a ridge, alone, and awaited the appearance of the biggest stag in Maine. Snow came instead, and, soon, a whiteout, with a squirrelly wind blowing thick wet flakes. He heard two rifle shots, signalling him to return to his brother's pickup. He lingered—hoping for a blind-chance encounter with the buck—while the fast-falling snow filled and eliminated his tracks. A compass was pinned to his lapel. He rubbed it, and squinted at it. He had left his reading glasses behind as well. The direction he had come from was east. He misread the compass and walked for two hours west.

By now, the snow was a foot deep, and the walking required effort. He was not yet uncomfortable. He was wearing three pairs of light wool socks, waterproof leather boots, insulated underwear, wool trousers, canvas hunting trousers, two wool shirts, a down jacket, an orange cotton hunting jacket, an orange wool hat, and fingered wool gloves. At last sensing a problem, he removed the compass from his lapel, rubbed it clear, and studied it closely. He set his rifle aside, where its metal could not affect the magnetism. When he saw his apparent error, he laboriously dug into an inner trouser pocket and came up with another compass. Its needle was stuck, and it was useless.

Returning the first compass to his lapel, he hung his rifle on his shoulder and began to retrace his way east. Some minutes later, he glanced down to check the compass and saw that it was gone. Evidently, he had failed to close its hasp, and the sling of the rifle had knocked it away. He turned to retrace his steps but realized with a glance that in all the accumulating snow he would never find the compass. He turned again, and tried to backtrack by following his westbound footprints, but soon they were faint and then invisible.

He kept going, reasoning that if he walked long enough he would come out somewhere. Sleet alternated with the snow. After going downhill for a time, he got into muskeg, soaking his legs and feet. The swampy ground frightened him, made him wonder if he could ever get away from it, because his clothing gradually became completely soaked, branches hit his face, and deadfalls blockaded him. One step would put him on solid earth, the next in thigh-deep water. After what he judged to be two hours in the muskeg, he saw in the snow a set of human footprints. He felt a rush of relief. People were looking for him. Help must be near. His steps quickened as he followed the footprints—for five minutes before he realized they were his own.

Sterling was making his fourth trip to the North Maine Woods. He was a mason-carpenter, fifty-eight years old, a small independent general contractor from Port Republic, New Jersey, in the eastern Pine Barrens. Now he followed an imaginary line intersected by two trees. He sloshed and struggled some distance, and then lined up the first pair with another tree. In this manner, he established and maintained a straight course of travel. He lengthened it a tree at a time—hurrying, and thus weakening himself, because dusk was coming down and he was still in the muskeg. Eventually, he beat the night, escaping to high ground.

He tore bark from a paper birch. He found a hollow tree, and with his folding knife cut out hunks of punky cortex. His matches—book matches—resembled a book of cold pasta, but he was carrying a small butane lighter that he had bought on impulse in a general store on his way into Maine. If he could get a fire going, he would owe his life to—among other things—the fact that he smoked cigarettes. His brand was Salem Lights. A pack of them was mush in his pocket. The wet bark fizzled and would not ignite.

To report him lost, his nephew had driven nearly fifty miles by tote road, and darkness had come before a searching flight could be made. Phil Dumond, the border warden from Estcourt Station, told the rest of the party to try to get some sleep, but they drove the tote roads through the night, firing their rifles, in hopes of a reply. Newt Sterling heard nothing. In the sleet, the wind, the thick wet snow, he could not have heard a howitzer a mile away. He knew that he was in for the night, and that he had to build a fire. From his wallet, therefore, he removed ten twenty-dollar bills. He crumpled them up, and placed upon them, like kindling wood, his plastic credit cards. He imagined them more flammable than they would prove to be. He added his weatherized Maine hunting license. He added twigs, and dry punk from another hollow tree—and he flicked his butane lighter. The two hundred dollars burned. The cards melted. The hunting license was even less flammable than his MasterCard. The twigs glowed. And everything went dark.

Midnight approached. The snow, intermittently, turned to rain. Oddly, he could see. So he moved on, knowing that if he stayed too long in one place he would chill and die. He did try resting from time to time, but the cold went through him quickly and he got up and moved. He found a pair of ruts—a long-abandoned track from the era when horses twitched logs from the woods. He followed the old road and came to a wide, rampaging brook. Opposite, the road broadened, climbed, looked like an avenue rising through the trees. Clearly, it would lead to safety, but he feared drowning, and waited until morning to ford the stream. All night, he walked back and forth on the old road, his hips in pain from lifting his feet above the deep snow. Suddenly, a bull moose came thrashing out of the woods and rushed by him, followed by two cows. A little closer and they would have killed him. They returned, and passed him several times during the night, breaking trail for him in the snow and improving his ability to walk. He felt no hunger but enormous thirst. When he took off his gloves and drank from a gully, his gloves froze. He thawed them in his armpits. Thereafter, he ate snow from a stick and ate so much he burned his mouth.

Heavy rain became snow again. The first gray light appeared, and within minutes Jack was in the air. There were clouds on all ridges. In varying densities, fog was everywhere. His first destination was Township 9, Range 10, and, flying alone, he picked his way toward it through gaps in the scud to search for another lost hunter. The man was found by ground wardens while the plane was on its way. So Jack turned and headed for the St. John country north of the Big Black River. He was there by seven-thirty. The lost man was in one of two "towns," somewhere in forty-six thousand acres, and finding him would not have been a particularly difficult assignment on a day of severe clarity, but the choice today was to fly on the treetops or fly in cloud. The snowstorm, with its hindering opacity, stopped rarely. He could see the white ground streaming along below him, and little more. Flakes were largest over the ridges. Elsewhere, he encountered some light rain. Unsuccessfully, he hunted for more than three hours—a hit-or-miss succession of closeup glimpses. Rodney Sirois, the border warden of St. Pamphile, came into the area to assist from the ground, and his first suggestion was that his colleague in the air go home. Speaking into his transceiver, he said, "Jack, if I were you, I'd leave." The conditions, in his opinion, did not even approach the marginal. Sirois himself is a pilot. Jack replied that he felt comfortable enough, because the St. John River was only a few miles to the east. He was much too socked in to see it, of course, but he could feel it there, and was sure that he could get to it, and knew that he could go down it, if necessary, just above the water, and follow it to Fort Kent, and then go up the Fish River to his home—as he had done on many a foul day.

During most of the search, he was so far away from Newton Sterling that Sterling did not hear the plane. After dawn, the hunter had forded the brook, figuring that if he fell it was the end. He was too discouraged by the sight of deadfalls and rapids to attempt to follow the brook to safety. Instead, he climbed the "avenue" he had seen in the night, but it narrowed and grew fainter and curved along a ridge and ended in a clearing. It had been built not as a way out of the woods but only to bring logs to the brook. Horses had once been kept at the clearing, in a cabinlike structure, which was now in a state of collapse, parts of it protruding above the snow. Sterling found some dry tarpaper, some dry grasses, weeds. From the old timbers he cut slivers with his knife. After he had constructed what he hoped would become a fire, he held the flame of his lighter below a piece of tarpaper—and went on holding it until the fuel was fading and his fingers were burned. Tar is petroleum, after all. Slowly, a drop welled up on the old dry paper, rolled off one edge, and blazed in the flame. The paper ignited. The grasses and the weeds ignited. He had a fire.

Since cloud was on the deck everywhere but in the little valleys, Jack for the most part stayed in them, trying to see ahead through a layer of condensation that was just above the trees. He flew on a time-distance formula, making many turns on instruments, holding his altitude and watching the rotation of the compass. In one of the valleys he saw what he thought must be the biggest buck he had ever seen in the state of Maine, and, passing the time of day, he told the ground wardens about it—Phil Dumond, Rod Sirois, John Caron. It was all he had to report.

He felt a strong need to set the plane down. Hours had passed since he drank his morning coffee. So he followed a compass heading for Lac de l'Est, the nearest large lake, where, in a manner of speaking, he could take a coffee break. The route took him past a ridge in Township 15, Range 14. Something in the fog on the ridge arrested his eye. He thought he saw "a slight difference in the cloudiness on the trees, a rich oaky look in contrast to the standard gray fog, a subtle difference—something you could look at for a while and decide, 'It's nothing.' " He altered his course for a close look.

"I didn't think anybody would be up flying," Sterling would say months later. "When I heard that airplane, it really surprised me that one was out there. It was just bad flying weather—at any moment, a whiteout. All at once, I saw a plane go just over the treetops." He would not remember what kind of plane it was, its colors or size, or even if it was equipped with floats. What he would never forget, though, were the canoe paddles, the incongruous canoe paddles wedged in the cross braces, a pair of canoe paddles passing over his head. The plane disappeared, turned, and came over him again. The wings dipped, and his eyes filled with tears.

Sirois drove his pickup to the nearest point of road and walked an hour and a half into the woods, sometimes in beaver flowages with water up to his chin. Dressed in State of Maine polyester —a uniform that Jack has described as "sapping heat away from you like a wick"—Sirois lost so much body heat that he thought it possible he would also lose his life. He walked a line traced by the airplane repeatedly passing overhead. Sirois, whose knowledge of woodcraft and wildlife is even more extensive than Jack's— Sirois, who with his wife, Judy, had raised two sons and two coyotes in a warden station so remote it is sixty feet from Quebec—had no idea who Sterling was. He had no idea that a Sterling Drive had been cut into the forest in New Jersey, and that Sterling had built nine imaginative homes there, one with a spiral staircase rising into an octagonal den. He didn't know that after the casinos came Sterling had built houses for Goldsmith of Playboy, Duberson of Harrah's. He didn't know that Sterling drove a diesel Olds with air, or that he also possessed an Indy 600 three-cylinder liquid-cooled snowmobile, which he had driven at speeds up to ninety miles an hour. Sirois, whose own history had become as endangered as Sterling's, didn't know any of that, nor did any of it matter. A man was lost, and another meant to save him.

The weather turned colder, snowier. An even higher percentage of cloud touched the deck. When Sirois had entered the clearing and was a hundred yards from the hunter, Jack banked away and sought the St. John.

Checking licenses and catches, and gathering biological data on fish, we flew various itineraries. The more remote they were, the more things differed from flights near the small valley towns. There were poachers and smugglers to watch for among the S-bends and oxbows of the St. Francis River, which serves as a segment of the international boundary and so much resembles tangled rope that it grossly confuses the jurisdictions. The snow would tell the story, though, if there was a story. Jack said, "In winter, these people who are crossing, for whatever reason, kind of have to leave a track. It gives you a clue as to what is going on." What is going on is sometimes nothing more than Canadians crossing the line to snare rabbits—an illegal practice in Maine. He called the tracks of snowshoes floats.

Few tracks, of course, were human. "Reading sign from the air is quite a technique," he remarked one day while we were flying low and northwest up the Machias River, in Township 12, Range 8. (There are two Machias Rivers in Maine, this one the lesser known—about forty miles north of Mt. Katahdin.) "Those are pretty good-sized canine tracks," he said, noticing some loops in the snow. "My guess would be those are coyotes. This is mating season for them. They go around pissing on sticks. From the air, a rabbit track, a white-tailed-deer track, and a coyote track are pretty much the same. I get fooled still, from time to time. There—see how far apart those tracks are on the river? Something was really moving. But what? A coyote chasing a deer? Whatever it was, it was right flat out. This is a nice, rich river: a lot of things to see." A bend or two later, we went over what was left of a coyote-killed deer, and Jack put us on our side for a tight, close look. Blood was spilled and spattered from one bank to the other. With the exception of some hide, the blood was about all that was left of the deer. "Amazing!" he said. "Amazing! An animal that weighed a hundred and fifty pounds—and in two or three days that sucker is gone."

The Eastern coyote is larger than the Western coyote, probably because it is a former Western coyote that came across Canada and acquired on the way some wolf. For many years, biologists noticed that some Eastern coyotes appeared to be part dog, hybrids they described as coydogs. Since then, the hybrids have all but died out. The pelt of an Eastern coyote has long, lupine fur and will typically measure five feet from the muzzle to the tip of the tail. Nothing about it suggests a domestic dog, and meanwhile its size confirms that it did not come off some little Western canine that bays at the moon.

Out in the backcountry, nothing differed so much as the style of the fishing. Jack was taking a kind of census. "Party of three. Second Musquacook Lake," he said, making notes. "An awful lot of people just don't bother with shacks up here." True, most of the fishermen on the Penobscot and Allagash headwater lakes were moving around, despite the cold, like fishermen in summer, trying this good spot or that—too mobile to be encumbered by something as unwieldy as a shack. Needless to say, they were fewer, and farther apart.

Party of five on Second Musquacook Lake. No shack. Party of five on Clear Lake. No shack. Party of two on Big Eagle Lake. No shack. The air temperature was seventeen degrees below zero. The fishermen were catching togue, brook trout, whitefish. "Whitefish are probably the best eating," Jack said. "They have sweet, white, flaky flesh. They're what a flounder would taste like if it lived in fresh water."

We saw two sleds, tandem, bucking the north winds of Chamberlain Lake in what seemed to be running smoke. I remembered fighting three-foot waves with canoe paddles, getting nowhere, in the same place. We saw a lone figure with a pack basket making his way without snowshoes across two miles of lake. Thick caps of snow sat on the boulders in the Chase Rapids of the Allagash River. A few miles away, we found a party of two, far out on Churchill Lake. Each man had his own airplane and his own folding lawn chair. Between the planes, at seventeen degrees below zero, the two men were sitting on the lake in the lawn chairs watching flag-loaded holes in the ice. "It's a different kind of activity working a lake fisherman than a brook fisherman," Jack commented. "A lake fisherman you can watch with a sixty-power scope. Like working Sunday hunters. Ground wardens watch ice fishermen taking more than their limit. They watch them hide the fish by burying them in the snow. Then they move in for the arrest. To work a brook fisherman, you have to get on your hands and knees and crawl very close. It's easy to dump fish if you're a brook fisherman. The Frenchmen from across the way, they just love to brook-fish. Maine people generally fish the lakes. I key in when the fish are biting. As a warden pilot, I don't get concerned about a fisherman who is not going to catch any fish."

At the edges of certain lakes, brook trout will go into a feeding frenzy when the ice recedes from the shoreline. The situation attracts "avid ice-out fishermen," and the wardens key in on them. Spring, after ice out, is the supreme time for what Jack looks upon as "fun fishin'." Fish are near the surface—even, to some extent, the togue (as lake trout are called in the region). "You can even troll with a fly rod," he said. "In summer, you'd have to use a lead line to catch a brook trout. In spring, the fishing gets good when the leaves on the alders are the size of a mouse's ear."

On the shore of Pillsbury Island, in Big Eagle Lake, we saw more sign of coyote-killed deer. The yards of Pillsbury Island were four feet deep in snow, a miring depth for deer. (When Thoreau travelled the Maine woods in bark canoes, Pillsbury Island was the northernmost landmark he reached.) Three or four miles up the lake, two coyotes had killed a moose earlier in the winter. Now there was nothing to be seen there except a party of four, who had taken shelter from the wind beside a small and treeless island. We descended in their direction, flared, and were about to touch down on the snow-covered ice when I said, "Don't scare the fish. You'll annoy the fishermen."

The skis rumbled, and Jack said, "Quite often, they get a bite when the plane lands."

The party of four was from Presque Isle, eighty miles to the east, and consisted of two women and two men, who had caught one wretched-looking and now frozen cusk—a soft-fleshed bottom-feeder, and all they had to show for a long cold day. The two women were huddled in a small nylon lean-to that appeared to be reducing the windchill by one degree. The two men were brothers, Dale and Dana Buck. They walked around in puffy jumpsuits watching their lines. The women—Dawn Nelson and Lisa Nickerson, who had never before found themselves in such a situation—had agreed to come along in order to see what ice fishing was all about. They had come. They had seen. They said as much, and added, with emphasis, that they were never coming back.

We taxied half a mile toward the middle of the lake to check another party of four. They were all men, and all from Ashland, about fifty miles away. They had runcible skimmers, ice chisels. One had icicles hanging from his beard. That they knew what they were doing was evidenced by two big togue lying on the ice. Each fish was about twenty-eight inches long, and their combined weight was sixteen pounds. As bait, other parties had been using chubs, shiners—so-called roughage fish. With chubs and shiners, other parties were catching nothing. These men were using smelts, and they were fishing the upper water about fourteen feet below the ice, in a total column of sixty feet. While Jack was measuring and weighing the togue, he said to me, "At this time of year, smelts are gearing up for their spawning runs, getting ready to go into shallow water, so they're up near the surface of the lake, and togue are up there feeding on them."

Vincent Malena, forty years old, was kneeling on the ice attending to a fish that had come onto one of his lines. Hand over hand, he would gently haul the line, and let it slip away when the fish decided to run. He knelt facing north—directly into the unabated wind—and to deliver the fish onto the ice with proper care he was working with his hands uncovered. Up, down, he patiently moved the line. The temperature was holding at minus seventeen degrees and the windchill factor was fifty below zero.

Malena was also known as Ashland One—a reference to the fact that he was the police chief of the small community that has now and again been called the capital of the North Maine Woods. Ashland One leads a force of three. At last, and with obstetrical competence, he brought the fish to the lower surface of the ice, and in the augered aperture the head became engaged. Lake ice varies in thickness from month to month and winter to winter, depending on the frequency and extent of thaws. Relatively speaking, this was thin ice—scarcely more than two feet thick—for the winter had been almost unremittingly cold. Firmly but without damaging force, Malena moved the head up into the shaft, his fingers flexible, his whole being evidently unaffected by the bone-cracking cold. It was 4 P.M. There was no shack, no protection of any kind from the wind. I asked him how long they had been fishing. Malena answered, "Oh, since about eight o'clock this morning."

The situation had become particularly delicate, and all eyes were concentrating on the now visible face in the cylindrical interior of the ice. I remembered Melford Pelletier telling me about a togue he'd had on a line that broke: he thought he had lost him, but the head was slightly wedged in the hole in the ice. Pelletier reached down, put a hand in the fish's mouth, expanded the hand like a toggle bolt, and brought the fish to the surface. Malena, for his part, was achieving a safe, normal delivery. The head moved toward him a centimetre at a time. At last, he slipped his fingers around the gills and lifted the creature into the world. Eight pounds four ounces. Male. Its length—twenty-six inches —exactly matched the thickness of the ice.

Jack and I took off. "In as nice a way as I can, I like to remind fishermen that the fish they are catching are, in a sense, as old as they are," he said. "There are togue in these lakes more than twenty years old. A lot of fishermen don't realize that. If we tell them, chances are sooner or later one of them might decide to throw a fish back. Those men have nearly twenty-four pounds of fish there. Chances are all three togue will end up in a freezer."

And now, on my last day (for a time) in Jack's backcountry, we were looking down on Third Matagamon Lake, and the spruce did not move. "We're indicating forty-five miles per hour," he

said. "There's your answer. That's how fast the wind is blowing."
We hung there some moments longer before he advanced the
throttle. The plane was full of skis, poles, boots, paper towels,
peanut butter, and other supplies off the shelves of a valley store:
Mélasse de Fantaisie, Pure de la Barbade; Scott Tissues; Sirop
d'Érable Pur, Produit du Québec; Ivory Liquid Detergent. After
completing an ice patrol, we unloaded the airplane. Then we
skied across the lake and into the woods. We went out onto the
ice of the shallow pond where, months before, we had tried calling
moose. Our double track, one trail, extended through the otherwise untraceried snow in a silence we left unbroken. An hour
or two later, with the sun dropping fast, we flew the seventy-five
miles to the nearest commercial airfield. As we were landing
there (on wheels below the skis), a pair of red foxes ran across
the runway in front of the plane. The late, slanting sunlight
transilluminated their fur. I watched Jack take off, watched his
plane until it was out of sight, and then, like a walking swastika,
carried my skis and poles to a twin-engined Beechcraft. Thirty
bucks to Bangor. Mt. Katahdin, backlighted, stood black in an
orange sky.

The correspondence continues. "I was thinking probably the
only reason we met was that article you did on the St. John," he
wrote not long ago. "You know, I really didn't believe you were
possible, because I was John McPhee."

We are not altogether the same. He is John Malcolm, son of
Malcolm, son of John. I am John Angus, son of Harry, son of
Angus. He is a pragmatist of the north woods. I am a landscapist
of the Suppressed Mudjekeewis and Muttering Hemlock School.
I have seen him carry briquettes into First Currier Pond. I have
seen him start a campfire with gasoline from the wing of his
airplane. (I learned something. In a paper cup, gasoline burns
quietly and does not blaze up in your face.) Whenever I think
about him, however, I feel such a strong sense of identification
that I wonder if it is not a touch of envy—an ancestral form of
envy, a benign and wistful envy, innocent of chagrin. As anyone
might, I wish I knew what he knows—and wish not merely for

his knowledge but for his compatibility with the backcountry and everything that lives there. I envy him his world, I suppose, in the way that one is sometimes drawn to be another person or live the life of a character encountered in a fiction. Time and again, when I think of him, and such thoughts start running through my mind, I invariably find myself wishing that I were John McPhee.

RISING FROM

THE PLAINS

(1 9 8 6)

[*In this* Reader, *the selections from three books*—Coming into the Country, Rising from the Plains, *and* Looking for a Ship—*have been adapted from public readings given by the author. McPhee has never published a piece of writing without having read it aloud to someone at some stage in the composition, customarily after the second of his usual four drafts. He has done some fifty or sixty public readings over the years—twenty-two of them with his wife, Yolanda Whitman, who speaks for Ethel Waxham of* Rising from the Plains, *coming in with Waxham's words whenever they are quoted and at whatever length. Waxham was twenty-three years old when she went into Wyoming in a stagecoach to teach in a one-room school. While* Rising from the Plains *is mainly about her son, a Yale Ph.D. and for many decades a preeminent Rocky Mountain geologist, this presentation is about her, and about ranch life at the turn of the century. Portions of it derive from her journal and her other writing, which was unpublished until 1993. Two of her granddaughters—Barbara Love and Frances Love Froidevaux—collected her journals and essays in a book called* Lady's Choice, *published by the University of New Mexico Press, the first of two projected volumes. Introducing the reading, McPhee says, "In the course of my research, after I had known Love for a couple of years and made a number of geological field trips in his company, he reached into a drawer in his office in Laramie and handed me a journal that had been started by his mother long before she was married—when she had first come to Wyoming. She would be well over a hundred years old now, and needless to say I never met her, but the admiration and affection I came to feel toward her is probably matched by no one I've encountered in my professional life.* Rising from the Plains *begins with her, a slim young woman arriving in Wyoming in the autumn of 1905. Her hair was so blond it looked white. In Massachusetts, a few months before, she had been graduated from Wellesley College and had been awarded a Phi Beta Kappa key, which now hung from a chain around her neck. Her field was classical studies. In addition to her skills in Latin and Greek, she could handle a horse expertly, but never had she made a journey into a region so remote as the one that lay before her."*]

On October 20, 1905, the two-horse stage left Rawlins soon after dawn. Eggs were packed under the seats, also grapes and oysters. There were so many boxes and mailbags that they were piled up beside the driver. On the waybill, the passengers were given exactly the same status as the oysters and the grapes. The young woman from Wellesley, running her eye down the list of merchandise, encountered her own name: Miss Ethel Waxham.

The passenger compartment had a canvas roof, and canvas curtains at the front and sides.

The driver, Bill Collins, a young fellow with a four days beard, untied the bow-knot of the reins around the wheel, and swung up on the seat, where he ensconced himself with one leg over the mail bags as high as his head and one arm over the back of his seat, putting up the curtain between. "Kind o' lonesome out here," he gave as his excuse.

There were two passengers. The other's name was Alice Amoss Welty, and she was the postmistress of Dubois, two hundred miles northwest. Her post office was unique, in that it was farther from a railroad than any other in the United States; but this did not inconvenience the style of Mrs. Welty. Not for her some false-fronted dress shop with a name like Tinnie Mercantile. She bought her clothes by mail from B. Altman & Co., Manhattan. Mrs. Welty was of upper middle age, and—"bless her white hairs"—her gossip range appeared to cover every living soul within thirty thousand square miles, an interesting handful of people. The remark about the white hairs—like the description of Bill Collins and the estimated radius of Mrs. Welty's gossip— is from the unpublished journal of Ethel Waxham.

The stage moved through town past houses built of railroad ties, past sheepfolds, and was soon in the dust of open country, rounding a couple of hills before assuming a northwesterly course. The hills above were the modest high points in a landscape that lacked exceptional relief. Here in the middle of the Rocky Mountains were no mountains worthy of the name.

Mountains were far away ahead of us, a range rising from the plains and sinking down again into them. Almost all the first day they were in sight.

As Wyoming ranges go, these distant summits were unprepossessing ridges, with altitudes of nine and ten thousand feet. In one sentence, though, Miss Waxham had intuitively written their geologic history, for they had indeed come out of the plains, and into the plains had in various ways returned.

The stage rolled onto Separation Flats—altitude seven thousand feet—still pursuing the chimeric mountains.

Lost Soldier was another sixteen miles and thus would take three hours.

We rattled into the place at last, and were glad to get in to the fire to warm ourselves while the driver changed the load from one coach to another. With every change of drivers the coach is changed, making each man responsible for repairs on his own coach. The Kirks keep Lost Soldier. Mrs. Kirk is a short stocky figureless woman with untidy hair. She furnished me with an old soldier's overcoat to wear during the night to come. . . . Before long, we were started again, with Peggy Dougherty for driver. He is tall and grizzled. They say that when he goes to dances they make him take the spike out of the bottom of his wooden leg.

There were four horses now—"a wicked little team"—and immediately they kicked over the traces, tried to run away, became tangled like sled dogs twisting in harness, and set Peggy Dougherty to swearing.

Ye gods, how he could swear.

[*Ethel Waxham's first destination was a place called Red Bluff Ranch, owned by a family named Mills, where she would live while she taught school.*]

Miss Waxham's school was a log cabin on Twin Creek near the mouth of Skull Gulch, a mile from the Mills ranch. Students came from much greater distances, even through deep snow. Many mornings, ink was frozen in the inkwells, and the day began with ink-thawing, followed by reading, spelling, chemistry, and civil government. Sometimes snow blew through the walls, forming drifts in the schoolroom. Water was carried from the creek—drawn from a hole that was chopped in the ice. If the creek was frozen to the bottom, the students melted snow. Their school was fourteen by sixteen feet—smaller than a bathroom at Wellesley. The door was perforated with bullet holes from "some passerby's six-shooter." Over the ceiling poles were old gunnysacks and overalls, to prevent the sod roof from shedding sediment on the students. Often, however, the air sparkled with descending dust, struck by sunlight coming in through the windows, which were all in the south wall. There was a table and chair for Miss Waxham, and eight desks for her pupils. Miss Waxham's job was to deliver a hundred per cent of the formal education available in District Eleven, Fremont County, Wyoming.

The first fifteen minutes or half hour are given to reading "Uncle Tom's Cabin" or "Kidnapped," while we all sit about the stove to keep warm. Usually in the middle of a reading the sound of a horse galloping down the frozen road distracts the attention of the boys, until a few moments later six-foot George opens the door, a sack of oats in one hand, his lunch tied up in a dish rag in the other. Cold from his five-mile ride, he sits down on the floor by the stove, unbuckles his spurs, pulls off his leather chaps, drops his hat, unwinds two or three red handkerchiefs from about his neck and ears, takes off one or two coats, according to the temperature, unbuttons his vest and straightens his leather cuffs. At last he is ready for business.

Sandford is the largest scholar, six feet, big, slow in the school room, careful of every move of his big hands and feet. His voice is subdued and full of awe as he calls me "ma'am." Outside while we play chickens he is another person—there is room for his bigness. Next largest of the boys is Otto Schlicting, thin and dark, a strange combination of shrewdness and stupidity. His problems always prove, whether they are right or not! He is a boaster, too, tries to make a big impression. But there is something very attractive about him. I was showing his little sister how to add and subtract by making little lines and adding or crossing off others. Later I found on the back of Otto's papers hundreds and hundreds of little lines—trying to add that way as far as a hundred evidently. He is nearly fifteen and studying division. . . . Arithmetic is the family failing. "How many eights in ninety-six?" I ask him. He thinks for a long time. Finally he says—with such a winsome smile that I wish with all my heart it were true—"Two." "What feeds the cells in your body?" I ask him. He thinks. He says, "I guess it's vinegar." He has no idea of form. His maps of North America on the board are all like turnips.

Students' ages ranged through one and two digits, and their intelligence even more widely. When Miss Waxham called upon Emmons Schlicting, asking, "Where does digestion take place?," Emmons answered, "In the Erie Canal." She developed a special interest in George Ehler, whose life at home was troubled.

He is only thirteen, but taller than Sandford, and fair and handsome. I should like to get him away from his family—kidnap him. To think that it was he who tried to kill his father! His face is good as can be.

At lunchtime, over beans, everyone traded the news of the country, news of whatever might have stirred in seven thousand square miles: a buffalo wolf trapped by Old Hanley; missing horses and cattle, brand by brand; the sheepherder most recently lost in a storm. If you went up Skull Gulch, behind the school, and climbed to the high ground beyond, you could see seventy, eighty, a hundred miles. You "could see the faint outlines of Crowheart Butte, against the Wind River Range." There was a Wyoming-history lesson in the naming of Crowheart Butte, which rises a thousand feet above the surrounding landscape and is capped with flat sandstone. To this day, there are tepee rings on Crowheart Butte. One of the more arresting sights in remote parts of the West are rings of stones that once resisted the wind and now recall what blew away. The Crows liked the hunting country in the area of the butte, and so did the Shoshonis. The two tribes fought, and lost a lot of blood, over this ground. Eventually, the chief of the Shoshonis said, in effect, to the chief of the Crows: this is pointless; I will fight you, one against one; the hunting ground goes to the winner. The chief of the Shoshonis was the great Washakie, whose name rests in six places on the map of Wyoming, including a mountain range and a county. Washakie was at least fifty, but fit. The Crow would have been wise to demur. Washakie destroyed him in the hand-to-hand combat, then cut out his heart and ate it.

Despite her relative disadvantages as a newcomer, an outlander, and an educational ingénue, Miss Waxham was a quick study. Insight was her long suit, and in no time she understood Wyoming. For example, an entry in her journal says of George Ehler's father, "He came to the country with one mare. The first summer, she had six colts! She must have had calves, too, by the way the Ehlers' cattle increased." These remarks were dated October 22, 1905—the day after her stagecoach arrived. In months that followed, she sketched her neighbors (the word applied over many tens of miles). "By the door was Mrs. Frink, about 18, with Frink junior, a large husky baby. Ida Franklin,

Mrs. Frink's sister and almost her double, was beside her, frivolous even in her silence." There was the story of Dirty Bill Collins, who had died as a result of taking a bath. And she fondly recorded Mrs. Mills' description of the libertine Guy Signor: "He has a cabbage heart with a leaf for every girl." She noted that the nearest barber had learned his trade shearing sheep, and a blacksmith doubled as dentist. Old Pelon, a French Canadian, impressed her, because he had refused to ask for money from the government after Indians killed his brother. "Him better dead," said Old Pelon. Old Pelon was fond of the masculine objective pronoun. Miss Waxham wrote, "Pelon used to have a wife, whom he spoke of always as 'him.' " Miss Waxham herself became a character in this tableau. People sometimes called her the White-Haired Kid.

"There's many a person I should be glad to meet," read an early entry in her journal. She wanted to meet Indian Dick, who had been raised by Indians and had no idea who he was—probably the orphan of emigrants the Indians killed. She wanted to meet "the woman called Sour Dough; Three Fingered Bill, or Suffering Jim; Sam Omera, Reub Roe. . . ." (Reub Roe held up wagons and stagecoaches looking for members of the Royal Family.) Meanwhile, there was one flockmaster and itinerant cowboy who seemed more than pleased to meet her.

In the first reference to him in her journal she calls him "Mr. Love—Johnny Love." His place was sixty miles away, and he had a good many sheep and cattle to look after, but somehow he managed to be right there when the new young schoolmarm arrived. In the days, weeks, and months that followed, he showed a pronounced tendency to reappear. He came, generally, in the dead of night, unexpected. Quietly he slipped into the corral, fed and watered his horse, slept in the bunkhouse, and was there at the table for breakfast in the morning—this dark-haired, blue-eyed, handsome man with a woolly Midlothian accent.

Mr. Love is a Scotchman about thirty-five years old. At first sight he made me think of a hired man, as he lounged stiffly on the couch, in overalls, his feet covered with enormous red and black striped stockings that reached to his knees, and were edged with blue around the top. He seemed to wear them instead of house shoes. His face was kindly, with shrewd blue twinkling eyes. A moustache grew over his mouth, like willows bending over a brook. But his voice was most peculiar and characteristic. . . . A little Scotch dialect, a little slow drawl, a little nasal quality, a bit of falsetto once in a while, and a tone as if he were speaking out of doors. There is a kind of twinkle in his voice as well as his eyes, and he is full of quaint turns of speech, and unusual expressions.

Mr. Love travelled eleven hours on these journeys, each way. He did not suffer from the tedium, in part because he frequently rode in a little buggy and, after telling his horses his destination, would lie on the seat and sleep. He may have been from Edinburgh, but he had adapted to the range as much as anyone from anywhere. He had slept out, in one stretch, under no shelter for seven years. On horseback, he was fit for his best horses: he had stamina for long distances at sustained high speed. When he used a gun, he hit what he was shooting at. In 1897, he had begun homesteading on Muskrat Creek, quite near the geographical center of Wyoming, and he had since proved up. One way and another, he had acquired a number of thousands of acres, but acreage was not what mattered most in a country of dry and open range. Water rights mattered most, and the area over which John Love controlled the water amounted to a thousand square miles—about one per cent of Wyoming. He had come into the country walking, in 1891, and now, in 1905, he had many horses, a couple of hundred cattle, and several thousand sheep. Miss Waxham, in her journal, called him a "muttonaire."

He was a mirthful Scot—in abiding contrast to the more prevalent kind. He was a wicked mimic, a connoisseur of the absurd. If he seemed to know everyone in the high country, he knew even better the conditions it imposed. After one of her conversations with him, Miss Waxham wrote in her journal:

It is a cruel country as well as beautiful. Men seem here only on sufferance. After every severe storm we hear of people's being lost. Yesterday it was a sheep camp mover who was lost in the Red Desert.

[*237*]

People had hunted for him for a week, and found no trace. Mr. Love —Johnny Love—told of a man who had just been lost up in his country, around the Muskrat. "Stranger?" asked Mr. Mills. "No; born and brought up here." "Old man?" "No; in the prime of life. Left Lost Cabin sober, too."

Mr. Love had been born near Portage, Wisconsin, on the farm of his uncle the environmentalist John Muir. The baby's mother died that day. His father, a Scottish physician who was also a professional photographer and lecturer on world travel, ended his travels and took his family home. The infant had three older sisters to look after him in Scotland. The doctor died when John was twelve. The sisters emigrated to Broken Bow, Nebraska, where in the eighteen-seventies and eighties they all proved up on homesteads. When John was in his middle teens, he joined them there, in time to experience the Blizzard of '88—a full week of blowing snow, with visibility so short that guide ropes led from house to barn.

He was expelled from the University of Nebraska for erecting a sign in a dean's flower bed, so he went to work as a cowboy, and soon began to think about moving farther west. When he had saved enough money, he bought matching black horses and a buggy, and set out for Wyoming. On his first night there, scarcely over the border, his horses drank from a poison spring and died. What he did next is probably the most encapsulating moment in his story. In Nebraska were three homes he could return to. He left the buggy beside the dead horses, abandoned almost every possession he had in the world, and walked on into Wyoming. He walked about two hundred miles. At Split Rock, on the Oregon Trail—near Crooks Gap, near Independence Rock—he signed on as a cowboy with the 71 Ranch. The year was 1891, and the State of Wyoming was ten months old.

Through the eighteen-nineties, there are various hiatuses in the résumé of John Love, but as cowboy and homesteader he very evidently prospered, and he also formed durable friendships—with Chief Washakie, for example, and with the stagecoach driver Peggy Dougherty, and with Robert LeRoy Parker and Harry Longabaugh (Butch Cassidy and the Sundance Kid). There came a day when Love could not contain his developed curiosity in the presence of the aging chief. He asked him what truth there was in the story of Crowheart Butte. Had Washakie really eaten his enemy's heart? The chief said, "Well, Johnny, when you're young and full of life you do strange things."

Robert LeRoy Parker was an occasional visitor at Love's homestead on Muskrat Creek, which was halfway between Hole-in-the-Wall and the Sweetwater River—that is, between Parker's hideout and his woman. Love's descendants sometimes stare bemusedly at a photograph discovered a few years ago in a cabin in Jackson Hole that had belonged to a member of the Wild Bunch. The photograph, made in the middle eighteen-nineties, shows eighteen men with Parker, who is wearing a dark business suit, a tie and a starchy white collar, a bowler hat. Two of the bunch are identified only by question marks. One of these is a jaunty man of middle height and strong frame, his hat at a rakish angle—a man with a kindly face, twinkling shrewd eyes, and a mustache growing over his mouth like willows bending over a brook. It may be doubtful whether John Love would have joined such a group, but when you are young and full of life you do strange things.

At Red Bluff Ranch, Mrs. Mills once twitted Mr. Love for being Scottish when other Scots were around and American in the presence of Americans. For a split second, Mr. Love thought this over before he said, "That leaves me eligible for the Presidency." Out of Mr. Love's buggy came a constant supply of delicacies and exotic gifts—including candy, nuts, apples—which he came by who knows where and liberally distributed to all. Miss Waxham began to look upon him as "a veritable Santa Claus"; and, predictably, at Christmastime Santa appeared.

And the next day was Christmas. . . . Just before supper the joyful cry went up that Mr. Love was coming, and actually in time for dinner. He had broken his record and arrived by day!

A pitch pine had been set up indoors and its boughs painted with dissolved alum to simulate frost. Hanging from the branches were wooden balls covered with tobacco tinfoil. Flakes of mica were glued to paper stars. On Christmas, Mr. Mills and Mr. Love dressed in linen collars and what Miss Waxham called "fried shirts." When Miss Waxham turned to a package from home that she knew contained pajamas, she went into her bedroom to open it.

The following day, Miss Waxham was meant to go to something called Institute, in Lander—a convocation of Fremont County schoolteachers for lectures, instruction, and professional review. By phenomenal coincidence, Mr. Love announced that he had business in Lander, too.

It was decided that I should go with him. I rather dreaded it. . . . I confess I was somewhat afraid of him. . . . I was wrapped up in a coat of my own with Mrs. Mills' sealskin over it, muffler, fur hat, fur gloves, leggings, and overshoes. Then truly I was so bundled up that it was next to impossible to move. "Absolutely helpless," laughed Mr. Love.

Whatever business Mr. Love had in Lander did not in any way seem to press him. Miss Waxham stayed with Miss Davis, the county superintendent, and while other people came and went from the premises Mr. Love was inclined to remain.

Supper time came and Mr. Love remained. We had a miserable canned goods cold supper. Miss MacBride left, Mr. Love remained.

In the afternoon, Mr. Love called. It certainly was a surprise. I explained why Miss Davis was out, but he didn't seem to mind. I said that she would be back soon. He asked if I should not like to take a drive and see the suburbs. Of course I would. . . . We went for a long drive in the reservation, with a box of chocolates between us, and a merry gossip we had. . . . He was bemoaning the fact that there is no place for a man to spend the evening in Lander except in a saloon. "Come and toast marshmallows," I said, and he took it as a good suggestion.

When she went to church on Sunday, Love was there—John Santa Love, who had not been to church in ten years. After the service, it was time to leave Lander.

There had been snow falling since morning, and the road was barely visible. The light faded to a soft whiteness that hardly grew darker when the sun set and the pale outline of the moon showed through the snow. Everywhere was the soft enveloping snow shutting out all sounds and sights. The horses knew the way and travelled on steadily. Fortunately it was not cold, and the multitudinous rugs and robes with the new footwarmer beneath kept us warm and comfortable. More pleasant it was travelling through the storm than sitting at home by the fire and watching it outside. When the conversation ran low and we travelled on quietly, Mr. Love discovered bags of candy under the robes . . . and he fed us both, for I was worse than entangled in wraps and the long sleeves of Mrs. Mills' sealskin. The miles fell away behind us easily and quietly.

As the winter continued, with its apparently inexhaustible resources of biting wind and blinding snow, temperatures now and again approached fifty below zero. Miss Waxham developed such an advanced case of cabin fever that she wrote in her journal, "My spirit has a chair sore." Even when drifts were at their deepest, though, Mr. Love somehow managed to get through. "Much wrapped up" on one occasion, he rode "all the way from Alkali Butte." On another, he spent an entire day advancing his education at the Twin Creek school.

These attentions went on in much the same way for five years. He pursued her to Colorado, and even to Wisconsin. They were married on the twentieth of June, 1910, and drove in a sheep wagon to his ranch, in the Wind River Basin. It was plain country with gently swelling hills. Looking around from almost any one of them, you could see eighty miles to the Wind River Range, thirty to the Owl Creeks, twenty to the Rattlesnake Hills, fifteen to the Beaver Divide, and a hundred into the Bighorns. No buildings were visible in any direction. In this place, they would flourish. Here, too, they would suffer calamitous loss. Here they would raise three children—a pair of sons close in age, and, a dozen years after them, a daughter. The county from time to time would supply a schoolmarm, but basically the children would be educated by their mother. One would become a petroleum chemist, another a design engineer for the New Jersey Turnpike and the New York State Thruway, another the preeminent geologist of the Rocky Mountains.

In the United States Geological Survey's seven-and-a-half-minute series of topographic maps is a quadrangle named Love Ranch. The landscape it depicts lies just under the forty-third parallel and west of the hundred-and-seventh meridian—coordinates that place it twelve miles from the geographic center of Wyoming. The names of its natural features are names that more or less materialized around the kitchen table when David Love was young: Corral Draw, Castle Gardens, Buffalo Wallows, Jumping-Off Draw. To the fact that he grew up there his vernacular, his outlook, his pragmatic skills, and his professional absorptions about equally attest. The term "store-bought" once brightened his eyes. When one or another of the cowpunchers used a revolver, the man did not so much fire a shot as "slam a bullet." If a ranch hand was tough enough, he would "ride anything with hair on it." Coffee had been brewed properly if it would "float a horseshoe." Blankets were "sougans." A tarpaulin was a "henskin." To be off in the distant ranges was to be "gouging around the mountains." In Love's stories of the ranch, horses come and go by the "cavvy." If they are unowned and untamed, they are a "wild bunch"—led to capture by a rider "riding point." In the flavor of his speech the word "ornery" endures.

He describes his father as a "rough, kindly, strong-willed man" who would put a small son on each knee and—reciting "Ride a cockhorse to Banbury Cross to see a fine lady upon a white horse"—give the children bronco rides after dinner, explaining that his purpose was "to settle their stomachs." Their mother's complaints went straight up the stovepipe and away with the wind. When their father was not reciting such Sassenach doggerel, he could draw Scottish poems out of the air like bolts of silk. He had the right voice, the Midlothian timbre. He knew every syllable of "The Lady of the Lake." Putting his arms around the shoulders of his wee lads, he would roll it to them by the canto, and when they tired of Scott there were in his memory more than enough ballads to sketch the whole of Scotland, from the Caithness headlands to the Lammermuir Hills.

David was fifteen months younger than his brother, Allan. Their sister, Phoebe, was born so many years later that she does not figure in most of these scenes. They were the only children in a thousand square miles, where children outnumbered the indigenous trees. From the ranch buildings, by Muskrat Creek, the Wind River Basin reached out in buffalo grass, grama grass, and edible salt sage across the cambered erosional swells of the vast dry range. When the wind dropped, this whole wide world was silent, and they could hear from a great distance the squeak of a horned lark. The nearest neighbor was thirteen miles away. On the clearest night, they saw no light but their own.

Old buffalo trails followed the creek and branched from the creek: old but not ancient—there were buffalo skulls beside them, and some were attached to hide. The boys used the buffalo trails when they rode off on ranch chores for their father. They rode young and rode long, and often went without water. Even now, six decades later, David will pass up a cool spring, saying, "If I drink now, I'll be thirsty all day."

· · ·

Even in October, a blizzard could cover the house and make a tunnel of the front veranda. As winter progressed, rime grew on the nailheads of interior walls until white spikes projected some inches into the rooms. There were eleven rooms. His mother could tell the outside temperature by the movement of the frost. It climbed the nails about an inch for each degree below zero. Sometimes there was frost on nailheads fifty-five inches up the walls. The house was chinked with slaked lime, wood shavings, and cow manure. In the wild wind, snow came through the slightest crack, and the nickel disks on the dampers of the heat stove were constantly jingling. There came a sound of hooves in cold dry snow, of heavy bodies slamming against the walls, seeking heat. John Love insulated his boots with newspapers—as like as not *The New York Times*. To warm the boys in their beds on cold nights, their mother wrapped heated flatirons in copies of *The New York Times*. The family were subscribers. Sundays only. The *Times*, David Love recalls, was "precious." They used it to insulate the house: pasted it against the walls beside *The Des Moines Register*, *The Tacoma News Tribune*—any paper from anywhere, without fine distinction. With the same indiscriminate voracity, any paper from anywhere was first read and reread by every literate eye in every cow camp and sheep camp within tens of miles, read to shreds and passed along, in tattered circulation on the range. There was, as Love expresses it, "a starvation of print." Almost anybody's first question on encountering a neighbor was "Have you got any newspapers?"

The ranch steadings were more than a dozen buildings facing south, and most of them were secondhand. When a stage route that ran through the ranch was abandoned, in 1905, John Love went down the line shopping for moribund towns. He bought Old Muskrat—including the hotel, the post office, Joe Lacey's Muskrat Saloon—and moved the whole of it eighteen miles. He bought Golden Lake and moved it thirty-three. He arranged the buildings in a rough semicircle that embraced a corral so large and solidly constructed that other ranchers travelled long distances to use it. Joe Lacey's place became the hay house, the hotel became in part a saddlery and cookhouse, and the other buildings, many of them connected, became all or parts of the blacksmith shop, the chicken hatchery, the ice shed, the buggy shed, the sod cellar, and the bunkhouse—social center for all the workingmen from a great many miles around. There was a granary made of gigantic cottonwood logs from the banks of the Wind River, thirty miles away. There were wool-sack towers, and a wooden windmill over a hand-dug well. The big house itself was a widespread log collage of old town parts and original construction. It had wings attached to wings. In the windows were air bubbles in distorted glass. For its twenty tiers of logs, John had journeyed a hundred miles to the lodgepole-pine groves of the Wind River Range, returning with ten logs at a time, each round trip requiring two weeks. He collected a hundred and fifty logs. There were no toilets, of course, and the family had to walk a hundred feet on a sometimes gumbo-slick path to a four-hole structure built by a ranch hand, with decorative panelling that matched the bookcases in the house. The cabinetmaker was Peggy Dougherty, the stagecoach driver who had first brought Miss Waxham through Crooks Gap and into the Wind River country.

The family grew weary of carrying water into the house from the well under the windmill. And so, as she would write in later years:

After experiments using an earth auger and sand point, John triumphantly installed a pitcher pump in the kitchen, a sink, and drain pipe to a barrel, buried in the ground at some distance from the house. This was the best, the first, and at that time the only water system in an area the size of Rhode Island.

In the evenings, kerosene lamps threw subdued yellow light. Framed needlework on a wall said "WASH & BE CLEAN." Everyone bathed in the portable galvanized tub, children last. The more expensive galvanized tubs of that era had built-in seats, but the Loves could not afford the top of the line. On the plank floor were horsehide rugs—a gray, a pinto—and the pelt of a large wolf, and two soft bobcat rugs. Chairs were woven with rawhide or cane.

The family's main sitting and dining room was a restaurant from Old Muskrat. The central piece of furniture was a gambling table from Joe Lacey's Muskrat Saloon. It was a poker-and-roulette table—round, covered with felt. Still intact were the subtle flanges that had caused the roulette wheel to stop just where the operator wished it to. And if you reached in under the table in the right place you could feel the brass slots where the dealer kept wild cards that he could call upon when the fiscal integrity of the house was threatened. If you put your nose down on the felt, you could almost smell the gunsmoke. At this table David Love received his basic education—his schoolroom a restaurant, his desk a gaming table from a saloon. His mother may have been trying to academize the table when she covered it with a red-and-white India print.

From time to time, other schoolmarms were provided by the district. They came for three months in summer. One came for the better part of a year. By and large, though, the boys were taught by their mother. She had a rolltop desk, and Peggy Dougherty's glassed-in bookcases. She had the 1911 Encyclopædia Britannica, the Redpath Library, a hundred volumes of Greek and Roman literature, Shakespeare, Dickens, Emerson, Thoreau, Longfellow, Kipling, Twain. She taught her sons French, Latin, and a bit of Greek. She read to them from books in German, translating as she went along. They read the Iliad and the Odyssey. The room was at the west end of the ranch house and was brightly illuminated by the setting sun. When David as a child saw sunbeams leaping off the books, he thought the contents were escaping.

In some ways, there was more chaos in this remote academic setting than there could ever be in a grade school in the heart of a city.

The house might be full of men, waiting out a storm, or riding on a round-up. I was baking, canning, washing clothes, making soap. Allan and David stood by the gasoline washing machine reading history or geography while I put sheets through the wringer. I ironed. They did spelling beside the ironing board, or while I kneaded bread; they gave the tables up to 15 times 15 to the treadle of the sewing machine. Mental problems, printed in figures on large cards, they solved while they raced across the . . . room to write the answers . . . and learned to think on their feet. Nine written problems done correctly, without help, meant no tenth problem. . . . It was surprising in how little time they finished their work—to watch the butchering, to help drive the bawling calves into the weaning pen, or to get to the corral, when they heard the hoofbeats of running horses and the cries of cowboys crossing the creek.

[*246*]

No amount of intellectual curiosity or academic discipline was ever going to hold a boy's attention if someone came in saying that the milk cow was mired in a bog hole or that old George was out by the wild-horse corral with the biggest coyote ever killed in the region, or if the door opened and, as David recalls an all too typical event, "they were carrying in a cowboy with guts ripped out by a saddle horn." The lessons stopped, the treadle stopped, and she sewed up the cowboy.

Across a short span of time, she had come a long way with these bunkhouse buckaroos. In her early years on the ranch, she had a lesser sense of fitting in than she would have had had she been a mare, a cow, or a ewe. She did not see another woman for as much as six months at a stretch, and if she happened to approach a group of working ranch hands they would loudly call out, "Church time!" She found "the sudden silence . . . appalling." Women were so rare in the country that when she lost a glove on the open range, at least twenty miles from home, a stranger who found it learned easily whose it must be and rode to the ranch to return it. Men did the housekeeping and the cooking, and went off to buy provisions at distant markets. Meals prepared in the bunkhouse were carried to a sheep wagon, where she and John lived while the big house was being built and otherwise assembled. The Wyoming sheep wagon was the ancestral Winnebago. It had a spring bed and a kitchenette.

After her two sons were born and became old enough to coin phrases, they called her Dainty Dish and sometimes Hooty the Owl. They renamed their food, calling it, for example, dog. They called other entrées caterpillar and coyote. The kitchen stool was Sam. They named a Christmas-tree ornament Hopping John. It had a talent for remaining unbroken. They assured each other that the cotton on the branches would not melt. David decided that he was a camel, but later changed his mind and insisted that he was "Mr. and Mrs. Booth." His mother noted his developing sense of scale when he said to her, "A coyote is the whole world to a flea."

One day, he asked her, "How long does a germ live?"

She answered, "A germ may become a grandfather in twenty minutes."

He said, "That's a long time to a germ, isn't it?"

She also made note that while David was the youngest person on the ranch he was nonetheless the most adroit at spotting arrowheads and chippings.

When David was five or six we began hunting arrowheads and chippings. While the rest of us labored along scanning gulches and anthills, David rushed by chattering and picking up arrowheads right and left. He told me once, "There's a god of chippings that sends us anthills. He lives in the sky and tinkers with the clouds."

When in a sense it was truly church time—when cowboys were badly injured and in need of help—they had long since learned where to go. David vividly remembers a moment in his education which was truncated when a cowboy rode up holding a bleeding hand. He had been roping a wild horse, and one of his fingers had become caught between the lariat and the saddle horn. The finger was still a part of his hand but was hanging by two tendons. His mother boiled water, sterilized a pair of surgical scissors, and scrubbed her hands and arms. With magisterial nonchalance, she "snipped the tendons, dropped the finger into the hot coals of the fire box, sewed a flap of skin over the stump, smiled sweetly, and said: 'Joe, in a month you'll never know the difference.' "

There was a pack of ferocious wolfhounds in the country, kept by another flockmaster for the purpose of killing coyotes. The dogs seemed to relish killing rattlesnakes as well, shaking the life out of them until the festive serpents hung from the hounds' jaws like fettuccine. The ranch hand in charge of them said, "They ain't happy in the spring till they've been bit. They're used to it now, and their heads don't swell up no more." Human beings (on foot) who happened to encounter these dogs might have preferred to encounter the rattlesnakes instead. One summer afternoon, John Love was working on a woodpile when he saw two of the wolfhounds streaking down the creek in the direction of his sons, whose ages were maybe three and four. "Laddies! Run! Run to the house!" he shouted. "Here come the hounds!" The boys ran, reached the door just ahead of the dogs, and slammed it in their faces. Their mother was in the kitchen:

The hounds, not to be thwarted so easily, leaped together furiously at the kitchen windows, high above the ground. They shattered the glass of the small panes, and tried to struggle through, their front feet catching over the inside ledge of the window frame, and their heads, with slavering mouths, reaching through the broken glass. I had only time to snatch a heavy iron frying pan from the stove and face them, beating at those clutching feet and snarling heads. The terrified boys cowered behind me. The window sashes held against the onslaught of the hounds, and my blows must have daunted them. They dropped back to the ground and raced away.

The milieu of Love Ranch was not all wind, snow, freezing cattle, and killer dogs. There were quiet, lyrical days on end under blue, unthreatening skies. There were the redwing black-birds on the corral fence, and the scent of moss flowers in spring. In a light breeze, the windmill turned slowly beside the wide log house, which was edged with flowers in bloom. Sometimes there were teal on the creek—and goldeneyes, pintails, mallards. When the wild hay was ready for cutting, the harvest lasted a week.

John liked to have me ride with them for the last load. Sometimes I held the reins and called "Whoa, Dan!" while the men pitched up the hay. Then while the wagon swayed slowly back over the uneven road, I lay nestled deeply beside Allan and David in the fragrant hay. The billowy white clouds moving across the wide blue sky were close, so close, it seemed there was nothing else in the universe but clouds and hay.

One fall, their mother went to Riverton, sixty-five miles away, to await the birth of Phoebe. For her sons, eleven and twelve, she left behind a carefully prepared program of study. In the weeks that followed, they were in effect enrolled in a correspondence school run by their mother. They did their French, their spelling, their arithmetic lessons, put them in envelopes, rode fifteen miles to the post office and mailed them to her. She graded the lessons and sent them back—before and after the birth of the baby.

Her hair was the color of my wedding ring. On her cheek the fingers of one hand were outspread like a small, pink starfish.

From time to time, dust would appear on the horizon, behind a figure coming toward the ranch. The boys, in their curiosity, would climb a rooftop to watch and wait as the rider covered the intervening miles. Almost everyone who went through the region stopped at Love Ranch. It had not only the sizable bunkhouse and the most capacious horse corrals in a thousand square miles but also a spring of good water.

Fugitive criminals stopped at the ranch fairly often. They had to—in much the way that fugitive criminals in lonely country today will sooner or later have to stop at a filling station. A lone rider arrived at the ranch one day with a big cloud of dust on the horizon behind him. The dust might as well have formed in the air the letters of the word "posse." John Love knew the rider, knew that he was wanted for murder, and knew that throughout the country the consensus was that the victim had "needed killing." The murderer asked John Love to give him five dollars, and said he would leave his pocket watch as collateral. If his offer was refused, the man said, he would find a way to take the money. The watch was as honest as the day is long. When David does his field geology, he has it in his pocket.

People like that came along with such frequency that David's mother eventually assembled a chronicle called "Murderers I Have Known." She did not publish the manuscript, or even give it much private circulation, in her regard for the sensitivities of some of the first families of Wyoming. As David would one day comment, "they were nice men, family friends, who had put away people who needed killing, and she did not wish to offend them—so many of them were such decent people."

One of these was Bill Grace. Homesteader and cowboy, he was one of the most celebrated murderers in central Wyoming, and he had served time, but people generally disagreed with the judiciary and felt that Bill, in the acts for which he was convicted, had only been "doing his civic duty." At the height of his fame, he stopped at the ranch one afternoon and stayed for dinner. Although David and Allan were young boys, they knew exactly who he was, and in his presence were struck dumb with awe. As it happened, they had come upon and dispatched a rattlesnake that day—a big one, over five feet long. Their mother decided to serve it creamed on toast for dinner. She and their father sternly instructed David and Allan not to use the word "rattlesnake" at the table. They were to refer to it as chicken, since a possibility existed that Bill Grace might not be an eater of adequate sophistication to enjoy the truth. The excitement was too much for the boys. Despite the parental injunction, gradually their conversation at the table fished its way toward the snake. Casually —while the meal was going down—the boys raised the subject of poisonous vipers, gave their estimates of the contents of local dens, told stories of snake encounters, and so forth. Finally, one of them remarked on how very good rattlers were to eat.

Bill Grace said, "By God, if anybody ever gave me rattlesnake meat I'd kill them."

The boys went into a state of catatonic paralysis. In the pure silence, their mother said, "More chicken, Bill?"

"Don't mind if I do," said Bill Grace.

Some years earlier, in the winter of 1912, winds with velocities up to a hundred miles an hour caused sheep to seek haven in dry gulches, where snows soon buried them as if in avalanche. Going without sleep for forty and fifty hours, John Love and his ranch hands struggled to rescue them. They dug some out, but many thousands died. Even on the milder days, when the temperature came up near zero, sheep could not penetrate the wind-crusted drifts and get at the grass below. The crust cut into their legs. Their tracks were reddened with blood. Cattle, lacking the brains even to imagine buried grass, ate their own value in cottonseed cake. John Love had to borrow from his bankers in Lander to pay his ranch hands and buy supplies.

That spring, a flood such as no one remembered all but destroyed the ranch.

Almost immediately, the bankers arrived from Lander. They stayed for several amiable days, looked over the herd tallies, counted surviving animals, checked John Love's accounts. Then, at dinner one evening, the bank's vice-president rubbed his hands together and said to his valued customer, his trusted borrower, his first-name-basis longtime friend, "Mr. Love, we need more collateral." The banker also said that while John Love was a reliable debtor, other ranchers were not, and others' losses were even greater than Love's. The bank, to protect its depositors, had to use Love Ranch to cover itself generally. "We are obliged to cash in on your sheep," the man went on. "We will let you keep your cattle—on one condition." The condition was a mortgage on the ranch. They were asking for an interest in the land of a homesteader who had proved up.

John Love shouted, "I'll have that land when your bones are rotting in the grave!" And he asked the man to step outside, where he could curse him. To the banker's credit, he got up and went out to be cursed. Buyers came over the hill as if on cue. All surviving sheep were taken, all surviving cattle, all horses—even dogs. The sheep wagons went, and a large amount of equipment and supplies. John Love paid the men in the bunkhouse, and they left. As his wife watched the finish of this scene, standing silent with Allan in her arms, the banker turned to her kindly and said, "What will you do with the baby?"

She said, "I think I'll keep him."

It was into this situation that John David Love was born—a family that had lost almost everything but itself, yet was not about to lose that. Slowly, his father assembled more modest cavvies and herds, beginning with the capture of wild horses in flat-out all-day rides, maneuvering them in ever tighter circles until they were beguiled into entering the wild-horse corral or—a few miles away—the natural cul-de-sac (a small box canyon) known to the family as the Corral Draw. Watching one day from the granary roof, the boys—four and five—in one moment saw their father on horseback crossing the terrain like the shadow of a cloud and in the next saw his body smash the ground. The horse had stepped in a badger hole. The rider—limp and full of greasewood punctures, covered with blood and grit—was unconscious and appeared to be dead. He was carried into the house. After some hours, he began to stir, and through his pain mumbled, "That damned horse. That damned horse—I never did trust him." It was the only time in their lives that his sons would hear him swear.

There were periods of drought, and more floods, and long, killing winters, but John Love never sold out. He contracted and survived Rocky Mountain spotted fever. One year, after he shipped cattle to Omaha he got back a bill for twenty-seven dollars, the amount by which the cost of shipment exceeded the sale price of the cattle. One spring, after a winter that killed many sheep, the boys and their father plucked good wool off the bloated and stinking corpses, sold the wool, and deposited the money in a bank in Shoshoni, where the words "STRENGTH," "SAFETY," and "SECURITY" made an arc above the door. The bank failed, and they lost the money. Of many bad winters, the worst began in 1919. Both David and his father nearly died of Spanish influenza, and were slow to recuperate, spending months in bed. There were no ranch hands. At the point when the patients seemed most in danger, his mother in her desperation decided to try to have them moved to a hospital (a hundred miles away), and prepared to ride for help. She had the Hobson's choice of a large, rebellious horse. She stood on a bench and tried to harness him. He kicked the bench from under her, and stepped on her feet. She gave up her plan.

The bull broke into the high granary. Our only, and small, supply of horse and chicken feed was there. Foolishly, I went in after him and drove him out down the step. Cows began to die, one here, one there.

Every morning some were unable to rise. By day, one walking would fall suddenly, as if it had no more life than a paper animal, blown over by a gust of wind.

The bull actually charged her in the granary and came close to crushing her against the back wall. She confused it, sweeping its eyes with a broom. It would probably have killed her, though, had it not stepped on a weak plank, which snapped. The animal panicked and turned for the door. (In decades to follow, John Love never fixed the plank.)

Snow hissed around the buildings, wind blew some snow into every room of the closed house, down the chimney, between window sashes, even in a straight shaft through a keyhole. The wood pile was buried in snow. The small heap of coal was frozen into an almost solid chunk of coal and ice. In the numbing cold, it took me five hours a day to bring in fuel, to carry water and feed to the chickens, to put out hay and cottonseed cake for the cattle and horses.

John began to complain, a favorable sign. Why was I outside so much? Why didn't I stay with him? To try to make up to him for being gone so long, I sat on the bed at night, wrapped in a blanket, reading to him by lamplight.

Somewhere among her possessions was a letter written to her by a Wellesley friend asking, "What do you do with your spare time?"

F R O M

THE CONTROL

OF NATURE

(1 9 8 9)

[*Three situations in which human beings, impelled by economic forces, are or have been engaged in flat-out battles with nature: a fight against flowing lava in Iceland; the fight against disintegrating mountains whose rock debris flows with destructive violence into neighborhoods of greater Los Angeles; a continuing war with the Mississippi River to keep it from making a natural and overdue move away from New Orleans and Baton Rouge and down a much shorter path to the sea. The selection here is from the part called "Los Angeles Against the Mountains."*]

F R O M

Los Angeles Against
the Mountains

In Los Angeles versus the San Gabriel Mountains, it is not always clear which side is losing. For example, the Genofiles, Bob and Jackie, can claim to have lost and won. They live on an acre of ground so high that they look across their pool and past the trunks of big pines at an aerial view over Glendale and across Los Angeles to the Pacific bays. The setting, in cool dry air, is serene and Mediterranean. It has not been everlastingly serene.

On a February night some years ago, the Genofiles were awakened by a crash of thunder—lightning striking the mountain front. Ordinarily, in their quiet neighborhood, only the creek beside them was likely to make much sound, dropping steeply out of Shields Canyon on its way to the Los Angeles River. The creek, like every component of all the river systems across the city from mountains to ocean, had not been left to nature. Its banks were concrete. Its bed was concrete. When boulders were running there, they sounded like a rolling freight. On a night like this, the boulders should have been running. The creek should have been a torrent. Its unnatural sound was unnaturally absent. There was, and had been, a lot of rain.

The Genofiles had two teen-age children, whose rooms were

on the uphill side of the one-story house. The window in Scott's room looked straight up Pine Cone Road, a cul-de-sac, which, with hundreds like it, defined the northern limit of the city, the confrontation of the urban and the wild. Los Angeles is over-matched on one side by the Pacific Ocean and on the other by very high mountains. With respect to these principal boundaries, Los Angeles is done sprawling. The San Gabriels, in their state of tectonic youth, are rising as rapidly as any range on earth. Their loose inimical slopes flout the tolerance of the angle of repose. Rising straight up out of the megalopolis, they stand ten thousand feet above the nearby sea, and they are not kidding with this city. Shedding, spalling, self-destructing, they are disinte-grating at a rate that is also among the fastest in the world. The phalanxed communities of Los Angeles have pushed themselves hard against these mountains, an aggression that requires a deep defense budget to contend with the results. Kimberlee Genofile called to her mother, who joined her in Scott's room as they looked up the street. From its high turnaround, Pine Cone Road plunges downhill like a ski run, bending left and then right and then left and then right in steep christiania turns for half a mile above a three-hundred-foot straightaway that aims directly at the Genofiles' house. Not far below the turnaround, Shields Creek passes under the street, and there a kink in its concrete profile had been plugged by a six-foot boulder. Hence the silence of the creek. The water was now spreading over the street. It descended in heavy sheets. As the young Genofiles and their mother glimpsed it in the all but total darkness, the scene was suddenly illuminated by a blue electrical flash. In the blue light they saw a massive blackness, moving. It was not a landslide, not a mud-slide, not a rock avalanche; nor by any means was it the front of a conventional flood. In Jackie's words, "It was just one big black thing coming at us, rolling, rolling with a lot of water in front of it, pushing the water, this big black thing. It was just one big black hill coming toward us."

In geology, it would be known as a debris flow. Debris flows amass in stream valleys and more or less resemble fresh concrete.

They consist of water mixed with a good deal of solid material, most of which is above sand size. Some of it is Chevrolet size. Boulders bigger than cars ride long distances in debris flows. Boulders grouped like fish eggs pour downhill in debris flows. The dark material coming toward the Genofiles was not only full of boulders; it was so full of automobiles it was like bread dough mixed with raisins. On its way down Pine Cone Road, it plucked up cars from driveways and the street. When it crashed into the Genofiles' house, the shattering of safety glass made terrific explosive sounds. A door burst open. Mud and boulders poured into the hall. We're going to go, Jackie thought. Oh, my God, what a hell of a way for the four of us to die together.

The parents' bedroom was on the far side of the house. Bob Genofile was in there kicking through white satin draperies at the panelled glass, smashing it to provide an outlet for water, when the three others ran in to join him. The walls of the house neither moved nor shook. As a general contractor, Bob had built dams, department stores, hospitals, six schools, seven churches, and this house. It was made of concrete block with steel reinforcement, sixteen inches on center. His wife had said it was stronger than any dam in California. His crew had called it "the fort." In those days, twenty years before, the Genofiles' acre was close by the edge of the mountain brush, but a developer had come along since then and knocked down thousands of trees and put Pine Cone Road up the slope. Now Bob Genofile was thinking, I hope the roof holds. I hope the roof is strong enough to hold. Debris was flowing over it. He told Scott to shut the bedroom door. No sooner was the door closed than it was battered down and fell into the room. Mud, rock, water poured in. It pushed everybody against the far wall. "Jump on the bed," Bob said. The bed began to rise. Kneeling on it—on a gold velvet spread—they could soon press their palms against the ceiling. The bed also moved toward the glass wall. The two teen-agers got off, to try to control the motion, and were pinned between the bed's brass railing and the wall. Boulders went up against the railing, pressed it into their legs, and held them fast. Bob dived into the muck to try to move the boulders, but he failed. The debris flow, entering through windows as well as doors, continued to rise. Escape was still possible for the parents but not for the children. The parents looked at each other and did not stir. Each reached for and held one of the children. Their mother felt suddenly resigned, sure that her son and daughter would die and she and her husband would quickly follow. The house became buried to the eaves. Boulders sat on the roof. Thirteen automobiles were packed around the building, including five in the pool. A din of rocks kept banging against them. The stuck horn of a buried car was blaring. The family in the darkness in their fixed tableau watched one another by the light of a directional signal, endlessly blinking. The house had filled up in six minutes, and the mud stopped rising near the children's chins.

Stories like that do not always have such happy endings. A man went outside to pick up his newspaper one morning, heard a sound, turned, and died of a heart attack as he saw his house crushed to pieces with his wife and two children inside. People have been buried alive in their beds. But such cases are infrequent. Debris flows generally are much less destructive of life than of property. People get out of the way.

If they try to escape by automobile, they have made an obvious but imperfect choice. Norman Reid backed his Pontiac into the street one January morning and was caught from behind by rock porridge. It embedded the car to the chrome strips. Fifty years of archival news photographs show cars of every vintage standing like hippos in chunky muck. The upper halves of their headlights peep above the surface. The late Roland Case Ross, an emeritus professor at California State University, told me of a day in the early thirties when he watched a couple rushing to escape by car. She got in first. While her husband was going around to get in his side, she got out and ran into the house for more silverware. When the car at last putt-putted downhill, a wall of debris was nudging the bumper. The debris stayed on the vehicle's heels all the way to Foothill Boulevard, where the car turned left.

Foothill Boulevard was U.S. Route 66—the western end of the rainbow. Through Glendora, Azusa, Pasadena, it paralleled the mountain front. It strung the metropolitan border towns. And it brought in emigrants to fill them up. The real-estate line of maximum advance now averages more than a mile above Foothill, but Foothill receives its share of rocks. A debris flow that passed through the Monrovia Nursery went on to Foothill and beyond. With its twenty million plants in twelve hundred varieties, Monrovia was the foremost container nursery in the world, and in its recovery has remained so. The debris flow went through the place picking up pots and cans. It got into a greenhouse two hundred feet long and smashed out the southern wall, taking bougainvillea and hibiscus with it. Arby's, below Foothill, blamed the nursery for damages, citing the hibiscus that had come with the rocks. Arby's sought compensation, but no one was buying beef that thin.

In the same storm, large tree trunks rode in the debris like javelins and broke through the sides of houses. Automobiles went in through picture windows. A debris flow hit the gym at Azusa Pacific College and knocked a large hole in the upslope wall. In the words of Cliff Hamlow, the basketball coach, "If we'd had students in there, it would have killed them. Someone said it sounded like the roar of a jet engine. It filled the gym up with mud, and with boulders two and three feet in diameter. It went out through the south doors and spread all over the football field and track. Chain-link fencing was sheared off—like it had been cut with a welder. The place looked like a war zone." Azusa Pacific College wins national championships in track, but Coach Hamlow's basketball team (12–18) can't get the boulders out of its game.

When a debris flow went through the Verdugo Hills Cemetery, which is up a couple of switchbacks on the mountain front, two of the central figures there, resting under impressive stones, were "Hiram F. Hatch, 1st Lieut. 6th Mich. Inf., December 24, 1843–October 12, 1922," and "Henry J. Hatch, Brigadier General, United States Army, April 28, 1869–December 31, 1931." The two Hatches held the hill while many of their comrades slid below. In all, thirty-five coffins came out of the cemetery and took off for lower ground. They went down Hillrose Street and were scattered over half a mile. One came to rest in the parking lot of a supermarket. Many were reburied by debris and, in various people's yards, were not immediately found. Three turned up in one yard. Don Sulots, who had moved into the fallout path two months before, said, "It sounded like thunder. By the time I made it to the front door and got it open, the muck was already three feet high. It's quite a way to start off life in a new home—mud, rocks, and bodies all around."

Most people along the mountain front are about as mindful of debris flows as those corpses were. Here today, gone tomorrow. Those who worry build barricades. They build things called deflection walls—a practice that raises legal antennae and, when the caroming debris breaks into the home of a neighbor, probes the wisdom of Robert Frost. At least one family has experienced so many debris flows coming through their back yard that they long ago installed overhead doors in the rear end of their built-in garage. To guide the flows, they put deflection walls in their back yard. Now when the boulders come they open both ends of their garage, and the debris goes through to the street.

Between Harrow Canyon and Englewild Canyon, a private street called Glencoe Heights teased the mountain front. Came a time of unprecedented rain, and the neighborhood grew ever more fearful—became in fact so infused with catastrophic anticipation that it sought the drastic sort of action that only a bulldozer could provide. A fire had swept the mountainsides, leaving them vulnerable, dark, and bare. Expecting floods of mud and rock, people had piled sandbags and built heavy wooden walls. Their anxiety was continuous for many months. "This threat is on your mind all the time," Gary Lukehart said. "Every time you leave the house, you stop and put up another sandbag, and you just hope everything will be all right when you get back." Lukehart was accustomed to losing in Los Angeles. In the 1957 Rose Bowl, he was Oregon State's quarterback. A private street could not call upon city or county for the use of heavy equipment, so in the dead of night, as steady rain was falling, a call was put in to John McCafferty—bulldozer for hire. McCafferty had a closeup knowledge of the dynamics of debris flows: he had worked the mountain front from San Dimas to Sierra Madre, which to him is Sarah Modri. ("In those canyons at night, you could hear them big boulders comin'. They sounded like thunder.") He arrived at Glencoe Heights within the hour and set about turning the middle of the street into the Grand Canal of Venice. His Cat was actually not a simple dozer but a 955 loader on tracks, with a two-and-a-quarter-yard bucket seven feet wide. Cutting water mains, gas mains, and sewers, he made a ditch that eventually extended five hundred feet and was deep enough to take in three thousand tons of debris. After working for five hours, he happened to be by John Caufield's place ("It had quit rainin', it looked like the worst was over") when Caufield came out and said, "Mac, you sure have saved my bacon."

McCafferty continues, "All of a sudden, we looked up at the mountains—it's not too far from his house to the mountains, maybe a hundred and fifty feet—and we could just see it all comin'. It seemed the whole mountain had come loose. It flowed like cement." In the ditch, he put the Cat in reverse and backed away from the oncoming debris. He backed three hundred feet. He went up one side of the ditch and was about halfway out of it when the mud and boulders caught the Cat and covered it over the hood. In the cab, the mud pushed against McCafferty's legs. At the same time, debris broke into Caufield's house through the front door and the dining-room window, and in five minutes filled it to the eaves.

Other houses were destroyed as well. A garage left the neighborhood with a car in it. One house was buried twice. (After McCafferty dug it out, it was covered again.) His ditch, however, was effective, and saved many places on slightly higher ground, among them Gary Lukehart's and the home of John Marcellino, the chief executive officer of Mackinac Island Fudge. McCafferty was promised a lifetime supply of fudge. He was on the scene for several days, and in one span worked twenty-four hours without a break. The people of the street brought him chocolate milk-shakes. He had left his lowbed parked around the corner. When at last he returned to it and prepared to go home, he discovered that a cop had given him a ticket.

A metropolis that exists in a semidesert, imports water three hundred miles, has inveterate flash floods, is at the grinding edges of two tectonic plates, and has a microclimate tenacious of noxious oxides will have its priorities among the aspects of its environment that it attempts to control. For example, Los Angeles makes money catching water. In a few days in 1983, it caught twenty-eight million dollars' worth of water. In one period of twenty-four hours, however, the ocean hit the city with twenty-foot waves, a tornado made its own freeway, debris flows poured from the San Gabriel front, and an earthquake shook the region. Nature's invoice was forty million dollars. Later, twenty million more was spent dealing with the mountain debris.

There were those who would be quick—and correct—in saying that were it not for the alert unflinching manner and imaginative strategies by which Los Angeles outwits the mountains, nature's invoices at such times would run into the billions. The rear-guard defenses are spread throughout the city and include more than two thousand miles of underground conduits and concrete-lined open stream channels—a web of engineering that does not so much reinforce as replace the natural river systems. The front line of battle is where the people meet the mountains—up the steep slopes where the subdivisions stop and the brush begins.

Strung out along the San Gabriel front are at least a hundred and twenty bowl-shaped excavations that resemble football stadiums and are often as large. Years ago, when a big storm left back yards and boulevards five feet deep in scree, one neighborhood came through amazingly unscathed, because it happened to surround a gravel pit that had filled up instead. A tungsten filament went on somewhere above Los Angeles. The county began digging pits to catch debris. They were quarries, in a sense, but exceedingly bizarre quarries, in that the rock was meant to come to them. They are known as debris basins. Blocked at their downstream ends with earthfill or concrete constructions, they are also known as debris dams. With clean spillways and empty reservoirs, they stand ready to capture rivers of boulders—these deep dry craters, lying close above the properties they protect. In the overflowing abundance of urban nomenclature, the individual names of such basins are obscure, until a day when they appear in a headline in the Los Angeles *Times*: Harrow, Englewild, Zachau, Dunsmuir, Shields, Big Dalton, Hog, Hook East, Hook West, Limekiln, Starfall, Sawpit, Santa Anita. For fifty miles, they mark the wild boundary like bulbs beside a mirror. Behind chain links, their idle ovate forms more than suggest defense. They are separated, on the average, by seven hundred yards. In aggregate, they are worth hundreds of millions of dollars. All this to keep the mountains from falling on Johnny Carson.

The principal agency that developed the debris basins was the hopefully named Los Angeles County Flood Control District, known familiarly through the region as Flood Control, and even more intimately as Flood. ("When I was at Flood, one of our dams filled with debris overnight," a former employee remarked to me. "If any more rain came, we were going to have to evacuate the whole of Pasadena.") There has been a semantic readjustment, obviously intended to acknowledge that when a flood pours out of the mountains it might be half rock. The debris basins are now in the charge of the newly titled Sedimentation Section of the Hydraulic Division of the Los Angeles County Department of Public Works. People still call it Flood. By whatever name the agency is called, its essential tactic remains unaltered. This was summarized for me in a few words by an engineer named Donald Nichols, who pointed out that eight million people live below the mountains on the urban coastal plain, within an area large enough to accommodate Philadelphia, Detroit, Chicago, St. Louis, Boston, and New York. He said, "To make the area inhabitable, you had to put in lined channels on the plain and halt the debris at the front. If you don't take it out at the front, it will come out in the plain, filling up channels. A filled channel won't carry diddly-boo."

To stabilize mountain streambeds and stop descending rocks even before they reach the debris basins, numerous crib structures (barriers made of concrete slats) have been emplaced in high canyons—the idea being to convert plunging streams into boulder staircases, and hypothetically cause erosion to work against itself. Farther into the mountains, a dozen dams of some magnitude were built in the nineteen-twenties and thirties to control floods and conserve water. Because they are in the San Gabriels, they inadvertently trap large volumes of debris. One of them—the San Gabriel Dam, in the San Gabriel River—was actually built as a debris-control structure. Its reservoir, which is regularly cleaned out, contained, just then, twenty million tons of mountain.

The San Gabriel River, the Los Angeles River, and the Big Tujunga (Bigta Hung-ga) are the principal streams that enter the urban plain, where a channel that filled with rock wouldn't carry diddly-boo. Three colossal debris basins—as different in style as in magnitude from those on the mountain front—have been constructed on the plain to greet these rivers. Where the San Gabriel goes past Azusa on its way to Alamitos Bay, the Army Corps of Engineers completed in the late nineteen-forties a dam ninety-two feet high and twenty-four thousand feet wide—this to stop a river that is often dry, and trickles most of the year. Santa Fe Dam, as it is called, gives up at a glance its own story, for it is made of boulders that are shaped like potatoes and are generally the size of watermelons. They imply a large volume of water flowing with high energy. They are stream-propelled, stream-rounded boulders, and the San Gabriel is the stream. In Santa Fe Basin, behind the dam, the dry bed of the San Gabriel is half a mile wide. The boulder-strewn basin in its entirety is four times as wide as that. It occupies eighteen hundred acres in all, nearly three square miles, of what would be prime real estate were it not for the recurrent arrival of rocks. The scene could have been radioed home from Mars, whose cobbly face is in part the result of debris flows dating to a time when Mars had surface water.

The equally vast Sepulveda Basin is where Los Angeles receives and restrains the Los Angeles River. In Sepulveda Basin are three golf courses, which lend ample support to the widespread notion that everything in Los Angeles is disposable. Advancing this national prejudice even further, debris flows, mudslides, and related phenomena have "provided literary minds with a ready-made metaphor of the alleged moral decay of Los Angeles." The words belong to Reyner Banham, late professor of the history of architecture at University College, London, whose passionate love of Los Angeles left him without visible peers. The decay was only "alleged," he said. Of such nonsense he was having none. With his "Los Angeles: The Architecture of Four Ecologies," Banham had become to this deprecated, defamed, traduced, and disparaged metropolis what Pericles was to Athens. Banham knew why the basins were there and what the people were defending. While all those neurasthenic literary minds are cowering somewhere in ethical crawl space, the quality of Los Angeles life rises up the mountain front. There is air there. Cool is the evening under the crumbling peaks. Cool descending air. Clean air. Air with a view. "The financial and topographical contours correspond almost exactly," Banham said. Among those "narrow, tortuous residential roads serving precipitous house-plots that often back up directly on unimproved wilderness" is "the fat life of the delectable mountains."

People of Gardena, Inglewood, and Watts no less than Azusa and Altadena pay for the defense of the mountain front, the rationale being that debris trapped near its source will not move down and choke the channels of the inner city, causing urban floods. The political City of Los Angeles—in its vague and tentacular configuration—actually abuts the San Gabriels for twenty miles or so, in much the way that it extends to touch the ocean in widely separated places like Venice, San Pedro, and Pacific Palisades. Los Angeles County reaches across the mountains and far into the Mojave Desert. The words "Los Angeles" as generally used here refer neither to the political city nor to the county but to the multinamed urban integrity that has a street in it seventy miles long (Sepulveda Boulevard) and, from the Pacific Ocean at least to Pomona, moves north against the mountains as a comprehensive town.

The debris basins vary greatly in size—not, of course, in relation to the populations they defend but in relation to the watersheds and washes above them in the mountains. For the most part, they are associated with small catchments, and the excavated basins are commensurately modest, with capacities under a hundred thousand cubic yards. In a typical empty reservoir—whatever its over-all dimensions may be—stands a columnar tower that resembles a campanile. Full of holes, it is known as a perforated riser. As the basin fills with a thick-flowing slurry of water, mud, and rock, the water goes into the tower and is drawn off below. The county calls this water harvesting.

Like the freeways, the debris-control system ordinarily functions but occasionally jams. When the Genofiles' swimming pool filled with cars, debris flows descended into other neighborhoods along that part of the front. One hit a culvert, plugged the culvert, crossed a road in a bouldery wave, flattened fences, filled a debris basin, went over the spillway, and spread among houses lying below, shoving them off their foundations. The debris basins have caught as much as six hundred thousand cubic yards in one storm. Over time, they have trapped some twenty million tons of mud and rock. Inevitably, sometimes something gets away.

At Devils Gate—just above the Rose Bowl, in Pasadena—a dam was built in 1920 with control of water its only objective. Yet its reservoir, with a surface of more than a hundred acres, has filled to the brim with four million tons of rock, gravel, and sand. A private operator has set up a sand-and-gravel quarry in the reservoir. Almost exactly, he takes out what the mountains put in. As one engineer has described it, "he pays Flood, and Flood makes out like a champ."

It was assumed that the Genofiles were dead. Firemen and paramedics who came into the neighborhood took one glance at the engulfed house and went elsewhere in search of people needing help. As the family remained trapped, perhaps an hour went by. They have no idea.

"We didn't know why it had come or how long it was going to last."

They lost all sense of time. The stuck horn went on blaring, the directional signal eerily blinking. They imagined that more debris was on the way.

"We didn't know if the whole mountain was coming down."

As they waited in the all but total darkness, Jackie thought of neighbors' children. "I thought, Oh, my gosh, all those little kids are dead. Actually, they were O.K. And the neighbors thought for sure we were all gone. All our neighbors thought we were gone."

At length, a neighbor approached their house and called out, "Are you alive?"

"Yes. But we need help."

As the debris flow hit the Genofiles' house, it also hit a six-ton truck from the L.A.C.F.C.D., the vigilant bureau called Flood. Vigilance was about all that the L.A.C.F.C.D. had been able to offer. The patrolling vehicle and its crew of two were as helpless as everyone else. Each of the crewmen had lived twenty-six years, and each came close to ending it there. Minutes before the flow arrived, the truck labored up Pine Cone Road—a forty-one-per-cent grade, steep enough to stiff a Maserati. The two men meant to check on a debris basin at the top. Known as Upper Shields, it was less than two years old, and had been built in anticipation of the event that was about to occur. Oddly enough, the Genofiles and their neighbors were bracketed with debris basins—Upper Shields above them, Shields itself below them, six times as large. Shields Debris Basin, with its arterial concrete feeder channels, was prepared to catch fifty thousand tons. The Genofiles' house looked out over Shields as if it were an empty lake, its shores hedged about with oleander. When the developer extended Pine Cone Road up into the brush, the need for Upper Shields was apparent. The new basin came in the nick of time but—with a capacity under six thousand cubic yards—not in the nick of space. Just below it was a chain-link gate. As the six-ton truck approached the gate, mud was oozing through. The basin above had filled in minutes, and now, suddenly, boulders shot like cannonballs over the crest of the dam, with mud, cobbles, water, and trees. Chris Terracciano, the driver, radioed to head-quarters, "It's coming over." Then he whipped the truck around and fled. The debris flow came through the chain-link barrier as if the links were made of paper. Steel posts broke off. As the truck accelerated down the steep hill, the debris flow chased and caught it. Boulders bounced against it. It was hit by empty automo-biles spinning and revolving in the muck. The whole descending complex gathered force with distance. Terracciano later said, "I thought I was dead the whole way." The truck finally stopped when it bashed against a tree and a cement-block wall. The rear window shattered. Terracciano's partner suffered a broken leg. The two men crawled out through the window and escaped over the wall.

Within a few miles, other trapped patrols were calling in to say, "It's coming over." Zachau went over—into Sunland. Haines went over—into Tujunga. Dunsmuir went over—into Highway Highlands. As bulldozers plow out the streets after events like these, the neighborhoods of northern Los Angeles assume a macabre resemblance to New England villages under deep snow: the cleared paths, the vehicular rights-of-way, the parking meters buried within the high banks, the half-covered drift-girt homes. A street that is lined with palms will have debris berms ten feet up the palms. In the Genofiles' front yard, the drift was twelve feet deep. A person, without climbing, could walk onto the roof. Scott's bedroom had a few inches of space left at the top. Kim-berlee's had mud on the ceiling. On the terrace, the crushed vehicles, the detached erratic wheels suggested bomb damage, artillery hits, the track of the Fifth Army. The place looked like a destroyed pillbox. No wonder people assumed that no one had survived inside.

There was a white sedan under the house eaves crushed to half its height, with two large boulders resting on top of it. Near the pool, a Volkswagen bug lay squashed. Another car was literally wrapped around a tree, like a C-clamp, its front and rear bumpers pointing in the same direction. A crushed pickup had boulders all over it, each a good deal heavier than anything a pickup could carry. One of the cars in the swimming pool was upside down, its tires in the air. A Volkswagen was on top of it. Bob Genofile—owner, contractor, victim—walked around in rubber boots, a visored construction cap, a foul-weather jacket, studying the damage, mostly guessing at what he couldn't see. A big, strongly built, leonine man with prematurely white hair, he looked like a middle linebacker near the end of a heavy day. He wondered if the house was still on its foundation, but there was no telling in this profound chaos, now hardening and cracking like bad concrete. In time, as his house was excavated from the inside, he would find that it had not budged. Not one wall had so much as cracked. He was uninsured, but down in the rubble was a compensation of greater value than insurance. Forever, he could say, as he quietly does when he tells the story, "I built it, man."

Kimberlee's birthday came two days after the debris. She was a college student, turning nineteen, and her father had had a gift for her that he was keeping in his wallet. "I had nineteen fifty-dollar bills to give her for her birthday, but my pants and everything was gone."

Young Scott, walking around in the wreckage, saw a belt sticking out of the muck like a night crawler after rain. He pulled at it, and the buried pants came with it. The wallet was still in the pants. The wallet still contained what every daughter wants for her birthday: an album of portraits of U.S. Grant, no matter if Ulysses is wet or dry.

The living room had just been decorated, and in six minutes the job had been destroyed—"the pale tangerines and greens, Italian-style furniture with marble, and all that." Jackie Genofile continues the story: "We had been out that night, and, you know, you wear your better jewelry. I came home like an idiot and put mine on the dresser. Bob put his on the dresser. Three weeks later, when some workers were cleaning debris out of the bedroom, they found his rings on the floor. They did not find mine. But—can you believe it?—a year and a half later Scott was down in the debris basin with one of his friends, and the Flood Control had these trucks there cleaning it out, and Scott saw this shiny thing, and he picked it up, and it was my ring that Bob had given me just before the storm."

Before the storm, they had not in any way felt threatened. Like their neighbors, they were confident of the debris basins, of the concrete liners of the nearby stream. After the storm, neighbors moved away. Where Pine Cone Road swung left or right, the debris had made centrifugal leaps, breaking into houses. A hydrant snapped off, and arcing water shot through an upstairs window. A child nearly drowned inside his own house. The family moved. "Another family that moved owned one of the cars that ended up in our pool," Jackie told me. "The husband said he'd never want to live here again, you know. And she was in real estate."

After the storm, the Genofiles tended to wake in the night, startled and anxious. They still do. "I wake up once in a while really uptight," Bob said. "I can just feel it—go through the whole thing, you know."

Jackie said that when rain pounds on a roof, anywhere she happens to be, she will become tense. Once, she took her dog and her pillow and went to sleep in Bob's office—which was then in Montrose, down beyond Foothill Boulevard.

Soon after the storm, she said, "Scotty woke up one night, and he had a real high temperature. You see, he was sixteen, and he kept hearing the mud and rock hitting the window. He kept thinking it was going to come again. Kim used to go four-wheeling, and cross streams, and she had to get out once, because they got stuck, and when she felt the flow of water and sand on her legs, she said, she could have panicked."

Soon after the storm, the family gathered to make a decision. Were they going to move or were they going to dig out their house and rebuild it? Each of them knew what might have happened. Bob said, "If it had been a frame house, we would be dead down in the basin below."

But it was not a frame house. It was the fort. "The kids said rebuild. So we rebuilt."

As he sat in his new living room telling the story, Bob was dressed in a Pierre Cardin jumper and pants, and Jackie was beside him in a pale-pink jumpsuit by Saint Germain. The house had a designer look as well, with its railings and balconies and Italianate marbles under the tall dry trees. It appeared to be worth a good deal more than the half-million dollars Bob said it might bring. He had added a second story and put all bedrooms there. The original roof spreads around them like a flaring skirt. He changed a floor-length window in the front hall, filling the lower half of it with cement block.

I asked what other structural changes he had made.

He said, "None."

The Genofiles sued Los Angeles County. They claimed that Upper Shields Debris Basin had not been cleaned out and that the channel below was improperly designed. Los Angeles settled for three hundred and thirty-seven thousand five hundred dollars.

From the local chamber of commerce the family later received the Beautification Award for Best Home. Two of the criteria by which houses are selected for this honor are "good maintenance" and "a sense of drama."

I have not been specific about the dates of the stories so far recounted. This was to create the impression that debris pours forth from the mountains continually, perennially, perpetually —which it does and does not, there being a great temporal disparity between the pace at which the mountains behave and the way people think. Debris flows do not occur in every possible season. When they do happen, they don't just spew from any canyon but come in certain places on the mountain front. The places change. Volumes differ. There are vintage years. The four most prominent in this century have been 1934, 1938, 1969, and 1978. Exceptional flows have occurred at least once a decade, and lesser ones in greater numbers. Exceptional flows are frequent, in other words, but not frequent enough to deter people from building pantiled mansions in the war zone, dingbats in the line of fire.

Why the debris moves when it does or where it does is not attributable to a single agent. The parent rock has been extensively broken up by earthquakes, but that alone will not make it flow. Heavy rainfall, the obvious factor, is not as obvious as it may seem. In 1980, some of the most intense storms ever measured in Los Angeles failed to produce debris flows of more than minimal size. The setting up of a debris flow is a little like the charging of an eighteenth-century muzzle-loader: the ramrod, the powder, the wadding, the shot. Nothing much would happen in the absence of any one component. In sequence and proportion each had to be correct.

On the geologic time scale, debris flows in the San Gabriel Mountains can be looked upon as constant. With all due respect, though, the geologic time scale doesn't mean a whole lot in a place like Los Angeles. In Los Angeles, even the Los Angeles time scale does not arouse general interest. A superevent in 1934? In 1938? In 1969? In 1978? Who is going to remember that? A relatively major outpouring—somewhere in fifty miles—about once every decade? Mountain time and city time appear to be bifocal. Even with a geology functioning at such remarkably short intervals, the people have ample time to forget it.

In February of 1978, while debris was still hardening in the home of the Genofiles, Wade Wells, of the United States Forest Service, went up and down Pine Cone Road knocking on doors, asking how long the people had lived there. He wondered who remembered, nine years back, the debris-flow inundations of Glendora and Azusa, scarcely twenty miles away. Only two did. Everyone else had arrived since 1969.

Wells is a hydrologist who works in the mountains, principally in San Dimas Experimental Forest, where he does research on erosion and sedimentation—the story of assembling debris. With a specialist's eye, he notes the mountain front, and in its passivity

can see the tension: "These guys here, they should be nervous
when it rains. Their houses are living on borrowed time. See that
dry ledge? It's a waterfall. I've seen hundreds of tons of rock falling
over it." More often, though, he is thousands of feet above the
nearest house, on slopes so steep he sometimes tumbles and rolls.
With his colleagues, he performs experiments with plants, rock,
water, fire. When I first became interested in Los Angeles' battle
with debris flows, I went up there with them a number of times.
The mountains, after all, are where the rocks come from. The
mountains shape the charge that will advance upon the city.
People come from odder places than the East Coast to see this
situation. One day, a couple of scientists arrived from the Cor-
dillera Cantábrica, in northwestern Spain. When they saw how
rapidly the San Gabriels were disintegrating, one of them said he
felt sorry for Wells, who would soon be out of work. When Wells
told him that the mountains were rising even faster than they
were coming down, the man said, *"Muy interesante. Sí, señor."*

From below, one look at the San Gabriels will suggest their
advantage. The look is sometimes hard to come by. You might
be driving up the San Gabriel River Freeway in the morning,
heading straight at the mountains at point-blank range, and not
be able to see them. A voice on KNX tells you that the day is
clear. There's not a cloud in the sky, as the blue straight up
confirms. A long incline rises into mist, not all of which is smog.
From time immemorial, this pocket of the coast has been full of
sea fog and persistent vapors. The early Spaniards called it the
Bay of Smokes. Smog, the action of sunlight on nitrogen oxides,
has only contributed to a preexisting veil. Sometimes you don't
see the San Gabriels until the streets stop and the mountains start.
The veil suddenly thins, and there they are, in height and magnitude overwhelming. You plunge into a canyon flanked with
soaring slopes before you realize you are out of town. The San
Gabriel Mountains are as rugged as any terrain in America, and
their extraordinary proximity to the city, the abruptness of the
transition from the one milieu to the other, cannot be exaggerated.
A lone hiker in the San Gabriels one winter—exhausted, snow-

blinded, hypothermic—staggered down a ridgeline out of the snow and directly into the parking lot of a shopping center, where he crawled to a phone booth, called 911, and slumped against the glass until an ambulance came to save him.

Hang-glider pilots go up the San Gabriels, step off crags, and, after a period of time proportional to their skills, land somewhere in the city. The San Gabriels are nearly twice as high as Mt. Katahdin or Mt. Washington, and are much closer to the sea. From base platform to summit, the San Gabriels are three thousand feet higher than the Rockies. To be up in the San Gabriels is to be both above and beside urban Los Angeles, only minutes from the streets, and to look north from ridge to dry ridge above deeply cut valleys filled with gulfs of clear air. Beyond the interior valleys—some fifty thousand feet away and a vertical mile above you—are the summits of Mt. Baldy, Mt. Hawkins, Mt. Baden-Powell. They are so clearly visible in the dry blue sky that just below their ridgelines you can almost count the boulders that are bunched there like grapes.

If you turn and face south, you look out over something like soft slate that reaches fifty miles to an imprecise horizon. The whole of Los Angeles is spread below you, and none of it is visible. It is lost absolutely in the slate-gray sea, grayer than a minesweeper, this climatic wonder, this megalopolitan featherbed a thousand feet thick, known as "the marine layer." Early in the day, it is for the most part the natural sea fog. As you watch it from above through the morning and into the afternoon, it turns yellow, and then ochre, and then brown, and sometimes nearly black—like butter darkening in a skillet.

Glancing down at it one day while working on an experiment, Wade Wells said it seemed to have reached the hue of a first-stage smog alert. Wells was helping Edwin Harp, a debris-flow specialist from the United States Geological Survey, collect "undisturbed" samples by hammering plastic tubes into the mountain soil.

"If the soil were nice and compliant, this would be nice and scientific," Harp said, smacking the plastic with a wooden-handled shovel. After a while, he extracted a tube full of uncompliant material, and said, "This isn't soil; it's regolith." Regolith is a stony blanket that lies under soil and over bedrock. It crumbled and was pebbly in the hand.

As they prepared to sink another tube, I said, "What's a first-stage smog alert?"

"Avoid driving, avoid strenuous activity," Wells answered.

Harp said, "Avoid breathing."

The slope they were sampling had an incline of eighty-five per cent. They were standing, and walking around, but I preferred —just there—to sit. Needle grass went through my trousers. The heads of needle grass detach from the stalks and have the barbed design of arrows. They were going by the quiver into my butt but I still preferred to sit. It was the better posture for writing notes. The San Gabriels are so steep and so extensively dissected by streams that some watersheds are smaller than a hundred acres. The slopes average sixty-five to seventy per cent. In numerous places, they are vertical. The angle of repose—the steepest angle that loose rocks can abide before they start to move, the steepest angle the soil can maintain before it starts to fail—will vary locally according to the mechanics of shape and strength. Many San Gabriel slopes are at the angle of repose or beyond it. The term "oversteepened" is often used to describe them. At the giddy extreme of oversteepening is the angle of maximum slope. Very large sections of the San Gabriels closely approach that angle. In such terrain, there is not much to hold the loose material except the plants that grow there.

Evergreen oaks were fingering up the creases in the mountainsides, pointing toward the ridgeline forests of big-cone Douglas fir, of knobcone and Coulter pine. The forests had an odd sort of timberline. They went down to it rather than up. Down from the ridges the conifers descended through nine thousand, seven thousand, six thousand feet, stopping roughly at five. The forests abruptly ended—the country below being too dry in summer to sustain tall trees. On down the slopes and all the way to the canyons was a thicket of varied shrubs that changed in character as altitude fell but was everywhere dense enough to stop an army. On its lower levels, it was all green, white, and yellow with buckwheat, burroweed, lotus and sage, deerweed, bindweed, yerba santa. There were wild morning glories, Canterbury bells, tree tobacco, miner's lettuce. The thicket's resistance to trespass, while everywhere formidable, stiffened considerably as it evolved upward. There were intertwining mixtures of manzanita, California lilac, scrub oak, chamise. There was buckthorn. There was mountain mahogany. Generally evergreen, the dark slopes were splashed here and there with dodder, its mustard color deepening to rust. Blossoms of the Spanish bayonet stood up like yellow flames. There were lemonade berries (relatives of poison ivy and poison oak). In canyons, there were alders, big-leaf-maple bushes, pug sycamores, and California bay. Whatever and wherever they were, these plants were prickly, thick, and dry, and a good deal tougher than tundra. Those evergreen oaks fingering up the creases in the mountains were known to the Spaniards as chaparros. Riders who worked in the related landscape wore leather overalls open at the back, and called them chaparajos. By extension, this all but impenetrable brush was known as chaparral.

The low stuff, at the buckwheat level, is often called soft chaparral. Up in the tough chamise, closer to the lofty timber, is high chaparral, which is also called hard chaparral. High or low— hard, soft, or mixed—all chaparral has in common an always developing, relentlessly intensifying, vital necessity to burst into flame. In a sense, chaparral consumes fire no less than fire consumes chaparral. Fire nourishes and rejuvenates the plants. There are seeds that fall into the soil, stay there indefinitely, and will not germinate except in the aftermath of fire. There are basal buds that sprout only after fire. Droughts are so long, rains so brief, that dead bits of wood and leaves scarcely decay. Instead, they accumulate, thicken, until the plant community is all but strangling in its own duff. The nutrients in the dead material are being withheld from the soil. When fire comes, it puts the nutrients back in the ground. It clears the terrain for fresh growth. When chaparral has not been burned for thirty years, about half the thicket will be dry dead stuff—twenty-five thousand tons of it in one square mile. The living plants are no less flammable. The chamise, the manzanita—in fact, most chaparral plants—are full of solvent extractives that burn intensely and ignite easily. Their leaves are glossy with oils and resins that seal in moisture during hot dry periods and serve the dual purpose of responding explosively to flame. In the long dry season, and particularly in the fall, air flows southwest toward Los Angeles from the Colorado Plateau and the Basin and Range. Extremely low in moisture, it comes out of the canyon lands and crosses the Mojave Desert. As it drops in altitude, it compresses, becoming even dryer and hotter. It advances in gusts. This is the wind that is sometimes called the foehn. The fire wind. The devil wind. In Los Angeles, it is known as Santa Ana. When chamise and other chaparral plants sense the presence of Santa Ana winds, their level of moisture drops, and they become even more flammable than they were before. The Santa Anas bring what has been described as "instant critical fire weather." Temperatures rise above a hundred degrees. Humidity drops very close to zero. According to Charles Colver, of the United States Forest Service, "moisture evaporates off your eyeballs so fast you have to keep blinking."

Ignitions are for the most part caused by people—through accident or arson. Ten per cent are lightning. Where the Santa Anas collide with local mountain winds, they become so erratic that they can scatter a fire in big flying brands for a long distance in any direction. The frequency and the intensity of the forest fires in the Southern California chaparral are the greatest in the United States, with the possible exception of the wildfires of the New Jersey Pine Barrens. The chaparral fires are considerably more potent than the forest fires Wade Wells saw when he was an undergraduate at the University of Idaho or when he worked as a firefighter in the Pacific Northwest. "Fires in the Pacific Northwest are nothing compared with these chaparral fires," he remarked. "Chaparral fires are almost vicious by comparison. They're so intense. Chaparral is one of the most flammable vegetation complexes there are."

It burns as if it were soaked with gasoline. Chaparral plants typically have multiple stems emerging from a single root crown, and this contributes not only to the density of the thickets but, ultimately, to the surface area of combustible material that stands prepared for flame. Hundreds of acres can be burned clean in minutes. In thick black smoke there is wild orange flame, rising through the canyons like explosion crowns. The canyons serve as chimneys, and in minutes whole mountains are aflame, resembling volcanoes, emitting high columns of fire and smoke. The smoke can rise twenty thousand feet. A force of two thousand people may fight the fire, plus dozens of machines, including squadrons in the air. But Santa Ana firestorms are so violent that they are really beyond all effort at control. From the edge of the city upward, sixteen miles of mountain front have burned to the ridgeline in a single day.

So momentous are these conflagrations that they are long remembered by name: the Canyon Inn Fire, August, 1968, nineteen thousand acres above Arby's by Foothill Boulevard, above the world's foremost container nursery, above the chief executive officer of Mackinac Island Fudge; the Village Fire and the Mill Fire, November, 1975, sixty-five thousand acres above Sunland, Tujunga, La Crescenta, La Cañada. The Mill Fire, in the words of a foreman at Flood, "burnt the whole front face off."

It is not a great rarity to pick up the *Los Angeles Times* and see a headline like this one, from September 27, 1970:

14 MAJOR FIRES RAGE OUT OF CONTROL
256 HOMES DESTROYED AS
FLAMES BURN 180,000 ACRES

In millennia before Los Angeles settled its plain, the chaparral burned every thirty years or so, as the chaparral does now. The burns of prehistory, in their natural mosaic, were smaller than the ones today. With cleared fire lanes, chemical retardants, and other means of suppressing what is not beyond control, people have conserved fuel in large acreages. When the inevitable fires come, they burn hotter, higher, faster than they ever did in a state of unhindered nature. When the fires end, there is nothing much left on the mountainsides but a thin blanket of ash. The burns are vast and bare. On the sheer declivities where the surface soils were held by chaparral, there is no chaparral.

Fine material tumbles downslope and collects in the waterless beds of streams. It forms large and bulky cones there, to some extent filling the canyons. Under green chaparral, the gravitational movement of bits of soil, particles of sand, and other loose debris goes on month after month, year after year, especially in oversteepened environments, where it can represent more than half of all erosion. After a burn, though, it increases exponentially. It may increase twentyfold, fortyfold, even sixtyfold. This steady tumbling descent of unconsolidated mountain crumbs is known as dry ravel. After a burn, so much dry ravel and other debris becomes piled up and ready to go that to live under one of those canyons is (as many have said) to look up the barrel of a gun.

One would imagine that the first rain would set the whole thing off, but it doesn't. The early-winter rains—and sometimes the rains of a whole season—are not enough to make the great bulk move. Actually, they add to it.

If you walk in a rainstorm on a freshly burned chaparral slope, you notice as you step on the wet ground that the tracks you are making are prints of dry dust. In the course of a conflagration, chaparral soil, which is not much for soaking up water in the first place, experiences a chemical change and, a little below its surface, becomes waterproof. In a Forest Service building at the foot of the mountains Wade Wells keeps some petri dishes and soil samples in order to demonstrate this phenomenon to passing unbelievers. In one dish he puts unburned chaparral soil. It is golden brown. He drips water on it from an eyedropper. The water beads up, stands there for a while, then collapses and spreads into the soil. Why the water hesitates is not well understood but is a great deal more credible than what happens next. Wells fills a dish with a dark soil from burned chaparral. He fills the eyedropper and empties it onto the soil. The water stands up in one large dome. Five minutes later, the dome is still there. Ten minutes later, the dome is still there. Sparkling, tumescent, mycophane, the big bead of water just stands there indefinitely, on top of the impermeable soil. Further demonstrating how waterproof this burned soil really is, Wells pours half a pound of it, like loose brown sugar, into a beaker of water. The soil instantly forms a homuncular blob—integral, immiscible—suspended in the water.

In the slow progression of normal decay, chaparral litter seems to give up to the soil what have been vaguely described as "waxlike complexes of long-chain aliphatic hydrocarbons." These waxy substances are what make unburned chaparral soil somewhat resistant to water, or "slightly nonwettable," as Wells and his colleagues are wont to describe it. When the wildfires burn, and temperatures at the surface of the ground are six or seven hundred centigrade degrees, the soil is so effective as an insulator that the temperature one centimetre below the surface may not be hot enough to boil water. The heavy waxlike substances vaporize at the surface and recondense in the cooler temperatures below. Acting like oil, they coat soil particles and establish the hydrophobic layer—one to six centimetres down. Above that layer, where the waxlike substances are gone, the veneer of burned soil is "wettable." When Wells drips water on a dishful of that, the water soaks in as if the dish were full of Kleenex. When rain falls on burned and denuded ground, it soaks the very thin upper layer but can penetrate no farther. Hiking boots strike hard enough to break through into the dust, but the rain is repelled and goes down the slope. Of all the assembling factors that eventually send debris flows rumbling down the canyons, none is more detonative than the waterproof soil.

In the first rains after a fire, water quickly saturates the thin permeable layer, and liquefied soil drips downhill like runs of excess paint. These miniature debris flows stripe the mountainsides with miniature streambeds—countless scarlike rills that are soon the predominant characteristic of the burned terrain. As more rain comes, each rill is going to deliver a little more debris to the accumulating load in the canyon below. But, more to the point, each rill—its natural levees framing its impermeable bed —will increase the speed of the surface water. As rain sheds off a mountainside like water off a tin roof, the rill network, as it is called, may actually triple the speed, and therefore greatly enhance the power of the runoff. The transport capacity of the watershed—how much bulk it can move—may increase a thousandfold. The rill network is prepared to deliver water with enough force and volume to mobilize the deposits lying in the canyons below. With the appearance of the rills, almost all prerequisites have now sequentially occurred. The muzzle-loader is charged. For a full-scale flat-out debris flow to burst forth from the mountains, the final requirement is a special-intensity storm.

Some of the most concentrated rainfall in the history of the United States has occurred in the San Gabriel Mountains. The oddity of this is about as intense as the rain. Months—seasons —go by in Los Angeles without a fallen drop. Los Angeles is one of the least-rained-upon places in the Western Hemisphere. The mountains are so dry they hum. Erosion by dry ravel greatly exceeds erosion by water. The celebrated Mediterranean climate of Los Angeles owes itself to aridity. While Seattle is receiving its average rainfall of thirty-nine inches a year, Chicago thirty-three, the District of Columbia thirty-nine, and New York City forty-four, Los Angeles is doing well if it gets fifteen. In one year out of every four over the past century, rainfall in Los Angeles has been under ten inches, and once or twice it was around five. That is pure Gobi. When certain storm systems approach Los Angeles, though—storms that come in on a very long reach from far out in the Pacific—they will pick up huge quantities of water from the ocean and just pump it into the mountains. These are by no means annual events, but when they occur they will stir even hydrologists to bandy the name of Noah. In January, 1969, for example, more rain than New York City sees in a year fell in the San Gabriels in nine days. In January, 1943, twenty-six inches fell in twenty-four hours. In February, 1978, just before the

Genofiles' house filled with debris, nearly an inch and a half of rain fell in twenty-five minutes. On April 5, 1926, a rain gauge in the San Gabriels collected one inch in one minute.

The really big events result from two, three, four, five storms in a row coming in off the Pacific. In 1980, there were six storms in nine days. Mystically, unnervingly, the heaviest downpours always occur on the watersheds most recently burned. Why this is so is a question that has not been answered. Meteorologists and hydrologists speculate about ash-particle nuclei and heat reflection, but they don't know. The storm cells are extremely compact, deluging typically about ten miles by ten. One inch of rain on a patch that size is seven million two hundred and thirty-two thousand tons of water. In most years, in most places, a winter rain will actually stabilize a mountainside. The water's surface tension helps to hold the slope together. Where there is antecedent fire, water that would otherwise become a binding force hits the rill network, caroms off the soil's waterproof layer, and rides the steep slopes in cataracts into the nearest canyon. It is now a lubricant, its binding properties repelled, its volume concentrating into great hydraulic power. The vintage years present themselves when at least five days of rain put seven inches on the country and immediately thereafter comes the heaviest rainfall of the series. That is when the flint hits the steel, when the sparks fly into the flashpan. On that day, the debris mobilizes.

Five miles into the mountains from the edge of the city is a small, obscure, steep-sided watershed of twenty-five hundred acres which is drained by the Middle Fork of Mill Creek, a tributary of the Big Tujunga. The place is so still you can hear the dry ravel. From time to time, you hear the dry cough of semi-automatic weapons. It is the sound of city folk pursuing a hobby. Recreational marksmanship is permitted on the Middle Fork. There are eight million people just down the wash, and they shoot some interesting guns. Amos Lewis, who covered the region as a deputy sheriff for twenty-five years, once found beside the Angeles Crest Highway "a gun you could hide behind your tie

—you'd think it was a tie clip." He has also seen enough muzzle-loaders to have made a difference in the Battle of Long Island. In an imaginative, life-loving city, there will always be people with a need to fire antique weapons. On July 24, 1977, a marksman on the Middle Fork rammed Kleenex down his barrel instead of cloth wadding. Under the Kleenex was black powder. In black powder there is more of an incendiary risk than there is in the smokeless kind. When the rifle fired, flaming Kleenex shot out the muzzle and burned down three thousand eight hundred and sixty acres, including the entire watershed of the Middle Fork.

It was a textbook situation—a bowl in the mountains filled with hard chaparral that had not been touched by fire in ninety-nine years. The older chaparral becomes, the hotter it burns. In its first ten years of new growth, it is all but incombustible. After twenty years, its renewed flammability curves sharply upward. It burns, usually, before it is forty years old. The hotter the fire, the more likely a debris flow—and the greater the volume when it comes. The century-old fuel of the Middle Fork was so combustible that afterward there were not even stumps. The slopes looked sandpapered. The streambed, already loaded, piled even higher with dry ravel. The Middle Fire, as the burn was known, was cause for particular alarm, because a small settlement was a mile downstream. Its name—Hidden Springs—contained more prophecy than its residents seemed prepared to imagine. Three hundred and ninety thousand cubic yards of loose debris was gathered just above them, awaiting mobilization.

Dan Davis and Hadi Norouzi, L.A.C.F.C.D. engineers, went up there after the burn to tell the people what they might expect. In midsummer, it is not a simple matter to envision a winter flood if you are leaning on a boulder by a desiccated creek. "We spent a lot of time trying to prevent a disaster from occurring," Davis said recently. "The fact that people would not believe what *could* happen was disappointing, actually. We held meetings. We said, 'There's nothing we can do for you. Telephones are going to go out. Mud will close the road. You're abandoned. If you're here, get to high ground.' " There was no debris basin, of course.

This was a hamlet in the mountains, not a subdivision at the front. Conditions were elemental and pristine. "We walked people through escape routes," he went on. "We told them the story of fire and rain. We said, 'If heavy rain starts, you've got fifteen to thirty minutes to get out.' "

Norouzi told them they were so heavily threatened that no amount of sandbags, barricades, or deflection walls was ever going to help them. "There is nothing you can build that will protect you."

Half a year went by, and nothing stirred. Cal Drake went on making jewelry in his streamside apartment. He and his wife, Mary, shared a one-story triplex with two other couples. The Drakes, from the city, had moved to Hidden Springs two years before, in quest of a "quiet life." Elva Lewis, wife of Amos the sheriff, went on running her roadside café. Gabe Hinterberg stayed open for business at the Hidden Springs Lodge. In December and January, there was an unusual amount of rain, but no flood. By the end of the first week of February, there had been eighteen inches in all. Then, in the next three days, came enough additional rain to make this the winter of the greatest rainfall of the twentieth century, exceeded only by 1884 and 1890 in the records of Los Angeles County. The National Oceanic and Atmospheric Administration selected the word "monstrous" to befit the culminating February storm, in which almost a foot of rain fell in twenty-four hours, and, in the greatest all-out burst, an inch and a half in five minutes. This was the storm that sent the debris down Pine Cone Road, overtopped the Zachau Basin, mobilized the corpses in the Verdugo Hills. In the small valley of the Middle Fork, upon the scorched impenetrable ground, three million tons of water fell in one day.

Toward midnight February 9, an accidental fire broke out in a small building of Gabe Hinterberg's. A fire truck eventually came. Half a dozen people fought the fire, assisted by the heavy rain. One of them was George Scribner. The five-minute spike of greatest downpour occurred at about one-thirty. Half an hour later, George said, "Hey, we got the fire put out."

[*286*]

Gabe said, "Good deal."

And then Gabe and George were dead.

Amos Lewis, nearby, was holding a fire hose in his hand and was attempting to prevent it from kinking. In his concentration, he did not see danger coming. He heard nothing ominous. He only felt the hose draw taut. Through his peripheral vision he became aware that the fire truck—with the hose connected to it—was somehow moving sideways. Seconds later, Amos Lewis, too, was swept away.

The snout of the debris flow was twenty feet high, tapering behind. Debris flows sometimes ooze along, and sometimes move as fast as the fastest river rapids. The huge dark snout was moving nearly five hundred feet a minute and the rest of the flow behind was coming twice as fast, making roll waves as it piled forward against itself—this great slug, as geologists would describe it, this discrete slug, this heaving violence of wet cement. Already included in the debris were propane tanks, outbuildings, picnic tables, canyon live oaks, alders, sycamores, cottonwoods, a Lincoln Continental, an Oldsmobile, and countless boulders five feet thick. All this was spread wide a couple of hundred feet, and as the debris flow went through Hidden Springs it tore out more trees, picked up house trailers and more cars and more boulders, and knocked Gabe Hinterberg's lodge completely off its foundation. Mary and Cal Drake were standing in their living room when a wall came off. "We got outside somehow," he said later. "I just got away. She was trying to follow me. Evidently, her feet slipped out from under her. She slid right down into the main channel." The family next door were picked up and pushed against their own ceiling. Two were carried away. Whole houses were torn loose with people inside them. A house was ripped in half. A bridge was obliterated. A large part of town was carried a mile downstream and buried in the reservoir behind Big Tujunga Dam. Thirteen people were part of the debris. Most of the bodies were never found.

As Amos Lewis suddenly found himself struggling in the viscous flow, he more or less bumped into a whirling pickup coming down in the debris from who knows where upstream. One of the roll waves picked him up and threw him into the back of the truck. As the vehicle spun around and around, it neared one bank. Lewis saw an overhanging limb. He reached for it, caught it, and pulled himself above the rocky flow. Years later, just about where this had happened, he told Wade Wells and me the story. "I got pushed to one side," he said as he finished. "I lucked out." Lewis is a prematurely white-haired man with a white beard and dark-brown eyes. On this day in late spring, his muscular build and deeply tanned skin were amply displayed by a general absence of clothing. He wore bluejean shorts, white socks, mountain boots, and nothing else. When people began to discover human remains in the reservoir, he had gone in his patrol car to investigate the fate of his neighbors. "I had to go roll on them calls," he said. "A deputy sheriff has to roll on any type of body being found. I carried out at least four, maybe five, skulls."

The thirteen people who died in Hidden Springs were roughly a third of the year-round community; there was a much larger summer population. The main house of Lutherglen, a resort-retreat of the First English Evangelical Lutheran Church, remained standing but in ruins. Houses that stayed put were gouged out like peppers and stuffed with rocks. Lewis gestured across the canyon—across foundations with no houses on them, bolts sticking up out of cinder blocks where sills had been ripped away—toward some skeletal frames made of two-by-fours. "They used to be trailer stalls," he said. "The people left their cars by the river and walked up the bank to the trailers. The cars ended up in the dam." The First English Evangelical Lutherans sued the Los Angeles County Flood Control District for twenty million dollars. The judge threw the case out of court—followed, moments later, by the collection plate. Since the act in question was God's, the defendant might as well have been the plaintiff, and the Plaintiff the target of the suit.

I remarked to Lewis, who is now retired as sheriff, that I thought I'd heard a machine gun earlier in the day. "I worked the canyon car here for twenty-five years," he said. "I probably rolled on a

minimum of a hundred and fifty calls where people said they
heard machine guns. I never saw a machine gun."

Wells was attentive to this remark, raising his eyes with interest.
Behind his mild ecological look—his tortoise-shell glasses, his
amiable scientific manner—lay a colonel's affection for ord-
nance. At the time, in the Reserve, he was a lieutenant colonel
and rising. He'd been on active duty seven years, two in Vietnam.
He told me one day that if California were to secede from the
United States it would be one of the richest countries in the world
and, with its present units of the National Guard, be among the
best defended. "You can take a file and in fifteen minutes make
an automatic weapon out of an M1," he said to Amos Lewis. "It
can sound like a machine gun."

This set off a long and highly technical discussion between the
scholarly hydrologist and the shirtless mountaineer, each slipping
into a second self against a backdrop of huge boulders that had
been somewhere else a short time before and had been delivered
by a force that was high in the kiloton range. Most of the mud,
sand, and rock had gone into the Big Tujunga, behind the dam,
and the county had spent more than two million dollars taking
it out. The debris that had stayed in the valley closely resembled
glacial debris—chaotic, unsorted till, a round-rock mélange. Far
up the hillsides framing the valley, some of it clung like bits of
plaster stuck to an old wall, thus recording the high edges of the
discrete slug, where six hundred thousand tons went by.

When you walk in the stream valleys of the San Gabriels, you
will see rocks the size of heads wedged among the branches of
trees. In a small tight valley called Trail Canyon, I saw two
boulders that were a good deal wider than the bed of the brook
that had carried and rounded them. They were bigger than school
buses. Surrounded by lesser debris, they had moved a long distance in its company. At a guess—from their dimensions and
specific gravity—the aggregate weight of the two rocks was a
hundred and sixty tons.

In February, 1978, a boulder weighing three hundred and

fifteen tons ended up on a residential street about a third of a mile inside the Los Angeles city limits. Through some neighborhoods, boulders in great numbers advance like Chinese checkers. People pile them up against fences, use them in retaining walls. When Dan Davis was working for Flood, he found debris—on an urban thoroughfare after a storm—a mile and a half from the nearest debris basin. ("When I saw that, I knew we had a real problem.") In 1938, a restaurant on the main street of Sierra Madre was destroyed by invading boulders. Two-foot boulders rumbled through Claremont, coming to a stop three miles from the mountain front. Five miles from the front you can see boulders a foot in diameter. If you ask people how the rocks got there, they assume it was by a process that is no longer functioning. If you suggest that the rocks may have come from the mountains, people say, "No way." Off the eastern end of the San Gabriels, rocks the size of soccer balls are eight miles south of the front.

Building stones in places like Glendora and Covina were delivered by streams from high in the mountains. The stream-rounded rock is more vulnerable to earthquake than bricks would be, but bricks are not shipped F.O.B. by God, and in a land of kaleidoscopic risks what is one more if the rocks are free? Mike Rubel's castle, in Glendora, is made of stream-rounded debris in sizes approximating cannonballs. Dunsinane was not much larger than this suburban home. The ground level of Rubel's castle is twenty-two thousand square feet. From its battlements rise towers sixty-seven feet high and seventy-four feet high, built with San Gabriel boulders and store-bought cement. There are six towers, four set in the walls and two in the courtyard freestanding. Bees live in the Bee Tower, and emerge through archery slits. All around the walls, muzzles of cannons protrude from crenels that are lined with shark-fin glass.

The intensity of the electronic surveillance is high, but the owner is not unfriendly. He likes to sit on a balcony above the courtyard, looking out over his walls and through the crowns of palms at the ridgeline of the mountains. He is a large man to the point of private tailoring. He began his castle in 1959 and completed it in 1985. When he had been working on the project ten years, he took an unexpected delivery of building materials in the form of a debris slug that breached his defenses, untimbered his portcullises, and got into the inner bailey.

"The ground was shaking just like an earthquake. In the washes, the water was going three billion miles an hour. You could hear the boulders rumbling. It was marvellous."

As a result, there is now a twelve-foot curtain wall on the periphery of the castle. Rubel calls his domain, which is surrounded by commoner houses on a most conventional street, the Kingdom of Rubelia. Numerous crafts are practiced there, and he has a hand-set-printing operation called the Pharm Press. In the Kingdom of Rubelia, F is Ph and Ph is F. There are hand-cranked phorges in the blacksmith phoundry. There are potters' wheels, looms, and lathes.

Sitting beside him on his balcony and dreamily looking at the mountain peaks, I said, "The castle is obviously the result of something."

Rubel said, "Yes. A genetic defect."

Rubel explained that he had built the castle with the help of numerous friends—friends from his days in Citrus High School, friends from his briefer days at Cal Poly. "We were twenty-year-old kids," he said. "And we were flunking out of school. We said, 'If we can't amount to anything, we might as well build a castle.'"

Prince Philip of Great Britain, who is not a Rubelian and gets no F, has made two visits to Rubel's castle.

Cal Poly—the California State Polytechnic University—is not to be confused with Caltech. I bring this up because I went to Caltech one day and, in a very impromptu manner, asked to see a geologist. Any geologist. It had not been my purpose, in pursuing the present theme, to get into the deep geology. I meant to roam the mountains and the mountain front with foresters and engineers, to talk to people living on the urban edge, to interview people who sell the edge—a foreign correspondent covering the battle from behind both lines. But not beneath them. This was a planned vacation from projects in geology—the continuation of a holiday that had begun with stream capture in the lower Mississippi and had spread forth into such innocent milieus as eruptions in Iceland and flowing red lava in Hawaii. Now, in Los Angeles, I had been avoiding geologists in the way that one tries to avoid visits to medical doctors. All had gone well for a matter of weeks, but then, one morning, I just happened to be in Pasadena looking up into the veiled chimeric mountains, and severe symptoms began to develop. Right off the street—in much the way that a needful patient would seek out a Doc-in-the-Box—I walked into the geology department of the California Institute of Technology, found the departmental office, and asked for professional help.

After a short wait, spent leafing through a magazine, I was shown into the office of Leon Silver, whom I knew only by reputation—an isotope geologist whose exacting contributions to geochronology have not repressed his interest in crustal settings, global tectonics, the Big Picture. An ebullient man, husky, in his sixties, he spread out the local sheets from the geologic map of California for a brief rehearsal of the rocks and faults before leading me to the roof of the building, where he continued his diagnosis in the panoramic presence of the rock itself. The roof was flat, a deck. Funnel vents and other apparatus gave the impression that the Caltech geology department was a cruise ship in the lee of seventy miles of mountains.

The institution as a whole, in its remarkable beauty and surprisingly compact size, is sort of a bonsai university—with pools, rialtos, inclined gardens—above which the mountains seem all the more immense. Silver said that if I was looking for first causes in the matter that concerned me I had come to the right place. "The geology provides the debris," he went on. "The San Gabes are a climber's nightmare. Several people a year die on the incompetent rock."

"Yes," I said. "The rock up there is really rotten."

Silver seemed offended. Drawing himself up, he said, "I beg your pardon, sir. It is not rotten. It is shattered." The region was a tracery of faults, like cracks in ancient paint. The mountains were divided by faults, defined by faults, and framed by them as well: on the near side, the Raymond Fault, the Sierra Madre Fault, the Cucamonga Fault; on the far side, the San Andreas Fault. The rock of the San Gabriels had been battered and broken by the earthquakes on these and related faults. In 1971, Silver had flown over the San Gabes immediately after an earthquake that reached 6.2 on the Richter scale. Like artillery shells randomly exploding, the aftershocks were sending up dust in puffs all over the landscape. Something like that would add quite a bit, he said, "to the debris potential." Some of the rock up there had become so unstable that whole hunks of the terrain were moving like glaciers. One mountaintop was heading south like a cap tipping down on a forehead. Things like that had been going on for so long that the mountains were in many places loaded with debris from ancient landslides—prime material, prepared to flow. "The ultimate origin of the debris flows," he said, "is the continuous tectonic front that has made this one of the steepest mountain fronts in North America and produced a wilderness situation not a hundred metres from people's houses."

The continuous tectonic front is where the North American and Pacific Plates are sliding past each other—where Bakersfield moves toward Mexico City while Burbank heads for Alaska. Between Bakersfield and Burbank lie the San Gabriel Mountains. With the San Bernardino Mountains east of them, they trend east-west, forming a kink in the coastal ranges that come down from San Francisco and go on to Baja California. The kink conforms to a bend in the San Andreas Fault, which runs along the inland base of the mountains. The kink looks like this:

It could be a tiptoeing h. It resembles a prize-winning chair. Los Angeles is like a wad of gum stuck to the bottom of the chair. The mountains are one continuous system, but its segments are variously named. The upper stretch is called the Coast Ranges.

The lower leg is called the Peninsular Ranges. The kink is called the Transverse Ranges.

My hieroglyph represents, of course, not only the mountains but the flanking San Andreas Fault, which comes up from the Gulf of California, bends left around Los Angeles, then goes on to San Francisco and north below the sea. As if this regional context were not large enough, Silver now placed it in a larger one. The East Pacific Rise, the ocean-basin spreading center away from which the Pacific Plate and other plates are moving, sinuously makes its way from the latitude of Tierra del Fuego all the way north to Mexico, where it enters the Gulf of California. The East Pacific Rise has splintered Mexico and carried Baja California away from the mainland—much as the Carlsberg Ridge has cracked open the deserts of Afro-Arabia and made the Red Sea. Baja is not moving due west, as one might guess from a glance at a map, but north by northwest, with the rest of the Pacific Plate. The cumulative power of this northward motion presses on the kink in the San Andreas, helping the mountains rise.

That much has long seemed obvious: as the two sides of the San Andreas slide by each other, they compress the landscape at the kink. It has been considerably less obvious that a compressional force accompanies the great fault wherever it goes. In the past, the building of the Coast Ranges and the Peninsular Ranges was in no way attributed to the San Andreas Fault. A paper published in *Science* in November, 1987—and signed by enough geologists to make a quorum at the Rose Bowl—offers evidence that the San Andreas has folded its flanking country, much as a moving boat crossing calm waters will send off lateral waves. The great compression at the kink is withal the most intense. The Coast Ranges and the Peninsular Ranges are generally smaller than the Transverse Ranges. The San Gabriels are being compressed about a tenth of an inch a year.

Why the kink is there in the first place is "not well understood." Just to the northeast, though, in the Great Basin of Utah and Nevada, the earth's mantle is close, the earth's crust is thin and stretching. In the past few million years, the geographic coordinates of Reno and Salt Lake—at the western and eastern extremes of the Great Basin—have moved apart sixty miles. This large new subdivision of the regional tectonics is in every way as entrancing as it is enigmatic. Almost all of California may be headed out to sea. Already, the east-west stretching of the Great Basin has put Reno west of Los Angeles, and it may be what has bent the San Andreas Fault.

Some of the rock of the San Gabriels is two hundred times as old as the San Andreas Fault, which has been in existence for less than a five-hundredth of the history of the world. Plates come and go—splitting, welding, changing through time, travelling long distances. Before the present North American and Pacific Plates began to work on this particular rock, Silver said, it may have been "bashed around in Mexico twice and perhaps across the Pacific before that." He continued, "It's a bedrock ridge up there. It's a weirdo wonderful block of rocks, the most complicated mountain range in North America. It includes the oldest rocks on the West Coast. The San Gabes look like a flake kicked around on plate boundaries for hundreds of millions of years."

The Santa Monica Mountains, a sort of footnote to the big contiguous ranges, stood off to the southwest of us, discrete and small. Like any number of lesser hills freestanding in the region, they were flexures of the San Andreas system. Oil people had found pay in the traps formed by such flexures. The Santa Monica Mountains were as shattered as the San Gabes. The several debris basins in the Santa Monicas had worked with varying success. People had died in their beds there, buried alive by debris.

The San Gabriels were rising faster than they were disintegrating, Silver said. The debris basins had given geomorphologists an unparalleled opportunity to calculate erosion rates. They could even determine how much mountain is removed by a single storm. On the average, about seven tons disappear from each acre each year—coming off the mountains and heading for town.

Between the geology-department roof and the San Gabriels, the city gradually rose. A very long, ramplike, and remarkably consistent incline ended in the sheerness of the mountain wall. This broad uniform slope is where the seven tons an acre had emerged from the mountains, year upon year for a number of millions of years—accumulating as detrital cones, also known as fans. Broad at the bottom, narrow at the top, the fans were like spilled grain piling up at the edge of a bin. There were so many of them, coming down from stream after stream, that they had long since coalesced, forming a tilted platform, which the Spaniards had called the bajada.

"I used to live on the mountain front," Silver said. "By Devils Gate, at the mouth of Arroyo Seco. We could hear the big knockers go by—the three-metre boulders. The whole front face of the San Gabes is processed."

"Processed?"

"Shattered and broken. It is therefore vulnerable to landsliding, to undercutting by the streams, to acceleration by local earthquakes, to debris flows."

"Why does anybody live there?"

"They're not well informed. Most folks don't know the story of the fire-flood sequence. When it happens in the next canyon, they say, 'Thank God it didn't happen here.' "

"Why would a geologist live there?"

"It's a calculated risk. The higher you build, the cooler it is. There are great views. And at night, up there, the cool air off the mountains flows down and pushes the dirty air masses back. The head of our seismological laboratory lives on the mountain front. In fact, most of the Caltech geology department lives on the mountain front."

"Where do *you* live?"

"Way out on the fan."

Silver passed me along to his colleague Barclay Kamb—the tectonophysicist, X-ray crystallographer, and glaciologist, who discovered, among other things, the structures of the high-pressure forms of ice: ice II through ice IX. Kamb once studied the Sierra Madre Fault Zone on the San Gabriel mountain front, and walked the relevant canyons. Recently, he has been using a surging glacier near Yakutat as a laboratory for the study of how rocks move, since ice deforms in much the way that rock does. He was about to leave for Alaska when I dropped in on him in his office. His mother was there, his father, and his son Linus, who was named for Kamb's father-in-law, Linus Pauling. In a swirl of ropes, ice axes, grad students, and relatives, Kamb, who has been described by another colleague as "the smartest man in the world," tracked six conversations simultaneously, one of which summarized concisely his sense of flowing debris. "There's a street in Altadena called Boulder," he began. "It is called Boulder for a very good reason. It is subject to severe threat. Boulder Road, below the Rubio Debris Basin, is the former course of Rubio Creek. You see encroachment of human habitation in many areas like that, which are most at risk. Above the debris basins, there are crib structures in the canyons. The theory is to prevent sediment from coming out of the mouths of the canyons. I think most geologists would say that is ridiculous. You're not changing the source of the sediment. You are just storing sediment. Those cribworks are less strong than nature's own constructs. The idea that you can prevent the sediment from coming out is meddling with the works of nature. Sooner or later, a flood will wipe out those small dams and scatter the debris. Everything you store might come out in one event. We're talking human time—not geologic time." Kamb lives in Pasadena, close by the mountain front.

Just upstairs was Andrew Ingersoll, the planetary scientist. In the San Gabriels, he had lived behind the lines. In the nineteen-sixties, he moved his family into a cabin that was so far up Big Santa Anita Canyon that they had to hike a mile and a quarter just to get to their car. They leased the place from the Forest Service. When they moved in, the children were three and four. Ingersoll was an assistant professor. "My colleagues in the geology department thought I was becoming a permanent hippie," he said. "But in those days everybody was some sort of hippie." The canyon was full of crib structures, arresting debris. Ingersoll did not know how to make sense of them unless they were "an example of bureaucracy doing something for its own sake." (In any case, the small wash above the Ingersoll's cabin was unprotected.) In January of 1969, during a nine-day series of storms, twelve inches of rain fell in one night. A debris flow hit the cabin, broke through a wall, and delivered three feet of mud, innumerable rocks, and one oak to the Ingersolls. The family regarded this as "just a lot of fun," he said, and continued, "Those little dams must have been nearly insignificant. They were based on the experience of Swiss farmers, and this may have been a totally different situation. It might have been a very poor concept to try to control the San Gabriels."

I also met Vito Vanoni, who is now a professor emeritus. A formal, small, wiry man with a husky voice and a sweet smile, he is a civil engineer, and a founding and still central figure in Caltech's Environmental Quality Laboratory. "That's an awful pile of rock and dirt up there, and we're proposing to hold it back," he said. "To do something like that is extremely expensive, but there are so many of us here to pay the bill, to protect those who insist on living up there. Our zoning is not strong enough to prevent this. The forces of development are hard to oppose. Most people who buy property in those areas never see the map and wouldn't know what they were looking at if they saw one. Very few are aware. When they see the concrete stream channels, I don't know what they think. How many people really realize why the channels are there and why they are as big as they are? You can't build a channel without a debris basin, or the debris will fill up the channel and then start sashaying back and forth. Debris basins have been built in response to the need of the community—after people have had sediment in their living rooms."

I asked Vanoni where he lived.

"Up there," he said. "Below Eaton Basin—since 1949. Like my neighbors, I figure that I'm protected. I haven't seen anything across my yard yet." After a pause, he added, "If they should have a failure up there, I'm afraid I'd get wet." There was a longer pause, then another sweet smile, and he said, "I live a hundred yards from the Raymond Fault."

F R O M

LOOKING FOR

A SHIP

(1 9 9 0)

[A *random ride with the Merchant Marine after the author haunts union
halls with a second mate looking for a ship. Work is scarce to the point of
non-existent, but the mate eventually gets a voyage—West Coast, South
America—on SS* Stella Lykes *under Paul Washburn, a captains' captain
and a character and a half. The farthest port is Valparaiso. Stowaways stow
away in Buenaventura. Southbound and northbound, pirates hit the ship
in Guayaquil. This selection is a montage of fifteen or sixteen segments, most
of them widely separated in the book.*]

Andy was worried about the Ben Sawyer Bridge. He thought of it stuck open, and saw in his mind's eye an unending line of stifled cars, his own among them. If his neurons seemed hyperactive, they had some reason to be. On the other hand, how often did this drawbridge get stuck? Once a year? Three times every two years? Whatever the statistics might be, they would make no difference to Andy. The drawbridge had stuck open one afternoon with him on the wrong side, and the delay was so prolonged that he checked into a motel and caught up on sleep. On that day, he wasn't going anywhere important. On this day, he allowed a minimum of three hours to complete a journey of thirty minutes. He was looking for a ship.

In Andy's wallet was a National Shipping Card that had been stamped in Boston ten and a half months before, registering under his name, George Anderson Chase, the date, the hour, and the minute when he arrived in a union hall after leaving his last ship. The older the card, the better the prospects for a new job. If the card were to go twelve months unused, it would roll over—lose all seniority, and begin again. Meanwhile strongly competitive, it had all but reached the status of a killer card. In the evolving decline of the United States Merchant Marine, qualified people

seeking work so greatly outnumbered the jobs there were to fill
that you almost had to hold a killer card or your chances were
slim for shipping out. You went to a union hall, presented the
card in person at a job call, and if someone tossed in an older
card you stayed on the beach. From his home, in Maine, Andy
had come to Charleston this time because he thought that shipping cards deadlier than his would be more numerous in Boston
or New York. On sheer speculation, I joined him, our idea being
that when he got himself a ship he would ask the shipping company if I could go along on the voyage as a P.A.C.—Person in
Addition to Crew. Andy said, "I probably have a better chance
out of Charleston. Fewer people. Less competition. A fairly steady
stream of ships." Besides, he had a place to stay. His wife's mother
lived on an island whose connection to the mainland was the
Ben Sawyer Bridge.

We had no idea where we would be going, if anywhere. We
had gear for cool weather and gear for the tropics. Looking for a
ship, Andy had once spent two months fruitlessly hanging around
the union hall in Charleston. He had put in many weeks in New
York with the same result. He once went as far as Puerto Rico.
He spent two weeks there going to the hall. He got no ship. He
tried Charleston on his way home, and with great luck got a ship
in two days. The ship he got in Charleston was called the Puerto
Rican. He was on it four months, sailing as third mate, coastwise.
A chemical tanker, it blew up, out of San Francisco, on a later
voyage. It broke in half.

       ·   ·   ·

The United States Merchant Marine, the name of which suggests an assault on a valuable foreign beach, is not, as a good
many people seem to think, a branch of military service. It is
essentially a collective enterprise of competing private companies,
flying the American flag on the sterns of their ships, employing
American-citizen crews, and transporting cargoes throughout the
world. Sail and steam, the United States grew in rank among
nations on the aggressive reach of its Merchant Marine. American
merchant ships once numbered in the thousands. The chimerical

ship that Andy Chase and I went to look for in Charleston would not be a selection from a field that large. Diminishing rapidly, the number of American dry-cargo ships was already below two hundred, and there were about as many tankers. Not one commercial vessel was under construction in an American shipyard.

[*After Andy Chase, weeks later, finally gets a chance to put down his killer card and secure a job, McPhee abruptly shifts the scene from South Carolina to the southeast Pacific Ocean in the middle of the voyage, and introduces Captain Washburn.*]

Four A.M., 32.25 degrees south, sky overcast, an almost total darkness on the bridge. To all horizons, no light. We have seen one ship in six days, since Guayaquil.

This is the tenth of August, the antipodal mirror of the tenth of February. The ocean air is cool. The momentum of more than forty thousand tons is as absolute as the darkness. In no hurried way is it going to change. If a target should appear on one of the radars, Andy, in avoiding it, would try to preserve a cushion of at least two miles. Very slowly, toward six, shapes will form in the developing light. Anyone coming or going through the passageway to the wheelhouse passes through two doors. When either door opens, the passageway lights go out. The bridge has to be dark, so that more than radar can see into the night. Andy is pacing around somewhere, invisible. Vernon McLaughlin is at the helm. The autopilot has the ship, but Mac stands by the helm.

I have attached myself to the four-to-eight watch. It is Andy's watch. It is the watch of both dawn and sunset. Mac will tell you, "It's the *only* watch." Mac is an able-bodied seaman. Calvin King, who is also an A.B., is far up in the bow, on lookout. William Kennedy, an ordinary seaman, will relieve Calvin at five. That Kennedy's name is William is as little known to the crew as the fact that his wife's name is Ethel. The crew, like his neighbors in Savannah, call him Peewee. Andy, Peewee, Calvin,

Mac: the second mate, the ordinary, the two A.B.s—the deck watch, four to eight.

Getting up at three-thirty every morning is not as difficult as one might think—not if, in the evening, you are asleep soon after eight. I wander around the ship all day, but I go to bed at eight. Suppose I were in Iceland—four time zones east—and were asleep by midnight and awake by seven-thirty. I would be setting and rising at the exact moments that I set and rise out here.

This is the twentieth day of the voyage. For this ship, a voyage is forty-two days and begins and ends in New York. Our present position is about as far south as the Cape of Good Hope. Almost all of Australia is farther north than we are. Halfway up a straight line between here and New York is a point in the mantle two thousand miles deep.

Mac's voice, in the dark, says, "This ship goes to coke country. This ship is hot as a potato."

The captain, who worries, can list dozens of disquietudes idiosyncratic to this run. Mac has just mentioned one. Steamship companies are responsible for what they carry even if they don't know it is there. Fines in six figures can make significant contributions to overhead. Stacked on the main deck and down in the hatches are five hundred boxes—the amphorae of this era, the containers that fit on highway trailers. The containers are sealed. Everywhere in the cargo manifests are the letters "STC" or the words "Said to Contain":

Said to Contain 16,636 pounds of shower curtains, telephones, and wall clocks.
Said to Contain 7,650 pounds of religious books.
STC 6,000 kits for assembling black-and-white TV sets.
STC panties de señora, five and a half tons.

Customs officials of six countries are interested in our ship. In Port Newark, they have turned out to greet her in very large numbers with dogs. Mac remarks that a white Cadillac with both front doors open was sitting on the pier once in Newark. When Mac went down the gangway and off the ship, someone inside the Cadillac asked him where he was going. "I said, 'Is that any of your God-damned business?' He said, 'Yes, it is.' He said he was the Man. He said, 'What have you got in there?' I said, 'Here, take it,' and threw it in the car. He said, 'Oh, it's your clothes.' I said, 'Whatever.' "

The first gray light will delineate the speaker at the helm—a man built strong and square-shouldered, with a large head, a regal paunch, an equitable mustache, and eyes that gleam with fun and anger. Not to mention moral indignation. Targets turn up on the radar. Fishing boats. Answering instructions from Andy, Mac turns off the autopilot and moves the wheel of the ship.

Andy is soon on the telephone: "Good morning, Captain, it's five-thirty. We are twenty miles out, and at our present rate of speed we should arrive at seven-ten." Normally—when we are at sea, and not about to intersect a continent—Andy calls the captain at half past six. No matter what the time is, the captain always answers quickly, and always sounds wide awake.

Gradually, the Fathometer has been sketching the steep slope of the Peru-Chile Trench, and the extremely narrow continental shelf. Electric lights come into view, rising high in sinuous lines, like ornamental strings in leafless trees. There are thousands of them, and they are beautiful. They define dark hills we cannot see.

We hear a door open and close. Another opens. Captain Washburn comes into the wheelhouse. "Good morning, good morning," he says. The first salutation may be for us, the second for the ship. More likely, the other way round. The captain routinely talks to the ship. Now, though, he goes directly to the radio. Channel 16. "Valparaiso pilots, Valparaiso pilots. This is the American steamship Stella Lykes. Stella Lykes. Whiskey, Mike, Romeo, Golf. Over." If you say those words—Whiskey, Mike, Romeo, Golf—in that order anywhere in the world, they mean this ship. In this part of the world, at the moment, no one seems to care. The captain waits in silence until his patience runs out. His patience could set a record at a hundred metres. Again he says, "Valparaiso pilots, Valparaiso pilots. This is the American steamship Stella Lykes. Stella Lykes. Whiskey, Mike, Romeo, Golf. Over."

No response.

"So much for moving ships at this hour in the morning," the captain says. "The port isn't even awake yet. When Ethan Allen was expiring, people said to him, 'Ethan, the angels expect you,' and Ethan said, 'God damn them. Let them wait.' Then he expired."

The complete resonance of the captain's parable passes above the head of the Person in Addition to Crew.

.   .   .

In front of the bridge telegraph and the redundant radars and the redundant steering mechanisms lies a long rubber mat, which firms the footsteps of anyone traversing the bridge. With the captain present, it is not a good place to linger. Back and forth through the wheelhouse he moves, from one bridge-wing door to the other—now indoors, now outdoors and a spin around a binnacle, now indoors, now outdoors and a look over the side. Occasionally, he stops and talks to someone. Sometimes he just stops and talks. Out of the blue, I have heard him say, "A little here, a little there." Out of the blue, I have heard him say, "If you don't like to do that, seek gainful employment elsewhere. The army of the unemployed has an opening." Out of nowhere, I have heard him say, "O.K., ye of little faith, there has been a change in the program; the regular cast has left and the stand-ins are taking over." With no related dialogue coming before or after, I have heard him say, "Any jackass can do that." Quite evidently speaking to the ship, he will sometimes say, "I don't like to lose and I never quit." Often he asks questions and then provides answers. One day, offering advice to all within earshot, he said, "In Rome, do as the Romanians do." His political opinions are unambiguous. Adlai Stevenson was "a wimpy little coward mumbling platitudes." The President of the Republic of Panama is "a pineapple-faced bum." The United States has been reduced to "a choice between being poor-and-weak and poor-and-strong." Pleasantly, he says, "You can get all the vitriol out of me you want, because I'm loaded with it."

This captain runs a happy ship. There are personnel aboard, both licensed and unlicensed, who have patterned their time and risked unemployment in order to sail with him. He has not won them over with fraternization. In the same unvarying manner in which Pinckney B. Ezekiel is called Zeke and Trevor Procter is called Kiwi and William Kennedy is called Peewee, Paul McHenry Washburn is called Captain Washburn. His family's early background is deep New England. His middle name relates to the fort of the star-spangled banner. He knows what a magisterial distance is, and he knows how to keep it.

"He's wrung more seawater out of his boots than I'll ever sail across," Andy says of the captain, awarding him the status of a marine cliché.

.   .   .

Now about to dock in a foreign city, he is wearing his more-or-less-dress blues. His shoes and trousers are dark and naval. His white short-sleeved shirt, open at the collar, has epaulets striped with gold. There is gold braid on his visor. His glasses are rimmed with gold. As he moves back and forth on the bridge, he takes things in with the comprehensive gaze of a boxer. He leans forward like a boxer, his mouth and jaw set firm. His body is chunky, his paunch under control, like a trimmed spinnaker. Wisps of gray edge his cap. His face—beardless, full-featured—appears to have been the site of an epic battle, wherein the vitriol he speaks of has at last been subdued by humor.

Few of the watches that begin at 4 A.M. turn up the lights of cities. Most watches have a rhythmic sameness, plunging through the dark, with the scent of coffee percolating on the bridge, the scent of bacon from five decks below, Mac or Calvin invisible at the wheel, Andy the Navigator—every inch an officer in his bluejeans, running shoes, rolled-up sleeves—working with dividers in the chartroom under a dim red lamp. In the first nine days on the Pacific, we put into port only once. One morning, a couple of hundred miles off the Colombian coast—at five-forty-nine, the hour of dawn—we heard in the wind a distinct whinny.

We saw whales on the way south, and were led by porpoises. Albatrosses flew beside us, motionless to the point of impudence, their eyes on our necks, their great wings fixed, their iron momentum matching the ship's. At bridge level, sixty-five feet above the water, an albatross flew beside us with his right leg up scratching his ear. But not even that was as weird as this whinny, in ocean air, so far from land. We knew, of course, where it came from—and the whinnies that followed as well—but knowledge didn't make the sound less strange. Andy said, "These are not the horse latitudes."

On Hatch 4, Bay 1, about halfway between the bridge and the bow, were four containers said to contain twenty-four thoroughbreds. One of them was Dr. Sab, out of White Reason by Seattle Slew. Undefeated in five starts, Dr. Sab was on his way to race in Guayaquil. So was The Admiral. So was Axe Lady. Most of the other horses were nameless two-year-olds on their way from Royal Eagle Farm, in Panama, to the stables of Silvio DeVoto, in Ecuador. To tote nine tons of horses eight hundred miles, Lykes Brothers was charging six thousand eight hundred dollars. For a few hundred more, the company was providing the food and lodging of Carlos Rolando Lopez, who described himself to me as the "assistant trainer of the principal horse, Dr. Sab." Carlos numbered among his intimate friends the Panamanian jockeys. Jacinto Vasquez. Lafitt Pincay, Jr. Walter Guerra. Jorge Velasquez. Carlos said that his own mentor was Luis Ferrugia the Magician, "the best trainer in Panama City." Carlos made these remarks, among other places, over meals—where, from a Xeroxed menu, I helped him choose what he wanted.

Carlos was eating better than his horses. I went to Hatch 4 with him in the afternoon. The containers were stowed amidships with their doors open. As many as seven horses were in one twenty-foot box—in narrow wooden stalls framed within the steel. The two-year-olds were cribbing as if their lives depended on it. They were chewing up the wood of the stalls. Five hundred miles from Guayaquil, they had already made crescent-shaped indentations larger than slices of watermelon. They were chewing the posts as well as the rails. Carlos explained that they were hungry. He said a very strict diet of hay and water was the Magician's formula for avoiding seasickness. Unfortunately, someone had taken the great trainer too much at his word and had sent to the ship just eight little packets of hay. Carlos was not being democratic. He had been giving a full ration to Dr. Sab, somewhat less to Axe Lady and The Admiral, and pittances to the others. Two and a half packets of hay were left. Carlos was reserving it all for Dr. Sab. This son of Seattle Slew—and brother of Slew City Slew—was a black horse that looked unpleasant, but the wood of his stall was whole.

I left Carlos and went to the bridge. The captain was attentive to the horses and asked how they were getting along. Vernon McLaughlin was at the ship's wheel, and as the story unfolded he burst out, "They're so cheap they won't feed their horses. With wood in their stomachs, they can't pass it. That's a sin!"

"Carlos says that is not a problem," I told him. "Carlos says, 'They could eat the whole ship.'"

Mac would not stoop to comment.

Time passed. A further thought occurred to me. "Dr. Sab is undefeated," I remarked. "Impressive as that may be, he has run in only five races, and he is five years old. What has he been doing?"

Captain Washburn said, "He's been eating."

Captain Washburn's family name derives from Great Washburne, near Evesham, in the English Midlands. The McHenrys in his background of course were Scots. John Washburn of Evesham immigrated to the Massachusetts Bay Colony in 1631. The family were in coastal shipping in the Boston area before going into timber and allied enterprises in Maine. In lake-and-river country near New Hampshire, they had a hilltop farm called Norlands—hundreds of acres and long deep views—that might as well have been called a plantation. It looks today much as it did a century ago. As Norlands Living History Center, it attracts school buses and preserves its first demeanor. There is a widow's walk on top of the house, for a widow with exceptional eyes, Norlands being fifty miles from the sea. Samuel Washburn (1824–90) was a skipper of clipper ships, a captain in the United States Merchant Marine. Elihu Washburn (1816–87) was named Secretary of State and minister to France by Ulysses S. Grant, whose portrait is prominent in the freestanding Washburn Memorial Library (1883), with its spinning wheels, its Britannica IX, its rose and pale-blue windows. Washburns went west, founded the Minneapolis Mill Company, and made Gold Medal Flour. They were involved in the beginnings of General Mills. Washburn College, in Topeka, Kansas, is named for Emory Washburn. The father of our Captain Washburn was a Washington lawyer. ("He had the trait of honesty. Hey, he didn't have a chance.") As a schoolboy in the District of Columbia, aged thirteen, Paul McHenry Washburn was told to write an essay about an ancestor. He wrote about Chief Justice John Marshall. He turned in the essay, but he was not for school. He ran away from home.

The captain learned from Leadline Dunn, from Terrible Terry Harmon, from Dirty Shirt George Price. These are the old skippers with whom he sailed when he was young, and on whose seamanship he modelled his own. They were not his only icons. He had plenty of admiration for Herbert P. High Pressure Erwin, for Clean Shirt George Price, and for Rebel Frazier. He even learned from Wacky Wacker. He had less affection for Jake the Snake Jacobs, Tanktop Evans, and Wild Buck Newsome. With the exception of Tanktop, who was an engineer, all were skippers.

Some were still mates when Washburn sailed with them. He sailed on Liberty ships. He sailed with the International Freighting Corporation, the Luckenbach Steamship Company, the United Fruit Company, the Mystic Steamship Company, the South Atlantic Mail Line. He sailed with Lykes Brothers Steamship Company. Dirty Shirt George Price and Clean Shirt George Price were not related. Each man, as it happened, was named George F. Price, Jr. Leadline was actually John Dunn. Among these first-class seamen, Dirty Shirt and Terrible Terry were especially gifted in the art of stowage and also had high reputations for "protecting ships and protecting people." Their example became Washburn's fixed priorities, which he lists as

> 1—people
> 2—ship
> 3—cargo.

When he himself became a master, and a difficult situation came up, he would think of the old skippers. He would think, If they threw this at Dirty Shirt, what would he do?

Dirty Shirt, Rebel, and Leadline instilled in Washburn the importance of confidence in your own dead reckoning: "Never doubt it. Never—as in do not ever—doubt it. Leadline came up in the twenties, when you didn't have a lot of navigation things to help you. You did it on your own or you fell by the wayside. Leadline had a sixth sense as to what types of wave action and sky action hint at coming weather. I learned to read the sky from him. From him I learned things not to do. Leadline was an aggressor in dealing with people. A steamship master—while he's there—*is* the master. Leadline and Dirty Shirt and Terrible Terry—they did not back off from anyone. I learned from them to maintain a gulf between yourself and the other officers. I learned, Never cross that gulf. I learned, Don't act like the other officers, dress like them, or socialize with them. I learned, Don't be like them. Whatever they are, be different. Never waver in your dealings with them. Don't vacillate. I learned, Never chastise people in public, even if they have earned it. I learned, Don't alibi, don't complain."

Tell it to the ship.

Now sixty-five years old, the captain began as an ordinary
seaman in a Merchant Marine of fewer than a thousand ships
and saw it rise above two thousand ships and then decline by
eighty per cent. He has seen at least fifteen American shipping
companies go ventral in the water. Only three major ones remain
alive in international shipping: American President Lines, Sea-
Land, and Lykes Brothers Steamship Company. Ship for ship,
crew lists have become much shorter as well—a process known
as reduced manning, which is the result of a combination of
automational technology and economic constraint. Ships that
might once have had fifty in the crew now have twenty-one.
Some ships are so undermanned that extra people have to come
out from land to help dock them.

If Dirty Shirt George Price had a shipful of starving horses,
what would Dirty Shirt do? If they threw this at Dirty Shirt, what
would he do? Captain Washburn found an answer. He sent word
to the galley that he wanted all the corn, cereal, bread, and other
foodstuffs that the cook could possibly spare. Toward noon, when
the cook had got it all together, the captain asked me to find
Carlos and bring him to the bridge. I went to Hatch 4, Bay 1,
where Carlos was offering the horses generous amounts of water,
and accompanied him to the bridge. The captain, with obvious
pleasure, asked me to tell Carlos that he had set aside for the
horses a hundred and twenty ears of corn.

Understand, I am by no means fluent. I have a fairly good
Spanish vocabulary, an ear that seems to reject incoming Spanish
sound, and grammar tartare. The pleasure in my voice must have
been clear enough, though, as I told Carlos about the corn.

Carlos said that racehorses do not eat corn—not *his* racehorses,
anyway. Absolutely, they were not to be given corn.

While the helmsman listened and the chief mate listened, I repeated this to Captain Washburn.

The captain's demeanor changed. In brusque staccato, he said, "Tell him to be my guest, then, if the horses prefer wood." Becoming even more sarcastic, he continued, "Tell him I'm sorry I don't have barley or oats."

I said that the captain had no other grains.

Carlos said that the captain needn't worry. The horses were not to be given other grains.

I told Carlos that the captain was sorry.

Carlos said, in English, "No problem." In Spanish he said to tell the captain that everything would be all right if we arrived on schedule in the morning. Was the captain quite certain that we would arrive in the morning?

Washburn said, "Tell him I can't say whether we will arrive at seven-fifty-five or eight."

Carlos remarked that by morning he would have one packet of hay left, which he would reserve for Dr. Sab.

To the captain I said, "Carlos feels confident that he can make it on one bale of hay and two cords of wood."

The captain said, "To each his own. Tell him I will no longer attempt to project myself into his business. Tell him I'm going to throw the corn over the side. Tell him I once had a rhinoceros on board."

Carlos said, "The captain has much experience."

Carlos went back to Hatch 4. When I saw him there a short time later, his hands were purple with gentian, and he was nursing a wound. In the wind, pieces of his trousers flapped like flags. Inside a container, he had been climbing from one stall to another when a two-year-old bit him in the crotch.

Sometimes I go on lookout with Peewee, Mac, or Calvin— go forward with a flashlight on the main deck at four, up the ladder to the fo'c'sle deck, around the windlasses and the anchor chains, and past the hawsepipes to the absolute point of the bow, where the lookout station conforms to the requirements of admiralty court, being "as far forward and as low down as conditions allow." The lookout stands in a roofless cupboard. A sheet of clear plastic deflects the wind. He is not quite like a fly on a bowsprit, but somewhere near it—projected far over the water, over the nose bulb, and riding up and down the Pacific swells.

· · ·

At 06:41:36, the telephone rang in the bow. Andy said to Peewee, "Good morning. This is the equator."

Andy drops money on the equator. I wondered how much he was dropping on it now. I imagined myself throwing money on the equator, and shivered at the thought.

I also shivered in the cool of the morning. At noon that day, one degree south, the Fahrenheit temperature was seventy-eight degrees, the relative humidity seventy-five per cent. At noon that day in New York City, I learned later, the temperature was eighty-five and climbing. The day's high humidity was ninety-one per cent. All through the summer, everybody in New York and its perisphere had been living in the sort of climate that seals the skin and pops veins in the head: They waded in humidity. Every day for weeks, the high temperatures remained between eighty-eight and ninety-seven. Before I shipped out, I met a Liberian who had come to Princeton on a fellowship. I asked him if he liked America. He said, "Everything but the heat. It is intolerable. Never in my country have I experienced such heat." By comparison with New York, Panama was cool. The canal, creeping through the forest, was cool. The evening we left Panama, the temperature in the North Pacific was in the seventies. The weather was almost unnerving. As soon as Stella crossed the equator, you heard people say, "It's winter now"—a technicality that is not persuasive there at the latitude of Borneo, with the hull's velvet slide over that soft ocean. We entered the Gulf of Guayaquil. Just the sound of that name—Guayaquil—spelled coffee and chocolate to me, spelled mangoes, bananas, guavas, and heat.

At four that afternoon, though, when the temperature in New York City was eighty-nine, the temperature in the Gulf of Guayaquil was seventy-five. I finally understood where the tropics are, why the nights of the iguana are on Forty-seventh Street, and Broadway steams with rain.

As the heavens fade, Andy has been out on the port bridge wing shooting Achernar, Mars, Sirius, and Venus—plucking them from the drift of clouds. Good with a sextant, he resembles a Castilian shepherd drinking wine. Ordinarily, he shoots the stars as an academic exercise, a way of keeping fresh his celestial navigation, which he figures out with his calculator and his dividers in the chartroom. As second mate, he enjoys his role as the ship's "navigator"—laying out courses on charts. However, the essence of the navigation has been purloined by the computer SatNav, which receives its intelligence from satellites. Some days ago, Andy said, "I almost wish the SatNav would bust down, so I could do something more challenging." This morning, he's got his wish. The SatNav's digital clock reads 10:08:19 Greenwich mean time. It has read 10:08:19 Greenwich mean time for two hours. As successive satellites have passed overhead, the SatNav has not accepted a fix. By taking fixes about once an hour, it ordinarily tells us, among other things, how far our next programmed way point is and where we are at the moment. In some places, such as the North Atlantic, there are redundant systems of electronic navigation—Decca, for example, in North Europe, in addition to loran and SatNav. A nervous ship may be using them all. Down here in the Southeast Pacific, SatNav is alone. Other electronic systems are not in place here, or anywhere near here. The SatNav includes a feature called automatic heading, but in fact it doesn't know what your heading is unless you tell it. Having shot the stars and now the rising sun, Andy knows where we are. He wants to tell SatNav, but he is unable to. Like a person whose cursor has ceased to blink, he is locked out of SatNav's keyboard. He has never before faced such a problem. He is speed-reading the SatNav manual.

Captain Washburn arrives on the bridge, previously informed and unconcerned. He says he never uses SatNav anyway. Like Dirty Shirt George Price and Rebel Frazier, he has an instinct for dead reckoning—the deduced reckoning of one's position from recorded course and speed. He says, "Every once in a while, we have to tell SatNav, 'Hey, fool. We're over here.' "

SatNav, in its time, has been known to reciprocate. The development of satellite navigation has brought some embarrassment to the hydrographic charts of the world. For example, we happen at the moment to be on the "Pisco to Arica" chart of the waters of Peru and Chile, which dates to the British survey conducted in 1836 by Captain Robert Fitzroy, of the Beagle, with additions and refinements through 1958. As a result of satellite navigation, a large purple box has been added to this chart warning that a stretch of coastline near Punta del Infiernillo is almost two miles closer to Australia than its charted position. New York is where it thinks it is, but, until recently, if you looked at the chart of the "Gulf of Mexico and Caribbean Sea" you discovered that the entire island of Antigua was "reported to lie one and a quarter miles northward of its charted position." When Andrew Marvell, in the sixteen-fifties, reported that "the remote Bermudas ride, in th' ocean's bosom unespied," he was singing the song of SatNav, which showed that Bermuda was not in its charted position. Satellite measurements found that several of the Caroline Islands were misplaced by as much as three miles. Cartographers have had to move Africa.

Andy and the captain discuss their sextants—comparing their astigmatizers, their ability to pluck bodies out of clouds, their need to filter the brilliance of first-magnitude stars. This may be the only sextant shootout I will ever see. The captain admits to the difficulties he has when he tries to work with a bubble sextant but asserts that he can sense the horizon even if he can't see it. He says, "I've got a bubble inside my head that the rest of you guys don't have."

.   .   .

In the eighteenth century and before, a ship's captain would almost always be the only person on the ship who could calculate the ship's position. He used the instruments and possessed the skills of navigation. The chronometer came into use in the seventeen-sixties. The sextant was invented in 1731. Cruder devices for measuring the angles between celestial bodies and the horizon—the astrolabe, the cross-staff—preceded the sextant. Whatever the instruments were, they were emblematic of the captain—the one person who could get the ship from A to C without veering off to G or wrecking it on B. This godlike knowledge helped to subordinate the crew and, if things went sour, to prevent mutiny. If you threw the captain overboard, who would get you home?

Nathaniel Bowditch, of Salem, Massachusetts, who was born in 1773, undertook to bring navigation out of the realm of mystery and into the understanding of ordinary seamen. His first pupil was himself. He did not go to school beyond the age of ten. He went to sea at twenty-one. He was the skipper of a merchant ship before he was thirty. He taught his sailors math. He taught them navigation. Like every other ship's master, he used John Hamilton Moore's "The Practical Navigator" as a text, but after he had found and corrected eight thousand errors in Moore's book he rewrote it completely and, in 1802, published it under his own name. This became the "American Practical Navigator," subtitled "An Epitome of Navigation." There is one on every Navy ship, one on every merchant ship—a copy in the chartroom of the Stella Lykes. The book has long since been taken over by the Defense Mapping Agency of the Department of Defense and is continually revised. Universally, it is known as Bowditch. It is two thousand pages long, includes vastly more than how to get from A to C, and, from its star charts to its discussion of relative bearings, is the Britannica of the sea.

Andy Chase owns Nathaniel Bowditch's sextant. This is not
the sort of thing he is likely to confide to the captain. When Andy
goes on ships, he doesn't take it with him. He takes another. He
leaves the heirloom at home and will someday present it to a
museum. I stumbled across this curious fact when Andy was trying
to teach me how to use a sextant, and I was looking for the angle
of Mimosa, a star of the Southern Cross. There were aspects of
Andy's background that had long puzzled me. For example, he
had studied in a New England prep school, just about the last
milieu one would imagine as a nursery for the Merchant Marine.
Yet he took off from the school and shipped out on a bulk carrier.
One of his grandfathers was a professor of history at Harvard. To
be sure, when Andy was born his father was running a boatyard
on Long Island Sound, and he later worked for a tuna company
and flew the world as a sort of water-pack diplomat, visiting the
tuna industries of numerous countries. But, for all that, I was
struck by the apparent paradox between the fabric of Andy's origins
and the romantic profundity of his attachment to the sea. And I
remained so until this morning, when I was trying to hold the
bright Mimosa in the index mirror of the sextant, and he told
me about the priceless old sextant at home, and explained that
it was there because Nathaniel Bowditch was his great-great-great-
grandfather. On page 3 of the current edition of the "American
Practical Navigator" a naval historian says that Bowditch learned
more than twenty languages in order to be able to acquire the
navigational knowledge that he passed along to American sailors.
When Andy called at Leningrad on the Waterman freighter
Thomas Jefferson, he studied the names on Russian ships from
the launch that carried him ashore. The names generally appeared
twice—in both Roman and Cyrillic characters. Before the launch
reached the dock, Andy had figured out the Cyrillic alphabet,
and he was able to get around in the city on buses. In common
with numerous sailors on the Stella Lykes, Andy has a tattoo on
his right forearm. Off the bulk carrier Kristin Brøvig, he went
ashore near Sydney, aged sixteen, and looked around for a parlor.
He explains that he chose to do this where he did for "the pure

sound" of the word "Australia"; that is, it would never do to be tattooed in a place like Scranton. "It was a romantic notion. I wasn't drunk. I wasn't impulsive. I damned well wanted a tattoo. My brother had a tattoo. Real sailors had tattoos. People tell me I'm supposed to regret it. Unless you're convinced you want it, you shouldn't do it. There ain't no turning back. I've never regretted it. I looked at the sketches all over the walls, and picked out the one that I wanted. It's a square-rigger coming over the horizon, coming out of the rising sun." When Andy was in his teens, he sailed five thousand miles working for his brother Carl, who was the skipper of a schooner called Nathaniel Bowditch.

Fourteen, fifteen, sixteen years old, Paul Washburn rode all over the United States as a hobo in freight cars. Where the freights stopped he would go into city libraries and read books. Primarily, he read history.

He read biographies of Christopher Columbus. And his favorite period was the century that followed. As he paces back and forth on the bridge, one can hear him speaking of Raleigh, of Mary Queen of Scots, of, by his description, "the occupation of France, the early ship movements, the beginning of commerce, the establishment of the colonies—the Drakes, the Hawkinses, the Frobishers, the Davises." He tells it to the ship.

Away for as much as eight months at a time, Washburn would eventually return home, resume life in Takoma Park, try another school, and then, one day, head out again. During that era, Siebrand Brothers Great Three Ring Piccadilly Circus & Carnival Combined had a sideshow freak who walked barefoot over broken glass and could accommodate with impunity any amount of current from an electric chair. This was Paul Washburn. Siebrand Brothers Great Three Ring Piccadilly Circus & Carnival Com-

bined was a truck show that made long stands in Southwestern
cities. After a crowd had been collected in the sideshow, the
barker introduced Washburn, saying, "And here we have a boy
from Asia. He believes in a strange religion: he believes the more
you torture the body, the quicker you go to Heaven. Sometimes
he punctures his body with nails, needles, and knives. Tonight
he walks on glass." When Washburn sat in the electric chair, his
upper arms were strapped, and he held a light bulb in one hand.
The switch was thrown. The bulb lighted. Any unbeliever who
stepped up and touched Washburn received a terrific shock. He
also did an "iron-tongue act." A weight was connected by a cord
to a hook that appeared to pass through his tongue. He raised his
head and lifted the weight.

Washburn worked his way east with Cole Brothers Circus as
a wagon hitcher. . . . From Jacksonville, for the first time, he
shipped out.

"I was down at the waterfront, and there was a banana boat
going to the Dominican Republic—an old ex-flush-decker from
World War I, eight dollars a month and all the bananas you
could eat. I heard that there were jobs. I asked for one—in the
clothes I was standing in. They were getting ready to go, and that
was under the Honduran flag."

"You went?"

"I went."

"What about your toothbrush?"

"I didn't have any."

"Extra clothes?"

"I didn't have any. We went down to the Dominican Republic
and brought some bananas back. Hard, green, tasteless bananas."

"And tarantulas."

"Tarantulas, small snakes."

In Jacksonville, he hung around with seamen and with prize-
fighters. In an out-of-the-way place like Jacksonville, there was
no regular fight card—no formal schedule of preliminary bouts.

"A bunch of us would go down to the arena, and the promoter,
Jimmy Murdock, would make up five or six fights out of the ones

who were there. You'd get four or five or six dollars, but it was eating money. You could eat three or four days. You could eat a week. You gave somebody a dollar for being in your corner and giving you the bandages and the tape."

He was looking for a ship, but this was before the Second World War, and ships were hard to get. He worked on a tugboat, a towboat, a homemade fishing boat, a paddle-wheel steamer called Gulf Mist. And he went on fighting.

In 1941, aged eighteen, he obtained his ordinary seaman's papers, and joined the oceangoing ranks of the Merchant Marine. He got a ship in Savannah. He got a ship in Charleston. He also shipped out of Port Arthur.

"I got a tanker out of there, coastwise."

He had no thought of a career at sea. Riding ships was like riding the rails.

"It was just something to do, some place to go, something that was moving."

One time, between ships, he went to West Palm Beach with a heavyweight friend who was fighting main event. The prelims were fought by servicemen picking up extra bucks, and that night all the prelim fighters' leaves were cancelled. The promoter—"Al Caroli, out of Boston"—was desperate to fill the card. Washburn and the heavyweight arrived at the National Guard Armory five minutes before the first prelim was supposed to begin. Caroli said to Washburn, "Give me a break. You fight a Mexican amateur, no big deal." Ten minutes later, the captain was on the canvas and his eyelids resembled coins.

"I got a whole twenty dollars for that," he told me. "That was the kid's last fight."

Three nights later, the Mexican amateur no-big-deal lost a ten-round decision in a Miami main event against the fourth-ranked welterweight in the world.

Looking for a ship in Charleston in January of 1943, Washburn got the John Harvey, a Liberty ship loaded with ammunition, C rations, tanks, and guns. A convoy collected at Cape Fear. Forty-five or fifty ships set out for Casablanca, soon after the

Allied invasion there. One general alarm followed another, the convoy was attacked, ships went down, escorts dropped depth charges every night. He then shipped out, as a wiper, on the Howard E. Coffin, on a run to England in the winter North Atlantic. He participated in the invasion of Sicily and in the delivery of matériel to the Italian mainland. On the Moses Rogers, of the Luckenbach Steamship Company, he crossed the ocean in a convoy of a hundred and eight ships.

"In New York, the Germans were waiting for you at the sea buoy. In San Juan, they hit you at the dock. Jap submarines were inefficient. Our freighters crossed the Pacific alone. After a certain point, they zigzagged. They formed convoys only near the front. In New York, the front was at the sea buoy."

On the John G. Tod, a Liberty ship, he did not set foot ashore for six months. He went to Kwajalein, and to Okinawa just after the American invasion. The John G. Tod stood off Okinawa for sixty-nine days. There were air raids every night, and two typhoons. Ships capsized, a couple went on reefs. The Tod was at Okinawa when the war ended.

"We paid off in San Francisco."

He had been married during the war. His wife was in Jacksonville. San Francisco was so jammed with travelling servicemen that there was no way to get out—no way to start for Florida by train or air. So he went to the union hall. Getting a ship was not difficult in 1945. Two days after arriving from the South Pacific, he was bosun of the Samuel W. Williston, and was sailing for home.

For home, but not for long. When Captain Washburn looks landward from the bridge of his ship, he will readily say, "I would rather be here for the worst that could be here than over there for the best that could be there. I've never felt comfortable or secure anywhere else. I once thought I was going to college and be a history teacher, but I have never been able to concentrate on anything else but this—not on business, family, anything. By the end of 1945, I had passed the point of no return. I was in the soup now good. Anything adverse that came up, this was my safety blanket: 'Hey, I can get a ship.' If I made plans and they went wrong, I was gone—looking for a ship."

His marriage was not pacific. Not even he could say if his draw to the Merchant Marine was more of a cause or a cure. Toward the end of 1946, he and his wife, Jacqueline, moved to the District of Columbia, and he became the manager of a dry-cleaning store—testing the possibilities of life on the beach. He worked there through Saturday, November 2nd. On Sunday, November 3rd, the Washington Redskins played a game of football against the Philadelphia Eagles. The Redskins are more important to Captain Washburn than any other group of people on land. They mattered no less to him then. He had developed an affectionate and protective sympathy for the Redskins after the Chicago Bears beat them 73–0 in their fourth Washington season. Washburn, who was at that game, had been following the team even before they came to Washington. He remembered them as the Boston Redskins. He remembered many of them as Duluth Eskimos. And now, on this significant Sunday in 1946, the Redskins led the Eagles 24–0 at the half. The final score was Philadelphia 28, Washington 24.

"I couldn't handle defeat like that," he says. "I can't now. I picked an argument with my wife. I remember saying, 'Listen, woman, I don't have to listen to this. I can go back to sea.' She said, 'Listen, jackass, if you go back to sea, if you come back to this house it will be so empty it will look like no one ever lived in it.' In those days, you didn't wave any red flags or throw gauntlets in front of the kid. November 7th, I was fireman and water tender on a ship out of Baltimore leaving for Poland."

"So what happened in the football game?"

"Washington sat on its lead. The Eagles' Tommy Thompson

—one eye and all—hit Blackjack Ferrante in the end zone, and that was that. I still feel a little pain."

The separation led to divorce.

.   .   .

Washburn first sailed as master on Lykes Brothers' Anadarko Victory. He has been the skipper of—among many other ships —the Sylvia Lykes, the Sue Lykes, the Charlotte Lykes ("She was a South and East African ship"), the Sheldon Lykes, the Jean Lykes, the Mallory Lykes, the Genevieve Lykes. In 1979, he took the Genevieve with a load of cotton to Tsingtao, in the Yellow Sea. A month earlier, the Letitia Lykes, under another master, had called at Shanghai. In thirty years, these were the first two American merchant ships to load for China. After Washburn secured the Genevieve, forty officials climbed the gangway to clear the ship, including naval architects. To the dockside came a very long line of children, walking two by two and holding hands. Thousands of people came to see the ship.

Across all the years, Washburn kept in touch with his former wife. He followed news of her as she remarried, as she gave birth to children, and, ultimately, as she suffered the dissolution of her second marriage as well. If she needed support in any form, he was always there to help. In 1976, between runs to South and East Africa as master of the Sheldon Lykes, he asked her to marry him. She decided that she could deal with him even if the Redskins lost.

[As McPhee has said in his introduction to public readings from Looking for a Ship, "Piracy seems to be about as rampant today as it has ever been. Pirates attack moving ships. They use grappling hooks. Crews fight them off with high-pressure hoses. Guayaquil is one of the most pirate-infested places in the world. After pirate attacks in the Malacca Strait, it has been reported

that the pirates were wearing uniforms. They use gunboats. They have sprayed
merchant ships with automatic weapons." On the way south, the Stella Lykes
was hit by pirates in Guayaquil. Northbound, as the ship went up the Guayas
River for the second time, the crew talked of almost nothing else.]

Having entered something called the Explosive Anchorage—
a piece of the river where ships wait for berths at the maritime
port of Guayaquil—Stella gives up her thrusting and slowly glides
to a stop. Bank to bank, the width here is nearly a mile. Beside
the water is little solid ground, just mangrove swamp: the *manglar*.
In one place there is firmness enough to support three tin shacks
on stilts. Otherwise the river on either side is backlashed with
vegetation, impenetrable—concealing in wilderness the seaport
that is around two bends and less than five miles away. Now,
after all the talk of world piracy from the Strait of Malacca to the
Bight of Benin, after the crescendo of pirate stories aboard this
ship as we have come ever farther up the Guayas River, we have
again reached the war-zone front, the precincts of Guayaquil.
The bosun has assembled the A.B.s and ordinaries of the idle
watches. They are spread around the deck like an army. The
slower the ship moves, the greater the tension grows. The anchor
is about to go down. Louis Smothers, in his Queen Mary cap,
says, "I ain't going to put a fire hose on nobody's child. You do
that and they'll send your name up and down the coast. They'll
break your legs. And when you go in the hospital this ship will
sail on with its cargo. When you're lying in the hospital, the
doctors and the nurses will finish you off."

Jim Gossett the electrician, tall and scant, who looks like an
old ranch hand with his frayed jeans and weathered face, says,
with a wild glint in his eye, "I'm a company man. I save the
cargo."

Murray the ordinary says, "I'm going to the stern. If anyone
comes up there, I'll point the way. I'll tell him where to go."

Pirogues have collected on the port side. Some call them beggar
boats. There are four, and one is a dugout. Paddlers, facing each
other, are in the bows and sterns, holding position in the current

with hand-carved paddles. Other people ride in the middle, with fold-open nets to catch the bars of soap, the cans of Coca-Cola, the bags of cookies that are raining down from the ship. Calvin King buys cookies at the duty-free shops in Balboa to throw to these people in Guayaquil. Skippers warn one another that the people in these pirogues could be the accomplices of pirates, here to create a diversion. There are children, old women, middle-aged men, a dog. In the bow of one boat is a supple young woman in red—red skirt, white blouse, red jacket, bare feet. Graham Ramsay says, "I wonder if she got my allotment check."

Trevor Procter retorts, "It wouldn't be the first time that some-one got an allotment check from two people."

A heaving line comes floating down the river and is picked up by the people in the dugout. Procter says, "That's our line!" On a transceiver he calls the bosun: "Hey, bose, I see your heaving line floating down the river."

The bosun tells him to notify the mate.

Pirates have boarded the ship, evidently up the anchor chain and through the hawsepipe to the fo'c'sle deck. How many of them? Where are they now? Who knows?

Understand: this ship is about the length of the Port Authority Bus Terminal, Rockefeller Center, Pennsylvania Station, Union Square. To berth her you need almost three city blocks. With her piled-high containers divided by canyons under the jumbo boom, she is, if nothing else, labyrinthine. She carries a crew of thirty-four. Thirty-four highly trained SWAT troops would have a hard time defending Rockefeller Center, so what can be expected of a militia of aging gourds? Moreover, there's so much of the ship and so few of them that the ship might as well be an open city. Action that occurs at Fifty-third Street escapes all notice at Fifty-sixth.

Confusion therefore occurs and follows. Fast-crackling rifle shots. Bullets slamming the mangroves. A pirogue full of pirates fleeing for the swamps, pursued by more bullets.

Very powerful boats appear. One of them circles the ship. Two lingering pirates cling to the bills of the anchor not in use. They stand on the flukes. They plunge into the river. Swiftly receding in the brown current, their heads bob. Their heads become dots in the water as they are swept away.

The pirates' forty-horse pirogue, with stores seized from the upper forepeak, reaches a sandspit at the edge of the *manglar*. There are six aboard. They take off, running.

An official launch from Guayaquil, making no apparent adjustment to the turn of events, comes alongside, business as usual: the port agent, the port officers, the necessary papers—the process known as clearing a ship. Short-sleeved, bureaucratic, the visitors climb the gangway from the launch. Smiles. Greetings. *Con mucho gusto. Encantado. Muy amigo mío.* Evidently, nothing that has occurred in the last fifteen minutes has surprised them, or even much interested them. They go into the thwartships passage. They follow one another up stairways to the boat deck. Captain Washburn descends from the bridge to meet them. The captain is in dress whites, white shoes. A .38 revolver is tucked in the back of his belt. The port agent hands him manifests and mail.

After a time, the powerful boat that was circling the ship pulls up at the bottom of the gangway. Sprawled on the floorboards are two wet prisoners with black bags over their heads. Their wrists are tied behind their backs. These were the swimmers who dived from the anchor flukes. The powerboat has a crew of four. Two of them carry .45s, another a shotgun. They wear sports shirts and ordinary trousers—nowhere a uniform, not a clue in the clothing to who is who or means to do what. A short, trim, serious man about thirty years of age comes up the gangway with a .45 tucked in his belt and under his unbuttoned shirt. If you are standing there beside him when he steps on the deck, you can be pardoned if you wonder who he is. Does he know those prisoners? Are the prisoners a ruse? Is he the pirate king? In the center of his finely structured and handsome face—set like a gem in one of his front teeth—is a gold star. He says that he is a naval officer. A colleague joins him. They ask to see the captain.

Captain Washburn is informed by walkie-talkie, "These two

say they are active-duty Navy men, but they are wearing no uniforms and are walking around the main deck with cocked .45s."

Washburn says, "That's the best uniform I know."

Scarce has this exchange occurred when the Guayaquil port officials reappear in the thwartships passage and, with nothing more than a frank glance at the trussed and hooded pirates, file down the gangway to their launch. Each port official carries two cartons of cigarettes and a six-pack of Coca-Cola. In the slop chest of the Stella Lykes there are many cigarettes and much cola for the visits of port officials. Sometimes they hand back unfiltered cigarettes and ask for filters.

The day settles down in the Explosive Anchorage. The Navy men patrol the main deck. Captain Washburn, in his office, pauses to read his mail. I leave the group of crewmen at the head of the gangway, go through the thwartships passage, and walk the starboard side. One of the Navy men is there—the one with the star in his incisor. He is intently watching the mangrove shore. He has seen six men shuttling among the plants, making their way toward the tin shacks. Around my neck is an eight-power monocular on a nylon cord. With a sweep of the *manglar*, I see them, too. He asks if he may borrow the glass. I lift the cord and drape it around his neck, tiptoeing away from the .45. He watches the walking pirates. He asks me to report them to the captain, so the captain can, in turn, radio the port.

Washburn, at his desk in his dress whites, is smoking a cigar. "Our security forces have seen a party of pirates on the beach," he says into a transceiver, and goes back to his mail. Ordinarily, Captain Washburn is not a smoker of anything. He bites off and lights up only when the Washington Redskins have won a football game. He looks down fondly at the letter before him. It contains the name of a new human being: Zachary David Howell. Jacqueline has written to the captain, "Smoke a cigar. Your great-grandson is at least as good as the Redskins."

F R O M

ASSEMBLING

CALIFORNIA

(1 9 9 3)

[It was appropriate that the four geology books should end with the story of California, because that is where the action is now. McPhee travelled with the tectonophysicist Eldridge Moores, of the University of California, Davis. A point reiterated with emphasis in this book is that the geologic time scale and the human time scale are generally, and in many ways, so far apart that they seem unrelated. A politician hurrying to keep a schedule is not thinking about deep time. Yet moments come when geologic time and human time intersect. In California, one such moment was the discovery of gold in 1848, and the rush that followed. In any significant earthquake, the time-lines cross as well. Two set pieces follow—one on the gold rush, the other on the Loma Prieta earthquake, of 1989.]

Now thirty miles west of Donner Summit, we were well into the country rock of California gold—the rock that was there when, in various ways, the gold itself arrived. The most obvious place to look for it was in fluviatile placers—the rubble of running streams. In such a setting it had been discovered. *Placer*, which is pronounced like Nasser and Vassar, was a Spanish nautical term meaning "sandbank." More commonly, it meant "pleasure." Both meanings seem relevant in the term "placer mining," for to separate free gold from loose sand is a good deal easier than to crack it out of hard rock. Some of the gold in the running streams of the western Sierra was traceable to the host formations from which it had eroded—traceable, for example, to nearby quartz veins that had grouted ancient fissures. Within two years of the discovery of gold in river gravel, gunpowder was blasting the hard-rock fissures. Into the quiet country of the low Sierra— between the elevations of one thousand and four thousand feet —gold seekers spread more rapidly than an explosion of moles. Their technology was as rampant as they were, and in its swift development anticipated the century to come. In 1848, the primary instrument for mining gold was a sheath knife. You pried yellow metal out of crevices. Within a year or two, successively, came the pan, the rocker, the long tom, and the sluice—variously invented, reinvented, and introduced.

There was also a third source of gold. It was found in dry gravel far above existing streams—on high slopes, sometimes even on ridges. The gravel lay in discontinuous pods. Geologists, with their dotted lines, would eventually connect them. In cross-section, they were hull-shaped or V-shaped, and in some places the deposits were more than a mile wide. They had the colors of American bunting: they were red to the point of rutilance, and white as well, and, in their lowest places, navy blue. They were the beds of fossil rivers, and the rivers were very much larger than the largest of the living streams of the Sierra. They were Yukons, Eocene in age. Fifty million years before the present, they had come down from the east off a very high plateau to cross low country that is now California and leave their sorted bedloads on a tropical coastal plain. Forty million years later, when the Sierra Nevada rose as a block tilting westward, it lifted what was left of that coastal plain. It included the beds of the Eocene rivers, which were fated to become so celebrated that they would be known in world geology less often as "the Eocene riverbeds of California" than as, simply, "the auriferous gravels." Foreset, bottomset, point bar to cutbank, under the suction eddies—gold in varying assay was everywhere you looked within the auriferous gravels: ten cents a ton in the high stuff, dollars a ton somewhat lower, concentrated riches in the deep "blue lead."

To separate gold from gravel, you wash it. But you don't wash a bone-dry enlofted Yukon with the flow of little streams bearing names like Shirt Tail Creek. Mining the auriferous gravels was the technological challenge of the eighteen-fifties. The miners impounded water in the high country, then brought it to the gravels in ditches and flumes. In five years, they built five thousand miles of ditches and flumes. From a ditch about four hundred feet above the bed of a fossil river, water would come down through a hose to a nozzle, from which it emerged as a jet at a hundred and twenty miles an hour. The jet had the diameter of a dinner plate and felt as hard. If you touched the water near the nozzle, your fingers were burned. This was hydraulic artillery. Turned against gravel slopes, it brought them down. In a contemporary account, it was described as "washing down the auriferous hills of the gravel range" and mining "the dead rivers of the Sierra Nevada." A hundred and six million ounces of gold —a third of all the gold that has ever been mined in the United States—came from the Sierra Nevada. A quarter of that was flushed out by hydraulic mining.

The dry bed of an Eocene river carries Interstate 80 past Gold Run. The roadside records the abrupt change. As if you were swinging off a riverbank and dropping into the water, you go out of the metavolcanic rock and into the auriferous gravels. We stopped, stood on the shoulder, and looked about a hundred feet up an escarpment that resembled an excavated roadcut but had not been excavated by highway engineers. It was capped by a mat of forest floor, raggedly overhanging. The forest, if you could call it that, was a narrow stand of ponderosas, above an understory of manzanita with round fleshy leaves and dark-red bark. The auriferous gravels were russet, and were full of cobbles the size of tomatoes—large stones of long transport by a most impressive river.

To the south, across the highway, the scene dropped off into a deep mountain valley. The near end of the valley was three hundred feet below the trees above us. The far end of the valley was nearly twice as deep. A mile wide, this was a valley that had not been a valley when wagons first crossed the Sierra. All of it had been water-dug by high-pressure hoses. It was man-made landscape on a Biblical scale. The stand of ponderosas at the northern rim was on the level of original ground.

The interstate was on a bench more than halfway up the gravel. Above us, behind the trees, were the tracks of the Southern Pacific. In the eighteen-sixties, when the railroad (then known as the Central Pacific) was about to work its way eastward across the mountains, it secured the rights to this ground before the nozzles reached it. Moores and I made our way up to the tracks, where the view to the north was over a hosed-out valley nearly as large as the one to the south, and bordered by white hydraulic cliffs. The railroad, with the interstate clinging to its hip, ran across a septum of the old terrain, an isthmus in the excavation, an unmined causeway hundreds of feet high made of gravel and gold.

This was the country of Iowa Hill, Lowell Hill, Poverty Hill, Poker Flat, Dutch Flat, Red Dog, You Bet, Yankee Jim's, Gouge Eye, Michigan Bluff, and Humbug City. It was the country of five hundred camps that sprang up for many dozens of miles to the north and south of the present route of I-80. For a year or two, it had been a center of world news, and for some decades had clanged with industry. Now, in the dry air, nothing was stirring, not even a transcontinental freight. But looking down the two sides into the artificial valleys you could almost hear the waterjets and the caving slide of gravel. Poverty Hill yielded four million dollars' worth of gold. You Bet yielded three. Humbug City got its name from a lack of confidence in the claims there, but when five million dollars came out of forty million cubic yards of flushed-away ground the name was changed to North Bloomfield. The water-dug valleys below the ground where we stood had yielded six million dollars in gold.

Yankee Jim was an Australian. A red-dog bank was a savings-and-loan ahead of its time. It issued notes in excess of its ability to redeem them. Across most of the Sierra, Interstate 80 runs close by the line of two counties—Placer and Nevada—which together produced five hundred and sixty million dollars in gold. Translated into modern values, that would be five billion. Yankee Jim was hanged in his eponymous town.

The ancient riverbed beneath us evidently passed through Gold Run, picked up a fossil tributary coming in through Dutch Flat, and went off to the northwest via Red Dog and You Bet. Before human beings appeared on earth, glacial ice and modern streams and other geologic agents had obliterated large parts of the Eocene river system. People had come near eliminating the rest. "Man is a geologic agent," Moores said, with a glance that swept the centennial valleys. Erosion occurs, for the most part, in what geologists call catastrophic events—hurricanes, rockslides, raging floods—and in that category full credentials belonged to hydraulic mining, for scouring out and taking away thirteen thousand million cubic yards of the Sierra.

I remember Moores rapping his geologic hammer on an outcrop of olivine in northern Greece. He was drawn to the rock for academic reasons, but he remarked that it might be gone before long, because of its use in a brick that is resistant to very high temperatures. I asked him how he felt about being in a profession that calls attention to the olivine that people tear up mountainsides to take away. He said, "Schizophrenic. I grew up in a mining family, a mining town, and when I got out of there I had had it with mining. Now I am a member of the Sierra Club. But you have to face the fact that if you are going to have an industrial society you must have places that will look terrible. Other places you set aside—to say, 'This is the way it was.'"

I remember him referring to the same disease in response to my asking him, one day in Davis, what effect his professionally developed sense of geologic time had had upon him. He said, "It makes you schizophrenic. The two time scales—the one human and emotional, the other geologic—are so disparate. But a sense of geologic time is the most important thing to get across to the non-geologist: the slow rate of geologic processes—centimetres per year—with huge effects if continued for enough years. A million years is a small number on the geologic time scale, while human experience is truly fleeting—all human experience, from its beginning, not just one lifetime. Only occasionally do the two time scales coincide."

When they do, the effects can be as lasting as they are pronounced. The human and the geologic time scales intersect each time an earthquake is felt by people. They intersect when mining, of any kind, begins. After 1848, when the two time scales intersected in the gold zone of the western Sierra, California was populated so rapidly that it became a state without ever being a territory. As the attraction diminished, newcomers ricocheted eastward, in sunburst pattern—to Idaho, to Arizona, to Nevada,

New Mexico, Montana, Wyoming, Utah, Colorado—finding zinc, lead, copper, silver, and gold, and transmogrifying the West in a manner more pervasive than the storied transition from bison to cattle. The event of 1848 in California led directly to the discovery of gold in Australia (after an Australian miner who rushed to the Sierra saw auriferous facsimiles of New South Wales). By 1865, at the end of the American Civil War, seven hundred and eighty-five million dollars had come out of the ground in California, making a difference—possibly *the* difference—in the Civil War. The early Californian John Bidwell, an emigrant of 1841, expressed this in his memoirs:

It is a question whether the United States could have stood the shock of the great rebellion of 1861 had the California gold discovery not been made. Bankers and business men of New York in 1864 did not hesitate to admit that but for the gold of California, which monthly poured its five or six millions into that financial center, the bottom would have dropped out of everything. These timely arrivals so strengthened the nerves of trade and stimulated business as to enable the government to sell its bonds at a time when its credit was its life-blood and the main reliance by which to feed, clothe, and maintain its armies. Once our bonds went down to thirty-eight cents on the dollar. California gold averted a total collapse and enabled a preserved Union to come forth from the great conflict.

Moores and I returned to the shoulder of the interstate and walked along the auriferous escarpment. The stream-rounded gravels, asparkle with quartz, are so compactly assembled there that they suggest the pebbly surface of a wide-wide screen. One does not need a director, a film, or rear projection to look into the bright stones and see the miners in motion: the four thousand who are in the region by the end of '48, the hundred and fifty thousand who follow in the years to 1884. With the obvious exception of the natives, no one is as sharply stricken by the convergences of time as Johann Augustus Sutter. He has come into a scene in which gold is unsuspected—this blue-eyed, blond and ruddy, bankrupt Swiss drygoods merchant, with his broad-brimmed hat and his broader belly and his exceptionally creative dream. He is thirty-six years old. He envisions a wilderness fiefdom—less than a kingdom but more than a colony—with himself as a kind of duke. On a ship called Clementine, he arrives in Monterey in 1839, accompanied by ten Hawaiians and an Indian boy once owned by Kit Carson and sold to Sutter for a hundred dollars. The Mexican government, which seeks some sort of buffer between coastal California and the encroaching United States, grants him, on an incremental schedule, a hundred thousand acres of land. Sailing around San Francisco Bay, he spends a week hunting for the mouth of the Sacramento River. Soon after he finds it, there is a collection of Hawaiian grass huts on what is now Twenty-seventh Street, in a section of downtown Sacramento still called New Helvetia. He has cannons. He builds a fort, with walls three feet thick. He does not overlook a dungeon. A roof slopes in above peripheral chambers to frame a parade ground of two acres. Sutter's goal is to develop an independent agricultural economy, and he prospers. He has a gristmill. He brings in cattle and builds a tannery. He hires weavers and makes textiles. He widens his fields of grain, and draws plans for a second gristmill. He attracts many people. He issues passports.

One of the attracted people is James Wilson Marshall, of Lambertville, New Jersey, a mechanic-carpenter-wheelwright-coachmaker who is experienced as a sawyer. Sutter sees possibilities in cutting lumber and floating it to San Francisco. Meanwhile, he needs boards for the new gristmill. He sends Marshall up the American River to a small valley framed in canyons and backed by a mountainside of sugar pines. Like many handsome moments in Western scenery, this one is prized by the natives, who think it is theirs. A bend in the river touches the mountains. Marshall lays a millrace across the bend.

He sees "blossom" in the stream gravel and remarks that he suspects the presence of metal.

A sawyer asks him, "What do you mean by 'blossom'?"

Marshall says, "Quartz."

As the sawmill nears completion, its wheel is too low. Water is ponding around it. The best correction is to deepen the tailrace down through the gravel to bedrock. Yalesumni tribesmen help dig out the tailrace, where, early in the morning of January 24, 1848, Marshall picks up small light chips that may not be stone.

Having some general knowledge of minerals, I could not call to mind more than two which in any way resembled this—*sulphuret of iron*, very bright and brittle; and *gold*, bright, yet malleable; I then tried it between two rocks, and found that it could be beaten into a different shape, but not broken.

He sets it on glowing coals, and he boils it in lye. The substance shows no change.

Carrying a folded cloth containing flakes the size of lentils, Marshall journeys to New Helvetia, and insists that he and Sutter talk behind a locked door. Sutter pours aquafortis on the flakes. They are unaffected. Sutter gets out his Encyclopedia Americana and looks under G. Using an apothecary's scales, he and Marshall are soon balancing the flakes with an equal weight of silver. Now they lower the scales into water. If the flakes are gold, their specific gravity will exceed the specific gravity of the silver. Underwater, the scales tip, and Marshall's flakes go down.

Sutter at once can see the future and is dismayed by the look of it. Who will work in his sawmill if gold lies in the stream beside it? Who will complete the gristmill? What will become of his New Helvetia, his field-and-forest canton, his discrete world, his agrarian dream? He and Marshall agree to urge others to keep the discovery a local if not total secret until the mills are finished.

Coincidentally in Mexico (that is, only five days after Marshall's visit to Sutter), Nicholas P. Trist, American special agent, who has defied orders recalling him to Washington and pressed on with negotiations, successfully concludes the Treaty of Guadalupe Hidalgo. For fifteen million dollars, Mexico, defeated in battle, turns over to the United States three hundred and thirty-four million acres of land, including California.

Sutter writes a twenty-year lease with the Yalesumni for the land around the sawmill. He agrees to grind their grain for them and to pay them, in clothing and tools, a hundred and fifty dollars a year. Seeking a validation of the lease, Sutter sends an envoy to Monterey—to Colonel Richard Mason, USA, military governor of California. The envoy sets on a table a number of yellow samples. Mason calls in Lieutenant William Sherman, West Point '40, his acting assistant adjutant general.

Mason: "What is that?"

Sherman: "Is it gold?"

Mason: "Have you ever seen native gold?"

Sherman: "In Georgia."

Sherman bites a sample. Then he asks a soldier to bring him an axe and a hatchet. With these he beats on another sample until—malleable, unbreakable—it is airy and thin. Sherman learned these tests in 1844, when he was twenty-four, on an investigative assignment in Georgia having to do with a military crime.

Mason sends a message to Sutter to the effect that the Indians, having no rights to the land, therefore have no right to lease it.

In an April memorandum, the editor of the *California Star* says, in large letters, "HUMBUG" to the idea that gold in any quantity lies in the Sierra. Six weeks later, the *Star* ceases publication, because there is no one left in the shop to print it. Thousands come through Sutter's Mill and spread into the country. On the American River at the discovery site, Marshall tries to charge tithes, but the forty-eighters ignore him and overrun his claims. They stand hip to hip like trout fishermen, crowding the stream. Like fishermen, too, they move on, restlessly, from cavern to canyon to flat to ravine, always imagining something big lying in the next pool. Indians using willow baskets wash sixteen thousand dollars. People are finding nuggets the size of eggs. "There is a chance now for every white man now in the country to make a fortune," says a letter written to the *New York Herald* on May 27, 1848. One white man, in some likelihood Scottish, is driven insane by the gold he finds, and wanders around shouting all day, "I am rich! I am rich!" Two miners in seven days take seventeen thousand dollars from a small gully.

In June, Colonel Mason travels from Monterey to San Francisco and on to New Helvetia to see for himself what is happening in the foothills. He takes Sherman with him. They find San Francisco "almost deserted," its harbors full of abandoned ships. Ministers have abandoned their churches, teachers their students, lawyers their victims. Shops are closed. Jobs of all kinds have been left unfinished. As Mason and Sherman cross the Coast Ranges and the Great Central Valley, they see gristmills and sawmills standing idle, loose livestock grazing in fields of ripe untended grain, "houses vacant, and farms going to waste." It is as if a devastating army had traversed a wide swath on its way to the foothills from the sea.

Sutter, in the shadow of his broad-brimmed hat—his silver-headed cane tucked under his arm—warmly greets the military officers. It is scarcely their fault that two thousand hides are rotting in the vats of his abandoned tannery, that forty thousand bushels of standing wheat are disintegrating on the stem, that work has ceased on the half-finished gristmill, that the weavers have abandoned their looms, that strangers without passports—here today, gone tomorrow—have turned his fort into a boarding house and taken his horses and killed his cattle. To short-term profit but long-term disaster his canton is doomed. His dream is drifting away like so much yellow smoke. We could follow him to his destitute farm on the Feather River and on to the East, where he dies insolvent in 1880, but better to leave him on July 4, 1848, sitting at the head of his table in the storehouse of his fort, host of a party he is giving to celebrate—for the first time in California—the independence of the United States. He has fifty guests. With toasts, entertainment, oratory, beef, fowl, champagne, Sauternes, sherry, Madeira, and brandy, he presents a dinner that costs him the equivalent of sixty thousand dollars (in the foothills' suddenly inflated prices converted into modern figures). In no way has he shown resentment that rejection has met his appeal to secure his claims in a discovery of sufficient magnitude to pay for a civil war. Seated on his right is Richard Barnes Mason. Seated on his left is William Tecumseh Sherman.

By the end of 1848, a few thousand people, spread out over a hundred and fifty miles, have removed from modern stream placers ten million dollars in gold. The forty-eighters have the best of it in 1849, because the forty-niners are travelling most of that season, at the end of which fifty thousand miners are in the country. There are a hundred and twenty thousand by the end of 1855. The lone miner all but disappears. To stay abreast of the sophisticating technologies, individuals necessarily form groups. Groups are crowded out by corporations. More and more miners make less and less money, until many independents are living hand-to-mouth and their way of life is called subsistence mining. Watching companions die of disease in Central American jungles or drown in Cape storms, they have travelled thousands of miles in pursuit of a golden goal that has now turned into "mining for beans." Always, though, there are fresh stories going east—stories that would cause almost anyone to start thinking about trying the overland route, the isthmus, the Horn.

Growlersburg is so named because of the sound of nuggets swirling in pans.

In a deep remote canyon on the east branch of the north fork of the Feather River, two Germans roll a boulder aside and under it find lump gold. Another couple of arriving miners wash four hundred ounces there in eight hours. A single pan yields fifteen hundred dollars. The ground is so rich that claims are limited to forty-eight inches square. In one week, the population grows from two to five hundred. The place is named Rich Bar.

At Goodyears Bar, on the Yuba, one wheelbarrow-load of placer is worth two thousand dollars.

From hard luck above Carson Creek comes a single piece of gold weighing a hundred and twelve pounds. After black powder is packed in a nearby crack, the blast throws out a hundred and ten thousand dollars in gold.

A miner is buried in Rough and Ready. As shovels move, gold

appears in his grave. Services continue while mourners stake claims. So goes the story, dust to dust.

From the auriferous gravels of Iowa Hill two men remove thirty thousand dollars in a single day.

A nugget weighing only a little less than Leland Stanford comes out of hard rock in Carson Hill. Size of a shoebox and nearly pure gold, it weighs just under two hundred pounds (troy)—the largest piece ever found in California. Carson Hill, in Calaveras County, is in the belt of the Mother Lode—an elongate swarm of gold-bearing quartz veins, running north-south for a hundred and fifty miles at about a thousand feet of altitude. There are Mother Lode quartz veins as much as fifty metres wide.

American miners come from every state, and virtually every county. Others have arrived from Mexico, India, France, Australia, Portugal, England, Scotland, Wales, Ireland, Germany, Switzerland, Russia, New Zealand, Canada, Hawaii, Peru. One bloc of several thousand is from Chile. The largest foreign group is from China. Over most other miners, the Chinese have an advantage even greater than their numbers: they don't drink. They smoke opium, certainly, but not nearly as much as the others like to think. The Chinese miners wear outsized boots and blue cotton. Their packs are light. They live on rice and dried fish. Their brothels thrive. They are the greatest gamblers in the Sierra. They make Caucasian gambling look like penny ante.

Some of the early gold camps are so deep in ravines, gulches, caverns, and canyons that the light of the winter sun never reaches the miners' tents. If you have no tent, you live in a hole in the ground. Your backpack includes a blanket roll, a pick, a shovel, a gold pan, maybe a small rocker in which to sift gravel, a coffeepot, a tobacco tin, saleratus bread, dried apples, and salt pork. You sleep beside your fire. When you get up, you "shake yourself and you are dressed." You wear a flannel shirt, probably red. You wear wool trousers, heavy leather boots, and a soft hat with a wide and flexible brim. You carry a pistol. Not everyone resembles you. There are miners in top hats, miners in panama hats, miners in sombreros, and French miners in berets, who have raised the tricolor over their claims. There are miners working in formal topcoats. There are miners in fringed buckskin, miners in brocaded vests, miners working claims in dress pumps (because their boots have worn out). There are numerous Indians, who are essentially naked. There are many black miners, all of them free. As individual prospecting gives way to gang labor, this could be a place for slaves, but in the nascent State of California slavery is forbidden. On Sundays, while you drink your tanglefoot whiskey, you can watch a dog kill a dog, a chicken kill a chicken, a man kill a man, a bull kill a bear. You can watch Shakespeare. You can visit a "public woman." The *Hydraulic Press* for October 30, 1858, says, "Nowhere do young men look so old as in California." They build white wooden churches with steeples.

In four months in Mokelumne Hill, there is a murder every week. In the absence of law, lynching is common. The camp that will be named Placerville is earlier called Hangtown. When a mob forgets to tie the hands of a condemned man and he clutches the rope above him, someone beats his hands with a pistol until he lets go. A Chinese miner wounds a white youth and is jailed. With a proffered gift of tobacco, lynchers lure the "Chinee" to his cell window, grab his head, slip a rope around his neck, and pull until he is dead. A young miner in Bear River kills an older man. A tribunal offers him death or banishment. He selects death, explaining that he is from Kentucky. In Kentucky, that would be the honorable thing to do.

Some miners' wives take in washing and make more money than their husbands do. In every gold rush from this one to the Klondike, the suppliers and service industries will gather up the dust while ninety-nine per cent of the miners go home with empty pokes. In 1853, Leland Stanford, twenty-nine years old, opens a general store in Michigan Bluff, about ten miles from Gold Run. John Studebaker makes wheelbarrows in Hangtown.

Stanford moves to Sacramento, where he sells "provisions, groceries, wines, liquors, cigars, oils & camphene, flour, grain & produce, mining implements, miners' supplies." Credit is not in Stanford's vocabulary. Miners must "come down with the dust." They come down with the dust to Mark Hopkins, a green-grocer who, sensing greater profit in picks, shovels, and pans, goes out of produce and into partnership at Collis P. Huntington, Hardware. They come down with the dust to Charles Crocker, Mining Supplies. When the engineer Theodore Judah comes down from a reconnaissance of the Sierra with the opinion that a railroad can be built across the mountains, these merchants of Sacramento have the imagination to believe him, and they form a corporation to construct the Central Pacific. The geologic time scale, rising out of the ground in the form of Cretaceous gold, has virtually conjured a transcontinental railroad.

It leaves Sacramento in 1863, and not a minute too soon, for in a sense—which is only a little fictive—it is racing the technology of mining. As the railroad advances toward Donner Summit at the rate of about twenty miles a year, the miners are doing what they can to remove the intervening landscape. Their ability to do so has been much accelerated in scarcely a dozen years. This is the evolution of technique:

Prospectors find the fossil rivers within two years of James Wilson Marshall's discovery, and soon afterward vast acreages are full of holes that seem to have been made by very large coyotes. In the early form of mining that becomes known as coyoting, you dig a deep hole through the overburden and lower yourself into it with a windlass. You hope that your mine will not become your grave. You dig through the gravel to bedrock, then drift to the side. Some coyote shafts go down a hundred feet. One goes down six hundred. When water first arrives by ditch and flume, it not only washes excavated pay dirt but is allowed to spill down-slope, gullying the gravel mountainsides and washing out resident gold. This is known as ground-sluicing, gouging, booming, or "picking down the bank." Even now the terrain is beginning to reflect the fact that these visitors are not the sort who carry out what they carry in. Jack London will write in "All Gold Canyon":

Before him was the smooth slope, spangled with flowers and made sweet with their breath. Behind him was devastation. It looked like some terrible eruption breaking out on the smooth skin of the hill. His slow progress was like that of a slug, befouling beauty with a monstrous trail.

So far, the technology is not new. From high reservoirs and dug canals, the Romans ground-sluiced for gold, as did Colombian Indians before 1500, and people in the eighteenth century in the region known as the Brazils. In the words and woodcuts of "De Re Metallica" (1556) the Saxon physician Georg Bauer, whose pen name was Georgius Agricola, comprehensively presented gold metallurgy, from panning and sluicing to the use of sheepskin:

Some people wash this kind of sand in a large bowl which can easily be shaken, the bowl being suspended by two ropes from a beam in a building. The sand is thrown into it, water is poured in, then the bowl is shaken, and the muddy water is poured out and clear water is again poured in, this being done again and again. In this way, the gold particles settle in the back part of the bowl because they are heavy, and the sand in the front part because it is light. . . . Miners frequently wash ore in a small bowl to test it.

A box which has a bottom made of a plate full of holes is placed over the upper end of a sluice, which is fairly long but of moderate width. The gold material to be washed is thrown into this box, and a great quantity of water is let in. . . . In this way the Moravians, especially, wash gold ore.

The Lusitanians fix to the sides of a sluice, which is about six feet long and a foot and a half broad, many cross-strips or riffles, which project backward and are a digit apart. The washer or his wife lets the water into the head of the sluice, where he throws the sand which contains the particles of gold.

The Colchians placed the skins of animals in the pools of springs; and since many particles of gold had clung to them when they were removed, the poets invented the "golden fleece" of the Colchians.

(Translation by Herbert Clark Hoover and Lou Henry Hoover, 1950.)

California's momentous innovation in placer mining comes in 1853, after Edward E. Matteson, a ground-sluicer, is nearly killed when saturated ground slides down upon him and knocks his pick from his hand. Matteson thinks of a way to dismantle a slope from a safe distance. With his colleagues Eli Miller and A. Chabot, he attaches a sheet-brass nozzle to a rawhide hose and bombards a hill near Red Dog with a shaped hydraulic charge. That first nozzle is only three feet long and its jet at origin three-quarters of an inch in diameter. Soon the nozzles are sixteen feet long, and are called dictators, monitors, or giants. They require ever more ditches and flumes. In the words of *Hutchings' California Magazine*, "The time may come when the whole of the water from our mountain streams will be needed for mining and manufacturing purposes, and will be sold at a price within the reach of all." Where two men working a rocker can wash a cubic yard a day, two men working a mountainside with a dictator can bring down and drive through a sluice box fifteen hundred tons in twelve hours, and this is the technology that the railroad is racing to the ground at Gold Run.

Although the nozzle has the appearance of a naval cannon, it is mounted on a ball socket and is so delicately counterbalanced with a "jockey box" full of small boulders that, for all its power, it can be controlled with one hand. Every vestige of what has lain before it—forest, soil, gravel—is driven asunder, washed over, piled high, and flushed away. At a hundred and twenty-five pounds of pressure per square inch, the column of shooting water seems to subdivide into braided pulses hypnotic to the eye, and where it crashes at the end of its parabola it sounds like a storm sea hammering a beach. In one year, the North Bloomfield Gravel Company uses fifteen thousand million gallons of water. Through the big nine-inch nozzles go thirty thousand gallons a minute. Benjamin Silliman, Jr., a founding professor of the Sheffield Scientific School, at Yale, writes in 1865, "Man has, in the hydraulic process, taken command of nature's agencies, employing them for his own benefit, compelling her to surrender the treasure locked up in the auriferous gravel by the use of the same forces which she employed in distributing it!"

To get at the deepest richest gravels, which lie in the hollows of bedrock channels, the miners dig tunnels under the beds of the fossil rivers. When they reach a point directly below the blue lead, they go straight up into the auriferous gravel, where they set up their nozzles and flush out the mountain from the inside. At Port Wine Ridge, Chinese miners make a tunnel in the gravel fifteen miles long. Surface excavations meanwhile deepen. Twelve million cubic yards of gravel are washed out of Scotts Flat, forty-seven million cubic yards of gravel out of You Bet and Red Dog, a hundred and five million cubic yards out of Dutch Flat, a hundred and twenty-eight million out of Gold Run. After a visit to Gold Run and Dutch Flat in 1868, W. A. Skidmore, of San Francisco, writes, "We will soon have deserted towns and a waste of country torn up by hydraulic washings, far more cheerless in appearance than the primitive wilderness of 1848." In the middle eighteen-sixties, hydraulic miners find it profitable to get thirty-four cents' worth of gold from a cubic yard of gravel. In a five-year period in the eighteen-seventies, the North Bloomfield Gravel Company washes down three and a quarter million yards to get $94,250. Soon the company is moving twelve million parts of gravel to get one part of gold.

As the mine tailings travel in floods, they thicken streambeds and fill valleys with hundreds of feet of gravel. In their blanched whiteness, spread wide, these gravels will appear to be lithic glaciers for a length of time on the human scale that might as well be forever. In a year and a half, hydraulic mining washes enough material into the Yuba River to fill the Erie Canal. By 1878 along the Yuba alone, eighteen thousand acres of farmland are covered. Mud, sand, cobbles—Yuba tailings and Feather River tailings spew ten miles into the Great Central Valley. Tailings of the American River reach farther than that. Broad moonscapes of unvegetated stream-rounded rubble conceal the original land. Before hydraulic mining, the normal elevation of the Sacramento River in the Great Valley was sea level. As more and more hydraulic detritus comes out of the mountains, the normal elevation of the river rises seven feet. In 1880, hydraulic mining puts forty-six million cubic yards into the Sacramento and the San Joaquin. The muds keep going toward San Francisco, where, ultimately, eleven hundred and forty-six million cubic yards are added to the bays. Navigation is impaired above Carquinez Strait. The ocean is brown at the Golden Gate.

In the early eighteen-eighties, a citizens' group called the Anti-Debris Association is formed to combat the hydraulic miners. On June 18, 1883, a dam built by the miners fails high in the mountains—apparently because it was insufficiently engineered to withstand the pressure of high explosives. Six hundred and fifty million cubic feet of water suddenly go down the Yuba, killing six people and creating a wasteland much like the miners'. On January 9, 1884, a United States Circuit Court bans the flushing of debris into streams and rivers. Although the future holds some hydraulic mining—with debris dams, catch basins, and the like—it is essentially over, and miners in California from this point forward will be delving into hard rock.

Edward E. Matteson—of whom the Nevada City *Transcript* said in 1860, "His labors, like the magic of Aladdin's lamp, have broken into the innermost caves of the gnomes, snatched their imprisoned treasures, and poured them, in golden showers, into the lap of civilized humanity"—spends the last days of his life at Gold Flat, near Nevada City, working as a nighttime mine watchman and a daytime bookseller. Even in the high years of his invention, he never applied for a patent. From 1848 onward, James Wilson Marshall has been literally haunted by the fact of his being the discoverer of California gold. William Tecumseh Sherman will remember him as "a half-crazy man at best," an impression that Marshall confirms across the years as he claims to consult with spirits, asking them where he might again find gold. Newcomers to California in mid-century believe that Marshall really does have some sort of divine intuition, and—to his bitter annoyance—follow him wherever he goes. With respect to further gold strikes, nowhere is where he goes. Drinking himself to heaven, he drips tobacco juice through his beard. It stains his shirt and dungarees. Looking so, he makes a visit home. From his family's house, on Bridge Street in Lambertville, he goes up into the country toward Marshall's Corner and the farmhouse where he was born, prospecting outcrops of New Jersey diabase, hoping to discover gold. He picks up rock samples. He carries them to a sister's house and roasts them in the oven.

At the end of the twentieth century, the small farmhouse where he was born is still standing. Part fieldstone, part frame, it has long since been divided into three apartments, enveloped in a parklike shopping center called Pennytown. A boldly lettered sign on a screen door indirectly recalls Marshall's compact with Sutter. It says, "Don't Let the Cat Out."

There is a swerve in the San Andreas Fault where it moves through the Santa Cruz Mountains. It bends a little and then straightens again, like the track of a tire that was turned to avoid an animal. Because deviations in transform faults retard the sliding and help strain to build, the most pronounced ones are known as tectonic knots, or great asperities, or prominent restraining bends. The two greatest known earthquakes on the fault occurred at or close to prominent restraining bends. The little jog in the Santa Cruz Mountains is a modest asperity, but enough to tighten the lock. As the strain rises through the years, the scales of geologic time and human time draw ever closer, until they coincide. An earthquake is not felt everywhere at once. It travels in every direction—up, down, and sideways—from its place and moment of beginning. In this example, the precise moment is in the sixteenth second of the fifth minute after five in the afternoon, as the scales touch and the tectonic knot lets go.

The epicenter is in the Forest of Nisene Marks, a few hundred yards from Trout Creek Gulch, five miles north of Monterey Bay. The most conspicuous nearby landmark is the mountain called Loma Prieta. In a curving small road in the gulch are closed gates and speed bumps. PRIVATE PROPERTY. KEEP OUT. This is steep terrain—roughed up, but to a greater extent serene. Under the redwoods are glades of maidenhair. There are fields of pampas grass, stands of tan madrone. A house worth two million dollars is under construction, and construction will continue when this is over. BEWARE OF DOG.

Motion occurs fifty-nine thousand eight hundred feet down—

the deepest hypocenter ever recorded on the San Andreas Fault. No drill hole made anywhere on earth for any purpose has reached so far. On the San Andreas, no earthquake is ever likely to reach deeper. Below sixty thousand feet, the rock is no longer brittle.

The epicenter, the point at the surface directly above the hypocenter, is four miles from the fault trace. Some geologists will wonder if the motion occurred in a blind thrust, but in the Santa Cruz Mountains the two sides of the San Andreas Fault are not vertical. The Pacific wall leans against the North American wall at about the angle of a ladder.

For seven to ten seconds, the deep rockfaces slide. The maximum jump is more than seven feet. Northwest and southeast, the slip propagates an aggregate twenty-five miles. This is not an especially large event. It is nothing like a plate-rupturing earthquake. Its upward motion stops twenty thousand feet below the surface. Even so, the slippage plane—where the two great slanting faces have moved against each other—is an irregular oval of nearly two hundred square miles. The released strain turns into waves, and they develop half a megaton of energy. Which is serious enough. In California argot, this is not a tickler—it's a slammer.

The pressure waves spread upward and outward about three and a half miles a second, expanding, compressing, expanding, compressing the crystal structures in the rock. The shear waves that follow are somewhat slower. Slower still (about two miles a second) are the surface waves: Rayleigh waves, in particle motion like a rolling sea, and Love waves, advancing like snakes. Wherever things shake, the shaking will consist of all these waves. Half a minute will pass before the light towers move at Candlestick Park. Meanwhile, dogs are barking in Trout Creek Gulch. Car alarms and house alarms are screaming. If, somehow, you could hear all such alarms coming on throughout the region, you could hear the spread of the earthquake. The redwoods are swaying. Some snap like asparagus. The restraining bend has forced the rock to rise. Here, west of the fault trace, the terrain has suddenly been elevated a foot and a half—a punch delivered from below. For some reason, it is felt most on the highest ground.

On Summit Road, near the Loma Prieta School, a man goes up in the air like a diver off a board. He lands on his head. Another man is thrown sideways through a picture window. A built-in oven leaves its niche and shoots across a kitchen. A refrigerator walks, bounces off a wall, and returns to its accustomed place. As Pearl Lake's seven-room house goes off its foundation, she stumbles in her kitchen and falls to the wooden floor. In 1906, the same house went off the same foundation. Her parents had moved in the day before. Lake lives alone and raises prunes. Ryan Moore, in bed under the covers, is still under the covers after his house travels a hundred feet and ends up in ruins around him.

People will come to think of this earthquake as an event that happened in San Francisco. But only from Watsonville to Santa Cruz—here in the region of the restraining bend, at least sixty miles south of the city—will the general intensity prove comparable to 1906. In this region are almost no freeway overpasses, major bridges, or exceptionally tall buildings. Along the narrow highland roads, innumerable houses are suddenly stoop-shouldered, atwist, bestrewn with splinters of wood and glass, even new ones "built to code." Because the movement on the fault occurs only at great depth, the surface is an enigma of weird random cracks. Few and incongruous, they will not contribute to the geologic record. If earthquakes like Loma Prieta are illegible, how many of them took place through the ages before the arrival of seismographs, and what does that do to geologists' frequency calculations?

Driveways are breaking like crushed shells. Through woods and fields, a ripping fissure as big as an arroyo crosses Morrill Road. Along Summit Road, a crack three feet wide, seven feet deep, and seventeen hundred feet long runs among houses and misses them all. Roads burst open as if they were being strafed. Humps rise. Double yellow lines are making left-lateral jumps. (Left-lateral: either way you look at it, the far side of the jump appears to have moved to the left.)

Cracks, fissures, fence posts are jumping left as well. What is going on? The San Andreas is the classic right-lateral fault. Is country going south that should be going north? Is plate tectonics going backward? Geologists will figure out an explanation. With their four-dimensional minds, and in their interdisciplinary ultra-verbal way, geologists can wiggle out of almost anything. They will say that while the fault motion far below is absolutely right lateral, blocks of rock overhead are rotating like ball bearings. If you look down on a field of circles that are all turning clockwise, you will see what the geologists mean.

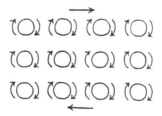

Between one circle and the next, the movement everywhere is left lateral. But the movement of the field as a whole is right lateral. The explanation has legerdemain. Harry Houdini had legerdemain when he got out of his ropes, chains, and handcuffs at the bottom of the Detroit River.

All compression resulting from the bend is highest near the bend, and the compression is called the Santa Cruz Mountains. Loma Prieta, near four thousand feet, is the highest peak. The words mean Hill Dark. This translation will gain in the shaking, and appear in the media as Dark Rolling Mountain.

At the University of California, Santa Cruz, three first-year students from the East Coast sit under redwoods on the forest campus. As the shock waves reach them and the trees whip overhead, the three students leap up and spontaneously dance and shout in a ring. Near the edge of town, a corral disintegrates, horses run onto a highway, a light truck crashes into them and the driver is killed. Bicyclists are falling to the streets and automobiles are bouncing. Santa Cruz has been recovering from severe economic depression, in large part through the success of the Pacific Garden Mall, six blocks of old unreinforced brick buildings lately turned into boutiques. The buildings are contiguous and are of different heights. As the shock waves reach them, the buildings react with differing periods of vibration and knock each other down. Twenty-one buildings collapse. Higher ones fall into lower ones like nesting boxes. Ten people die. The Hotel Metropol, seventy years old, crashes through the ceiling of the department store below it. The Pacific Garden Mall is on very-young-floodplain river silts that amplify the shaking—as the same deposits did in 1906.

Landslides are moving away from the epicenter in synchrony with the car alarms. As if from explosions, brown clouds rise into the air. A hundred and eighty-five acres go in one block slide, dozens of houses included. Hollister's clock tower falls. Coastal bluffs fall. Mountain cliffs and roadcuts fall.

The shock waves move up the peninsula. Reaching Los Gatos, they give a wrenching spin to houses that cost seven hundred and fifty thousand dollars and have no earthquake insurance. A man is at work in a bicycle shop. In words that *Time* will print in twenty-four-point type, he will refer to the earthquake as "my best near-death experience." (For a number of unpublished fragments here, I am indebted to editors at Time Warner, who have shared with me a boxful of their correspondents' files.)

Thirteen seconds north of the epicenter is Los Altos, where Harriet and David Schnur live. They grew up in New York City and have the familiar sense that an I.R.T. train is passing under their home. It is a "million-dollar Cape Cod," and glass is breaking in every room. This is scarcely their first earthquake.

David: "Why is it taking so long?"

Harriet: "This could be the last one. Thank God we went to *shul* during the holidays."

The piano moves. Jars filled with beans shatter. Wine pours from breaking bottles. A grandfather clock, falling—its hands stopping at 5:04—lands on a metronome, which begins to tick.

The shock reaches Stanford University, and sixty buildings receive a hundred and sixty million dollars' worth of damage. The university does not have earthquake insurance.

The waves move on to San Mateo, where a woman in a sixteenth-floor apartment has poured a cup of coffee and sat down to watch the third game of the World Series. When the shock arrives, the apartment is suddenly like an airplane in a wind shear. The jolt whips her head to one side. A lamp crashes. Books fall. Doors open. Dishes fall. Separately, the coffee and the cup fly across the room.

People are dead in Santa Cruz, Watsonville has rubble on the ground, and San Francisco has yet to feel anything. The waves approach the city directly from the hypocenter and indirectly via the Moho. Waves that begin this deep touch the Moho—the geophysical boundary between crust and mantle—at so slight an angle that they carom upward, a phenomenon known as critical reflection. As the shaking begins in San Francisco, it is twice as strong as would generally be expected for an earthquake of this magnitude at that distance from the epicenter.

Two men are on a motor scooter on Sixteenth Street. The driver, glancing over his shoulder, says, "Michael, stop bouncing." A woman walking on Bush Street sees a Cadillac undulating like a water bed. She thinks, What are those people *doing* in there? Then the windows fall out of a nearby café. The sidewalks are moving. Chimneys fall in Haight-Ashbury, landing on cars. In Asbury Heights, a man is watering his patch of grass. He suddenly feels faint, his knees weaken, and his front lawn flutters like water under wind. Inside, his wife is seated at her seven-foot grand. The piano levitates, comes right up off the floor as she plays. She is thinking, I'm good but not this good. A blimp is in the air above. The pilot feels vibration. He feels four distinct bumps.

In Golden Gate Park, high-school girls are practicing field hockey. Their coach sees the playing field move, sees "huge trees

. . . bending like windshield wipers." She thinks, This is the end, I'm about to fall into the earth, this is the way to go. Her players freeze in place. They are silent. They just look at one another.

In the zoo, the spider monkeys begin to scream. The birdhouse is full of midair collisions. The snow leopards, lazy in the sun with the ground shaking, are evidently unimpressed. In any case, their muscles don't move. Pachy, the approximately calico cat who lives inside the elephant house, is outside the elephant house. She refused to enter the building all day yesterday and all day today. When someone carried her inside to try to feed her, she ran outside, hungry.

At Chez Panisse, in Berkeley, cupboard doors open and a chef's personal collection of pickles and preserves crashes. The restaurant, renowned and booked solid, will be half full this evening. Those who come will order exceptionally expensive wine. Meanwhile, early patrons at a restaurant in Oakland suddenly feel as if they were in the dining car of a train that has lurched left. When it is over, they will all get up and shake hands.

In the San Francisco Tennis Club, balls are flying without being hit. Players are falling down. The ceilings and the walls seem to be flowing. Nearby, at Sixth and Bluxome, the walls of a warehouse are falling. Bricks crush a car and decapitate the driver. Four others are killed in this avalanche as well.

In the hundred miles of the San Andreas Fault closest to San Francisco, no energy has been released. The accumulated strain is unrelieved. The U.S. Geological Survey will continue to expect within thirty years an earthquake in San Francisco as much as fifty times as powerful. In the Survey's offices in Menlo Park, a seismologist will say, "This was not a big earthquake, but we hope it's the biggest we deal with in our careers." The Pacific Stock Exchange, too vital to suffer as much as a single day off, will trade by candlelight all day tomorrow.

Passengers on a rapid-transit train in a tube under the bay feel as if they had left the rails and were running over rocks. The Interstate 80 tunnel through Yerba Buena Island moves like a slightly writhing hose. Linda Lamb, in a sailboat below the Bay

Bridge, feels as if something had grabbed her keel. Cars on the bridge are sliding. The entire superstructure is moving, first to the west about a foot, and then back east, bending the steel, sending large concentric ripples out from the towers, and shearing through bolts thicker than cucumbers. This is the moment in which a five-hundred-ton road section at one tower comes loose and hinges downward, killing the driver of a car below and breaking open the lower deck, so that space gapes to the bay. Heading toward Oakland on the lower deck, an Alameda County Transit driver thinks that all his tires have blown, fights the careening bus for control, and stops eight feet from a plunge to the water. Smashed cars vibrate on the edge but do not fall. Simultaneously, the Golden Gate Bridge is undulating, fluctuating, oscillating, pendulating. Daniel Mohn—in his car heading north, commuting home—is halfway across. From the first tremor, he knows what is happening, and his response to his situation is the exact opposite of panic. He feels very lucky. He thinks, as he has often thought before, If I had the choice, this is where I would be. Reporters will seek him later, and he will tell them, "We never close down." He is the current chief engineer of the Golden Gate Bridge.

Peggy Iacovini, having crossed the bridge, is a minute ahead of the chief engineer and a few seconds into the Marin Headlands. In her fluent Anglo-Calif she will tell the reporters, "My car jumped over like half a lane. It felt like my tire blew out. Everybody opened their car doors or stuck their heads out their windows to see if it was their tires. There were also a couple of girls holding their chests going oh my God. All the things on the freeway were just blowing up and stuff. It was like when you light dynamite —you know, on the stick—it just goes down and then it blows up. The communication wires were just sparking. I mean my heart was beating. I was like oh my God. But I had no idea of the extent that it had done."

At Candlestick Park, the poles at the ends of the foul lines throb like fishing rods. The overhead lights are swaying. The upper deck is in sickening motion. The crowd stands as one.

Some people are screaming. Steel bolts fall. Chunks of concrete
fall. A chunk weighing fifty pounds lands in a seat that a fan just
left to get a hot dog. Of sixty thousand people amassed for the
World Series, not one will die. Candlestick is anchored in radiolarian chert.

The tall buildings downtown rise out of landfill but are deeply
founded in bedrock, and, with their shear walls and moment
frames and steel-and-rubber isolation bearings, they sway, shiver,
sway again, but do not fall. A woman forty-six floors up feels as
if she were swinging through space. A woman twenty-nine floors
up, in deafening sound, gets under her desk in fetal position and
thinks of the running feet of elephants. Cabinets, vases, com-
puters, and law books are flying. Pictures drop. Pipes bend. Nearly
five minutes after five. Elevators full of people are banging in
their shafts.

On the high floors of the Hyatt, guests sliding on their bellies
think of it as surfing.

A quick-thinking clerk in Saks herds a customer into the safety
of a doorjamb and has her sign the sales slip there.

Room service has just brought shrimp, oysters, and a bucket
of champagne to Cybill Shepherd, on the seventh floor of the
Campton Place Hotel. Foot of Nob Hill. Solid Franciscan sandstone. Earthquakes are not unknown to Shepherd. At her home
in Los Angeles, pictures are framed under Plexiglas, windowpanes
are safety glass, and the water heater is bolted to a wall. Beside
every bed are a flashlight, a radio, and a hard hat. Now, on Nob
Hill, Shepherd and company decide to eat the oysters and the
shrimp before fleeing, but to leave the champagne. There was a
phone message earlier, from her astrologer. Please call. Shepherd
didn't call. Now she is wondering what the astrologer had in
mind.

A stairway collapses between the tenth and eleventh floors of
an office building in Oakland. Three people are trapped. When
they discover that there is no way to shout for help, one of them
will dial her daughter in Fairfax County, Virginia. The daughter
will dial 911. Fairfax County Police will teletype the Oakland

police, who will climb the building, knock down a wall, and make the rescue.

Meanwhile, at sea off Point Reyes, the U.S. Naval Ship Walter S. Diehl is shaking so violently that the officers think they are running aground. Near Monterey, the Moss Landing Marine Laboratory has been destroyed. A sea cliff has fallen in Big Sur —eighty-one miles south of the epicenter. In another minute, clothes in closets will be swinging on their hangers in Reno. Soon thereafter, water will form confused ripples in San Fernando Valley swimming pools. The skyscrapers of Los Angeles will sway.

After the earthquake on the Hayward Fault in 1868, geologists clearly saw that dangers varied with the geologic map, and they wrote in a State Earthquake Investigation Commission Report, "The portion of the city which suffered most was . . . on made ground." In one minute in 1906, made ground in San Francisco sank as much as three feet. Where landfill touched natural terrain, cable-car rails bent down. Maps printed and distributed well before 1989—stippled and cross-hatched where geologists saw the greatest violence to come—singled out not only the Nimitz Freeway in Oakland but also, in San Francisco, the Marina district, the Embarcadero, and the Laocoönic freeways near Second and Stillman. Generally speaking, shaking declines with distance from the hypocenter, but where landfill lies on loose sediment the shaking can amplify, as if it were an explosion set off from afar with a plunger and a wire. If a lot of water is present in the sediment and the fill, they can be changed in an instant into gray quicksand—the effect known as liquefaction. Compared with what happens on bedrock, the damage can be something like a hundredfold, as it was on the lakefill of Mexico City in 1985, even though the hypocenter was far to the west, under the Pacific shore.

In a plane that has just landed at San Francisco International Airport, passengers standing up to remove luggage from the overhead racks have the luggage removed for them by the earthquake. Ceilings fall in the control tower, and windows break. The airport is on landfill, as is Oakland International, across the bay. Sand boils break out all over both airfields. In downtown San Francisco, big cracks appear in the elevated I-280, the Embarcadero Freeway, and U.S. 101, where they rest on bayfill and on filled-in tidal creek and filled-in riparian bog. They do not collapse. Across the bay, but west of the natural shoreline, the Cypress section of the Nimitz Freeway—the double-decked I-880—is vibrating at the same frequency as the landfill mud it sits on. This coincidence produces a shaking amplification near eight hundred per cent. Concrete support columns begin to fail. Reinforcing rods an inch and a half thick spring out of them like wires. The highway is not of recent construction. At the tops of the columns, where they meet the upper deck, the joints have inadequate shear reinforcement. By a large margin, they would not meet present codes. This is well known to state engineers, who have blueprinted the reinforcements, but the work has not been done, for lack of funds.

The under road is northbound, and so is disaster. One after the last, the slabs of the upper roadway are falling. Each weighs six hundred tons. Reinforcing rods connect them, and seem to be helping to pull the highway down. Some drivers on the under road, seeing or sensing what is happening behind them, stop, set their emergency brakes, leave their cars, run toward daylight, and are killed by other cars. Some drivers apparently decide that the very columns that are about to give way are possible locations of safety, like doorjambs. They pull over, hover by the columns, and are crushed. A bank customer-service representative whose 1968 Mustang has just come out of a repair shop feels the jolting roadway and decides that the shop has done a terrible job, that her power steering is about to fail, and that she had better get off this high-speed road as fast as she can. A ramp presents itself. She swerves onto it and off the freeway. She hears a huge sound. In her rearview mirror she sees the upper roadway crash flat upon the lower.

As the immense slabs fall, people in cars below hold up their hands to try to stop them. A man eating peanuts in his white pickup feels what he thinks are two flat tires. A moment later, his pickup is two feet high. Somehow, he survives. In an airport shuttle, everyone dies. A man in another car guns his engine, keeps his foot to the floor, and races the slabs that are successively falling behind him. His wife is yelling, "Get out of here! Get out of here!" Miraculously, he gets out of here. Many race the slabs, but few escape. Through twenty-two hundred yards the slabs fall. They began falling where the highway leaves natural sediments and goes onto a bed of landfill. They stop where the highway leaves landfill and returns to natural sediments.

Five minutes after five, and San Francisco's Red Cross Volunteer Disaster Services Committee is in the middle of a disaster-preparedness meeting. The Red Cross Building is shivering. The committee has reconvened underneath its table.

In yards and parks in the Marina, sand boils are spitting muds from orifices that resemble the bell rims of bugles. In architectural terminology, the Marina at street level is full of soft stories. A soft story has at least one open wall and is not well supported. Numerous ground floors in the Marina are garages. As buildings collapse upon themselves, the soft stories vanish. In a fourth-floor apartment, a woman in her kitchen has been cooking Rice-A-Roni. She has put on long johns and a sweatshirt and turned on the television to watch the World Series. As the building shakes, she moves with experience into a doorway and grips the jamb. Nevertheless, the vibrations are so intense that she is thrown to the floor. When the shaking stops, she will notice a man's legs, standing upright, outside her fourth-story window, as if he were floating in air. She will think that she is hallucinating. But the three floors below her no longer exist, and the collapsing building has carried her apartment to the sidewalk. Aqueducts are breaking, and water pressure is falling. Flames from broken gas mains will rise two hundred feet. As in 1906, water to fight fires will be scarce. There are numbers of deaths in the Marina, including a man and woman later found hand in hand. A man feels the ground move under his bicycle. When he returns from his ride, he will find his wife severely injured and his infant son dead. An apartment building at Fillmore and Bay has pitched forward onto the street. Beds inside the building are standing on end.

The Marina in 1906 was a salt lagoon. After the Panama Canal opened, in 1914, San Francisco planned its Panama-Pacific International Exposition for the following year, not only to demonstrate that the city had recovered from the great earthquake to end all earthquakes but also to show itself off as a golden destination for shipping. The site chosen for the Exposition was the lagoon. To fill it up, fine sands were hydraulically pumped into it and mixed with miscellaneous debris, creating the hundred and sixty-five dry acres that flourished under the Exposition and are now the Marina. Nearly a minute has passed since the rock slipped at the hypocenter. In San Francisco, the tremors this time will last fifteen seconds. As the ground violently shakes and the sand boils of the Marina discharge material from the liquefying depths, the things they spit up include tarpaper and bits of redwood—the charred remains of houses from the earthquake of 1906.

FROM

THE RANSOM OF

RUSSIAN ART

(1 9 9 4)

[*The story of Norton T. Dodge, an American professor who travelled in the Soviet Union in the nineteen-fifties, sixties, and seventies collecting material on economics by day and the work of underground, dissident artists at night, which he smuggled—or arranged to have smuggled—to his farm in southern Maryland. One way and another, he ultimately amassed nine thousand works of "unofficial" art—in the chronological window 1956–1986—from the Soviet Union.*]

Norton Townshend Dodge, born in Oklahoma City in 1927, first presented his curriculum vitae to officials of the Union of Soviet Socialist Republics in the early spring of 1955. They let him in for thirty days. His stated purpose was to travel with his father (a retired college president) and assist him in a study of Soviet education. Norton did not reveal his real mission. In a journey that encompassed three hundred thousand square miles, he gathered material for what eventually became a nine-hundred-page monograph on Soviet tractors. It served as his doctoral dissertation in economics at Harvard, where he already held an M.A. from the Russian Regional Studies Program, regarded by the K.G.B. as the academic wellhead of American spies.

In this country, Norton Dodge was (and still is) looked upon by his doting friends as a person who has difficulty getting from A to C without stumbling over D and forgetting B. On his own, he returned to the Soviet Union in the nineteen-sixties. He had become a professor of economics at the University of Maryland. His initial and primary travelling purpose was to learn all he could about (as his book was eventually called) "Women in the Soviet Economy—Their Role in Economic, Scientific, and Technical Development" (Johns Hopkins, 1966). Some of his colleagues said that he was studying "the position of Russian women under Stalin." But Stalin, of course, was gone, and Dodge was obviously far ahead of those colleagues, not to mention almost everybody else, in his absorption in the topic of opportunity for women. He suspected that this was one sociopolitical area in which the American situation might benefit from Soviet example. In those Khrushchev and Brezhnev years, he went from republic to republic, calling on state farms, collective farms, universities, and research institutes, and asking to see hierarchical charts. He could not always count on Intourist to broker these interviews. Tentative at first, he soon became aggressive. He says he would just take a cab to this or that institute and ask to see its leading woman scientist. A K.G.B. person met him at the door and put him in touch with the leading woman.

He had, as well, a hidden and unrelated interest. At Harvard, at the Russian Research Center, he had known a graduate student who had studied economics at Moscow University and had shared living quarters there with a Russian artist. The grad student told Dodge that the Russian, Valery Kuznetsov, had once been enrolled at one of the Moscow art institutes, learning the techniques of Socialist Realism on his way to becoming an official artist. The style was so repellent, though, that Kuznetsov went underground and painted what he was moved to paint, as an "unofficial artist," a "nonconformist artist," and therefore a "dissident artist"—all terms that were applied to the clandestine painters and sculptors of the Soviet Union in the era from Stalin to glasnost. They consisted of small, close circles, in Moscow and elsewhere, and those that did not have a covering occupation—like, say, student of economics—could be harassed not only as dissidents but as unemployed parasites and be sent to labor camps or mental hospitals, where some of them continued their artistic work. In time, their secrecy diminished and their circles overlapped, but 1962—when Norton Dodge went to the Soviet Union with Kuznetsov's name, address, and telephone number in his pocket—was early in this parabola. Slipping away from Intourist, he called from a public telephone and was soon visiting not only Kuznetsov but also the apartments of Kuznetsov's unofficial-artist friends. They took him to an apartment-exhibition of the work of Lev Kropivnitsky. The informality and the secretiveness notwithstanding, this was apparently the first abstract-art show in Moscow since the nineteen-twenties. In time, the unofficial artists became heroic figures through the drumlike telegraphy of Soviet culture. Kropivnitsky was the brother-in-law of Oskar Rabin, who was especially revered. Middle-aged and essentially hairless, Rabin developed the incongruous status of a bald rock star. Dodge bought works of these artists and either carried them in his suitcase or, with larger items, found ways of having them smuggled out. Meanwhile, the Moscow painters gave him the names of underground artists in other cities.

While Norton Dodge is behind a steering wheel on Interstate 95 between New York City and his home in Maryland, he has been observed reading the newspaper. Funnies first. Looking up at his surroundings, he tends to concentrate on the rearview mirror, explaining, "I'm keeping the car aligned." Sometimes the vehicle has been a white pickup with a boxed-in plywood back, full of paintings. Before he retired from college teaching, he sometimes went south on the interstate, writing his lectures with one hand and driving with the other. When he travels by air, archway metal detectors routinely rebuff him. He empties pockets, more pockets; but, back in the A.M.D., he fails. He continues to search himself from knee to chin, not missing the linings loose from the inner tweed. On the tray, he builds a pyramid of metal, with incidental plastic, wood, paper, rubber, and glass. For a third time, he submits himself to the electromagnetic inductors, the result being a bzzzzzzzzzzt, a clang, and a flashing red light. In such a moment, his wife, Nancy, has said to him, "How could you ever get around the Soviet Union if you can't beat your way out of the St. Louis airport?"

In Ukraine, Georgia, Byelorussia, Soviet Central Asia, Dodge went around in the daytime collecting material for what he calls his "women book," meanwhile figuring out how to contact artists at night. There were no city maps. But he had his Baedeker with him, naturally—the 1914 edition. Although most street names had been changed, the Baedeker was useful. In Dodge's words, "The layout of transportation was not far different." He carried a flashlight—incredible as this seems to people who knew the country in those years—and he used it to find numbers in dim corridors and lightless streets. "When travelling under the aegis of Intourist, it was worthwhile to take one of the general trips around the city and spot the numbers of various streetcars and other things," he recalls. "Not only was I pursuing art but also my other research, so I liked to know where universities or re-search institutes or the Academy of Sciences were, so that I could go and visit them directly if I felt that I wasn't threatening directly the people I would suddenly descend on." He was, to say the least, somewhat threatening to the artists, but they were willing to accept the risk. "We were all scared to death, all of us, including him," one of the artists has said. "Maybe he needed excitement in his life. It was a threat, a constant physical threat. He could have been killed. He introduced himself as an American professor interested in Russian art. Nobody could make anything of him. He was a mysterious figure—a professor obviously with money. We couldn't understand. He was strange, clumsy. He kept drop-ping things. He was afraid to reveal a name. We didn't know if he worked for the K.G.B., or if somebody who brought him did. He kept his connections quite secretive. He didn't mention his contacts. We didn't ask him. His appearance may have saved him. He didn't look like an American. He was sloppy. He was more like a Russian. If he was Russian, he would have been normal."

Dodge had a great deal more hair on his upper lip than else-where on his head. With his grand odobene mustache, he had everything but the tusks. He dressed professor, in tie, jacket—used clothing. Various friends have likened him to an unmade bed. He is absentminded to a level that no competing professor may yet have reached. He has called a locksmith to come and get him out of a situation that could have been alleviated by a key he later found in his pocket. But he got around Leningrad.

He got around Kharkov. He got around Kiev, Odessa, Tbilisi, Baku, Yerevan. By the late nineteen-seventies, he had become too anxious to continue these travels. By then, he possessed a thousand works of Soviet unofficial art. Through his network of contacts, in following years, he multiplied that number by nine. All within the chronological window 1956 to 1986, his collection of nonconformist art from the Soviet Union became by far the largest and (in the scholarly sense) most exhaustive in the world. This way and that, he brought it to his farm, in southern Maryland.

Cremona Farm, broadly peninsular, lies between two creeks, fronts the Patuxent River, and consists of nine hundred and sixty acres. There are long-range views over fields to treelines and water. In early morning on the flat pastures, a ground fog will all but conceal the dark shapes of horses. Beyond them are stands of maple, hickory, beech, sycamore, pine, sweetgum, poplar, oak. Half the farm is wooded. Certain of the owner's friends refer to the place as "his plantation." People ride to hounds there. The owner has known horses since his youth, but does not ride to hounds. The main house is Georgian, brick, with six chimneys, and with columned porticoes on both the land and the river sides. There is a pool, emerald with algae, and rosebushes, rampant, going wild beside it. Thorns gradually enveloped a piece of sculpture cast in zinc—bold, not easily movable, a little more than semi-abstract—titled *The Prophet* by the nonconformist sculptor Ernst Neizvestny, who once survived what Dodge describes as a "toe-to-toe, face-to-face, knockdown discussion" with Nikita Khrushchev about the themes of unofficial art. Later, Khrushchev's family chose Neizvestny to design Khrushchev's gravestone. The sculpture beside the Cremona pool was spirited out of the Soviet Union with the help of a German diplomat.

It's a short walk to the edge of the Patuxent, which is more than a mile wide and much like the Chesapeake it feeds— drowned rivers, both of them, widely and enduringly flooded when ice melted in the north. Cremona's dock is six hundred feet long, extending straight out in the shallow water to reach the one-fathom curve. The far shore is as wooded and rural as the near one. This panorama is not seriously blemished by the coal-fired power plant a few miles upstream.

The farm's driveway is a terrestrial version of the farm's dock. One straight stretch of it runs more than a mile. West of the flat pastures, it meanders through hilly woods and comes to brick pillars at Maryland 6. Dodge once employed a tenant's young son to fetch the newspaper at Maryland 6. Each morning, the boy's round trip was more than two and a half miles. Dodge paid him seven cents a week. About halfway up the drive, at an intersection of farm roads, are eleven mailboxes in a row, one larger than the others. There are about forty buildings on Cremona, well spread, eleven of which are human habitations. There are hip-roofed barns, louvered tobacco barns, tall saltbox gabled barns—silver weathered-cypress barns, covered in part with carriage vine. The music barn. The brick horse barn. Under its tall cupolas and outsize weathervanes, the brick horse barn resembles a stable that President Washington built at Mount Vernon. To Russian artists visiting Cremona Farm, the milieu it has brought to mind is from a deeper stratum: "His tenants seem to be serfs. He lives in a pre-capitalist era. He's still in the feudal system. Artists who served feudalists were better off than artists are now."

In a general way, Dodge refers to himself as an "on-the-site absentee landowner." Wine is made at Cremona, from Mediterranean hybrid grapes: Vidal, Villard Blanc, Seyval, Chambourcin, Villard Noir. The winemaker is a retired professor from the University of Maryland, whose name, as it happens, is not Norton Dodge. While Walter Deshler comes each year as visiting vigneron, Norton Dodge has yet to crush his first grape, but of course he is the labelled *propriétaire*. Billy Morgan farms Cremona, paying rent like the tenants, and growing more than a hundred thousand dollars' worth of soybeans, barley, wheat, and tobacco, and sharing proceeds with the landlord. Of Deshler's efforts, Morgan says, "Some of that wine is good wine and some will take your head off."

Norton Dodge spent more than three million of his own dollars on the art of the Soviet underground, but in all other ways he is the antonym of spendthrift. Surveying the broad Patuxent, the long boatless dock, he will say, "The best way to do your yachting is to look at other people's yachts." To attain an antebellum polish, Cremona would require a large staff of gardeners, housemaids, and handymen, who are not there. Professor Dodge is there, alone much of the time, struggling indoors to keep up with his paperwork, while the carriage vine grows, the cypress weathers, and Cremona itself ferments. Sarah Burke, a professor of Slavic languages and literature at Trinity University in San Antonio, has said, "Cremona could be one of the estates in 'Dead Souls.'"

Ante-Norton, Cremona was owned by an army officer whose very rich mother-in-law had offered to buy her daughter and son-in-law a house if it was within fifty miles of Washington. The officer went up in a small plane, flew around, spotted what he wanted, and marked it on a map. He drove there. It was Mount Vernon. He took off again, and found Cremona. President Franklin Roosevelt came to visit, in the yacht Sequoia. When Dodge, between travels, bought Cremona in 1966 and began to stuff its barns with Russian paintings, he was an untenured professor still in his thirties.

I met him on an Amtrak train in Union Station, Washington, in January, 1993. Casual as that. He came into an empty car and sat down beside me, explaining that the car would before long fill up. It did. He didn't know me from Chichikov, nor I him. His button-down buttons weren't buttoned. He wore khaki trousers, a green tie, a salmon shirt, a tweed jacket with leather elbows, and a rubber band as a bracelet. An ample fringe of hair all but covered his collar. His words filtered softly through the Guinness Book mustache. It was really a sight to see, like a barrel on his lip. Two hundred miles of track lie between Union Station and Trenton, where I got off, and over that distance he uttered about forty thousand words. After I left him, I went home and called a friend who teaches Russian literature at Princeton University, and asked her who could help me assess what I had heard,

[*371*]

since my qualifications, with respect to the relevant topics, consisted of a used train ticket. She mentioned Marian Burleigh-Motley.

Burleigh-Motley is an art historian in the Education Division of New York's Metropolitan Museum, and her special field within modern art is Russian painting, particularly of the late nineteenth and early twentieth centuries. She told me that Dodge's collection was unique, and that in amassing it over the years he could not have had any sense that it was a good investment. "He could not have anticipated that it was worth money. He likes the stuff, and that is why he did it. What he collected is therefore more idiosyncratic and more admirable." In a later conversation, she said, "I would stress the joy that he got out of collecting," and she added, "If he hadn't collected these works, many of them might have been destroyed. This was a great moment in Russian art—the sixties and seventies. They [the younger artists] never talk about it now. It's the sons and the fathers." In passing, she referred to Dodge as "a cuddly teddy bear of a man."

The art critic Victor Tupitsyn, who is Russian, said to me, "It wouldn't be an exaggeration to say that Norton singlehandedly saved contemporary Russian art from total oblivion. This makes him an evangelical figure."

On March 23, I went to Cremona for the first time. It was a raw day on the edge of the Patuxent. The farm appeared to be the sort of place where you would expect to find something other than pie filling inside the pumpkins. A door would slide open. The figure that emerged was Russian. There were Russians in the library, Russians in the barns—transient, here-today, gone-tomorrow, nonresident Russians. And there was Dodge, said to *look* Russian, in his luffing corduroys, his perennial tweed, his wine-dust sweater, his once-white shirt and abused red tie. On his head was a blue fits-all baseball cap lettered CREMONA FARM.

Drawings were in the library, a small freestanding building; the paintings were in a tobacco barn and the brick horse barn. At least from the standpoint of preservation, you would not have compared these barns with the Beinecke rare-books library at Yale.

A cat had once gone round-the-bend and damaged some of the paintings. Others had been stained by raccoon urine and raccoon feces. But such accidents had affected a minuscule percentage of the whole nine thousand works of art. "The Russians thought the paintings were better off here than in their homes in Russia," Dodge remarked. Stretched canvases of various dimensions were stacked vertically in horse stalls, or in bins in ceilinged rooms made of plywood. There were air conditioners, dehumidifiers, heaters. The collection represented more than six hundred un-official artists.

The interior of the tobacco barn was an artwork in itself, with its lofted complexity of hewn beams and pole beams, its moted space, its illusion of volume. Some of the art was too large for the plywood rooms. In the tobacco barn's great central space was a Yakerson six and a half feet high, thirteen feet wide. To the question "Who on earth could have smuggled that out of any-where?" the answer was "Josef Yakerson": he had rolled it in a carpet, and had rolled a dozen other large canvases in other carpets, and had taken them all with him when he went to Beer-sheba in 1973. The theme of the painting was classical but scarcely official. A mostly human figure with a demented coun-tenance and a huge double set of hairy bull testicles was shoving a swan aside and addressing his parts to Leda-Europa from behind. He had a firm grip on her abundant hair. Dodge critiqued the piece, saying, "One can see why that was not favored."

This was by no means the only outsize painting he had, but the majority were of modest dimensions, and many were quite small. A good many were abstract. Dodge pulled canvases ran-domly from bins: Nazarenkos, Bulgakovas, Shteinbergs; work of Kopystianskaya, of Kabakov the superstar, of the photo-realist Faibisovich, the Sotsartist Sundukov, the iconic architec-tonic Shvartsman, the organic Yankilevsky (heads emerging from anuses). Abstractions aside, themes ranged from pornography through religion to politics (a red star with a nail through it). A Pivovarov consisted of twenty-one words: "Go and wash your face. People are coming soon. It is not good for them to see you looking like this." He came upon a Rukhin; and he came upon a painting by Galina Popova, who was married to Rukhin. They lived in Leningrad. He died in a fire in his studio in 1976. In 1978, she had done this portrait of him, in which his great ursine head with its ruff of dark hair stood forth against a broad red cross. Dodge said, "They had three children. He supported them on his work. That is probably why they killed him—as an example." In a stall in the brick horse barn was Yakhnin's post-modern Schick razor blade, done in 1986, at the far side of Dodge's temporal window. "They would be very aware by the nineteen-eighties of what had gone on in the U.S.," he said. "In the fifties and sixties, some would be getting art journals from cultural attachés, but most would not. Mikhail Roginsky did pop art, and early examples of the satirical Sotsart, in the fifties. So he was up with the West. While Warhol was doing soup cans, he was doing toilets, chunks of wall—nauseous-looking walls with electrical fixtures proliferating: what you would see, if you were Russian, when you woke up. Doesn't seem like much to us, but there he was, shutting off his career, transcending all kinds of rules. He could be picked up any time and sent off to a labor camp."

In the bins were numerous paintings with coarse or subtle connotations in contempt of the Soviet regime, only a few of which, I thought, had risen past the level of political cartoons. It was not to be my purpose, however, even to approach an evaluation of the art in this collection. My interest would lie almost wholly in the collecting. What Dodge had evidently assembled was not so much *of* an era as the era itself. It was the whole tree—the growing cambium with the dead wood. If his motive was higher than money, it was also higher than the aesthetic level of any given work. He had released into the general light a creativity whose products had been all the more concealed because they were untranslatable and awkward to move. With it, he had released the creators.

The farmer Billy Morgan had once or twice seen the pictures. One morning, he told me, "I never really did take interest into 'em. They tell me most of 'em came from Russia. I swear to God

I don't know where they came from. Some of 'em caught your eye, some of it didn't. If you had six girls standing in front of you, one of 'em would catch your eye quicker than the other five."

Dodge was still adding to his collection, filling gaps in its definitive spread. A panel truck covered with graffiti arrived on one of those gloomy March days and parked beside a tobacco barn. The driver was a young Russian and the truck was full of paintings by an artist from Irkutsk. They were in stacks, like mats or rugs, for the most part unframed. One after another, the driver drew them out for Dodge to view. Dodge bought one that was the size of a bedspread, and a large stretched one, and four small ones. It was as if he were buying fish.

In the barns, in the stalls and bins, some of the works that Dodge pulled out had been painted on stretched tablecloths. Some were framed in wooden rulers. The underground artists would paint on anything. There were works done on burlap sacks. One was on a Cuban sugar sack. The artist had incorporated its logo into the art. There were works on scraps of metal, on wood, on cardboard. A painting that Dodge described as "a phantasmagoria, a potpourri of humanoid monsters," had been done on oilcloth in 1973. The "oil" side, checked, was now the back of the painting. It appeared to have spent innumerable years spread on a kitchen table.

Official artists had access to paints, canvases, and other art materials in official stores. Unofficial artists did not. In Dodge's words, "They had to wangle things one way or another. Or they had to use oilcloth or wallboard or something. The paint might be automobile paint. To get gouache or acrylics, they had to have foreign connections, or friends who were official artists. Members of the Artists Union could get stretchers and frames, but nonconformists had to improvise with rulers, yardsticks, plain strips of wood. A typical nonconformist frame used no more than a handful of tacks. They didn't have staple guns. I often took a staple gun with me, and a bunch of staples. Sometimes they painted on wood, or on the back sides of posters or the back sides of scrap paper. Tonis Vint did prints on what we would consider to be poor-quality wrapping paper. They painted canvases on both sides if the first side was not liked. They painted over earlier paintings." (When Dodge was about ten years old and his father was dean of the graduate school at the University of Oklahoma, his father helped set up a campus art studio for native tribes. "The idea was to give the Indians something better than wrapping paper or sacks to work on. My interest in art developed there. I began collecting Indian art in my college years.") In the sixties in the Soviet Union, there was a story that spread from artist to artist, circle to circle, city to city, about a small golden fish. It was based on a Russian fairy tale. An artist catches the golden fish. The fish says to the artist: You are to be granted three wishes. What do you wish?

Artist: A dacha by the sea.

Fish: Granted. What more do you wish?

Artist: A woman to go with the dacha.

Fish: Granted. What more do you wish?

Artist: To be a member of the Artists Union.

Fish: Granted. You no longer have any talent.

Dodge himself may have helped to circulate the story, moving from one to another of the small circles that were geographically scattered or had not yet coalesced. Only their friends knew of the artworks jamming the artists' apartments—tessellated up the walls, nailed to ceilings, thickly piled under beds. In a new building intended to relieve crowding, he called on an artist who was living in one bedroom with his mother while another family lived in the main room of the apartment and shared the kitchen and bathroom. If an unofficial artist had a separate "studio," it was typically under big low pipes in a basement. To see the work of Ilya Kabakov, Dodge climbed six flights of stairs to the attic of an apartment building, went through an extremely narrow door, and somehow kept his balance on planks set on rafters, avoiding a fall through the ceiling of the apartment below. Finally, a door opened into a wide workplace. Some of Kabakov's paintings on pressboard were so large that there was no way to remove them.

Male artists were, in the main, supported by their wives. Since the Decree Against Parasitism was both formal and enforced, some male artists bestirred themselves to stoke coal or run elevators. But the women, generally speaking, had a heavy burden, a double burden. Not a few of them were artists, too. In Moscow, Lydia Masterkova was married to Vladimir Nemukhin. Valery Gerlovin was married to Rima Gerlovina. Olga Potapova was married to Evgeny Kropivnitsky, and their daughter Valentina Kropivnitskaya was married to Oskar Rabin. In Riga, Dzemma Skulme was married to Ojars Abols. In Tallinn, Sirjee Runge was married to Leonhard Lapin. In Tbilisi, Nino Morbedadze was the wife of Dato Shushanja. And so forth, wherever Dodge's travels took him. The women often had at least as much talent as their husbands did, and the women prepared the sandwiches while the men drank vodka and held forth on art theory.

On Dodge's first journey, in 1955, the Intourist escorts had been so closely attentive that visiting people in their homes was out of the question. Even had it not been, Dodge and his father would have had a difficult search if they had wished to find unofficial artists. "They were just starting to emerge. This was before Khrushchev denounced Stalin. Stalin was still too close. The circumstances of the police state were still very strong. There's not much likelihood that very much was going on in the way of underground art." A few unofficial painters were doing landscapes, still lifes, and portraiture, but little more. At that time, there was essentially no abstract art. After painting furtively and showing only to close friends, artists were destroying their own work. In the twenty previous years—before, during, and after the Great Patriotic War—materials were unobtainable and there was no unofficial art. The artist Alexander Melamid, who grew up in Moscow, asserts that in any case nothing much would have been produced, because in Stalin's Soviet Union no artist would have thought to defy the system: "The society was united then, in a strange, ideal way." Melamid was eight when Stalin died and ten when Dodge first went to Moscow. Interested in learning how much Western art there might be in Soviet galleries in 1955, Dodge found very little in Moscow's Tretyakov, but in Leningrad at the Hermitage "Picassos, Matisses, Cézannes, and Gauguins had just been brought up from the storage cellars for the public to see." Later in the fifties, after Khrushchev denounced Stalin, things thawed to the extent that Rockwell Kent was put on display in museums of modern art. Unofficial artists began to paint unofficially. The period in art history that is now represented by Norton Dodge's collection had opened.

In 1960–62, the junior economics officer in the American embassy in Moscow was a school friend of Norton Dodge named Julian F. ("Pete") MacDonald. Dodge and MacDonald were graduates of Deep Springs, a small California ranch school in an isolated valley so far east of the Sierra that it seemed to be in Nevada. In 1950, they had worked together as waiters in the Russian dining hall in the summer language school at Middlebury. Both earned degrees in the Russian Regional Studies Program at Harvard. While Dodge was going around Moscow talking to and about women, he gravitated to the embassy, where he could eat hamburgers and talk to MacDonald. He mentioned his interest in artists. MacDonald mentioned George Costakis, who had been born in Moscow in 1912, was married to a Russian, presented himself as a Greek citizen, and worked as an administrative clerk in the Canadian embassy. MacDonald's wife, Allen, was tutoring two of Costakis's children in English and had found Costakis's apartment of more than routine interest because—a large one by Soviet standards—it was crammed fuller than a warehouse with Russian art. A chunky, bespectacled, Attic man, Costakis was the liaison between the Canadian embassy and the Soviet government. From the viewpoint of the foreign diplomatic community, it went without saying that he reported to the K.G.B.

"When I first got his address and first visited him, I was hardly prepared for the elaborate strap-iron-covered doors and multiple locks, like an impregnable-fortress entrance, that he had his art behind," Dodge recalls. There were three rooms, furnished with the modern sofa and Danish tables that seemed to Allen

[*378*]

MacDonald to be "like an American existence." Costakis's collection, like so many others, started under the beds and went up the walls and over the ceilings. Unlike others, though, it was worth untold millions of dollars, because it consisted almost wholly of antique icons and of paintings from the early twentieth century by the Russian avant-garde. Kandinskys. Chagalls. Rodchenkos. In words of Costakis's biographer, the former Canadian diplomat Peter Roberts, "Their paintings and sculptures and designs were lost or hidden. To exhibit or collect their works, or even to possess them, was highly dangerous. Costakis collected them anyway. He saved thousands of works from almost certain loss, and did much of this at a time when Stalin's persecution of art and artists was at its peak of frenzy. He was finally hounded out of the country by the K.G.B., as at about the same time were Solzhenitsyn, Rostropovich, Brodsky, Sinyavsky." In the hunt for his trophies from the avant-garde, Costakis had become acquainted with contemporary artists. He gave parties in his apartment for them. He bought the work of a selected few. Dodge continues, "I could see on his wall the works of nonconformist artists I had yet to meet. Plavinsky. Krasnopevtsev. Nemukhin. Zverev's self-portrait, with his slashing strokes of paint. Out of it emerged his face; he looked like a madman." Dodge's friend the Leningrad poet Konstantin Kuzminsky says of Costakis that "he collected the cream of Moscow underground art, only the cream—he left the milk."

Costakis put Dodge in touch with whey, milk, cream, and butter, and also mentioned Nina Stevens. She was Russian, and she had once dealt in foreign merchandise on the general level of nylon stockings. Inspired by Costakis, she had begun collecting nonconformist art and artists. In the seventies, Dodge would pay her fifty thousand dollars for some of her collection, on the average of a thousand dollars a painting. Meanwhile, he was invited to the art-viewing parties that she gave in her home on Saturday afternoons—events tantamount to a salon. Her husband was the American journalist Ed Stevens, who had been assigned to the Soviet Union in the nineteen-thirties and, essentially, had never left. He worked variously for *Life, Time, Look, Newsday, The Saturday Evening Post,* NBC radio, *The Times* of London, *The Manchester Guardian,* and *The Christian Science Monitor.* Across the river from the Kremlin, they lived in what she fondly remembers as "a fantastic *izba,*" a log cabin—large, rambling, picturesque—where they served caviar in great dollops out of ten-kilo tins. Later, they moved into a stone mansion with tall stately windows, which Nina caused to resemble an art museum. For many years, it seemed to foreigners in Moscow that this was the only place you could go where you could meet Russians, the fact notwithstanding that the K.G.B. clearly knew that she was supporting unofficial artists. Dodge remembers Ed Stevens and his companions drinking full tumblers of vodka in a few gulps. "He would then pull out a sharp knife and start slicing tomatoes, never catching his finger." The presence of an artist or two was a part of the salon's attraction. In 1965, Dodge met Vasily Sitnikov there. Bearded, byelobohemian, he was dressed in peasant boots and peasant blouse. Dodge remarks, "She was showing him—using him as dancing bear."

Sitnikov's apartment, where several families lived, was very close to Dzerzhinsky Square and the K.G.B. headquarters at Lubyanka Prison. The eccentric artist had had numerous difficulties with the authorities. In order to be sure that an approaching caller was his own specific invitee, he dangled from a window a small artistic decoration at the end of a string. Dodge pulled the string. This caused a bell to ring. Sitnikov came down and let him in. "The place had one bathroom, one kitchen, food on the windowsills to keep it cool, uneven floors—it was a rattletrap. He was crammed in with all his artworks. He was dressed in a less peasanty costume than at Nina's, but he had a rough country-boy look about him, the product of a life in the outdoors." A light kayak hung from the ceiling—"in itself a work of art." Sitnikov was an early key figure among unofficial artists. Others had their beginnings with him. With regard to Sitnikov himself, Dodge was equally drawn to art and artist. He admired Sitnikov's religious themes, his "impressionistic, almost ethereal nudes," his "snowy wintry scenes of kremlins and churchyards and churches, in the foreground cats and dogs fighting or a militiaman dragging a drunk to a police car." As if these things were not enough to pull a bell at Lubyanka, there were Sitnikov's "scatological paintings, which, if he had ever tried to show them, would have gotten him into even bigger trouble." Sitnikov had at one time been imprisoned in a mental institution so that he might "shape up ideologically." He had done a pencil drawing of an inmate there, in straitjacket. The face had no mouth. Because of the circumstances of composition, he said, he could never complete the mouth. In the course of things, Sitnikov would sell his work not only to Norton Dodge but to Augusto Pinochet, Gina Lollobrigida, Elizabeth Taylor, Carlo Ponti, and Sophia Loren. Sitnikov is dead. Nothing of his is in Russia now. The drawing with no mouth made its way to Maryland.

In the nineteen-sixties, the artists were not competitive in the way that, with glasnost, they were destined to become. In those early years, they freely gave Dodge any information they might have about work being done in Moscow and other cities. An artist's name would be mentioned and someone would say, for example, "He's a fine young man in Leningrad. Here is his phone number. Don't call him from your hotel." With his flashlight, his safety pins, his Scotch tape, and his other high-tech devices, Dodge carried in his pockets as many two-kopeck pieces as he could gather, because they alone would work in a public telephone.

"Norton just pushed every envelope," Pete MacDonald recollects. "He had a visa with limited access, but he would push the envelope further, push it as far as it would go. The Soviet government kept things away from the outsider. As the embassy's economics officer, I got to go to a cement plant, a fish cannery, a ladies' underwear establishment, and a collective farm. It was like pulling teeth to get under the surface. But Norton would just go into some bureau and say, 'I want to learn about cotton production in Kazakhstan.' And he went to Kazakhstan. Not being in the government, Norton was coming from a different direction. He was like a naturalist in a country for the first time."

Dodge was sometimes the first American the artists had encountered, and certainly the first they sold things to. Professor Sarah Burke remembers from her own experience in the Soviet Union in those years that "Americans were almost worshipped," and she goes on to say that "Norton—with money, buying paintings—would have been one of the most desirable people anyone wanted to see." According to Elena Kornetchuk, whose gallery in Sewickley, Pennsylvania, is probably the only one in the world that specializes in Soviet unofficial art, "Norton, to the artists, was a man out of nowhere, a prince on a white horse. They felt some amusement when he liked bad things. He wanted the art to be dissident—to be outrageous: utterly unacceptable [to the regime]." In Lithuania, for example, he was engrossed by the work of Vladas Zilius, not only because some of it was so abstract that it was officially considered pornography, but also because Zilius had painted people with fresh bullet holes through them despite their raised hands.

Dodge would outline his own itinerary and arrange it with Intourist, with the stated purpose of interviewing women. Soviet economists put him in touch with them in the way that artists led him to other artists. He was trying to see what he could learn about the fortunes of women during the first, second, and third five-year plans, and in the postwar period. "Technically and legally, and in terms of access to careers, it was much more open for them in the Soviet Union. A lot of doors were open to women. But it didn't reduce their load of family responsibilities. The men often would never lift a finger. The reality was that although women in Russia had career opportunities opened up to them they still had to carry the burden of all the cooking, all the washing, all the cleaning, and all the child care except insofar as there might be public child care. Our child-care facilities were abysmal. In the Soviet Union, child care was also rather abysmal; but at least on paper they had high purpose, and they actually provided at the factories child care that was connected with the place that the women worked, and they had other child-care facilities for the day and also for whole periods of time when people were in seasonal work, like herders and so on that would go off into the mountains; and in summer on the farms they would have in-the-field child-care facilities. Another thing was abortion. Lacking other means of contraception, a lot of Russian women were overly dependent on abortion. Care may not have been very good, anesthetics often were not provided. But it was legal. The principle of legalized abortion was accepted—at a time when women in the United States had to go to quacks or abroad. I felt that in many ways women were discriminated against in the United States in a rather shameful fashion. Many areas that were closed to American women by tradition or convention had been opened up in the Soviet Union, legally, so that the proportion of women was positively increased. Forty percent of engineers were women. In mathematics, the percentage of women was well above ours. The percentage in the legal profession was substantially higher. At the peak of a profession, though, you could see the winnowing out of women. You might have a lot of women doctors—seventy-five percent—but by the time you got to the membership in the Academy of Medicine there might be two or three percent." Dodge obtained counts of the percentages of women at various levels in universities, and in different fields at universities. He determined the percentage of research articles written by women. None of this had been published. He just went around and found out.

In his hidden mission, he was not infrequently frustrated. In Baku and in Kiev, for example, he attempted to make contact with artists but failed. He knew their names but could not get to them. In tufa-built, desert Yerevan—the snowcap of Ararat floating on the southern horizon—artists outnumbered goats. In stone and stuccoed crumbling Tbilisi—its funicular rising to the statue of the mythical mother of Georgia—he saw the widow of Kakabadze. Her husband had exhibited in Paris in his youth with Picasso and Matisse. When he came back to Russia, after the revolution, he had to alter his style to fit the strictures of Socialist Realism. His impressionistic landscapes of the Caucasus changed little in their backgrounds, but in their foregrounds they developed steel smelters, factories, and cement plants. Kakabadze's son was

[*383*]

now working in three-dimensional assemblage—bits of metal, clothing, real hair, a fish spine on a plate—and was in the mainstream of nonconformist Georgian art. In the dim courtyards of Tbilisi buildings dating from the fifteenth and sixteenth centuries, Dodge felt "peculiar," as he puts it, blinking his flashlight, and "trying not to stumble in on too many people," because his Russian was not the best, his Georgian was nonexistent, and in any case it would be difficult to explain what he was doing. One night, shuffling forward in the dark from one door to the next along a courtyard's second-floor balcony, he was looking for Alexander Bazhbeuk-Melikian's young widow. Peering through a window, he saw a woman sleeping, half-disrobed. "I thought: This is the address. Here I am. Will I ever be back? What should I do?" He cleared his throat. He stepped heavily. He coughed. He tapped on the window. She woke up and showed him her late husband's paintings.

When he bought small paintings or drawings and other paper things, he packed them flat or rolled them up and took them with him. Larger works, he says—his thick eyebrows merging with his mustache—"had to go through channels." In or out of his suitcase, the accumulation of art gave him a logistical problem, compounding all the other problems of being on his own in the dark and cabless streets of strange cities, "finding your way around, finding apartments in the outskirts, stumbling through all this, and after midnight asking yourself, How do you get back? When you add it all up, you wonder how you did all that."

Notes made one summer day that could have been made in any season:

On top of a small fire extinguisher on the kitchen wall at Cremona Farm are thirteen hats, hung there offhandedly, one upon another, each a sign of fresh arrival, each a distinct moment in epicranial time, as random and as ordered as any stratigraphy, and all belonging to Norton T. Dodge. One ignores, of course, the great formal portico and enters the house through the kitchen—a fairly large room, square, with a professional range, a countertopped island, a refrigerator six feet wide. There is topography in this kitchen—hills, valleys. Mail, for example, on the central island, appears to represent a wedge of time from the present backward two years. Spices in little unracked cans, enough for twenty farms. Bottles, boxes, bags in great profusion, contents half consumed. West of Anatolia, there may be no bazaar denser than Dodge's kitchen. On a corner table is a heap of newspaper clippings and other printed materials that date back—riffling reveals —at least seven years. What is all that? One can't help asking. "Inert stuff that needs to be processed," the owner says. "Meanwhile, the cat lies on it." Posted on the door to the kitchen porch are many bulletins. One lists a hundred and fourteen bird species seen on Cremona Farm in a six-week period twenty years ago.

The kitchen porch is long, narrow, glassed-in, full of canoe paddles and climbing vines. The table where Dodge works and takes his meals requires plowing to get down to surfaces level enough for the meals. Within the eight-year-old stack on a second table is a blackboard eraser, a book called "Self Management and Efficiency—Large Corporations in Yugoslavia," a three-year-old *Washington Post*, and a seven-year-old letter signed "Vladimir Urban."

Nancy Dodge has said of her husband: "Norton is a collector in all respects. Books. Magazines. Art catalogues. It's like living with the Sorcerer's Apprentice. If you clear a place it fills right back up."

For Christmas, Norton has given her notes promising order, promising reform. He might as well promise a farm on the moon. Walter Deshler, vintner of Cremona wine, says, "The sweet bastard can't throw anything away. He is obsessive. Anal retentive. He'll never sort through the debris. When Norton departs this earth, his yard sale will be wild. Eternally, he sits at the kitchen-porch table, with papers in front of him, saying, 'I'm behind.' "

He works there much of the day. Nancy says that with respect to exercise Norton's outer envelope is a one-way swim across the pool. His idea of a hike, she says, is to take two shopping bags full of books, and go off somewhere and read them. They have paddled fair distances, mainly in the Thousand Islands. With his father, Norton paddled down the Green and the Yampa and the Colorado through Glen Canyon when the dam was not there. "Papa was always in the stern," Nancy remarks. "Now Norton is in the stern."

He calls her each evening from a phone in the old pantry, on the way to the dining room. She works in Washington and is intermittent at Cremona. On the wall above the pantry telephone are posted notices dating back twenty years, far down into the time when he was travelling in the Soviet Union. Piles of papers, bottles, and cans are even more dense in the pantry than the kitchen. These include about a dozen plastic jugs for transporting Cremona well water to their apartment in the District of Columbia.

The dining room is the command post of Dodge's personal sorting, filing, processing, and retrieval system, which long ago achieved the level of terminal dysfunction. The dining room— with its tall draperies, its extended elegance, its marble fireplace—would not be amiss in a governor's mansion. One can almost see the gowned guests at state dinners ante-Norton. He says now, with a certain wistfulness, "There was a time when our dining-room table was usable." He is referring to high-rise piles of exhibition catalogues, books, magazines, and papers that at least include alleys of visible tabletop between semi-organized zones. "Physics Today" is represented. Today is four years old. There's a suggestive copy of Allan Kulikoff's "Tobacco and Slaves" (University of North Carolina, 1986). The dining room, Dodge says, is his "assembly point" for the several hundred stacks of material that are elsewhere in the house, and which, as they are "processed," are moved by Dodge from way station to way station on their long yellowing journey toward cryptic preservation. From a geologic perspective, the dining-room table is active. I have not found much of anything on it more than six years old.

Ambivalent as it may seem, the guided-tour groups of Maryland House and Gardens Pilgrimage have visited Dodge's Cremona. The central hall, three stories high, which runs from portico to portico—pasture to river—under the floating bridges and airy balustrades of a nearly abstract set of stairways, is surely worth the ticket no matter what may be piled to the sides. And then a doorway frames an unexpected neat and tidy parlor scene in a pool of clear light: a style "O" 1902 Steinway grand piano under a tall English mirror from the eighteenth century, a Hepplewhite table, English music stands, an eighteenth-century English secretary, Audubon prints above the fireplaces. I feel compelled to say that what I see in this suddenly kempt and becalming picture is the space of Nancy Dodge. It is one of a number of spaces like it elsewhere in the house. Upstairs, on the two sides of the great central staircase, are high-ceilinged bedrooms with fireplaces. One is ready for the American Wing of the Metropolitan Museum and the other is ready for an oceangoing barge—things in it everywhere stacked to waist- and shoulder-height, and books fifteen deep and cardboard boxes and shoes and copies of *Art News* and ties and bowls and sleigh beds. More than a few of the books are encyclopedias of art.

Nancy, trim as a trapeze, refreshing in voice and manner, could be mistaken for a flight attendant but actually is the dean of the Washington chapter of the American Guild of Organists. Her weekdays are very busy as she tries to solve the problems of those who play in churches, and on many Sundays she plays as well, freelance through the region, lured in each instance by the quality of the instrument. The music barn at Cremona contains a Rodgers organ. Nancy first happened into Cremona in 1975 to pick grapes. She knew a friend of the vintner Deshler. She worked for the Encyclopaedia Britannica Educational Corporation, which had sent her from Chicago to Washington to sell films to the federal government. At Cremona as in Washington, she is at the keyboard hours a day.

Dodge acknowledges that the parlor reflects Nancy's world, and in a tone of faint shame points out that he is gradually penetrating it, his sign creeping relentlessly toward the grand piano from the southeast corner and also from the far end of the room, where a samovar stands on a small table near a Broadwood pianoforte, and a Socialist Realist painting leans against a sofa. By having some Socialist Realist official art mixed into his underground collection, he establishes a kind of control group. In this example, two militiamen are being honored for thirty years of service. They are without expression and their skins are blue-gray. "Those faces look dead," Dodge observes. "The artist maybe had some slightly ulterior motive." A couple of Warhol Maos, each a metre square, stand in a fireplace. In the offending corner are several dozen shopping bags (some full, some empty), the molded interior of a carton that once held thirty-six eggs, a complete newspaper nine years old, maybe a hundred other items having to do with art and exhibitions, and a pillow embroidered in homage to Dodge: "God made only so many perfect heads. The rest he covered with hair."

Asked for a state-of-the-pile report on this particular midden, Dodge says, "It hasn't been processed yet. That's high among my priorities, as it has been for the last ten years."

Beyond the parlor is a small impacted space that may once have been a den but now is an outcrop of stacked periodicals and a collection of recorded music about as large as his collection of Soviet art; and beyond that is a former kitchen, dating from 1819, with a stand-up walk-in fireplace, a spinning wheel, a cutlass, a Navajo rug in the form of an American flag, hanging dried herbs and hanging dried corn and a hand of tobacco, and stockpiles of what Dodge describes as "art material in transition toward a permanent home; it's being assembled here." It's all Russian.

Of her "collector in all respects," Nancy Dodge has said, "He doesn't function in any disciplined way that I've ever been able to determine. Norton takes in information like a whale taking in krill," but he could serve as a case study in "competency linked with absentmindedness—Norton *is* distractible." She has also said that he is accident-prone. And we are back to her question: "How could you ever get around the Soviet Union if you can't beat your way out of the St. Louis airport?"

He has rolled over in a convertible Porsche on Mallorca. As a delayed result of a pedestrian accident in New York City, his right eye is blind. Sitting beside him as he drives, Nancy will say, "Norton, I hope you have the other eye open." Describing a typical crisis on the road, she says, "There's a great honking, and he just floats through. The cars around him just part. He drives everywhere. He weaves around. Police stop him. He has an accident every other year." At stoplights, he tears clippings out of the newspapers he has been reading while driving. "Norton is critical of other people on the highway."

Not a few interior doors at Cremona normally stand open, forming unintentional closets with adjacent walls. Behind the doors are tons of Russian detritus, countless mailing tubes, maps, posters, a baby violin. Nancy once told me that from the beginning of their life together Norton kept rifles and shotguns in the house behind doors. He assured her repeatedly that the guns were not loaded. Came a day when, just outside the house, a dog treed a groundhog. The groundhog went up the tree like a cat, fifteen feet, and froze there. Norton went into the house, saying, as he left, that he was going for a gun. While the dog kept the groundhog in place, Nancy held her breath. Silence extended itself. The dog's nose remained high. The groundhog tried to be its own shadow. From inside the house came the sound of a great explosion. Nancy imagined Norton dead. Norton, in his confidence, had pulled a trigger just for checking purposes, and had shot a hole in the dining-room floor. The renewed silence seemed endless to Nancy. Then a door stirred. He emerged from the house and shot a hole in the groundhog.

To the question "What impelled Norton Dodge to run the risks he did in extricating so much unofficial art from the Soviet Union?" answers come in as many varieties as there are words in the question. Almost anyone hearing his story cannot help think-ing that he could have been more than an economist collecting art and information. Anyone he met in the Soviet Union would have thought the same. In the words of one artist, "We never knew where he came from or where he was going, and we didn't show interest. Those were the rules. Everyone could have been an agent, including us, including Norton Dodge. Only now that it is past do we realize how strange and paranoid it was. There is no exaggeration in Orwell."

Did the K.G.B. know everything about him?

"No doubt about it. They were efficient. They threatened him enough so that he didn't come back."

A helping friend has passed along to me a handwritten note from a person I have been counselled to describe as "a reliable Soviet defector from the Second Chief Directorate of the K.G.B." (The mission of the Second Chief Directorate was the defense of Mother Russia. The First Chief Directorate did espionage over-seas.) The K.G.B. defector writes, "I do not know Mr. Norton T. Dodge, but taking into account the supplied information about his trips to Russia I have serious suspicions. (1) The fact that the man is a specialist on Soviet economy. The K.G.B. was always paying special attentions to all American specialists on any field of Russia or Soviet Union from the beginning of a foreign tourism to the U.S.S.R. in 1955. By the way, the first recruitment by the K.G.B. of an American tourist was in 1956, who a profes-sor of an American university—a specialist on Russian history. (2) The man visited the U.S.S.R. over 20 years (1955–1977) on many occasions. The K.G.B. was extremely suspicious to Amer-icans who were coming second and time to the U.S.S.R. (3) The man on his trips to the U.S.S.R. was visiting unofficial artists in different cities throughout the U.S.S.R. (4) The Soviets were and still are very strict with any pieces of art going abroad."

Americans had suspicions, too, as Professor Sarah Burke reveals in discussing her own feintings and shiftings with the K.G.B.: "You tried to blend in with the population. You could be arrested. You could be walking down the street and a car would pull up.

Almost anything you did was illegal. It was a game. For me, it was like risky living. I was very cautious and very careful. Seeing artists was a reason for taking you and interrogating you. They thought everybody was a spy. They must have thought Norton was a spy. I thought Norton was a spy. Why? Because people his age who taught Russian subjects were connected somehow to the C.I.A. He's so bumbling. No one would think he was. His Russian is just ghastly. The flashlight cracked me up. Russians don't have flashlights. You just wouldn't do that—look for them with a flashlight. You'd meet somebody somewhere. Besides, you endear yourself to Russians if you're completely discreet."

To numerous people, in fact, Norton Dodge sounds so much like a spy that they find it almost impossible to believe that he was not. For his part, he dismisses the idea as romantic nonsense. Other sources, looked into, assert themselves dry. So you are left with an assemblage of story blocks and dotted lines, a write-it-yourself novel—"Burnt Norton"—in which he bumbles around Khrushchev's Soviet Union and Brezhnev's Soviet Union, first as an economist interested in tractors and women, and later as a tourist collecting and smuggling underground art. Creatively, you give him all that as developed cover, and try to imagine what he was doing as an operative (with flashlight) from the C.I.A. Or, you see him merely as an economist interested in clandestine art, female employment, and tractors. And, or, maybe—why not?— you see him as a double agent. You tell your reader, "Either (1) the Soviet Union was a great deal easier to get around in than most of us imagined or (2) Norton was in the K.G.B." What is common to all plots you may construct, however, is that in the denouement the art comes out. Nine thousand works of art come out.

When he went to the Soviet Union in 1955, he had a sense of the stirrings already going on there in literature and poetry— stirrings that increased greatly, in the following year, after the Stalin-denunciation speech and the beginning of the relative thaw. Thinking about it, Dodge decided that if such things were happening in literature something analogous must be occurring in art: "You knew that since people had been writing for the drawer there must have been people who were painting for themselves and their friends." An article in *Life* mentioned unofficial artists, confirming his extrapolations, and the thought occurred to him that while "it was easy to smuggle poetry out, and novels, and manifestos, and to have conferences ad nauseam, in the art field there was a whole branch of the dissident or underground movement that wasn't visible here or being discussed here." Before he made his first women trip, in 1962, he had had further thoughts, which he recalls as follows: "It would be tragic if these artists were to die without their work being seen outside Russia. The courage of these people . . . They worked often in isolation with no audience other than their wives and families and a small circle of friends. They risked harassment and interrogation. Also, I thought, if anything is going to happen to change the system for the better it had to be through greater freedom of expression. These people were sticking their necks out. They were risking everything."

He tried to interest, among others, the American Association for the Advancement of Slavic Studies, but essentially failed. The Western art world, in its various manifestations, seemed even more indifferent than the A.A.A.S.S. Asked why this would be so, Dodge delivers an analysis that ultimately fixes himself in the context and meanwhile sounds like one of his lectures on Soviet economics: "The nexus that is necessary for the development of an interest in some sort of art movement was missing. Much of the nexus is involved around the marketing of art, the buying and selling of art, the mechanism able to make the artist able to survive and produce. This did not exist in Russia. The Americans were not interested because art historians like dead artists, dealers want a steady supply, and critics review exhibits, they don't go off digging up artists. Museums don't collect artists unless they have been anointed by having many shows with good reviews. I felt it was left to an economist who goes to Russia. I thought, If anybody's going to do it I guess I'll have to do it. That's why I was first attracted. The people who should have been doing it weren't doing it; and I thought, If the right people aren't doing it, then who else but me?"

When he began his collecting, his friends the MacDonalds at once understood what he was doing. Allen MacDonald used to leave copies of American magazines in Moscow subway cars so that people would pick them up and have them. "The Soviets wanted to hide everything, and they would use strong-arm stuff if they felt they needed to," Pete MacDonald has said. "Those of us not on the military side felt challenged to dig out anything they hid. With so much stifling of information and stifling of the human spirit, all of us felt a bond with the Russians and wanted to help them. We wanted to bring out the truth. Norton was in contact with the artists. He *knew* them. He felt that here was a whole creative force being bottled up, and he wanted to get it to the outside."

Dodge continues, "I started out thinking, I really don't care too much whether the art is good or bad. I just am interested in getting it out and then people will have something to form their judgment on. But I soon found I thought it was very good, much of it—although, surely, large parts of the collection aren't very good." Jon Showe, husband of the gallery owner Elena Kornet-chuk, describes Dodge as having had a "holistic approach to art—more than the sum of the parts." Art collectors often specialize, he explains, "but Norton is broad gauge." The most important aspect of him as a collector of Soviet unofficial art "is Norton's appreciation of the milieu that gave rise to all this: someone else gets interested in a certain period in painting and goes and looks up the history, the political and economic and social systems; Norton went at it the other way around."

Dodge told the artists that he wanted to collect the art so that at least some of it would be available somewhere no matter what happened to them or to their collections in the Soviet Union. He added that he was not just interested in collecting; he wanted the art to be publicly exhibited. The artists, for their part, seemed to yearn for Western validation. Touchingly, they even sought the opinions of embassy people, which may have been like seeking mariners' opinions of climbing routes in the Alps. Dodge was often embarrassed when the artists he sought out earnestly asked for comments. He would say, "It's very interesting. Very interesting, indeed." He was like an obstetrician saying, "Now there *is* a baby!"

Father Alipy, abbot of the monastery of Pskov-Pechersky, was collecting the work of unofficial artists in the same years that Dodge was. Father Alipy had been an artist himself. His collection of underground painting grew to include the work of several hundred artists. He died in 1975. Almost immediately, the monks of the monastery, in cooperation with the state, destroyed the collection.

Asked why Dodge did what he did, Victor Tupitsyn says, "To help this art be survived."

"To survive," Margarita Tupitsyn says, correcting him.

Victor: "To come to life. He is compassionate."

Margarita: "He sometimes feels first for the artist and then for the art. You can't imagine how many Russian émigrés are surviving because of him. He supports them and their families."

Taking into account the fortune he spent for his collection, Dodge said, not long ago, "We didn't have children or expect to have children. It was not a matter of robbing any children or grandchildren. It was interesting to see your assets giving support to those who were undermining the monolithic thought-control apparatus of the Soviet Union. This was one factor among the many in the breakup." He would appear to have been a spy for the humanities. In a conversation I had with Elena Kornetchuk and Jon Showe, Kornetchuk said of Norton Dodge, "He's the Lorenzo de' Medici of Russian art."

Showe said, "A Maecenas."